GUNS O NEW WEST

A Close-Up Look At Modern Replica Firearms

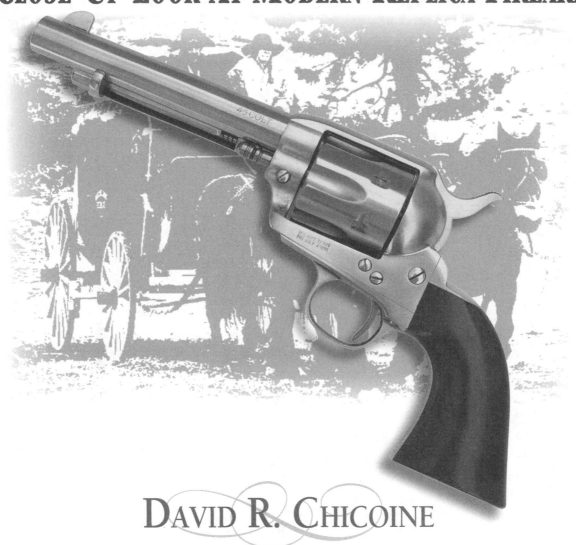

David R. Chicoine

Gun Digest Books
An imprint of F+W Publications

700 East State Street • Iola, WI 54990-0001
715-445-2214 • 888-457-2873

Our toll-free number to place an order or obtain
a free catalog is (800) 258-0929.

Library of Congress Catalog Number: 2004114243

ISBN: 0-87349-768-6

Designed by Paul Birling
Edited by Kevin Michalowski

Printed in United States of America

Table of Contents

Dedication And Notes Of Thanks

This book is dedicated to my three terrific children; Dallas Jan, David Theodore and Margaret Rose, of whom I am extremely proud. Words could not express the gratitude I feel to have been blessed to be the person that such wonderful individuals call "Daddy."

A very special note of thanks goes out to my dear friend Ed Wade, who by generously giving of his time, his expertise, firearms, accessories, his shooting ability and most especially his wonderful sense of humor has made the production of this book so much easier. It could not have been accomplished without him. A big thank you also goes to my talented son, David T. Chicoine, whose wonderful artwork provided the basis for some of the illustrations for this book.

My thanks to Peter Pedone (Palaver Pete) for answering my questions about SASS history, for his support of the writer and of this project. Most of all, thank you for writing the enthusiastic foreword for this book, you have done a wonderful job of introducing the subject.

Personal thanks go out the following individuals whose help in so many and varied ways, has contributed so much toward the production of this book. To: Tommy Abernathy, James Allen, Frank Brownell, Bill Cottingham, John Culligan, Bill English, Delbert Fentress, Cristie Gates, Gary Germaine, Don Gulbrandsen, Mike Harvey, Bobby James, Edward Janis, Lisa Keller, John Kopec, Kevin Michalowski, Amy Navitski, Walt Penner, General John Pickett, Allessandro Pietta, John Powell, Ken Ramage, Margaret Sheldon, Ron Smith, Fred Stann, Gary Stift, Jim Supica, Art Tobias, Maria Uberti, John Watts, Suzanne Webb, Larry Weeks and last alphabetically, but certainly not least, the late Butch Winter.

To Giacomo Merlino, Managing Director, and Suzanne Webb, Sales Manager, of A. Uberti S.R.L. in Brescia, Italy for helping me to assemble such a wide variety of Uberti-made firearms for us to inspect and to test fire for this book and for their generosity in sharing company sales and historical information. Thank you both for all your time and effort.

The following companies have been extremely generous and supportive, unselfishly providing us with the loan of product, illustrations, and/or technical assistance and historical information that have helped to make this book possible:

James Allen, leather (featured products)

Black Hills Ammunition (featured products)

Brownell's Inc. (featured products)

C&R Hard Chrome and
    Electroless Nickel Service, Inc.

Cimarron Firearms (featured firearms)

Colt Firearms (featured firearms)

Coltparts.com (Ed Cox)

Dixie Gun Works (featured products)

EMF Corp. (featured products)

Hornady Ammunition (featured products)

Kirkpatrick Leather (featured products)

Krause Publications

Marlin Firearms (featured firearms)

Numrich Gun Parts Corporation

Peacemaker Specialists

Davide Pedersoli (featured products)

Pietta (featured products)

Roy Rugers (featured products)

Smith Enterprise (featured products)

Stoeger Industries/Benelli USA
    (featured products)

Sturm, Ruger and Co. (featured firearms)

United States Firearms Mfg. Co.
    (featured products)

A. Uberti S.R.L. (featured firearms)

VTI Gun Parts (featured products)

Winchester Ammunition (featured products)

Foreword

Ah, the New West—what a great feeling just to be part of it! What a great feeling simply to say it, **"The New West!"** Yes, all of us who play the game of cowboy action shooting (CAS) are part of the New West. Collectively we members of SASS (the Single Action Shooting Society) represent a resurgence of America's love of our Western heritage. I ask you, What other nation in the world can claim any history similar to our Western migration? The answer is none. We clashed with Native Americans—we explored new regions, we panned for gold—we homesteaded barren land. With the exception of the treatment of our Native Americans, we take pride in what we accomplished. We relish what we did—we rejoice in it—we play it! This is our West. This is our game, this is our time, and we say to the rest of the world, "If you really love our West as we do, then come on in and play with us."

And now, with this book titled *Guns of the New West,* David Chicoine has given us a bible of the "new" toys we use in playing this game. Toys we cherish as much as our Western heritage. Toys we love to caress. Toys we "tune up" in order to make them shoot quicker and straighter, than did their forefathers, the guns of the Old West. Like cowboy action shooters around the world, we Americans love our Western guns. We love to hold them—we love to shoot them, and we like to "strut" with them strapped to our hips. And as we strut, and as we shoot these guns of the New West, we marvel at the ingenuity of our forefathers who invented these works of art, especially Sam Colt. Listen, as the hammer is pulled back—the click, click, click, and click. As we listen to the clicks, our minds race back to the time when the West was indeed wild, and now we are part of it—we are part of what Mr. Chicoine calls the New West—Hallelujah, we love it—bring it on!

Our author reminds us that CAS has brought about the need for high-quality replicas of firearms used on the frontier. CAS has not only created a resurgence of our Western heritage, it has created a very competitive sport, resulting in participants practicing daily, and in so doing, burning up 500 or more rounds per week (oh heck, make that 1,000). This hard use of our firearms has created a need for manufacturers to achieve the highest of metallurgical standards in their construction. They have met our demands, and today's replicas are built to accept the challenge of daily CAS use. The guns of the New West are not only beautiful in their design, they are now as durable as any found in the modern world. They are ready for the use and abuse we may foster upon them and they will respond with the same dependability as their forefathers.

Chicoine, an experienced writer, who has already brought us such books as *Gunsmithing Guns of the Old West,* and *Smith & Wesson Sixguns of the Old West,* has arranged the new guns in easy-to-read order and provided plenty of photos. Does "chuck-full" of photos sound good enough? I think we CAS people understand "chuck-full."

Chicoine has also integrated the names of the new manufacturers and retailers, such as: Uberti, Pietta, Rossi, Cimarron Firearms, Dixie Gun Works, EMF, and Navy Arms, along with the more frequently heard names like Colt, Smith & Wesson, Winchester, Remington, Marlin, and Ruger. Just the sound of those names, like the sounds of the click, click, click, I mentioned above, makes me want to read the *Guns of the New West* all over again. I'm sure it will have the same effect on you, pard! Enjoy this book, as I know you will.

Peter J. Pedone
AKA: Palaver Pete,
SASS Life/Regulator #4375,
Sunriver, Oregon.

Introduction

Our "New West" isn't really a location. What we are referring to is the state of mind surrounding the relatively new and increasingly popular sport of cowboy action shooting. Cowboy action shooting, or CAS, is an outdoor shooting sport where shooters compete against the clock, using guns like those used by real characters in the Old West, all the while playing the role dressed in period garb and speaking in that peculiar 19th century cowboy vernacular. CAS could be likened to what IPSC shooting competitions might have looked like, that is, if they had been started 100 years earlier. During these shooting meets, the colorfully dressed competitors adopt stage names such as "Jake Slade" or "Palaver Pete."

In the early days of CAS many competitors made use of original 19th century firearms, sometimes with smokeless powder ammunition, and the hard use involved in the competition took a heavy toll on some great old guns. Guns, which, the truth be told, had probably never been put to such extreme use in their entire 125-year lives. Just how extreme is this use? If we try to discount hard use from the matches themselves, which remember, are being fired against the clock, we must also remember that to be competitive these people have to practice a lot. That means firing 500 to 1,000 rounds or more a week in situations that simulate the real competition. At least that is what a couple of good friends of mine do. They practice that much to help make them, sometimes, what we might term "reasonably competitive" at regional matches. How many practice shots the consistent winners have to shoot each week to stay in tip-top shape is anyone's guess. One sure fact that jumps out at you; this much shooting, especially when the "pressure is on" to fire the weapon as fast and as accurately as possible and all the while not make a mistake in the process, is, to understate it, incredibly hard on the equipment. I do not think I am out of line when I say that a month in modern CAS competition would be roughly the equivalent of a lifetime of service for most 19th century guns that were actually used in any capacity on the frontier.

Given that rigorous use, what these competitors really needed were high-quality replicas of the guns used on the frontier. They needed guns that were not nearly so dear, or in many cases so valuable, as the originals. They needed guns that could be easily replaced, but also that were made with good enough quality to enable them to be used heavily. When CAS started to get popular, we had many variations of replica percussion revolvers and rifles, one or two copies of the Colt SAA, a trapdoor Springfield copy and one or two lever-actions. That was because in the early 1980s, the replica firearms market was still being directed more toward the Civil War battlefield reenactor. As the demand for these types of weapons increased, shooters began to ask for more and better replica firearms. Replica firearms retailers like Cimarron Firearms, Dixie Gun Works, EMF and Navy Arms, some of the Italian arms makers such as ASM, Aldo Uberti, Pedersoli and Pietta, who were already making shoot-able replica firearms, responded and began expand their lines.

As a direct result of the demand created by CAS shooters, the shooting public today has a terrific selection of replica weaponry that is, at the least, styled after guns from the 19th century. Today we have a large variety of Colt SAA clones (including several variants that never existed before) and the genuine article of current manufacture. There are a couple of nice copies of the large-caliber S&W top-break revolvers and the promise of more to come. Even Ruger has gotten into the cowboy act with its ultra-tough Vaquero line. At this juncture, we have an entire line of replicas of the Winchester lever-action rifles. Marlin is producing an ever-expanding line of new lever guns specifically for CAS shooters, and there is quite a selection of single-shot rifles available as well as a copy of the Colt pump rifle. These then are the *Guns of the New West,* and whether you are involved in cowboy action shooting or not, if you enjoy the guns used in the Old West and cowboy gear, then you will benefit from this wonderful selection.

As many of us found out, usually the hard way, some of the early replica firearms exhibited varying degrees of quality in their manufacture. When you set out to use a gun this hard if there is any part of the mechanism that is not just right it will become readily apparent. In the heat of competition any weapons that made it that far with inherent flaws quickly gave up the ghost. Companies like Uberti, Pietta and Davide Pedersoli paid attention when shooters and gun writers complained about these problems, they made the necessary corrections and today offer shooters much better products. Other companies such as ASM, failed to heed the call from shooters to provide a quality gun and have fallen by the wayside.

People often ask me if such-and-such a replica gun is even half the gun the original that it is styled after was. That is certainly a fair question and to be perfectly honest, 20 years ago, without hesitating, I would have unequivocally said no, it sure isn't. But friend, things have changed. Now, it depends on exactly what your gauge of quality is. Are fit and finish the criteria you use? For what it's worth, quality hand labor was very inexpensive in the 19th century, but as we all know, that is surely not the case today. Unless shooters get rich enough so they can afford to pay $2,000 or more per gun for fancy fit and finishing, we will have to accept the fact that most weapons made today just will not measure up for "sheer pretty" to a Winchester made in 1880.

On the other hand, great strides have been made mechanically. Not only are modern replica firearms being made from steel of unimaginably better quality than the steel available back in the 1880s, the replica arms makers have actually upped the ante by improving their overall quality, in some instances dramatically. So then, if we use dependability as the criteria for quality, we begin to see a very different picture. I will give you a couple of good examples of this. The first are a pair of Uberti-made Schofields that have fired over 10,000 rounds each. I know the owner spent some money on gunsmithing for both guns just after he purchased them new and that was in order to get them operating up to a satisfactory level of dependability. Since then these guns have been fired an average of probably 300 shots each, per week. I am told both guns break cylinder stop springs about every 2,000-2,500 shots and both still have the original mainsprings. In my experience, if these were original S&W revolvers, they would be breaking cylinder stop springs about every 200-500 shots and mainsprings would be breaking at a similar rate. Sure, without a doubt the old Smith & Wesson's are beautifully made firearms; far more beautiful than any replica that has yet been produced and likely no one will ever duplicate that gorgeous machine work! However, I have been shooting, repairing and restoring the originals for more than 30 years and I have to tell you truly, the originals require far more maintenance to keep going in the face of the kind of hard use these Italian replicas have endured.

I also have a close friend who owns and shoots replicas of the model 1866 Winchester hard and fast in CAS competition, sometimes burning up 500 rounds or more in a week practicing. One of these rifles has fired in excess of 20,000 rounds with only one minor part failure in all that time. That is incredible performance and I know for a fact that is not the only Uberti-made replica that has shown this kind of dependability. To be quite blunt, I do not believe an original 19th century Winchester would deliver that sort of dependable performance under similar circumstances. Moreover, these replicas are more than just efficient ammo burners. In most cases they also deliver accuracy that is on par with the originals and in some cases better. We cannot overlook Marlin's modern-made lever-actions and the incredible single-actions made by Sturm, Ruger & Co. Perhaps we can't quite call them unbreakable, but they are the closest thing to being unbreakable that we have seen. Back to the important question. Do the replica firearms in general measure up to their 19th century counterparts? Well now, sometimes they may not look quite as pretty (but sometimes they look better!). Some of the replicas might not operate quite as smoothly, but yes indeed, from a practical standpoint, as a general rule many of the modern replicas will outperform the originals and sometimes they will do this handsomely.

The growing popularity of CAS is such that whole industries are sprouting up around this intriguing new sport. Industries that include not only firearms, but ammunition, reloading supplies, repair tools, clothing, hats, boots, leather, gun carts, steel targets, not to mention the never-ending plethora of gizmos and gadgets, running the gamut between the ridiculous and the sublime, that seem to go hand-in-hand with almost any exciting hobby. CAS is a healthy, competitive pastime that is here to stay and I am delighted to see that. Now, let's have a look at some of the guns and gear being used by the modern cowboy in today's New West.

David R. Chicoine
North Carolina
September 2004

Chapter 1

Where do we find the New West?

What in the world is the New West? Here's just a little background.

Out on the back porch of the infamous "Wade Ranch and Saloon", cowboy shooter Jake Slade (Ed Wade) demonstrates his one-handed "duelist" stance. The revolver is a 7 1/2-inch Colt Single Action Army in .45 Colt. All the leather was hand-made by James Allen.

What we have termed the New West is, in fact, the huge resurgence of interest in the American West when that region was the frontier. This love of all things "cowboy" has been driven over the last 20-plus years by the sport of cowboy action shooting. And just where are these cowboy action shooting activities taking place, where is the "New West"? Well, it certainly sounds a lot like something that must be happening somewhere west of the Mississippi River, but I am happy to report that is not the case. Cowboy action shooting was officially started in the early 1980s in California. Since then it has spread rapidly all over the United States to include competitions in such very "Eastern" places as Charlotte, N.C., and Augusta, Maine. Considered the fastest growing outdoor shooting sport in the country, probably in the world, CAS provides competitors with a sport that tests the shooter's accuracy, attention, dexterity and equipment in a setting purposely created to have the look and feel of the Old West and the lifestyle of the American cowboy and frontiersman.

The Single Action Shooting Society (SASS) is the prominent governing organization for the sport of cowboy action shooting. Today, SASS is an international organization that is headquartered in Yorba Linda, Calif. More than 53,000 SASS members share not only a love of shooting, but a love of the history of the American West or, as it is most often called, the Old West. They are linked by a common bond at SASS-sponsored regional matches being run by more than 450 SASS-affiliated clubs in all 50 states and in 18 foreign countries. Perhaps of even greater importance is the fact that the organization and its affiliated clubs are governed by a set of procedures and rules which, from what we have seen, are practiced faithfully. Understanding first that CAS is a live-ammunition action-shooting sport, we can see how the code of conduct and those safety rules have contributed immeasurably to cowboy action shooting's excellent, and consistent safety record.

To use their own words, taken directly from the *SASS Shooter's Handbook,* April 2003 edition, "Cowboy Action Shooting is a multifaceted shooting sport in which contestants compete with firearms typical of those used in the taming of the Old West: single-action revolvers, lever-action rifles, and side-by-side double-barreled, pre-1899 pump, or lever-action shotguns. The shooting competition is staged in a unique, characterized, "Old West" style. Contestants shoot in several one- to four-gun stages (courses of fire) in which they engage reactive steel and cardboard silhouette targets. Scoring is based on accuracy and speed."

One activity that sets SASS-approved cowboy action shooting apart, and helps to make it fun, is the costume requirement. Participants have to adopt a unique alias and must dress in a manner fitting of that character. Your cowboy name may be that of some authentic or fictional Western personality such as Palaver Pete or Jake Slade. It may even be the name of a Hollywood Western star, real or imagined, like Roy Rugers (who of course, shoots Ruger Vaquero revolvers!) Whatever name you chose for an alias, it has to be unique; the rules state that just like old cattle brands, there should be no two alike.

Based on a desire to maintain the authenticity of the characters, costuming rules are very specific. Therefore, even if those characters are fictional, participants should try to look as correct as possible in order to fit the role they are playing. Moreover, all clothing has to be worn for the duration of the match. "Duration" includes later awards ceremonies, so you a person can't compete, then go back to the SUV and change into shorts and a Grateful Dead t-shirt and come back to roam among the contestants. Participants must select from at least three costume requirements. Their clothing may include (from the list given in the SASS Shooter's Handbook, April 2003 edition) "Chaps, spurs, cuffs, scarf worn loosely around the neck or with scarf slide, tie, vest, pocket watch with full-length chain, jacket, no straw hats allowed. In addition to the above items, ladies may choose from the items listed below in order to compete within this category: Period watch, split riding skirt, bustle, hoops, corset, Victorian-style hat (straw allowed), period jewelry, period hair ornaments (e.g. feathers), snood, reticule (period handbag), period lace up shoes, camisole, bloomers, fishnet stockings, feather boa, cape." Boots have to be of traditional design with plain soles and hats (how could you be a cowboy without a hat, one of the main necessities!) should be worn for the duration of the match.

Here is a big part of why these cowboy action events are fun; you get to wear all your gear. Heck, even the horses can get in on the action. This is Roy Rugers (Fred Stann) and his pal Rusty. Both are dressed in period garb and ready for some serious cowboyin'.

CAS participants also have a code that they rely on in all the matches called "The Spirit of the Game" and this really injects a great sense of fair play into all the events. As the sport evolved, the SASS members developed an attitude towards their competitions. To use SASS's own words "it is a code by which we live." To practice "The Spirit of the Game" is to participate fully in whatever the rules of the competition ask and to practice good sportsmanship and fair play. They are very serious about this and the fact that they are, I believe, genuinely helps to level the playing field and is a big reason the sport feels so friendly.

Another unique aspect of SASS is that the sport is not just for adult men, SASS encourages men, women, children and folks of varied age groups to be a part of this and the rules have a good selection of events tailored specifically for their safe participation. This is an active shooting sport that places the heaviest emphasis on the safe "recreational use of firearms" and is, at the same time, geared toward the theme of the opening of the American West. Participation in these events takes you back into a much simpler time in our history, a time that has always been universally fascinating. SASS activities are based around the idea of wholesome, honest camaraderie, injected with something that almost everyone seems to enjoy; a little bit of play-acting.

Just sitting around, waiting to be test fired. From left, EMF Hartford stainless 92, Marlin's 1894 Cowboy Competition, Cimarron Lightning 32-20 in a Texas Jack rig, Dixie Gun Works/Uberti Henry 44-40 and a Uberti 1866 carbine engraved by Ken Hurst.

Understandably, the sport also has definite rules concerning what kinds of firearms, ammunition and leather can be used in the events. For instance, firearms should look like the ones used during the Old West period. Revolvers should be traditional single-action, original or replica and with fixed sights. No visible external modifications are permitted other than (non-rubber) grips, recoil pads on shotguns, and leather wrapping of rifle finger levers. Modern soft-rubber or wooden target grips or grip tape are not allowed. Then there are the basic, common sense safety rules that are rigidly enforced. These include the old "load-five" rule; where six-shot revolvers are always loaded with only five rounds, the hammer is always placed back down on the empty chamber. That, by the way, is a very fine safety rule to practice on the range or off, its the only safe way to carry almost all conventional single-action revolvers loaded.

As to ammunition, here is another area where careful self-policing is helping to keep cowboy action shooting among the safest of shooting sports. For revolvers, only ammunition with a muzzle velocity of less than 1,000 fps is permitted and rifle ammunition must have a muzzle velocity of less than 1,400 fps. The SASS rules say shooters can be instantly disqualified and ejected from the match (ouch!) for damage or injury due to "bounce-back" caused by the use of "inappropriate ammunition" (We suppose that means ammo with too high a muzzle velocity.) All bullets must be lead, whether used in rifle or handgun. Black powder, its equivalents or smokeless powder are allowed.

It is easy to see why there are some necessary rules concerning gunleather. Rules state handguns must be carried in a safe holster that is capable of "retaining the firearm throughout a normal range of motion." Holster angles also cannot deviate from the vertical more than 30 degrees. Spare ammo for reloads during the events must be carried on the shooter in a bandoleer, a pistol belt, ammo pouch or pocket. All cartridge belts, bandoleers and pouches also must be of a traditional-looking design. Modern so-called drop pouches, combat-style shotgun loops, wrist or forearm bandoleers can't be utilized.

I don't know if anyone has an accurate handle on exactly how many people are involved in CAS around the world, but I believe there are at least as many people participating as a personal hobby in un-official groups as there are participating in officially sanctioned matches. Suffice to say, the numbers of people interested in cowboy shooting, reenacting, or who simply really enjoy the Old West and its weaponry, would be larger than most of us imagine. Because of this unprecedented amount of interest, all sorts of companies and individuals have popped up around the edges of the sport to support the

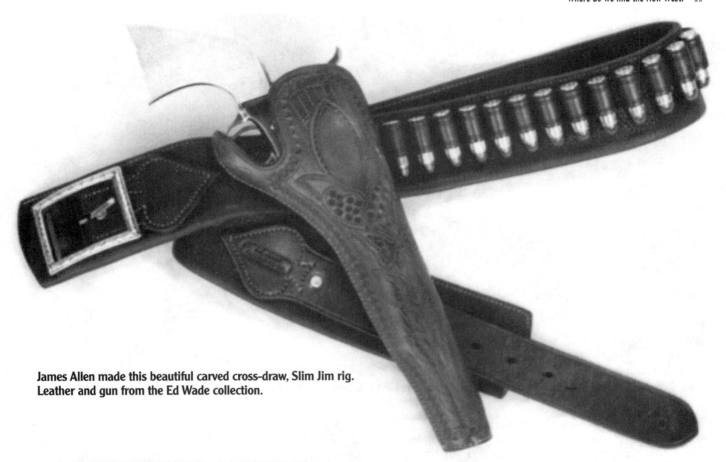

James Allen made this beautiful carved cross-draw, Slim Jim rig. Leather and gun from the Ed Wade collection.

Two of the percussion revolvers we tested for this book, the .36-caliber Uberti 1851 Navy (left) and the .44-caliber Model 1860 Army, also by Uberti, sit beside a couple Hornady Frontier cartridge boxes. Both revolvers are loaded, capped and ready to go. Revolvers courtesy Stoeger Industries.

many and varied needs of its ever-growing ranks. Not the least of these are gun companies, who are introducing, or should we say, re-introducing models with an Old West flavor. New and old holster makers and leather workers, boot makers, saddlery, clothing suppliers are producing "cowboy action gear" of every sort. The ammo companies are certainly all on the "chuck-wagon," offering cowboy action shooting loads for many calibers. To our delight these now include calibers that had been too long obsolete. Some companies are even decorating the ammo packaging with period artwork.

Think about it, where else could you go and dress up like a cowboy or Western movie actor, talk like you were from Wyoming, even though you grew up in Brooklyn, enjoy your favorite sport (shooting) and play the ham all at the same time without the slightest chance of being ridiculed? CAS is a wonderful sport. These activities promote honesty, moral correctness, a love of history and on top of that it's one heckuva' lot of fun. We predict it will only continue to experience even more rapid growth than it has seen thus far.

SASS maintains a very informative, user-friendly and colorful web site that you may access by going to www.sassnet.com on the Internet. The web site says they receive on average 1.5 million visits per month and the activity just continues to grow.

The EMF .45 Colt caliber Great Western II in satin nickel is being cleaned up after firing more than 100 rounds.

Incidentally, the SASS web site makes an excellent springboard to use when trying to locate suppliers for virtually anything that you might require to get started in this exciting sport. SASS also publishes a monthly newspaper for its membership, *The Cowboy Chronicle,* which prints more than 30,000 copies and carries ads from some 150 advertisers.

As we move through the book, we will be taking a closer look at some of the typical firearms being used in CAS competitions. We'll see how they look, feel and operate on the range. The concentration is on Main Guns, their ammunition and holsters, not on pocket pistols. With very few exceptions, these firearms are brand-new, just-out-of-the-box guns, so the readers can get an idea what to expect from factory-fresh firearms that have had no "extra work" whatsoever done to them. We'll also look at how they performed on paper targets, in most cases with two or more kinds of factory ammunition and we will offer our opinions on what we found. There is a look at contemporary cowboy ammunition and what is available to the shooter. We also take a look at gunleather (mainly holsters and belts, with a just a few chaps, cuffs and etc.) for cowboy shooters, but this is purposely not presented in a catalog form. Shown are several basic styles of holsters, with many variations on some of the styles, each of them with its own good features and points. Some of those features are very practical. Many are seen as purely aesthetic and in the eye of the beholder. For the SASS shooter both can be equally as important. What we've done is to offer you up a

Some of the handguns we tested on a cold April morning: (left row from top) Cimarron Stainelss Model P, Colt Cowboy, Cimarron Bisley, and Lightning, (right, top) Cimarron Richards-Mason conversion and Cimarron Open-Top .44.

selection of the many popular styles of holsters and gun rigs, both of traditional style and those that were inspired by the cowboys and gunfighters of the large and the small screen.

You will notice we did not attempt to examine every gun and holster that is available today. To be sure, there are many other brands, types, calibers and models of each, so to look at them all in-depth would have required a much larger volume, and perhaps this could have led to a not-so-careful look at each. In some cases, the choices of products or brands tested or examined were based solely on their availability, or the lack thereof, to the author at the time the book was written. This may or may not reflect their availability in your part of the country and at the time you read this book. In any event, with the heaviest emphasis placed on firearms, we have taken a selection of many of the most popular of each category, and reported the results based on what we actually saw. As a rule, what we saw was good. Sometimes it was not. Along with the good, the bad is also reported. The whole idea is to help you, the shooter, make up your own mind as to what not only looks good and works well, but what might be best suited for your own individual needs.

Single Action Shooting Society
23255 La Palma Avenue,
Yorba Linda, California 92887
(714) 694-1800, fax (714) 694-1815

Web resources:
SASS: www.sassnet.com
CAS-CITY: www.CasCity.com
    Kjell Heilevang aka: Marshal Halloway,
    SASS #3411 Regulator
    Email: marshal@cascity.com (620) 374-2093

Civil War Reenactors: www.cwreenactors.com
National Muzzle Loading Rifle Assn.: www.nmlra.org
World Fast Draw Assn.: WFDA-Info@fastdraw.org

Chapter 2

Replica vs. Original: The guns and a few shooters

This trio, Dusty, Brad and Cliff, could have been photographed in the 1880s, but they weren't. The photograph is actually one of Will Dunniway's remarkable modern tintypes.

When cowboy action shooting was in its infancy only a very few types of replica weapons were available for shooters to use. Not all of these replicas were of very good quality. That, of course, meant the brunt of the shooting was done using original 19th century weapons. Boy, how the scenery has changed since then. Today we are blessed to have a truly wonderful array of replica firearms to choose from. And, in the main, these firearms are of very good quality. Even so, some shooters still insist on being purists, they will settle for nothing less, competing regularly with original weapons that either they or their gunsmith work hard to keep running and up to snuff. Not that there is anything wrong with this. Those who shoot original guns know they are taking the chance of ruining an original firearm that has some historical significance, albeit often of minor importance. They know that, even if the gun doesn't actually break right away or get destroyed because of an accident or faulty ammunition, if they keep on shooting them in competition these guns will eventually wear out, finally deteriorating mechanically past the point where they could be successfully rebuilt. Hence, the physical loss is the owner's, although, as some would argue, there is a loss for posterity in this as well since there were only a limited number of these 19th century original weapons manufactured and when one is ruined it cannot be replaced. If that one less original were a rare Colt Walker revolver, then the loss to posterity would be truly significant. Certainly, such a loss is needless and would generate quite a stir. If however, the loss is just one more 1873 Winchester out of the 720,000 odd guns manufactured, its loss might be thought of as sustainable. These are great old rifles and yes, it's a shame, but its definitely not the end of the world.

El Paso Marshall, Dallas Stoudenmire preferred the Smith & Wesson .44 American for his serious business work. He owned a pair. Photo; *Guns of the Gunfighters*, Petersen Publishing Co.

Here is a rare Moore .32 rimfire single-action. A revolver just like this one was taken from Cole Younger after he was captured in Minnesota. From the David Fox collection. Author photo.

The famous S&W .44 American Model No. 3 single-action featured a top-break action and simultaneous ejection. This is a revolver much like the ones Marshal Dallas Stoudenmire used. Wyatt Earp is also known to have carried an American S&W. This is one revolver many shooters would love to have as a shooting replica. From the Ed Massenburg collection. Author photo.

For a long time I have supposed that I would fall somewhere in the middle on this argument. I have always thought it was a terrible shame to have a wonderful old gun fall victim to wear and tear. Having been a gunsmith for so many years I have witnessed more than my share of that. As I think about it, I can see that there is also a valid point on the other side of the coin. To what better use could you possibly put that original gun? From a practical viewpoint, the gun is being used–actually fired in realistic competition and this is something its owner is getting a lot of good clean fun out of. In many cases, the gun is getting used to a far greater degree than it ever would have been lounging in a gun rack somewhere, maybe getting hauled out to be shown off to the relatives once a year. Looking at it that way, I guess maybe I object a lot less to the use of originals in competition than I used to think I did. Regarding ruined firearms, to be perfectly truthful I have seen many more fine old firearms ruined forever by atrocious workmanship than I have seen wrecked by honest wear and tear. Those weapons having fallen prey not to hard use from shooting, but to the thoughtless tinkerer whose level of competency is too often far less than was required for the task.

This is Fred Stann striking a happy pose as Roy Rugers on his South Carolina horse farm. Fred is standing in front of several of the weapons tested for this book. As his alias hints, Roy prefers Ruger single-actions. Author photo.

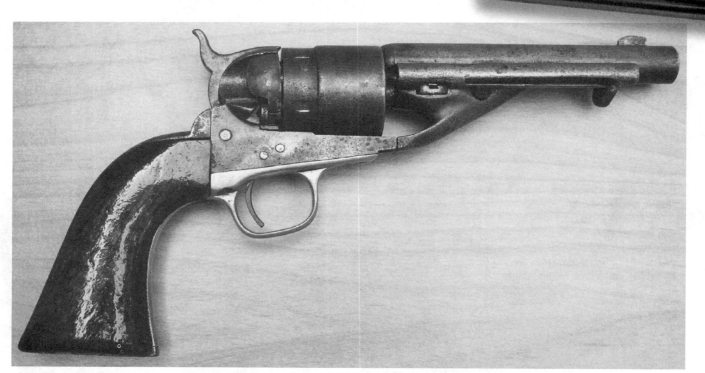

A genuine Civil War veteran Colt 1860 Army .44 that has been "gunsmith" converted to .44 Colt centerfire. This pup has seen some hard use, it's exactly the kind of gun we wish could talk. Maybe it would tell us all about its life on the American frontier. Uberti makes an excellent replica of the Colt Richards-Mason conversion revolver. From the Walt Penner collection. Author photo.

What's "right" with replica firearms?

Is there an argument for using them instead of originals that makes any sense? There is a lot "right" with replica firearms, and yes, there are several very sound reasons for using them, including what we just spoke about. To start with, modern, replica firearms can be readily replaced, so there is a sound argument that you can tear up as many modern replicas as you like, and history will still not be the worse off for it. We have often heard complaints about the quality of replica guns and the statement that the imported replicas were junk compared to the old, American originals. I think to some extent at least, that used to be true as a blanket statement for almost all the imported arms in this category. In all sincerity, in my experience for quite a few years now, what once may have been true is for the most part no longer the case. Times have changed and the replica arms makers have either changed with them, or gone out of business. Many of the replicas I have been shooting or that I have taken apart for repair, especially over the past, I will say four years or so, are standing up as well, and in some cases even better, yes I really did say better, than an original may have under similar situations of hard use and

This desperate-looking character is Floyd Oydegaard, aka Black Bart. Here, he looks like someone you might not want to cross paths with! From a modern tintype by Will Dunniway.

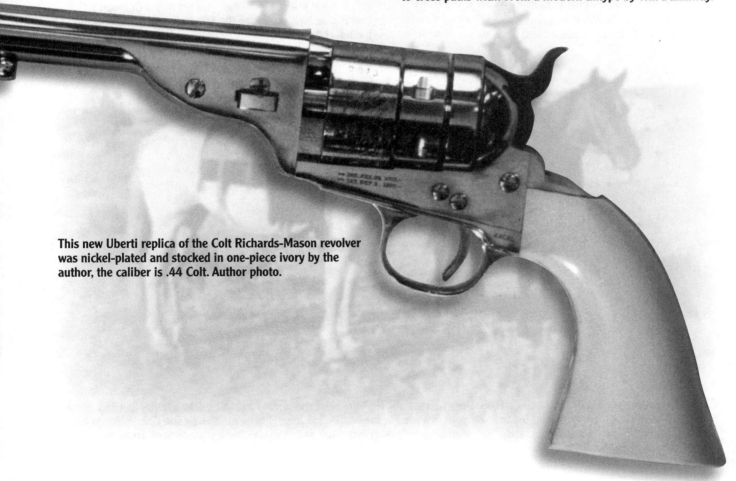

This new Uberti replica of the Colt Richards-Mason revolver was nickel-plated and stocked in one-piece ivory by the author, the caliber is .44 Colt. Author photo.

abuse. The steels in barrels, cylinders and receivers are 1000 percent better and for the most part, the springs in replicas are a world improved over 19th century springs. That does not mean the replica springs are of the correct tension or shape. Often they are not. It means in many cases you can count on the replica spring to operate the part it drives from four to six times longer than an original spring would have before it broke.

Just as it did with original guns, modern cowboy competition pushed the replica guns for all they were worth. Some of them couldn't cut the mustard; many of them developed problems ranging from annoying broken springs to some more serious timing issues that caused guns to blow up. We've watched how most of the Italian makers have responded to these complaints and frankly, I believe they all dragged their feet for more than a few years, perhaps hoping the problems would go away. Of course, the issues didn't go away and to their credit, companies like Uberti, Pietta and Pedersoli eventually did respond to the requests and complaints of American shooters. Once again, we've watched as these companies have made great strides to "clean up their act" over the last few years, trying to produce a more mechanically sound firearm. From what I have seen so far, the results are very promising. We have also noticed a definite improvement in the areas of fit-up (metal-to-metal and wood-to-metal fit) along with a dramatic improvement in external finish work. Oh no, in most (but not all) of these cases, the finish work is still

This is what it looks like when you are about to load-up the Colt Richards, can you see the firing pin just in front of the hammer? Author photo.

C.B. Richards conversions of the 1860 Colt .44 Army percussion revolvers were chambered in .44 Colt. Notice the hammer has a flat face? The Richards used a spring-loaded firing pin mounted in the conversion ring. This gun is an original Colt-Richards that someone restored years ago. Unfortunately, the original cylinder was lost. The one in the photo is a replacement. From the Walt Penner collection. Author photo.

Jake Slade (Ed Wade) ridin' the range with Rusty. The genuine Colt 7-1/2-inch .45 is nestled in a hand-carved James Allen slim-jim holster, while his primary weaponry is a modern, Pedersoli-made replica of the .45-70 caliber model 1873 U.S. Springfield carbine. Author photo.

not up to 1870s Smith & Wesson quality. On the other hand, replica finish quality today is pretty darn good by any measure, I can tell you its a marked improvement over the looks of some of those 1970s and 1980s imports.

Modern replica firearms also come with something the 100-year-old originals do not, and cannot come with; something that is called accountability. No one would argue with the fact that the guarantee on the S&W Schofield and that 1873 Winchester ran out quite a few generations ago. If you have a problem of any sort with one of these old-timers, there is no one that you can turn to for warranty assurance; you own the problem just as you own the gun. If you have a problem with a replica firearm, you may take your grievance back to the importer, who in my experience, will usually respond to your complaint.

Kaboom! The very shootable replica of the 1860 Colt .44 Army made by Uberti is shown here in full recoil. With 28 grains of FFFg black powder, it sure does make a wonderful smoke screen! Author photo.

There is one excellent aspect of replica firearms that we have not really touched on yet; an idea that I for one enjoy very much. This would be that the old "coulda, woulda, shoulda" speculation can now be made to come true. You know, those "wish-guns" we've so often sat around with the bunch talking about, saying they shoulda been made back in the day, but, too bad doggon' it, they weren't!" Well, now those "wish guns" are, to some extent, being manufactured. There are guns such as the neat little Cimarron Lightning single-action, which is similar in size and shape to the medium-framed Colt 1877 double-action (they share an almost identical grip shape and size), yet the 1877 itself will probably never be reproduced. This is both because the 1877 is a double-action, so its usefulness for SASS would be nil and because its mechanism is a nightmarish conglomeration of continually breaking parts. There are also the large-framed single-actions with rounded-butts and bird's-head grips that are built on the 1873 SAA frame. The shape of the grips are likened to the 1877 or the bigger 1878 Colt double-action, this was another double-action revolver of the same time period, one that had a sound mechanical design, but alas, its a DA.

Another good coulda, shoulda example would be the lever-action, short rifle concept that has become the hot-ticket in competition. Not really a wish-gun, in the old days Winchester actually made small numbers of lever-actions in this configuration, so this is not a replica of something that wasn't, but it is a replica of something that originally was produced in very small numbers. From a practical standpoint, the short rifle is one of the better ideas to come along and it works perfectly for Cowboy competition; it's short and easy to swing like a carbine yet with its stiff octagon barrel, the little rifle is front-heavy

Smith & Wesson's .44 double-action top-break was first introduced in 1881 chambered in .44 S&W Russian caliber, later they made a slightly elongated version (pictured) in .44-40 Winchester that was called the Double Action Frontier. In later years John Wesley Hardin owned one. Author photo.

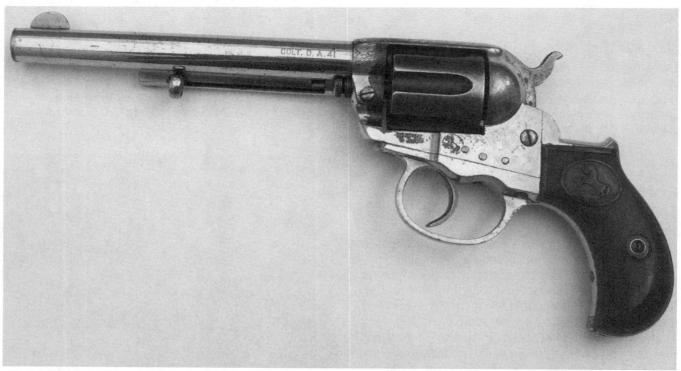

The 1877 Colt double-action was offered in .41 Colt and .38 Colt. This one is a .41 caliber, aka the Thunderer, it is very much like the one Cole Younger gave to a museum after he was released from prison. Billy the Kid and John Wesley Hardin are also reported to have owned 1877 Colts. Cimarron's Lightning single-action is almost the same size and shape as the 1877. From the Walt Penner collection. Author photo.

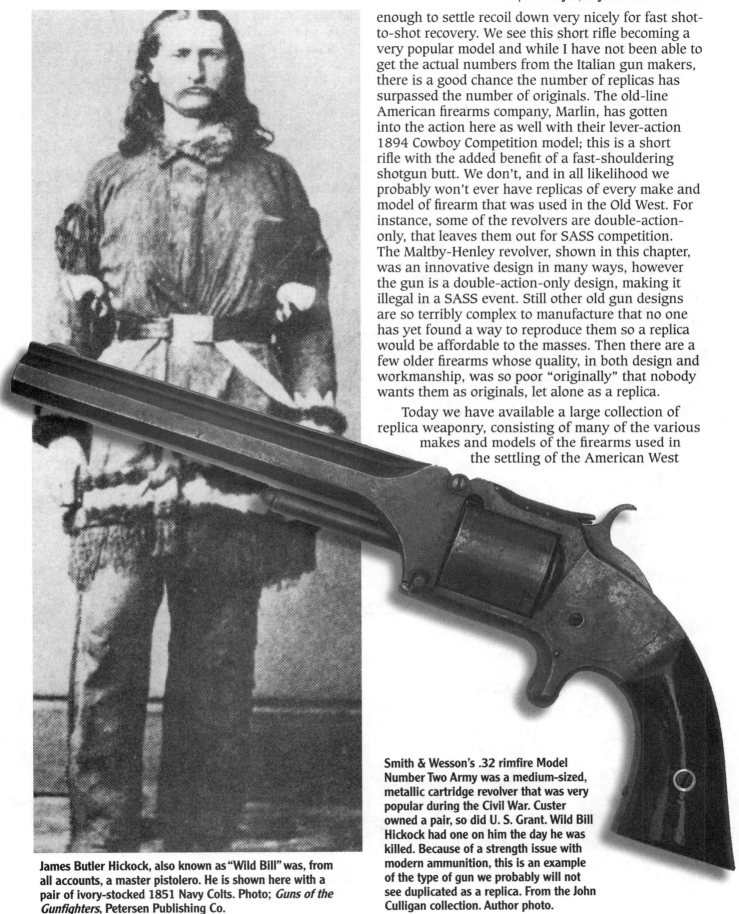

enough to settle recoil down very nicely for fast shot-to-shot recovery. We see this short rifle becoming a very popular model and while I have not been able to get the actual numbers from the Italian gun makers, there is a good chance the number of replicas has surpassed the number of originals. The old-line American firearms company, Marlin, has gotten into the action here as well with their lever-action 1894 Cowboy Competition model; this is a short rifle with the added benefit of a fast-shouldering shotgun butt. We don't, and in all likelihood we probably won't ever have replicas of every make and model of firearm that was used in the Old West. For instance, some of the revolvers are double-action-only, that leaves them out for SASS competition. The Maltby-Henley revolver, shown in this chapter, was an innovative design in many ways, however the gun is a double-action-only design, making it illegal in a SASS event. Still other old gun designs are so terribly complex to manufacture that no one has yet found a way to reproduce them so a replica would be affordable to the masses. Then there are a few older firearms whose quality, in both design and workmanship, was so poor "originally" that nobody wants them as originals, let alone as a replica.

Today we have available a large collection of replica weaponry, consisting of many of the various makes and models of the firearms used in the settling of the American West

James Butler Hickock, also known as "Wild Bill" was, from all accounts, a master pistolero. He is shown here with a pair of ivory-stocked 1851 Navy Colts. Photo; *Guns of the Gunfighters*, Petersen Publishing Co.

Smith & Wesson's .32 rimfire Model Number Two Army was a medium-sized, metallic cartridge revolver that was very popular during the Civil War. Custer owned a pair, so did U. S. Grant. Wild Bill Hickock had one on him the day he was killed. Because of a strength issue with modern ammunition, this is an example of the type of gun we probably will not see duplicated as a replica. From the John Culligan collection. Author photo.

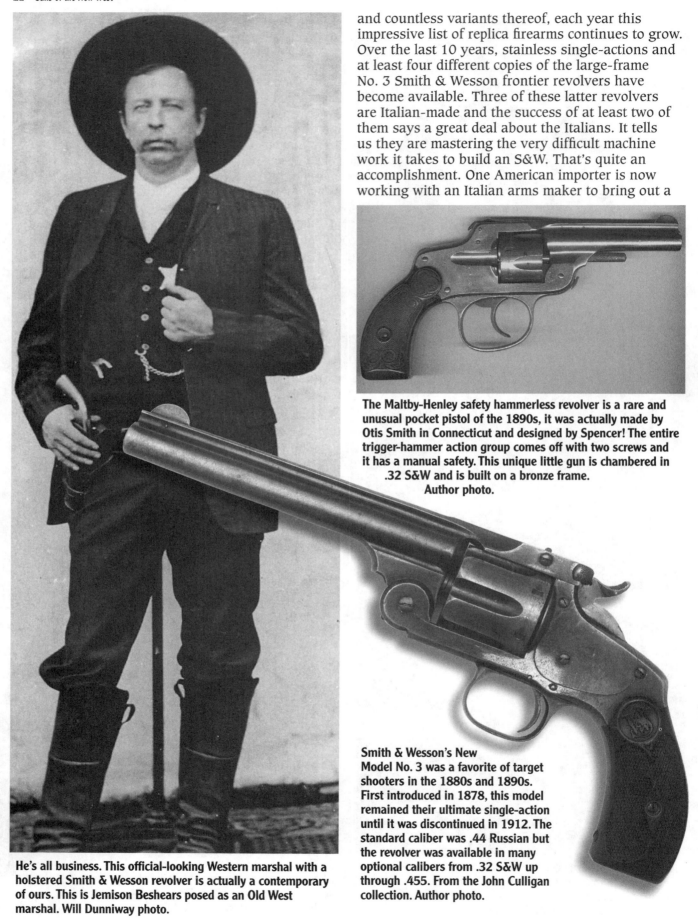

and countless variants thereof, each year this impressive list of replica firearms continues to grow. Over the last 10 years, stainless single-actions and at least four different copies of the large-frame No. 3 Smith & Wesson frontier revolvers have become available. Three of these latter revolvers are Italian-made and the success of at least two of them says a great deal about the Italians. It tells us they are mastering the very difficult machine work it takes to build an S&W. That's quite an accomplishment. One American importer is now working with an Italian arms maker to bring out a

The Maltby-Henley safety hammerless revolver is a rare and unusual pocket pistol of the 1890s, it was actually made by Otis Smith in Connecticut and designed by Spencer! The entire trigger-hammer action group comes off with two screws and it has a manual safety. This unique little gun is chambered in .32 S&W and is built on a bronze frame. Author photo.

Smith & Wesson's New Model No. 3 was a favorite of target shooters in the 1880s and 1890s. First introduced in 1878, this model remained their ultimate single-action until it was discontinued in 1912. The standard caliber was .44 Russian but the revolver was available in many optional calibers from .32 S&W up through .455. From the John Culligan collection. Author photo.

He's all business. This official-looking Western marshal with a holstered Smith & Wesson revolver is actually a contemporary of ours. This is Jemison Beshears posed as an Old West marshal. Will Dunniway photo.

replica of the Merwin-Hulbert single-action (now you talk about complicated machine work!) and an 1876 Winchester rifle. That one I want to see! We also got hold of a replica Colt Lightning the 1880s Colt pump-action design. This is an all American-made weapon, produced by USFA in Hartford, competitively priced, it will be available in several grades and chambered for .44-40 or .45 Colt.

I have often been asked the question, "Just how many of these Italian-made replica firearms are there in the United States?" It's a question I have not yet been able to answer, but it is a valid question and something that I have long wondered about, so I made some inquiries. We were not able to obtain the figures from all the companies who make replica firearms, nor could we get a grand total on such short notice. I would like to express

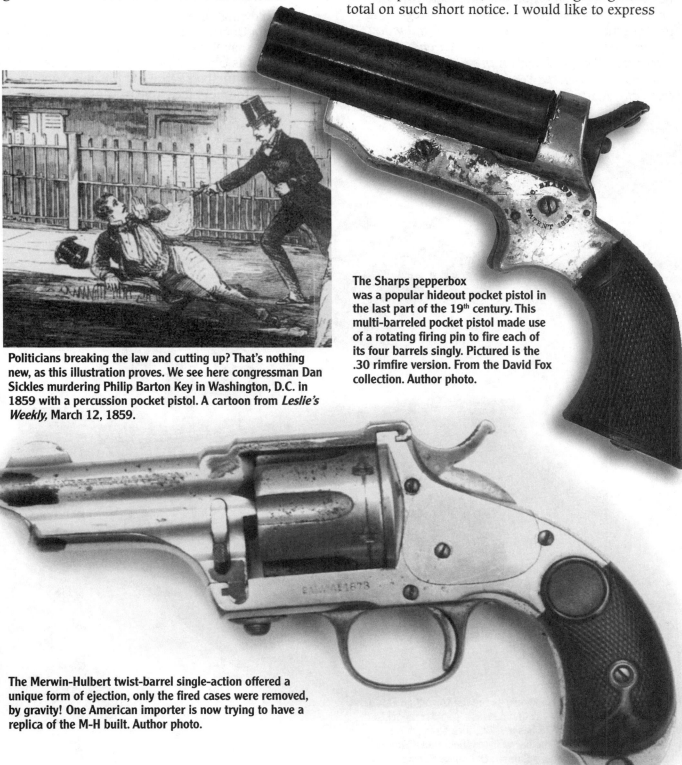

Politicians breaking the law and cutting up? That's nothing new, as this illustration proves. We see here congressman Dan Sickles murdering Philip Barton Key in Washington, D.C. in 1859 with a percussion pocket pistol. A cartoon from *Leslie's Weekly,* March 12, 1859.

The Sharps pepperbox was a popular hideout pocket pistol in the last part of the 19th century. This multi-barreled pocket pistol made use of a rotating firing pin to fire each of its four barrels singly. Pictured is the .30 rimfire version. From the David Fox collection. Author photo.

The Merwin-Hulbert twist-barrel single-action offered a unique form of ejection, only the fired cases were removed, by gravity! One American importer is now trying to have a replica of the M-H built. Author photo.

my gratitude to Mr. Merlino and to Suzanne Webb of A. Uberti Spa in Italy, who were generous enough to provide me with some approximate sales figures. These figures reflect only Uberti firearms that have been exported to the U. S. for the last 10 years, but some of this is eye-opening.

I asked the question, "How many single actions has Uberti made based on the 1873 pattern?" In an e-mail response from Suzanne Webb regarding that question, she says; *Between 1994 and today we have produced 142,500 Single Actions. Another interesting thing to know on these Cattleman is that Uberti is able to make 800,000 variants if we take into consideration all the different calibers, barrel* *lengths, finishes, engravings, different grips. Maybe there is only a small difference between them but there is a difference. We could lay out 800,000 different Single Actions. I don't think anyone else could do this!! Mr. Merlino has checked the quantity of all Single Actions made right from the beginning when they started production. We are now at 300,000 pcs!!*

The following table represents approximate exports from Uberti to the United States over the last 10 years, the smaller numbers represent sales in the earlier years, as Uberti says, closer to 10 years ago and the larger numbers represent the approximate sales figures for more recent years.

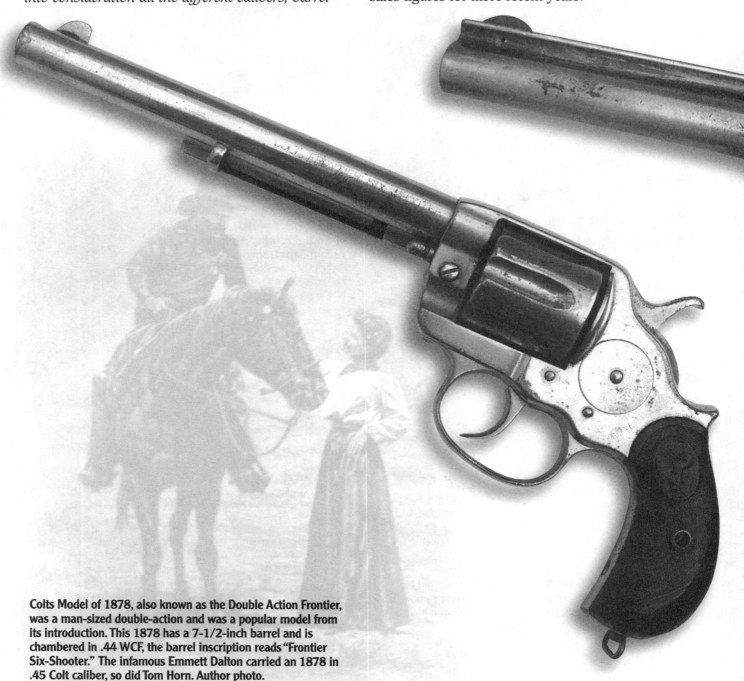

Colts Model of 1878, also known as the Double Action Frontier, was a man-sized double-action and was a popular model from its introduction. This 1878 has a 7-1/2-inch barrel and is chambered in .44 WCF, the barrel inscription reads "Frontier Six-Shooter." The infamous Emmett Dalton carried an 1878 in .45 Colt caliber, so did Tom Horn. Author photo.

Uberti firearm model	Per year, early years	Per year, later years
1851 Navy	400	900
1860 Army	500	1,500
Remington New Model	1,500	3,000
Colt 1873 type SAA variants	11,000	24,000
S&W Top-Break types	2,000	4,000
Henry lever-action	1,300	2,100
1866 lever-action	800	2,800
1873 lever-action	1,400	3,600
1885 High-Wall	500	1,200

This book. . . is a look at a few of the original weapons used in the Old West along with a few of the original characters who used them, interspersed with visits from a few of our own, modern-day but quite authentic-looking cowboy shooters and Old West reenactors.

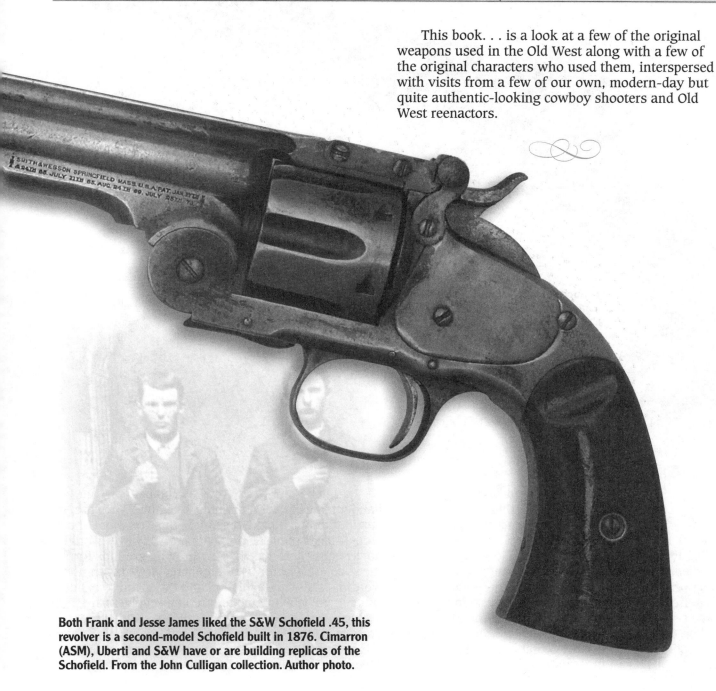

Both Frank and Jesse James liked the S&W Schofield .45, this revolver is a second-model Schofield built in 1876. Cimarron (ASM), Uberti and S&W have or are building replicas of the Schofield. From the John Culligan collection. Author photo.

Chapter 3

Handguns of the New West; where today's Cowboy Competiton revolvers came from.

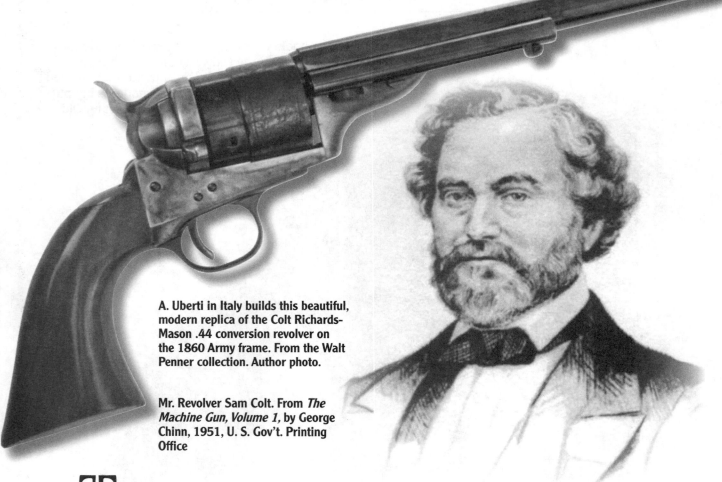

A. Uberti in Italy builds this beautiful, modern replica of the Colt Richards-Mason .44 conversion revolver on the 1860 Army frame. From the Walt Penner collection. Author photo.

Mr. Revolver Sam Colt. From *The Machine Gun, Volume 1,* by George Chinn, 1951, U. S. Gov't. Printing Office

The handguns used in cowboy competition shooting mimic, to a large degree, the actual weapons used on the American frontier during the period of western expansion. Not represented are the double-action handguns, which aren't permitted under SASS rules. These handguns range from the very slow-to-load percussion pistols, of the type from the antebellum era, to the ultra-fast-loading top-break cartridge revolvers; copies of Smith & Wesson's Model Number 3 that in the 1870s, were the state-of-the-art firearms.

In this kind of heavy cowboy competition, the handguns really end up taking a beating. They are, in fact, put to much more demanding use on more of a regular basis than the originals probably ever would have been. These matches are proving grounds for the shooters and for the equipment. Any sixgun not worth its salt will rapidly fail and fall by the wayside. Quite literally, many modern replica revolvers are seeing more action in a weekend shoot and in the practice leading up to that weekend, than most original revolvers actually saw in their existence. Given that fact, we have to admit that it is really a

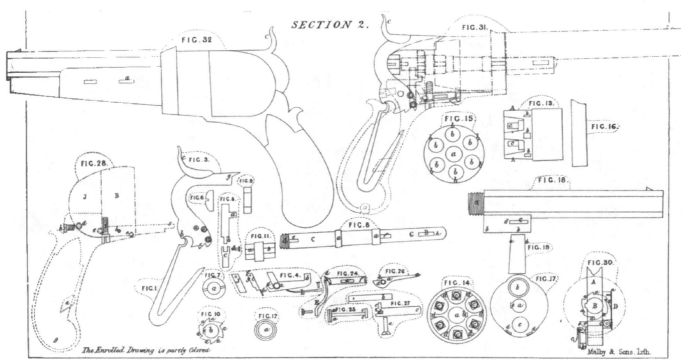

The original revolver patent shown here is from the lower portion of Colt's British patent, granted in 1835.

testimony to the inherent quality of some modern-made replica firearms and this may cause some shooters to pause for a moment. That statement is especially true for those who may have, in the past, offered vocal opposition to the quality of those copies from Italy. The times they are a changin'!

Real cowboys did carry percussion revolvers!

Oh yes, in the real Old West, typical handguns included a goodly portion of single-action and even some double-action percussion revolvers of Civil War or pre-war vintage. The Colt percussion revolver seems to have been the most prominent and it, of course, stems from the original Paterson revolver and the Colt's revolver patent of 1835. Colt's cap-and-ball revolvers really reached their zenith of mechanical perfection and beauty with the 1848-1849 pocket models, although innovations continued to evolve, such as the geared ramming lever used on the 1860

Remington's .44 caliber New Model Army was a very popular revolver both during and after the Civil War. This photo and the one below showing the ramrod down for cylinder removal are both of a fine-quality modern replica manufactured in Italy by Pietta. Author photos.

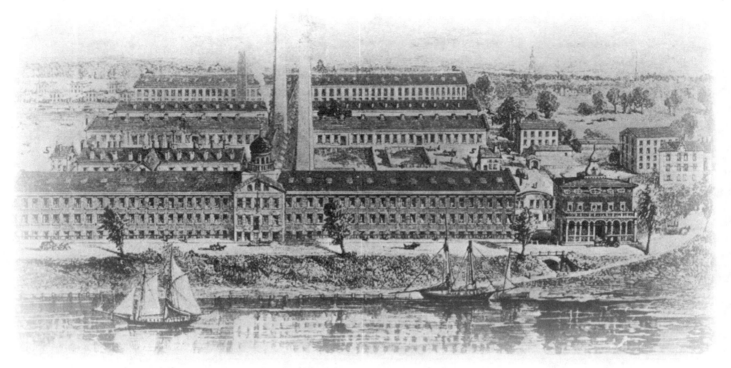

The Colt Armory at the height of war production as it looked circa 1862-1864 before being destroyed by a monstrous fire.

Elisha K. Root worked for Colt for many years and after Sam Colt's death succeeded him as president. An ingenious man, Root invented many of the machines used to produce Colt's revolvers. From *A History of the Colt Revolver* by Haven & Belden, 1940, Bonanza.

and 1861 models. Our Civil War caused an upsurge in the mass production of cap-and-ball revolvers and the appearance of many other makes and models, such as the well-liked Remington single-action and the Starr revolver. The latter was available in both double- and single-action versions.

Colt's percussion revolvers and the copies were for the most part, open-topped. In other words, they had no frame top-strap and the barrel was very much a separate component part, being fastened in place on the frame's arbor with a simple steel wedge device. Revolvers such as the Remington, on the other hand, had the advantage of being solid-framed. That meant the frame girded the cylinder, enabling the barrel to be firmly screwed into the frame, this offered the shooter a revolver with greater strength, and without the potential of a barrel becoming loose and interfering with either accuracy or dependability. On the whole, percussion revolvers of both types proved their mettle in the war. The poor guns fell by the wayside into disuse, while the good ones proved themselves outstanding. When the war ended, large numbers of these so-called obsolete weapons were carried westward by veterans into the new American frontier, and you can be sure that those revolvers played a much more prominent role than they are generally given credit for in the winning of the American West.

After making that statement, I am often asked: Why were there so many percussion revolvers still in use well into the time when everyone could have had modern metallic cartridge revolvers? The answers may be debatable, but I think there were at least three very good reasons for this. First, because during the 20 or so years that followed the Civil War, a percussion revolver was much less expensive and would have been very easy to come by compared to a cartridge revolver. This was not only because of the huge wartime production of percussion weapons, but on account of the metallic cartridge technology born just before the war. These two factors combined to create a glut of these percussion weapons that the market now considered obsolete: Hence, less expensive. Also, so many war veterans were intimately familiar with their percussion revolvers, having used them with success in combat for years. These folks did not feel in any way inadequate or under-gunned and others simply saw no earthly reason to make such a drastic, and expensive change. The financial consideration part of that last sentence makes even more sense when you understand that the majority of people who moved west after the war were dirt-poor. Buying a new weapon when they already had one that was perfectly serviceable would not have been an option for most people. Finally and from a very practical standpoint, although these percussion revolvers were far slower to load, the fact remains that until the cylinder chambers were emptied, they were every bit as deadly as the new metallic cartridge revolvers. So, there continued to be a demand for cap-and-ball revolvers well into the metallic cartridge era.

Wild Bill Hickock would probably be happy to attest to that fact, if we could ask him. Hickock is actually a good example of what we are talking about. This noted gunman carried a pair of unaltered 1851 Colt Navy models well into the cartridge era. And, just so we don't think of him as totally old-fashioned, Wild Bill also owned a Smith & Wesson Model 2 in .32 Rimfire caliber. In fact, he had this gun on him the day he was murdered. Colt actually continued to make percussion revolvers into the mid-1870s and Remington did so until nearly 1880. Buffalo Bill Cody is said to have used a New Model Remington Army percussion revolver throughout his stint as a scout in the Indian Wars and as a buffalo hunter, he said of his Remington revolver, *"It never failed me."*[1]

Colt's huge Walker Dragoon revolver was truly the magnum handgun of its day. Its cavernous chambers could be loaded with as much as 60 grains of black powder; as much as many contemporary muzzle loading carbines! The revolver shown is a faithful, replica by A. Uberti of Italy. Author photo.

One contemporary of the 1850s Colt was the British designed Beaumont-Adams revolver. This particular revolver was built in the U.S.A. by Massachusetts Arms. It's a percussion, five-shot .31 caliber, double- and single-action revolver equipped with a manual safety device. Very advanced for its day and exceedingly well made by anyone's standards. From the Bob Brecht collection. Author photo.

Colt made percussion revolvers that ranged in size from the diminutive five-shot .31 caliber pocket pistols on up to the oversized .44 caliber Dragoon models which had longer than normal cylinders, allowing great charges of powder to be loaded under the ball. The little pocket models were small enough that they might be concealed in a jacket pocket, but those Dragoon pistols where generally too large and heavy to be carried comfortably in belt holsters. They were more easily slung in a holster off the saddle of a horse, as their name implied. The most popular Colt revolvers were of "belt-size." These were medium in stature, in between the pocket models and the Dragoons. They were the revolvers that were to prove

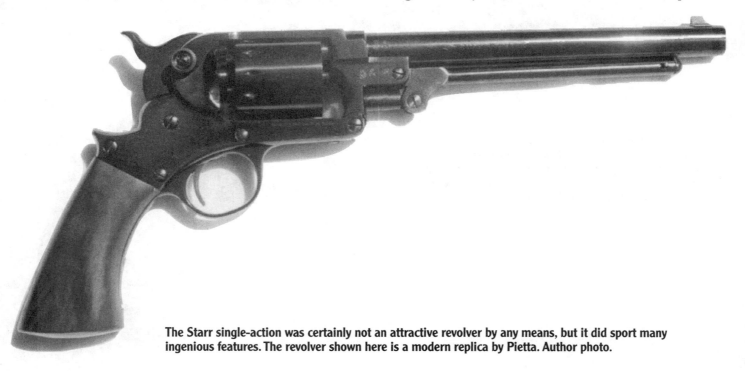

The Starr single-action was certainly not an attractive revolver by any means, but it did sport many ingenious features. The revolver shown here is a modern replica by Pietta. Author photo.

the most useful in a fight. Belt-sized revolvers like the .36 caliber 1851 and 1861 Navy Models and the .44 caliber Model 1860 Army were of heavy enough caliber to be effective man-stoppers but without the massive bulk of the Dragoons, so they could be comfortably carried in a belt holster.

The equivalent "belt" sized percussion revolvers from Remington were their Remington-Beals or New Model revolvers, which were available in both .36 Navy chambering and .44 Army calibers. Like the Colt, Remington also made a full range of percussion revolvers that ran from tiny pocket-sized .31 calibers up to full, belt-sized .44s, although they did not attempt to duplicate the ultra-large Colt Dragoon pistols. The upstate New York-based company, E. Remington & Sons, developed a reputation for making a dependable revolver early on. Despite the fact that the many 1860s and 1870s vintage Remington's the author has viewed apart displayed machine work that was not quite up to the same quality as contemporary S&Ws, or even that of Colts, the Remingtons worked well. They were strong and thought of as very good revolvers by both soldiers and civilians. Indeed, the .44 Remington Army was the second most popular revolver used during the Civil War and it was often held up as the example to compare other revolvers with. Our government actually kept many thousand on hand after the turn of the century, that was more than 35 years after the Civil War ended[2]! Because of the high demand for revolvers during the Civil War there were literally dozens of other, lesser-known gun makers offering belt-sized Army and Navy caliber percussion revolvers. These included better known names such as Starr in New York who produced innovative revolvers of their own design in double- and single-action. Metropolitan Arms, also of New York made copies of the several Colt revolvers and Rogers and Spencer in Utica, N.Y. made percussion revolvers that were similar to the Remington pattern.

The South was not the manufacturing giant that the North was during the Civil War, but they also produced percussion revolvers for their military, albeit on a comparatively limited scale, in Georgia, North Carolina, Virginia, Tennessee and Texas. Most of these revolvers were, in one form or another, copies of the Colt system then in fashion. Without a doubt, the most famous and legendary of all revolvers associated with the South would have to be the colorful Le Mat two-barreled revolver, also known as the "grape shot" revolver. Even though these percussion revolvers were manufactured overseas, an American designed the weapon and the Le Mat was popular with some Confederate officers, especially in the cavalry, for reasons that will quickly become obvious. The intimidating and unique Le Mat pistol featured a nine-shot, .42 caliber cylinder that rotated on a .63 caliber (about 20-gauge) shotgun barrel! An ingenious design, it featured a hammer with a pivoting head that could quickly be set to fire either the cylinder chambers or the center shotgun barrel.

The percussion enthusiasts of this new millennia are indeed fortunate to have a such wide array of very well made, replica percussion revolvers easily available to them. Last time I looked, I believe that everything Colt ever made as a percussion revolver, with the exception of the 1855 Root, is available today as a modern, fully functioning reproduction firearm. The available inventory doesn't stop with Colt replicas. We also have copies of a nice variety of other old guns, including Remington, Rogers & Spencer, as well as many other southern Civil War revolvers.

The dreaded confederate LeMat revolver held nine shots in its cylinder of .42 caliber and the cylinder revolved on a 20-gauge shotgun barrel. This is the high-quality replica manufactured in Italy by Pietta and it is actually a nine-shot .45! Revolver courtesy Dixie Gun Works. Author photo.

Horace Smith and Daniel Baird Wesson, founders of the Smith & Wesson arms dynasty. From *The Machine Gun, Volume 1,* by George Chinn, 1951, U. S. Gov't. Printing Office

The first cartridge revolvers...

Not all revolvers made during the so-called percussion era were percussion. The notable exceptions are the revolvers manufactured by Smith & Wesson in Springfield, Mass. The S&W was the first American metallic cartridge revolver. Beginning in 1857 when Colt's patent protection on the revolver expired, S&W invented, manufactured and sold successful metallic cartridge revolvers in .22 and .32 rimfire caliber. Although these revolvers were not purchased by the U.S. government for use in the war, many thousands of S&Ws were used during the Civil War by individuals and several hundred of the larger Model No. 2 revolvers were purchased by the State of Kentucky. The S&W revolvers were extremely well made and functioned beautifully. The down side was they had a weak design and the small-caliber rimfire ammunition they used was very underpowered when compared to the larger percussion revolvers then in common use. Nevertheless, the S&W system offered the shooter the ability to load a revolver with much greater speed and efficiency than any muzzle-loading system up to that point and the little S&Ws were highly sought after from the day they were introduced.

What set Smith & Wesson apart from anything else during that time was that they had the rights to a patent which covered the only sound method of loading a rimmed, metallic cartridge into a bored-through cylinder chamber from the rear. This infamous patent, the brainchild of an inventor named Rollin White, gave Smith & Wesson an effective monopoly on that concept, and hence, also on the ability to produce and sell metallic cartridge revolvers until its expiration in 1869. Such patent protection, for an idea based on commonly known principals, would likely not be possible to secure in modern times, yet somehow it was granted to White. The same thought might also apply to Colt's famous revolver patent, itself based on an ancient windlass, the mechanical principals of which had been common knowledge for millennia.

There are many original S&W tip-up revolvers floating around today and at first glance they might seem like a perfect candidate for SASS side matches. Please think again. These guns were all manufactured in the black-powder era, none of them were designed or proved for use with smokeless powder ammunition. We won't even get deeply into the fact that the design was considered really weak, even by the standards of yesteryear. So, even with mild smokeless loads the shooter stands a good chance of breaking the gun, or at the least having that little tip-up barrel unlatch upon discharging the weapon; when that happens the barrel ends up pointing straight at you, the shooter. That event by itself may cause you to think twice about firing these great little antique pocket guns again.

Smith & Wesson began manufacturing metallic cartridge revolvers in 1857 and they made tip-up revolvers like this one in .22 and .32 rimfire calibers until 1881. The revolver pictured is a seven- shot, .22 caliber Model No. 1, third issue built in 1872. Author photo.

This is Smith & Wesson's .44 caliber Model Number 3, introduced in 1870. This advanced top-break was the first metallic cartridge revolver to be used by the U.S. Army and predates the Colt SAA by three years. Author photo.

What was Colt thinking?

With that pesky S&W patent expiring in 1869, you would think Colt and the other large gun makers would have been waiting in the wings with new designs for cartridge revolvers in their hot little hands, but that just did not happen as quickly as you might suppose. It seems the watchword was frugality. We mentioned that "glut" of percussion revolvers left over from the Civil War; guns that had been pretty much made obsolete and devalued by the advent of metallic cartridges. That situation would only get worse as the market accepted the new metallic cartridge system to a greater degree. By the early 1870s, no one was more anxious to do something with the inventories of those old-time pistols than the Colt Firearms Company. One solution they tried for many years was to "pretty-up" the percussion revolvers by nickel plating them and offering them for sale equipped with an array of accessories at bargain prices. By the mid 1880s, C. J. Godfrey, a Colt distributor in New York was selling new, nickel-plated 1860 Army models for $4.50. That same company listed a nickel-plated Colt Dragoon for $5.50 or with detachable shoulder stock for $6.50, this was at a time when the Single Action Army was bringing a whopping $20.

Other marketing solutions came in the form of cartridge conversions as methods were devised to

Alexander Thuer the inventor. Photo from *A Study of Colt Conversions* by R. Bruce McDowell, Krause Publications.

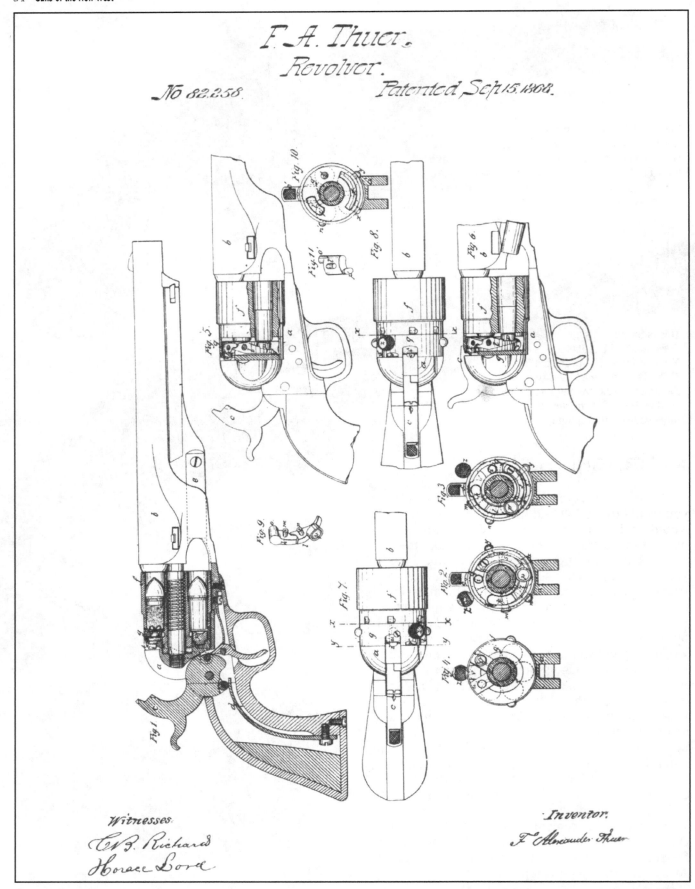

F. A. Thuer.
Revolver.
No 82,258.
Patented Sep 15. 1868.

Witnesses.
C. B. Richard
Horace Lord

Inventor.
F. Alexander Thuer

This 1868 patent to Alex Thuer shows how his conversion used tapered cartridges that were loaded from the front of the cylinder. A neat idea, but it was obsolete before the ink was dry.

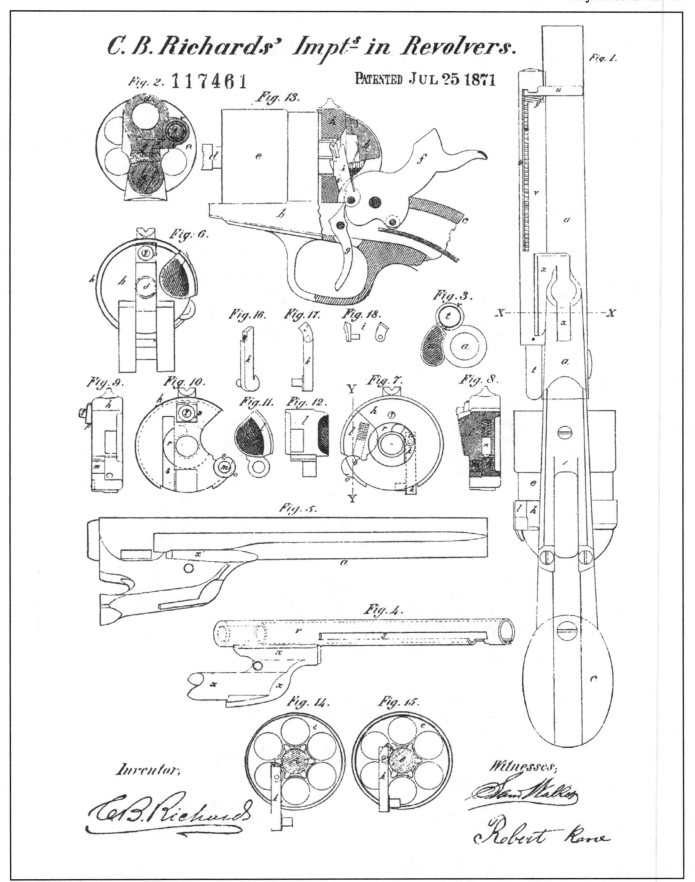

C.B. Richards very complete 1871 patent drawing gives the viewer a good look at how the Richards conversion worked.

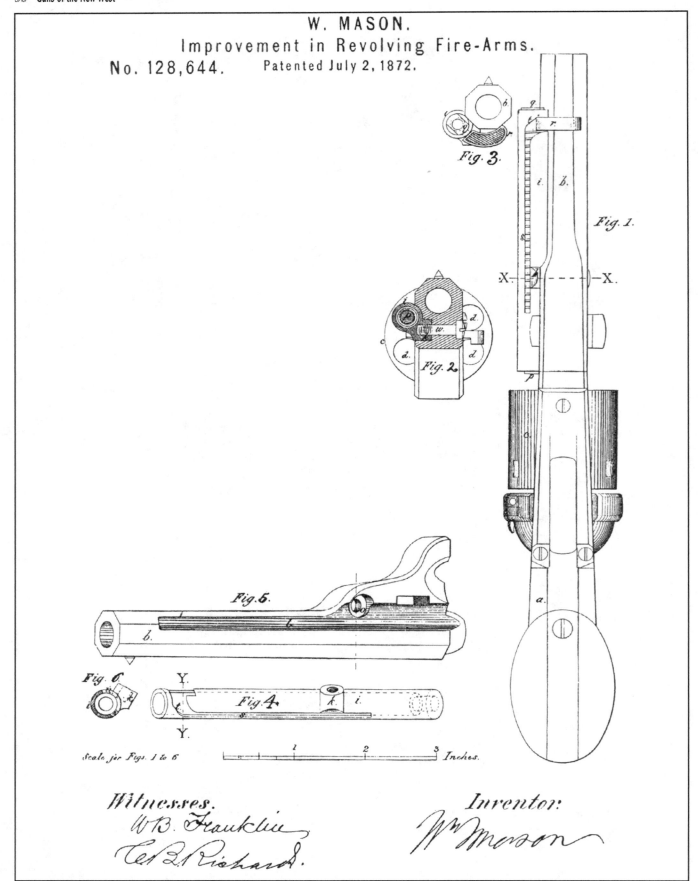

W. MASON.
Improvement in Revolving Fire-Arms.
No. 128,644.   Patented July 2, 1872.

Fig. 3.

Fig. 1.

Fig. 2.

Fig. 5.

Fig. 6.

Fig. 4.

Scale for Figs. 1 to 6.

Inches.

Witnesses.
W.B. Franklin
C.B. Richards.

Inventor:
Wm Mason

This 1872 William Mason patent covers the excellent tube ejector used on the Richards-Mason, the 1872 Open-Top and in modified form, on the Single Action Army of 1873. The patent drawing shows its application on an 1851 Navy.

COLT'S,
New Breech Loading
METALLIC CARTRIDGE REVOLVERS.
FOR SALE BY THE TRADE GENERALLY.
— MANUFACTURED BY —
Colt's Patent Fire Arms Manufg. Co.,
HARTFORD, CONN.

COLT'S,
METALLIC CARTRIDGE,
Army Six Shot Revolving Pistol.

.44 Calibre, Weight 2 lbs. 11 oz., Weight of ball 212 grains or 33 to the pound.

The Drawing is one-half the size of the Pistol.

PRICE $16.

COLT'S,
METALLIC CARTRIDGE,
Navy Six Shot Revolving Pistol.

.36 Calibre, Weight 2 lbs. 11oz.. Weight of ball 140 grains or 50 to the pound.

The general appearance of the Pistol is the same as that of the Army Pistol. See cut above.

PRICE $15.

This advertising broadsheet from 1872 shows the 1860 Army .44 with a C. B. Richards conversion. This one has the rare 12-notch cylinder.

convert these guns from the percussion system so they would accept metallic cartridges. Remington presented the first of the conversions in 1868 and it was actually licensed by Smith & Wesson under the Rollin White patent, where Remington, under license, converted 4,574 New Model .44 caliber Army revolvers to caliber .46 rimfire with five-shots. These revolvers were subsequently sent to Smith & Wesson for inspection where they were paid $1 per revolver[3]. After the Rollin White patent expired, other kinds of conversions, grown at the Remington factory, were soon put into use.

Of the Colt conversions, the Colt Thuer conversion patented Sept. 15, 1868, was the first. It was an oddity that actually got around the Rollin White patent but in so doing required a special Thuer cartridge, which loaded from the front, in order to fire the gun. The next, and more successful conversion, was the C.B. Richards Colt conversion. This one used a more conventional .44 centerfire cartridge along with a rod ejector mounted on the barrel. Of note was the Richards frame-mounted firing pin that was certainly ahead of its time. Last on the short list of Colt conversions was the Richards-Mason type. This conversion combined the efforts of C.B. Richards with a new barrel-mounted extractor mechanism from William Mason and a simplified, (read that; less expensive to make) hammer-mounted firing pin. Both the latter types of conversion made use of a specially machined frame plate or "conversion" plate, which was equipped with a loading gate. This required the factory to machine away a portion of the frame's breech face so the conversion plate could be attached to the frame. These revolvers also had the rear of their cylinders (but not the ratchet teeth) machined away. This exposed the rear of the cylinder chambers so

the cartridges could be inserted. A good number of these types of conversions were made using the .44 caliber 1860 Army Model revolvers as the basis. Lesser numbers were assembled on 1851 Navy and on the small pocket model frames. Cartridge conversions from percussion revolvers were sold by Colt, Remington and other makers until the middle to the late 1870s. By that time metallic cartridge revolvers really started to take over the market.

Colt's first actual made-for-cartridges revolver was the gun we know now as the 1871-1872 Open-Top. This revolver, as nicely balanced as it was, remained a bastard of sorts. It retained the open-top frame and a barrel held on with a wedge, just like the old percussion pistols. Well, at least the Open-Top's frame was actually machined to accept a loading gate, without the requirement of a separate conversion plate. Unlike the conversions, the 7,000 or so Open-Tops manufactured were chambered to fire the .44 rimfire cartridge. The world would have to wait for another year, until 1873, for Colt to introduce the now famous Single Action Army, a revolver that would combine the best features and lines of the percussion models along with a strong solid-topped frame and screwed in barrel. Now, we all know the rest of this story, so let's not jump too far ahead. . .more on that later.

The cowboy shooter has several nice Uberti-manufactured replicas to choose from that cover the gamut from several of the Richards-Mason conversions to the 1871-72 Open-Tops. A few short years ago there were copies of the Richards conversion on the market that were being built by ASM in Italy. Regrettably, their quality was not as high as we had hoped and they are prone to breakage. Since ASM has apparently gone bankrupt, there is today no easy source for parts.

S&W very quickly managed to export this new American technology with their Model Number 3 revolver as the Russian military contracts began in 1871. The revolver shown here is a .44 Russian Second Model made in 1873 with its distinctive Russian features; the hooked trigger guard and grip shape. Author photo.

Smith & Wesson decided not to wait

While other American arms companies concentrated on how to improve their obsolete percussion revolvers to make them more salable, S&W was already looking in other directions. After all, these guys, who worked just up the Connecticut River from Colt, did not have inventories of obsolete revolvers to worry about, never having produced any of those in the first place! As their precious patent protection expired in 1869, the two ingenious New Englanders, Horace Smith and D.B. Wesson, apparently already had their heads in high gear and in late 1869 they introduced something so radical that it is still marveled at today; the Smith & Wesson .44 caliber, top-break Model Number 3 revolver. This new S&W was a large-framed single-action revolver that was about the size and shape of the Colt Army Model belt-sized percussion revolver, but its resemblance to any previous revolver stopped right there. The amazing Model Number 3 was totally different from anything before it. A top-break revolver, the S&W used a large hinge at the bottom front of the frame. When the barrel was manually unlatched and opened from the top, it was tilted down like a shotgun. When you did this, the tilting barrel brought the cylinder along with it and as the barrel opened all the way down, the fired cartridges were then automatically extracted and expelled from the weapon. What that meant was, in 1870, before their competitors had even started to react to their expired revolver cylinder patent,

S&W had managed to patent and produce the world's fastest-loading and unloading metallic cartridge revolver. This looked like it would be (and was) a hard act to follow.

The U.S. Army tested the No. 3 in 1870 and subsequently bought 1,000 S&W .44 caliber Model Number 3 revolvers for field trials, however by the end of the trials they had decided the S&W was just too complicated, and too apt to get out of order to warrant further orders. In spite of that, the S&W became the first U.S. Army metallic cartridge service revolver. Then as we know, in 1873, after another

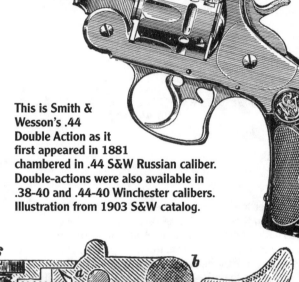

This is Smith & Wesson's .44 Double Action as it first appeared in 1881 chambered in .44 S&W Russian caliber. Double-actions were also available in .38-40 and .44-40 Winchester calibers. Illustration from 1903 S&W catalog.

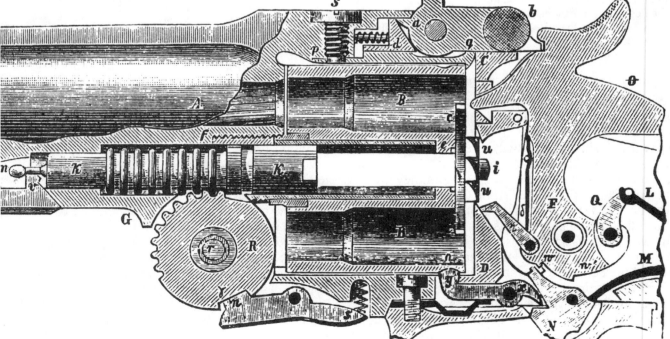

These early illustrations show the workings of the S&W New or Third Model Russian. From *Handguns of the World* by Edward C. Ezell, 1993, Barnes & Noble Books.

By the time Smith & Wesson's Second Model .38 single-action was introduced in 1877 it carried most of the features that would stay with S&W top-break production until 1940. Illustration from 1903 S&W catalog.

The .44 caliber New Model Number 3 of 1878 was the most refined of their large-frame single-actions. It was equipped with a rebounding hammer and many of the improvements learned from constructing so many revolvers for the Russians. The New Model was also available in a wide array of calibers and with optional, adjustable target sights. Illustration from 1903 S&W catalog.

series of tests, the Army decided to accept Colt's new Single Action Army in .45 Colt caliber as the official service revolver. However, as history shows, the S&W didn't simply fade away after this slight from the U.S. Army. The Russian government had gotten a good look at the Smith & Wesson, and they loved the design. Starting in 1871, the Czar's Army bought well over 100,000 .44 caliber Number 3 revolvers in three distinctly separate "Russian" models. Along the way, the Russian Czar's representatives at S&W insisted on making engineering changes that altered the S&W revolver somewhat internally. The result of this process ended up making the Smith & Wesson Model Number 3 into a very dependable and battle-worthy weapon. Largely because of those early Russian contracts, S&W's were purchased, and used, for years by the military organizations of other nations around the globe.

Early in the 1870s, a U.S. Army officer named George W. Schofield, also a staunch supporter of the S&W top-break system, patented several improvements and changes to the Model Number 3. These changes included an alteration to allow the revolver to be opened by pulling back on the latch instead of lifting it up, enabling a mounted cavalryman to open the revolver one-handed. Schofield also modified and substantially improved the extraction system, greatly simplifying the mechanism. The U.S. Army tested model Number 3 revolvers with the Schofield alterations and liked them. The Army subsequently purchased about 8,000 S&W Schofield revolvers in .45 S&W caliber. These guns were delivered from 1875 to 1877. Some would disagree, but there are many shooters and

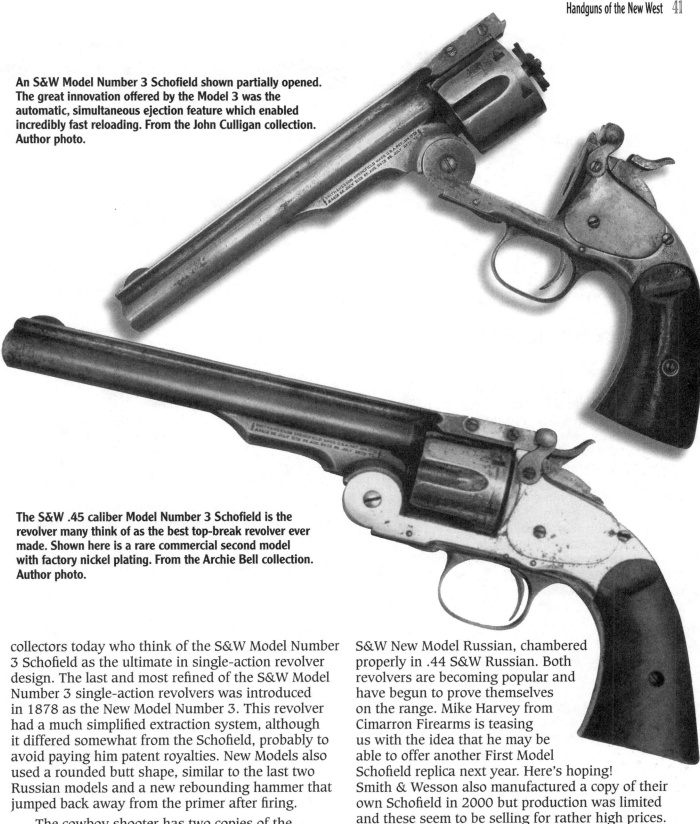

An S&W Model Number 3 Schofield shown partially opened. The great innovation offered by the Model 3 was the automatic, simultaneous ejection feature which enabled incredibly fast reloading. From the John Culligan collection. Author photo.

The S&W .45 caliber Model Number 3 Schofield is the revolver many think of as the best top-break revolver ever made. Shown here is a rare commercial second model with factory nickel plating. From the Archie Bell collection. Author photo.

collectors today who think of the S&W Model Number 3 Schofield as the ultimate in single-action revolver design. The last and most refined of the S&W Model Number 3 single-action revolvers was introduced in 1878 as the New Model Number 3. This revolver had a much simplified extraction system, although it differed somewhat from the Schofield, probably to avoid paying him patent royalties. New Models also used a rounded butt shape, similar to the last two Russian models and a new rebounding hammer that jumped back away from the primer after firing.

The cowboy shooter has two copies of the S&W top-break available at this time. Both are manufactured by Aldo Uberti in Italy. The first is the replica of the S&W .45 caliber Second Model Schofield, originally imported by Navy Arms. This gun is available in .44-40 as well. The second is also a Navy Arms innovation, a nice copy of the S&W New Model Russian, chambered properly in .44 S&W Russian. Both revolvers are becoming popular and have begun to prove themselves on the range. Mike Harvey from Cimarron Firearms is teasing us with the idea that he may be able to offer another First Model Schofield replica next year. Here's hoping! Smith & Wesson also manufactured a copy of their own Schofield in 2000 but production was limited and these seem to be selling for rather high prices. This Schofield S&W is not a faithful copy of their own 1875 revolver by any means but it is a ruggedly built gun and if the price moderates somewhat, it would likely make a very good shooter.

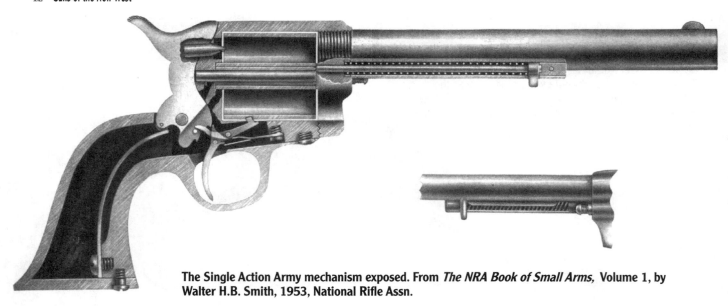

The Single Action Army mechanism exposed. From *The NRA Book of Small Arms*, Volume 1, by Walter H.B. Smith, 1953, National Rifle Assn.

Getting back to the Model 1873 Colt...

The Colt Model 1873 or Single Action Army was surely not as mechanically refined as the S&W, nor was it anywhere near as fast to load and unload. Still it managed to become an instant success. It remained so until shortly before World War II when, by that time, its popularity had been largely usurped by double-action side-swing revolvers, semi-automatic pistols and the looming demands of having to supply the free world with more modern weapons. The revolver was discontinued in 1940. Colt reintroduced the SAA (as the second-generation) in the mid-1950s and it remains in production, albeit having undergone several minor engineering changes. To this day, its image helped immeasurably along the way by Hollywood, the venerable Peacemaker serves as the official, yet unofficial symbol of the western frontier and all things cowboy.

Those western movies aside, a big reason the Colt SAA was so popular from the start was that its basic design was very simple. The 1873 shares proven, dependable lock-works that trace back to when Sam Colt perfected his single-action lock-works in the late 1840s with percussion revolvers. We also believe that another important reason for the Colt's popularity has always been its superb looks and its amazingly good balance, which of course, lend to its excellent shooting qualities. I have never heard anyone argue that the SAA is not a great-looking firearm, and there is certainly something oddly compelling about its classic profile that we really have trouble putting into words. There will always be a few people who don't find the Single Action Army a comfortable gun to hold, but these folks seem to make up an incredibly small minority. It is those two aesthetic features of the Colt that I will confess, although this author leans heavily toward the S&W

Remington's Rolling Block pistol was actually pitted against revolvers in U.S. Army tests. It was a great gun and worked flawlessly but alas, it was only a single-shot.

top-break revolvers, have left me and many others with a big soft spot for the old Peacemaker.

The above does say a lot about why we have so many replicas, or as they are often called today, clones, of the Colt Single Action Army. With so many copies from so many manufacturers, including the genuine article, I suspect we can look for even more in the coming years. These replicas range from nearly exact copies of the early first-generation cavalry revolvers, to guns that Colt never got around to building, but very likely should have. Revolvers such as the 2/3-scale Cimarron Lightning Model with its bird's-head grip and the Model P Jr. with a conventional grip shape are just about the size of the Colt 1877 Double Action Lightning. That's a size that fits small and medium-sized hands perfectly. The only thing is these new revolvers are single-action-only and infinitely more dependable than the originals ever were. We started out with only one or two Italian-made replicas that were of, at best, mediocre quality. Times have certainly changed. The quality and the variety available to us have vastly improved over those early copies. Today it is to the point where, as you will see, many of the

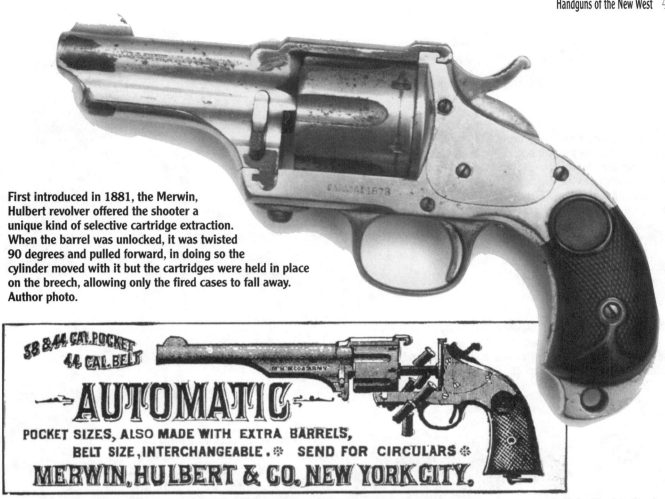

First introduced in 1881, the Merwin, Hulbert revolver offered the shooter a unique kind of selective cartridge extraction. When the barrel was unlocked, it was twisted 90 degrees and pulled forward, in doing so the cylinder moved with it but the cartridges were held in place on the breech, allowing only the fired cases to fall away. Author photo.

Merwin, Hulbert & Co. advertisement from about 1882 showing the extraction system. M-H revolvers were built by Hopkins and Allen in Norwich, Conn.

copies we tested for this book were nothing short of outstanding in both performance and looks. We also have the stainless steel replicas. It is 100 years too late to participate in the opening of the west, but we finally have the perfect black powder cartridge revolver!

Remington and other gun makers gradually got on the bandwagon and produced revolvers of their own that were specifically intended for metallic cartridge use. Some of those "other makers" included Ethan Allen, American Arms Co., Bacon Manufacturing Co., Cummings, Connecticut Arms Co., Deringer, Forehand & Wadsworth, Hopkins and Allen, Moore, Plant, Prescott, James Reid, Otis Smith, Spencer, Rollin White and Whitney.

Entering into the large-framed, metallic cartridge revolver field with both feet, Remington's Single Action Army of 1875 was, like its own previous percussion revolvers, a solid-framed single-action that used a simple, barrel-mounted rod ejector system. In this case Remington elected to provide a long, girder-shaped tube as support for the ejector rod, which itself was actually mounted outside of the tube. In keeping with their New Model percussion

revolvers, Remington retained the small, separate trigger guard that was held with only one screw at its front, while unlike the Colt, its grip straps were forged as one piece with the frame, also in the fashion of its percussion ancestors. A scarcer model was produced from 1891 to 1896. Known as the 1890 Single Action Army, it featured a more streamlined ejector and was sold in .44-40 caliber only. We are lucky to have some very well made, handsome replicas of both versions of the Remington cartridge revolvers on the market today. But I have noticed many shooters are overlooking them, possibly just because they are a little different from the run-of-the-mill Colt SAA types that every Tom, Dick and Ned seems to shoot. Take a second look. These are great, colorful guns. And just like the Colt copies, they will require some fine tuning to make them competition-ready, but hey, a Remington was good enough for Jesse James. . .right?

A contemporary of Colt and Remington sold another interesting line of revolvers, these were the revolvers marketed by Merwin, Hulbert & Company of New York (formerly Merwin and Bray) during the 1890s. These intriguing revolvers featured

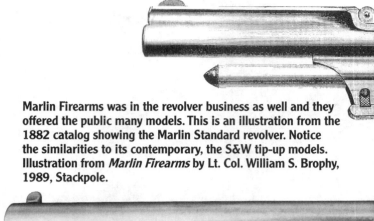

Marlin Firearms was in the revolver business as well and they offered the public many models. This is an illustration from the 1882 catalog showing the Marlin Standard revolver. Notice the similarities to its contemporary, the S&W tip-up models. Illustration from *Marlin Firearms* by Lt. Col. William S. Brophy, 1989, Stackpole.

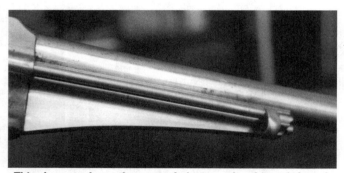

Remington's Model 1875 Single Action Army available in .45 Colt, .44 Remington and .44-40 Winchester. A favorite of Jesse James, the Remington was a strong gun and the company produced between 25,000 and 30,000 from 1875-1889. Author photo.

This close-up shows the unusual ejector rod and its reinforced tube. Notice the rod is mounted outside the tube. Part of the ejector rod head forms a ring around the base pin, which extends to the end of the ejector tube. Author photo.

a barrel and cylinder that, once unlatched, were twisted 90 degrees to the right and pulled forward for unloading. The Merwin, Hulbert revolvers were extremely well designed and well made. They also used a sliding loading gate on the right recoil shield.

The revolvers were manufactured for Merwin, Hulbert by Hopkins and Allen in Norwich, Conn. and they were offered in .32, .38 and .44 calibers, in both single- and double-action variations and in many different styles. One popular M-H model was called the "Pocket Army." Offered in .44 caliber, the Pocket Army came equipped with a built-in head basher at the bottom of its grip frame. M-H also offered a seven-shot tip-up revolver in .22 rimfire (made by O. S. Cummings) that was nearly identical to the S&W Model Number 1 third issue.

Unfortunately, there are no replicas of those cool Merwin, Hulbert revolvers today. . .at least, not yet. I have heard rumors along with a couple of fairly sound reports that at least two American companies are experimenting with the idea of reproducing the M-H Pocket Army single-action and are talking to some Italian gun factories about the prospect. Hmmm.

Endnotes

[1] Flayderman's Guide to Antique American Firearms, 8th Ed., 2001, Krause Publications

[2] Civil War Pistols by John D. McAulay, 1992, Andrew Mowbray Inc.

[3] A Study of Colt Conversions, by R. Bruce McDowell, 1997, Krause Publications

A quick look at percussion revolvers

Percussion revolvers have a much smaller role in our competitions than do cartridge guns. Nonetheless they have a strong following and are, without a doubt, an awfully important piece of the history of the American West. The truth is, after the Civil War countless thousands of percussion revolvers, the hand-held mainstay of that conflict, went west with many adventurers, explorers, settler families, bad guys and lawmen. Percussion revolvers, no doubt, played a far greater role in the winning of the West than many today imagine.

Even though percussion revolvers were made obsolete, at least from a practical standpoint, in 1857 by Smith & Wesson's Model No. 1 metallic cartridge revolver, it is a fact that the metallic cartridge concept, as advanced as it was, for many reasons took a while to catch on. Thus, percussion weapons continued to be made and successfully used on a daily basis. During the 1850s and 1860s, and most especially during the 1861-65 period of the Civil War, revolvers using percussion ignition were manufactured in the hundreds of thousands and by a long list of famous international gun manufacturers

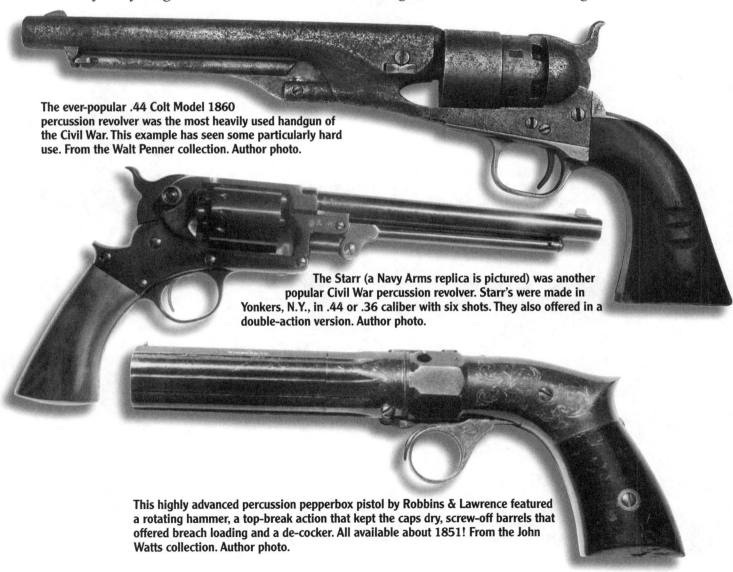

The ever-popular .44 Colt Model 1860 percussion revolver was the most heavily used handgun of the Civil War. This example has seen some particularly hard use. From the Walt Penner collection. Author photo.

The Starr (a Navy Arms replica is pictured) was another popular Civil War percussion revolver. Starr's were made in Yonkers, N.Y., in .44 or .36 caliber with six shots. They also offered in a double-action version. Author photo.

This highly advanced percussion pepperbox pistol by Robbins & Lawrence featured a rotating hammer, a top-break action that kept the caps dry, screw-off barrels that offered breach loading and a de-cocker. All available about 1851! From the John Watts collection. Author photo.

such as; Adams, Bacon, Colt, Cooper, Hopkins & Allen, Metropolitan, Remington, Savage, Starr and Whitney. With the Civil War coming to an end in 1865, uncounted thousands of soldiers; comprising the entirety of the Confederate forces as well as much of the Union Army, were quickly mustered out of the military services. Given the injection of such a huge number of men back into American society, and the fact that most of the southeast was in ruins, many of those folks decided in was in their best interest to seek new ground, so they headed west to the wide open frontiers. It would be inconceivable to believe that large numbers of these percussion revolvers were not carried west by these veterans who, having recently used these weapons in combat, were absolutely convinced of their dependability.

Handguns with revolving cylinders were not always considered the ultimate form of repeating handgun, indeed, from the 1830s on up to the mid-1850s, the pepperbox form had a strong following. These were multi-barreled weapons that either had rotating barrels like the Allen & Thurber or Darling pepperboxes, or fixed barrels with a rotating firing pin or hammer, like the unique Robbins & Lawrence pistol.

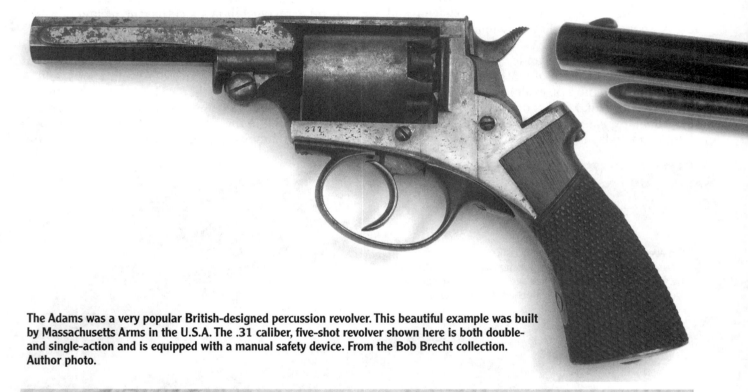

The Adams was a very popular British-designed percussion revolver. This beautiful example was built by Massachusetts Arms in the U.S.A. The .31 caliber, five-shot revolver shown here is both double- and single-action and is equipped with a manual safety device. From the Bob Brecht collection. Author photo.

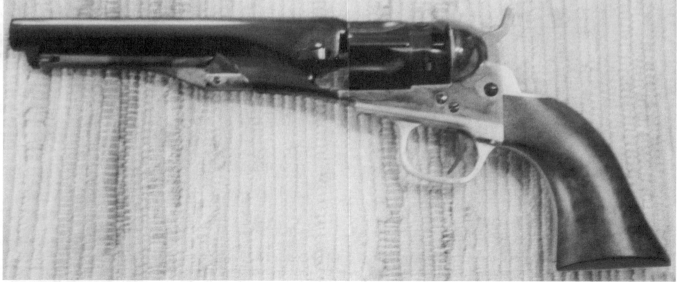

The 1862 Colt Pocket Police was a five-shot .36 caliber pistol built on the 1849 pocket model frame. Revolver courtesy Cimarron Firearms. Author photo.

A big marketing obstacle that Colt had to overcome with his revolvers was, in fact, the pepperbox, a design that was already in place when he invented the Paterson revolver in 1836. As popular as we think the early Colt revolvers were, it was only with the introduction of his really practical pistol designs, such as the pocket pistols in 1848, and the Navy model in 1851 that public opinion switched decidedly from multi-barreled repeating pistols to the sort of repeating revolvers we know today. These, of course, make use of a single barrel with a revolving cylinder.

Percussion revolvers, as we now know them, were originally offered in three distinct patterns or sizes. From the smallest or pocket size (like the .31 caliber 1849 Colt Pocket), up through the medium or "belt" size (such as the .36 caliber Colt 1851 Navy) then, they went on up to the massive Dragoon size (as the .44 caliber Colt Walker and Dragoon series revolvers.) The latter were so large and heavy, they were meant to be carried in a saddle holster. Eventually, variants of these "sizes" were offered. For instance, the so-called pocket model frame was offered as a five-shot .36 caliber revolver, so you could have a more powerful "belt caliber" in a pocket-sized revolver, albeit with a reduced powder charge. Probably the most well-known of these "size variants" is the Colt Model 1860 Army, which offered a .44 or Dragoon caliber with a lesser powder charge but still carrying six shots, built on the 1851 Navy belt frame. This revolver size variant, with its heavy caliber in such a lightweight package, was actually more popular than the previous Dragoon-size pistols.

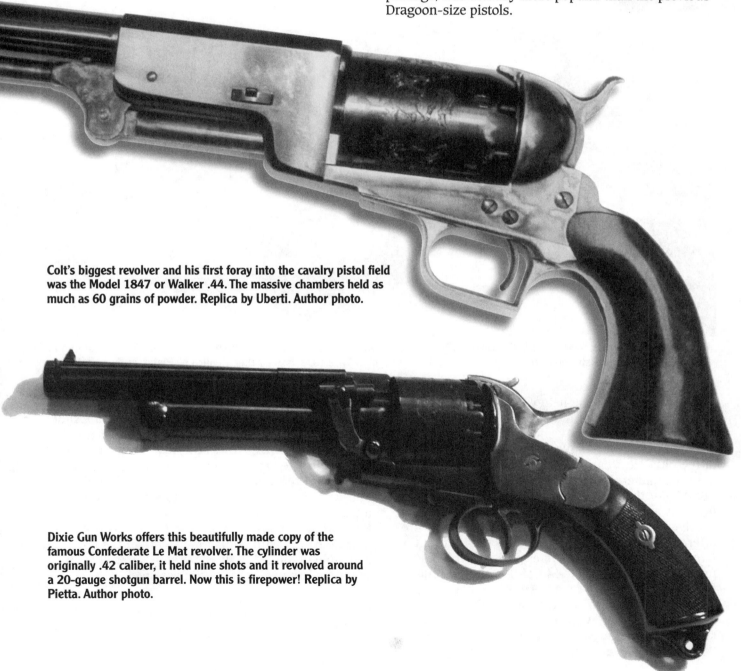

Colt's biggest revolver and his first foray into the cavalry pistol field was the Model 1847 or Walker .44. The massive chambers held as much as 60 grains of powder. Replica by Uberti. Author photo.

Dixie Gun Works offers this beautifully made copy of the famous Confederate Le Mat revolver. The cylinder was originally .42 caliber, it held nine shots and it revolved around a 20-gauge shotgun barrel. Now this is firepower! Replica by Pietta. Author photo.

The Remington New Model Army is a good example of a belt-sized pistol in the heavier Dragoon .44 caliber. Remingtons were Colt's primary competition during the Civil War. Replica by Pietta. Author photo.

Remington's percussion revolvers, unlike Colt, used a solid frame with a top-strap and many shooters preferred the added strength. Colt finally settled on a stronger solid frame too, when they brought out the 1873 Peacemaker. Replica by Pietta. Author photo.

As the result of the heavy interest in Civil War reenactments and spurred on to some extent now by interest from the Cowboy shooting fraternity, replica arms manufacturers have filled out a good portion of the old Colt, Remington and other percussion firearms makers' catalog lines of the 1850s and 1860s. For the most part, these black powder firearms are good-quality copies of those famous revolvers. Modern replica percussion revolvers are offered in sizes and in calibers that range from the miniscule five-shot .31 caliber pocket revolvers up to the huge six-shot .44 Colt Dragoons. Today there are copies of the Starr Arms revolvers, the Union Rogers and Spencer, plenty of Colts and Remingtons, along with replicas of a few lesser-known Confederate arms makers, like Spiller & Burr. There is even a great copy of the magnum opus of all black powder cavalry revolvers; the famous Confederate 10-shot Le Mat; the grapeshot revolver. The most popular of these replicas are the medium frame size Army and Navy Colts and the New Model Remingtons in .36 and .44 caliber. In addition to these modern-made copies of originals and variations thereof Sturm, Ruger manufactures a truly modern .44 caliber percussion revolver that they call the Old Army. The Old Army was originally available only with adjustable sights but is now available in a fixed-sighted version, as well as in other models made from stainless steel.

This variety of revolvers gives the modern black powder shooter quite a selection and the opportunity to, if he so desires, create a collection of modern replica arms.

Colt 1851 Navy model

Colt first manufactured the famous 1851 Navy revolver in 1850. From then, up through 1873, the company manufactured about 215,000 of these six-shot, .36 caliber percussion pistols in Hartford, Conn. In addition, another roughly 42,000 Navy Colts were manufactured in England by Colt's London factory. The pistol's beautiful lines and perfect balance with its 7 1/2-inch octagon barrel and comfortable grip shape made the 1851 Navy a popular handgun from the beginning. It was quickly taken into combat by officers of the British military and used in the Crimean War. Later, soldiers on both sides of the conflict used their Navy Colts with telling effect in the U.S. Civil War. Navy Colts were also popular on the American frontier well after the Civil War. One such instance is the notorious frontiersman and gunfighter Wild Bill Hickock, who is known to have preferred an ivory-stocked pair of .36 caliber, 1851

The 1851 Navy was one of the prettiest and best-handling revolvers Colt ever made. Uberti's replica captures much of the original beauty and balance with modern steel. Revolver courtesy Stoeger Industries. Author photos

I am told the 1851 Navy was Uberti's very first replica, produced in the 1950s for Val Forgett. This replica has good-looking finishes that set one another off nicely, the manufacturer has managed to produce a good-looking and slick-operating revolver.

Navy model Colts. One of the things everyone has always seemed to enjoy about the '51 Navy was, and is, its wonderful balance. These great old revolvers just drop into your hand and point as if they were an extension of your forearm.

Colt's Navy model cylinders were roll-engraved with a scene created by W. Ormsby depicting the Texas Navy's victory over the Mexican fleet in 1843. Though the majority of the 1851 Navy production was manufactured with rounded trigger guards, approximately the first 4,200 were produced with a square-backed trigger guard. All of them use a one-piece walnut grip. The exact size and shape of this universally comfortable Navy grip were retained and used again by Colt on the famous Single Action Army. . .where the grip lives on today.

Our test revolver is a replica of the model 1851 Navy manufactured in Italy by the Aldo Uberti Co. and imported and sold in the U.S.A. by Stoeger Industries. The gun is, in most respects, a very faithful copy of the original Colt revolver. Furnished with a nicely blued 7 1/2-inch octagon barrel and a cylinder roll-engraved with an excellent likeness of the original Ormsby naval scene, the lines of the original pistol have been very well maintained by the modern-day maker. Blueing used is a modern caustic black-blue but we did not think the metal was as well prepared as many Uberti replicas of this type we have handled. Still, the blue work is very good and the gun does make a fine presentation. The barrel has no visible stamped markings at all, that is until the loading lever is dropped, then we

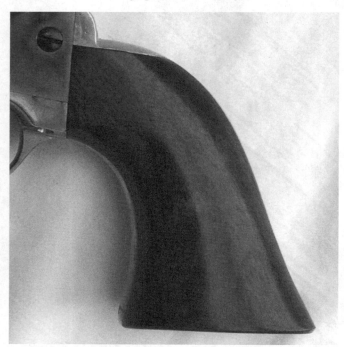

Colt's 1851 Navy was the most popular grip shape and size ever conceived, it is still used today on the SAA and its copies.

The Navy cylinder is roll-engraved like the originals, with a naval battle scene between the Texan and Mexican navies that was originally done by W.L. Ormsby.

It's a pretty easy procedure to break open one of these Colt-designed, open-topped percussion revolvers for cleaning.

1851-load.tif: The 1851 Navy loading levers worked just like the 1849 Pocket models, they simply pivoted on a screw in the barrel. Check out those great case colors!

find the caliber marking, a black powder-only warning and the maker's name and country of origin stamped on the lower barrel flat. Like the original Colt, the lock-frame, hammer and loading lever are color case hardened. The case hardening process Uberti is using is obviously different from the bone and charcoal method used by Colt and the colors are far more subdued and somewhat washed-out looking. Nevertheless, the colors actually look very nice. Original Colts used brass trigger guards and backstraps that were silver-plated. Our replica Navy's straps were unplated brass. The one-piece grips are made of walnut nicely stained a dark orange-brown color and well filled. These were fitted only fairly well to the grip straps, with some annoying sharp overhang along the front and rear edges and at the heel. All the screws are nicely domed, polished and blued. They fit the gun frame very well and have an appearance like the originals.

The replica Navy's sights are a crude notch in the hammer top and a brass "nub" on the barrel that honestly gave us a truly awful sight picture. Sighting was done by very careful use of North Carolina kenyigisswat-tawindajiz.

Checkering on the hammer's spur is very similar to original checkering and it is sharp and functional.

Both the 1851 Navy and the shooter (Ed Wade) are shrouded in a pawl of black powder.

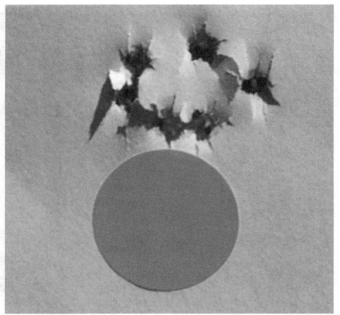

We didn't expect the 1851 to give us groups this small with its poor sight picture, nevertheless, the gun shot up to its reputation in spite of the sights!

The sights on this replica Navy model are also much like the originals. The front sight consists of a small brass conical "bead" and the rear sight a simple V notch cut into the top of the hammer face, becoming visible only when the hammer is cocked. The front sight on this particular revolver was much too wide at the top for it to fit between the rear sight notch, so there was effectively no sight picture; or at least a very poor one. We could tell this would present a challenge on the range. The action in our Navy replica worked very well. The timing and indexing were perfect and lock-up was tight. We noticed that when the hammer was placed in the half-cocked or loading position, the nipples were not parked as close to the center of the frame's loading cut as we would have liked. This meant that when capping the piece, the cylinder had to be manually rotated a bit farther each time in order to comfortably install the cap, this turned out to be only a minor inconvenience and not a big deal. The trigger let-off was quite crisp, with very little noticeable creep and the hammer falling at just under 4 pounds. All in all a nice trigger and the hammer had good, quick lock-time. We measured the bore on our 1851 replica and its groove diameter was .379" while the chamber mouths measured .377".

This Navy did have an unusual problem, one that was shared with the Uberti 1860 we were testing at the same time. The barrel was fitted much too tight to the arbor pin and frame. When we attempted to take the barrel off it would not pull off by hand and even after trying the usual trick of using the leverage of the ramrod with the rammer placed between two chambers it would not budge. Being a gunsmith, I

eventually got the barrel off to clean it up after the shooting, but this was no small task and one I would not recommend to an amateur! This is the sort of thing that should not have gotten by the factory fitters. We were surprised that it did. Most of the Uberti cap-and-ball revolvers I've seen are pretty well fitted in this area so it was strange to find this on two of the same production vintage revolvers.

We wiped the chambers clean and fired a percussion cap on each to dry out any remaining oil before charging them with powder. The tests of this 1851 Navy were fired with .375" round balls over 20 grains (measured) of GOEX brand FFFg black powder, ignited with RWS No. 1075 percussion caps. The latter portion of the firing was done with CCI No. 11 caps which were reliable but all too often fell into pieces which once or twice went down into the action, jamming the hammer. I sealed the chambers over the balls with thick, white Lubriplate Marine Lube "A" grease. The .375" round balls were used only because a larger size was not readily available. We would hard-seat each ball (that is, to attempt to crush and up-set each ball by pushing on it extra hard with the loading lever) then carefully seal each chamber with grease to help prevent the possibility of a chain fire. Uberti suggests a target charge of 16 grains with the round ball and a maximum charge of 25 grains. We used 20 grains for two reasons. First, you should make it a practice never to fire a maximum load in any black powder revolver that is new or untested. I always start about 20 percent under the published maximum. Secondly, this load of 20 grains of FFFg has been a very accurate charge in almost every 1851 Navy model I have owned in the past.

Uberti 1851 Navy
.36cal

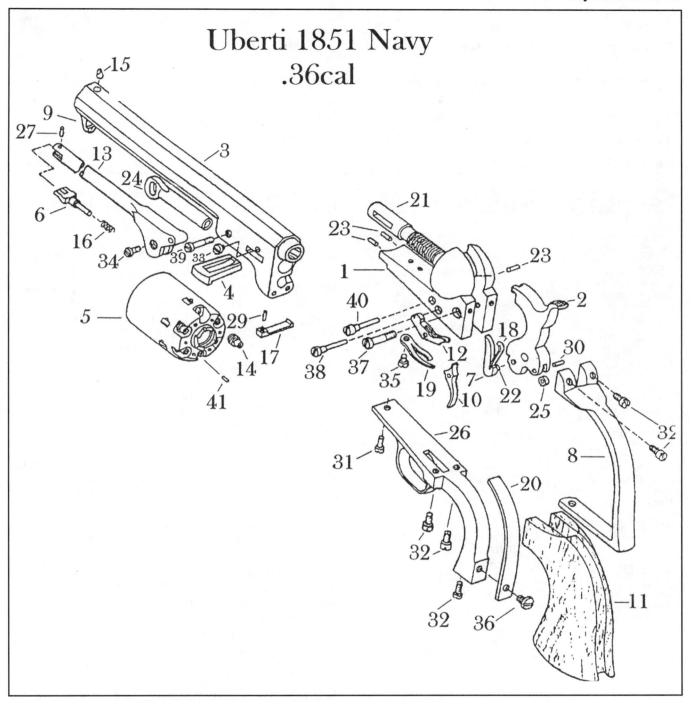

Parts for the Uberti 1851 Navy, Illustration used with permission from A. Uberti.

1. Frame	12. Bolt	22. Hand spring pin	33. Wedge screw
2. Hammer	13. Loading lever assembly	23. Barrel pin	34. Plunger screw
3. Barrel	14. Nipple	24. Plunger	35. Trigger bolt spring screw
4. Wedge	15. Sight	25. Roller	36. Main spring screw
5. Cylinder	16. Loading lever latch spring	26. Triggerguard	37. Hammer screw
6. Loading lever latch	17. Wedge spring	27. Loading lever latch pin	38. Trigger screw
7. Hand assembly	18. Hand spring	28. None	39. Loading lever screw
8. Backstrap	19. Trigger bolt spring	29. Wedge pin	40. Bolt screw
9. Barrel stud	20. Mainspring	30. Roller pin	41. Cylinder pin
10. Trigger	21. Base pin (arbor)	31. Front triggerguard screw	
11. Grip	22. Rear backstrap screw	32. Rear backstrap screw	

Caliber:	.36 (.377" actual chamber diameter)
Barrel Lengths:	7 1/2"
Frame:	Forged steel
Stocks:	One-piece walnut
Finishes:	Blue and case color
Backstrap:	Round or square guard-- brass or optional silver
Suggested Retail:	Starting at $250

1851 Navy specs, as tested	
Model	340000
Name	1851 Navy
Finish(s)	Blue & color case hardened
Barrel length	7 1/2"
Overall length	13"
Caliber	.36, black powder
Capacity	6 shots
Action	Single
Front sight	Fixed blade
Rear sight	Fixed notch
Grips	1-pc walnut, smooth
Chamber mouth	.377" (actual)
Barrel groove	.379" (actual)
Retail as tested	$250
Available from	Stoeger Industries, 17603 Indian Head Highway, Accokeek, MD 20607 301-283-6300.

Our little Navy performed very well on the range. Despite the sight picture, we soon found that we could do pretty good work if we filled the sight notch completely with the front sight (which wasn't hard to do, the front sight is too large for the rear notch) then leveled the whole thing, off using a six o-clock hold on the bottom on an 1 1/2-inch orange paster. In this way we managed to shoot some pretty fair little groups, averaging 1 1/2 inches for six shots and the darned thing actually hit right were you pointed it and perhaps an inch high. Aside from some problems with those fragile CCI caps sending fragments into the action and jamming up the gun a couple of times, the Uberti Navy performed beautifully throughout the shooting tests and gave us no trouble whatever, even in rapid fire.

I would say without hesitation that Uberti's 1851 Navy .36 is a great-shooting little gun, in many ways just like the original; it feels good in your hand, looks great and it has that wonderful balance that made the original Colt Navy so popular. Overall, it left a very good impression. Yes, we would like to have seen a little better fit-up of the wood to metal around the grip edges but really, for a percussion revolver in this retail price range the gun is a darn good buy. The one criticism I have is that the factory needs to attend to this overly tight barrel thing. After seeing it on two guns I wonder if they don't have a problem they need to address on the production line. We would hate to see this lack of attention be the reason for such a great revolver to acquire a bad image. The 1851 Navy is, after all, Uberti's signature revolver being their very first replica model to be imported into the U.S.

The 1860 Army

Colt introduced its Army revolver in 1860, and it was made using what they called superior silver spring steel. The 1860 Army was a .44 caliber revolver built on the lightweight frame of the smaller, .36 caliber Navy model. They did this by using a cylinder that was rebated, or stepped down from the large .44 caliber size in front, to the Navy diameter at its rear. The frame had a similar step to allow the larger cylinder in. Previous Army models had been built on the large, heavy Dragoon frames but the 1860 successor produced a much lighter, easier-handling revolver. Colt's 1860 also featured a "creeping" loading lever whose top had gear teeth that meshed with corresponding holes in the bottom of the more streamlined, round barrel. This feature not only provided the shooter with greater leverage during loading, it also used fewer parts. The first 1860 models used 7 1/2-inch round barrels and had fluted cylinders but later, and for the majority of production, Colt settled on 8-inch round barrels with unfluted, round, roll-stamped cylinders.

The 1860 was the acme of Colt's percussion Army revolvers, made from 1860 through 1873, and in total, Colt manufactured over 200,000 of this model with about 127,000 of them purchased for issue to Union troops during the Civil War. Another key feature of the 1860 is its grip, which is identical in shape with the popular 1851 Navy, however, the

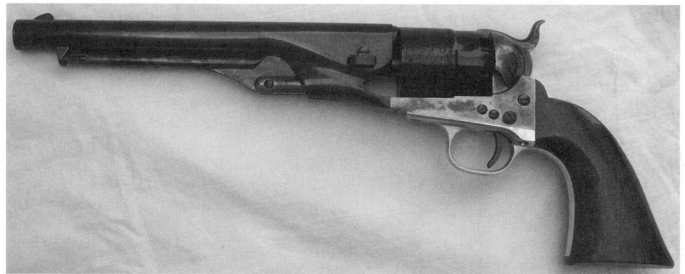

Uberti's 1860 Army model, shown here, is a very faithful replica of the most-used Colt revolver in the Union Army during the Civil War. Revolver courtesy Stoeger Industries. Author photos.

In this close-up view, you can make out the machined cuts in the recoil shield and the "extra" screw to attach a shoulder stock. The case colors, while attractive, were somewhat faded looking.

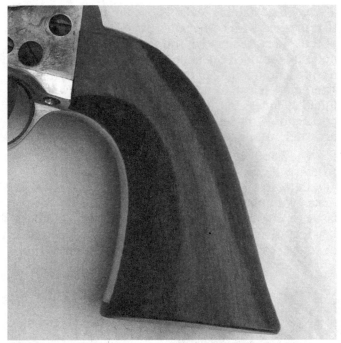

Grips on the 1860 are one-piece walnut, nicely shaped and finished to look surprisingly like a Colt job. The only flaw in fitting was the tiny gap you can see at the left front of the grip where it meets the back of the trigger guard.

Like an original Colt, the Uberti replica carries a beautiful naval battle scene originally engraved by Wm. Ormsby.

Here's what the 1860 looks like with the barrel and cylinder pulled apart for cleaning.

1860's grip, while it retains the Navy shape, was made just a bit longer. This model used a brass trigger guard with a blue steel back strap. Some 1860 revolvers were fitted to accept shoulder stocks. On these the recoil shields were specially machined and an additional screw installed on each frame side for stock attachment.

We obtained the Uberti-made 1860 replica used for these tests from Stoeger Industries and it is a standard 8-inch barreled revolver with an un-fluted cylinder. The cylinder carries a very good reproduction of the same naval scene used on the 1851 Navy models, as originally engraved for Colt by W.L. Ormsby. The revolver is furnished in blue and case colors, in other words, the fame, hammer

and loading lever are color case hardened while the barrel, cylinder and back strap and blued. Overall, the metal surfaces of the revolver were nicely prepared, with lines and edges sharp and professional looking and not over-polished. The blue is of course, accomplished by modern "hot blue" methods but its overall appearance is one of a very good, high-gloss blue. Color case hardening was apparently done using some method other than the traditional bone and charcoal system. Nevertheless, the colors were pleasing, although quite faded looking. The fit of the metal parts (grip straps to the frame, etc.) was superb, with only the differences in the color of the metals betraying a seam. Our test

This shot of the hammer offers a good look at the very original looking checkering on its spur. Notice the additional screw for attaching the shoulder stock protruding from the frame side just below.

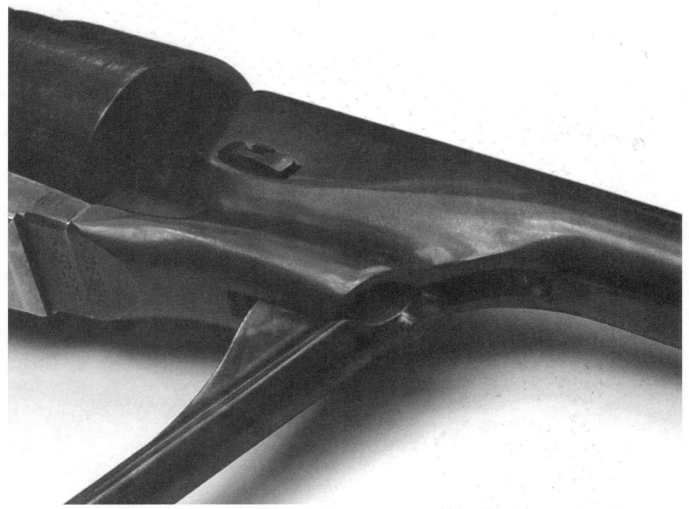

Looking up from the underside of the barrel with the loading lever pulled down, you can clearly see the gear teeth on the top of the lever. These teeth meshed with holes in the bottom of the barrel, to create a very effective and inexpensive method of loading lever operation.

model 1860 Army came fitted (like the original) with a one-piece walnut grip that showed a small amount of figure and was finished with a deep, varnish-like coating that is not unlike an original Colt. These grips were reasonably well-fitted to the grip straps and shaped in the typical Colt minimalist fashion to fit the shooter's hand beautifully. The one small exception was the fit of the grip at the trigger guard where it met the frame at the rear, but even this tiny flaw produced but a miniscule gap that you really have to look close to see.

Parts for the Uberti 1860 Army. Illustration used with permission from A. Uberti.

1. Frame	13. Loading lever assembly	24. Plunger	36. Main spring screw
2. Hammer	14. Nipple	25. Roller	37. Hammer screw
3. Barrel	15. Sight	26. Triggerguard	38. Trigger screw
4. Wedge	16. Loading lever latch	27. Loading lever latch pin	39. Loading lever screw
5. Cylinder	spring	28. None	40. Bolt screw
6. Loading lever latch	17. Wedge spring	29. Wedge pin	41. Cylinder pin
7. Hand assembly	18. Hand spring	30. Roller pin	455. Backstrap screw,
8. Backstrap	19. Trigger bolt spring	31. Front triggerguard screw	lower
9. Barrel stud	20. Mainspring	32. Rear backstrap screw	
10. Trigger	21. Base pin (arbor)	33. Wedge screw	
11. Grip	22. Hand spring pin	34. Plunger screw	
12. Bolt	23. Barrel pin	35. Trigger bolt spring screw	

Uberti 1860 Army
.44cal

Uberti's sights also look much like the originals. A simple notch in the hammer top forms the rear and the front is a very low, brass blade.

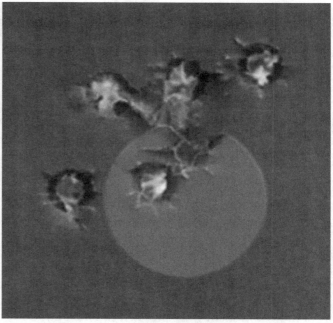

This 1860 shot very well. This is a typical group shot by the author with a casual one-handed hold at 7 yards. The load is 25 grains of black powder with round balls and RWS caps.

The screws on this gun were domed, with smallish screwdriver slots and just the right amount of protrusion. In appearance they are indeed very good replicas of original, period Colt screws. We did notice the screws were all a bit short for the width of the frame. This revolver is the so-called four-screw frame, cut to accept a shoulder stock. Sights are typical percussion Colt, with the rear sight being a small V notch in the top face of the hammer and visible only when the hammer is cocked. For a front sight the gun has a small brass, oblong sight. Taken together the sight picture should be awful but its not. As a matter of fact, this combination managed to produce one of the better sight pictures of all the handguns tested in this book. It was; clear, fairly sharp and very fast to acquire. The groove diameter of the barrel rifling measured .459" while the cylinder chambers were .452", this is a wide variation and frankly, its a combination that is encountered more often on original Colts than on replicas. As we would soon see, this had no effect on accuracy.

We found our 1860 had a very smooth action overall. It cocked smoothly and precisely, although we noticed the timing was just a bit "much." In other words; it over-timed with the hammer reaching full cock just after the cylinder was rotated into the locked position. This caused the shooter to have to pull the hammer harder than should have been necessary to bring the hammer into full cock. This sort of problem can usually be cured by a minor internal adjustment and that should have been done at the factory. With the hammer placed in the half-cocked or loading position we noted the nipples were stopping very near the center of the frame's loading port. That's good; making for easy capping. When cocked the cylinder locked quite snugly with almost no perceptible radial play. Also good. Trigger pull was exceptionally light, letting the hammer fall

abruptly at just about 1 1/2 pounds and with very little pre-break movement or creep. We could actually feel the hammer hitting the trigger sear tip as it fell all the way forward, an indication of a problem that will eventually break the trigger sear. Again, this is probably a minor adjustment but it is one that the factory should have caught since it directly effects a safety concern.

I dislike beating a horse that's already down but, while we are on a sour note, taking the barrel off a Colt-type percussion revolver is a simple process. You push out the wedge and pull the barrel and then the cylinder off the front of the frame. Sometimes if the barrel is a tight fit, you may have to use leverage from the ram rod to force the barrel off but it shouldn't take much, and even such tight barrels usually can be re-stalled by hand. Not so here. The barrel on this particular revolver was fitted much too tightly. We not only had to force the barrel off, but it had to be beaten back on with considerable force applied by a plastic mallet. This problem must have been obvious to the person at the factory who fitted the gun for assembly, and again, it's not such a big deal for a gunsmith to adjust, so why did the factory let this slip by?

We test fired the 1860 with 25 grains of FFFg, Elephant brand black powder under a .454" lead round ball with water pump grease covering the ball faces. Prior to charging the chambers, we fired caps on each, to dry off any oil and grease. The firing was done using the dependable RWS No. 1075 percussion caps until I exhausted my supply and we finished up using CCI No. 11 caps. Both gave

Caliber:	.44 (.452" actual chamber size)
Barrel Lengths:	8"
Frame:	Forged steel
Stocks:	One piece walnut
Finishes:	Blue and case color
Backstrap:	Blued steel
Trigger guard	Brass, round

us dependable ignition. We did notice the CCI caps tended to come apart readily when fired, with the consequence that we had to stop shooting every two or three shots to clean pieces of cap debris from the action to keep the gun working. This did not occur with RWS the caps. As with all black powder revolvers, it's important to select the correct sized ball for the chambers and since our chamber mouths measured .452 inches, we selected the next larger, readily available, off-the-shelf ball size of .454. As I expected, the excellent Colt "creeping" loading lever worked perfectly. It made ramming the balls home an easy task. Uberti's literature that comes supplied with the gun shows a minimum or target charge of 22 grains with the round ball and a maximum charge of 30 grains. We opted for 25 grains because, first of all, you should never fire maximum loads in any black powder weapon that is new or as yet untested, also because 25 grains of FFFg powder has already proven to be a dependable, accurate round-ball load in many 1860 models I have previously fired, both original and replica.

On the range the Army .44 performed very well. That light trigger did take some getting used to and the first few shots from both shooters were, at best, flyers. Once we settled into that touchy trigger, both shooters found that it was easy to do very good work with it. Even in the bright sunlight the sight picture remained very good and surprisingly effective. This revolver would consistently place all six balls within a 1 1/2-inch circle at 7 yards, and it did this fired in the traditional off-hand fashion with one hand and with all the groups hitting the paper about over the point of aim. When fired from a bench rest, the groups shrank to just 1 inch with all shots touching.

What's the verdict? Well, as we mentioned earlier, this revolver had some problems that need attention, such as that ultra-light trigger and the fact that the take-down of the barrel and frame were so difficult the average shooter could not have performed this

1860 Army, as tested	
Model	340480
Name	1860 Army
Finish(s)	Blue & color case hardened
Barrel length	8"
Overall length	13 ¾"
Caliber	.44, black powder
Capacity	6 shots
Action	Single
Front sight	Fixed blade
Rear sight	Fixed notch
Grips	1-pc walnut, smooth
Chamber mouth	.452" (actual)
Barrel groove	.459" (actual)
Retail as tested	$260
Available from	Stoeger Industries, 17603 Indian Head Highway, Accokeek, MD 20607 301-283-6300.

basic task without the benefit of tools. This latter was a surprise, in fact this and the 1851 we tested at the same time were the first Uberti replicas I had ever seen with this problem and I have no hesitation in saying its something the factory should not have released. I'll try to be fair about this because there is another side to this coin. The Uberti 1860 is one very handsome revolver, it was very well finished and fitted and it really did perform outstandingly on the target range. Overall, this is a very good 1860 Army replica and, for the money (about $260) the revolver is a good buy, even if it required some basic gunsmithing to get it back on track.

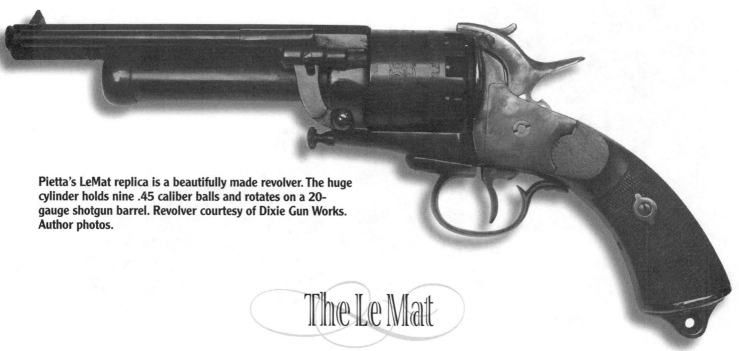

Pietta's LeMat replica is a beautifully made revolver. The huge cylinder holds nine .45 caliber balls and rotates on a 20-gauge shotgun barrel. Revolver courtesy of Dixie Gun Works. Author photos.

The Le Mat

Some have called this remarkable pistol "the most awesome hand-held weapon ever produced." There's some truth in that statement. Used to some extent by the Confederacy during the American Civil War, the original Le Mat was a unique two-barreled percussion revolver. One of its nicknames was the "Grapeshot Revolver." Le Mat revolvers had a .42 caliber cylinder that held nine shots, if that wasn't enough, the massive cylinder rotated on a .63 caliber (or about 20-gauge) smooth-bored shotgun barrel. Immediately the idea of the percussion revolver as

a personal defense weapon takes on a whole new image! Le Mat hammers were fitted with a moveable hammer nose that was pivoted up or down, allowing shooters to fire the shotgun barrel separately from the revolver cylinder. As far as we know[1] less than 2,900 Le Mat revolvers were manufactured during the years from 1856 through 1865 and they were made in several countries; in about 1859 some were made in the United States, then in Liege, Belgium during 1862, to Paris, France in 1864-65, and finally in Birmingham, England 1865. On account of

Here you can see the excellent cylinder engraving. Notice how the loading lever is mounted at the bottom-rear of the barrel. The lever arrangement was not the easiest to use. We took this photo after the shoot so you will notice some black powder residue and grease.

This is one view of the big LeMat that will win any argument!

difficulties imposed by the Union Naval blockade of the southern states, the revolvers made in Belgium and France were sent to England to be proofed, then shipped on to Bermuda, from there the Le Mat revolvers were run (hopefully) through the Union blockade and on into Southern ports.

Dr. Jean Alexandre Francois Le Mat of New Orleans first patented the design for the Le Mat in the United States in 1856. He later patented the unusual revolver in several European countries. At the start, P.G.T. Beauregard, who would later turn out to be one of the Confederacy's best known, and most flamboyant generals, aided Le Mat in manufacture and sale of his revolver. Folks even say that Beauregard had a hand in its design, or at least in its improvements. There were roughly 25 prototypes of the Le Mat made in 1859 by John Krider in Philadelphia. It has been reported that a fairly substantial number of Le Mat's amazing revolvers were sold to the Confederate States of America. Certainly we know that several well known officers, including General J.E.B. Stuart, were very fond of the Le Mat. And why wouldn't they be, with its nine-shot capacity and that "surprise" the shot barrel! According to Norm Flayderman in Flayderman's Guide, 900 of the Belgian production went to the Confederate Army and 600 were issued to the Confederate Navy.

A modern-made, shooting replica of the Le Mat® is being manufactured in Italy by F.F.L. Pietta and sold here in the states by Dixie Gun Works. This Pietta-made replica is chambered to accept the .451" round ball, if anything, I guess that makes this modern Le Mat even more formidable than the original. We tested the Le Mat Navy Model sold by

Pietta did a very professional job with the grips, they look just like originals, are nicely hand checkered and well fitted.

In the left photo the hammer is cocked and its nose is tilted "down" to allow the shotgun barrel to be fired, you can see the nipple for the shot barrel on the frame just to the left. In the right photo the hammer is down and the nose has been tilted back into the "up" position so it can fire the nipples on the revolver cylinder.

Dixie Gun Works in Union City, Tenn. This version uses a 6 1/2-inch octagon barrel in .45 caliber (.451") over a 5-inch round shotgun barrel with a .640" bore. The Pietta-Le Mat's huge cylinder is 1.95 inches in diameter, 1.72 inches long and holds nine balls of true .45 caliber. Even though this is a percussion weapon, any way you look at it, these dimensions are impressive.

Our revolver was finished in high-luster blue. The metal parts were very well polished, showing well-defined edges and corners. The cylinder was nicely engraved with vine-scrolls around its periphery and the barrel to is marked Col. Le Mat within a scroll format. Pietta's name and country of origin appear on the revolver barrel side and under the shotgun barrel. The Italian government proofs appear on the right side of the frame and on the sides of both barrels. Grips are nicely checkered European walnut that look just like pictures of the originals I have seen and the wood-to-metal fit is excellent. The butt of the Navy model is formed with an integral

hole, which is meant to accept a lanyard. Color case hardening was used to finish the hammer and the trigger and the colors have a very strong tan hue. In appearance, the Le Mat is finished very nicely, with superior workmanship in evidence everywhere we looked.

The sights on the Le Mat are crude, the rear being a rather large notch in the hammer nose, the front is sort of an inverted V with a flat top, dovetailed into the top flat of the octagon barrel. Together, the two created, shall we say, an interesting and very indefinite sight picture, which as we were soon to see, actually worked. The hammer itself has a broad, sharply checkered spur that turned out to be a good thing, because this gun has a very strong mainspring! On the hammer top is a small lever that, if pushed forward, swings the hammer nose down putting it in a position where it can reach the percussion cap for the shotgun barrel. The Le Mat trigger pull was short, only slightly creepy and the hammer fell off quickly at about 4 pounds pressure.

Top; Ed Wade is just about to touch off the first shot of the day from the LeMat. Above; Kaboom! And the world is white smoke.

That fast hammer fall was a welcome occurrence, since holding this heavy revolver out at arm's length for any period of time quickly becomes a workout. Action operation was very positive and smooth, albeit the mainspring had quite a bit of tension so the hammer required some effort to pull back. In cocking the revolver we noticed that the ultra-large cylinder rotated into battery at the right moment; just as the hammer reached its fully cocked position, proving the gun is nicely timed and cylinder lock-up was tight with almost no perceptible radial play.

We test fired the Le Mat at 7 yards using 25 grains of FFFg GOEX black powder under a .451" diameter lead round ball. The chambers were sealed with a thick coat of Lubriplate Marine Lube "A" white grease and capped with reliable RWS No. 1075 percussion caps. Yeah, before you ask, it took us a long-time to load all nine chambers! This task was not made easier by the loading lever. This we discovered, was not the LeMat's best feature! The lever offers, at best, poor leverage and it sure made

the job of ramming round balls into the cylinder a tough chore. This made me appreciate how easy the Colt 1860 Army loading lever is to use. Touching off the Le Mat for the first time quickly drew the attention of nearby shooters, who, unable to see their own targets on account of our billowing clouds of black powder smoke, gathered close around to laugh at us and to watch the beautiful behemoth do her buck and roll. One guy noticed the gun was still shooting after six shots and wondered what in the heck kind of gun that was. The laughing stopped abruptly as the wind blew the smoke away and the target became visible; those first nine shots had dropped into a group that I measured as not quite 2 inches from center to center. Later in the day, and this despite my on going fight with this gun to try to get some kind of definite sight picture, I fired six shots into a group that measured 2 inches, I ruined the last shot or it would have been much smaller, the first five shots stayed under an inch.

LeMat Parts (Pietta nomenclature)

1. SHOT BARREL RAMROD
2. LOADING LEVER TUBE
3. LOADING LEVER
4. PLUNGER SCREW
5. PLUNGER
6. LOADING LEVER SCREW
7. FRONT SIGHT
8. BARREL
9A. TAKEDOWN PIN (ARMY/NAVY)
9B. TAKEDOWN LEVER (CAVALRY) .
9C. TAKEDOWN LEVER SPRING
10. TAKEDOWN PIN SPRING
11. TAKEDOWN PIN SPRING SCREW
12. CYLINDER
13. NIPPLE
14. SHOT BARREL .20 GA.
15. BREECH PLUG
16. TENSION SPRING ADJ. SCREW
17. SIDE PLATE NUT
18. HAMMER SCREW

19. CYLINDER STOP
20. CYLINDER STOP RETURN SPRING
21. CYLINDER STOP RETAINING NUT
22. TRIGGER SPRING
23. FRAME
24. SIDE PLATE
25. TAKEDOWN LEVER PIN
26. TRIGGER
27. TRIGGER PIN
28. TRIGGER GUARD
29. FRONT TRIGGER GUARD SCREW
30. REAR TRIGGER GUARD SCREW
31. HAMMER NOSE
32. HAMMER
33. HAMMER NOSE SPRING SCREW
34. HAMMER NOSE SPRING
35. HAMMER NOSE SCREW
36. CYLINDER STOP TENSION SPRING
37. CYL. STOP TENSION SPRING SCREW

38. MAINSPRING RETAINER
39. MAINSPRING RETAINER PIN
40. HAND & SPRING
41. HAND BRACKET
42. HAND BRACKET SCREW
43. MAINSPRING
44. MAINSPRING SCREW
45. GRIP SCREW
46. RIGHT GRIP LOCKING NUT
47. LEFT GRIP NUT
48-49. LEFT/RIGHT GRIP
50. LOADING LEVER RETAINING SPRING SCREW
51. LOADING LEVER RETAINING SPRING
52. LANYARD BASE
53. LANYARD RING
54. CYLINDER STOP SCREW
55. HAMMER NOSE PIN

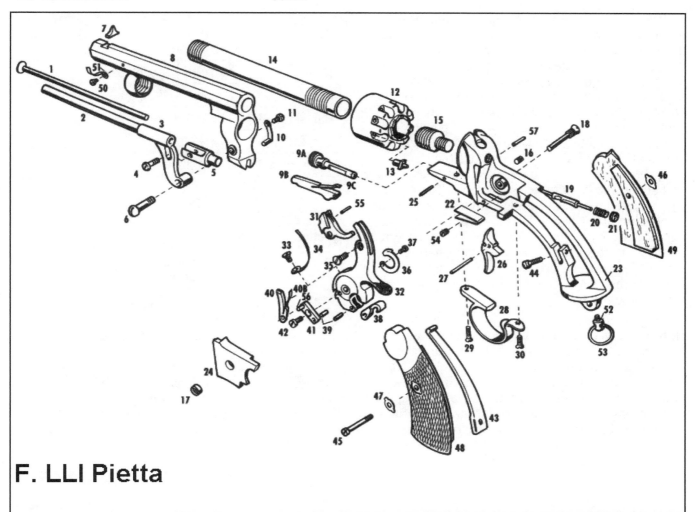

F. LLI Pietta

The first target fired consists of nine-shots. The paper was not well supported so the holes are ragged but the group measured about 2 inches.

This group is six shots and five of them went into the 1-inch cluster at the bottom, the author threw the sixth.

We regret that, owing to a lack of time, we did not have the chance to make proper wads and develop a charge for the shot barrel. In spite of that, curiosity got the best of me, so I admit to firing the shotgun barrel, just once. This was with a quickly made-up affair of corrugated cardboard wads, 50 grains of FFg and about 3/4 ounce of #6 shot. Not knowing the exact charge of powder or shot, the thought was to keep it all on the light side. This makeshift affair did not produce the tightly compacted load I would have liked, but I have to say that single shot was rather impressive. There was a good amount of recoil along with a huge cloud of smoke and fire. The gun actually produced a much tighter pattern on paper than we expected, covering only about the spread of the palm your hand at 7 yards. This performance has got me really curious to see what the Le Mat can do with properly developed loads and tight wads.

Bottom line. The Le Mat is a very well made replica revolver and after using it I can see where the idea of having a nine-shot percussion revolver was a real advantage to the Civil War soldier, let alone the fact that it still had that tenth shot waiting underneath. Shooting the LeMat cured my skepticism about its sights too, which I still think are awful, but so what. Evidently they work a whole lot better than

LeMat specs	
Model	LMN44
Name	Navy Model LeMat
Caliber	.45 and 20 gauge
Barrel length	6 3/4" revolver, 5" sg
O.A.L.	13 1/2"
Weight	3 lbs. 7 oz.
Chamber mouth	.450"
Barrel groove	.450"
Retail	$625
From	Dixie Gun Works, Inc. Gunpowder Lane Union City, TN 38281 (731) 885-0700 fax (731) 885-0440 www.dixiegunworks.com

they look. This is a well-made replica and, aside from the loading lever operation, which is only rated at fair, the gun operated and shot beautifully. I think the colonel would be proud.

Endnotes

1   Flayderman's Guide to Antique American Firearms, 8th Edition, 2001, Krause Publications

Ruger Old Army

Ruger's Old Army with fixed sights is a very good-looking gun, the author calls it "over-built" like all Ruger single-actions.

Ruger's Old Army, while not a replica of anything, is a very usable black powder sixgun and suitable in every way for modern percussion shooting events. This modern blackpowder revolver is built on the Ruger Blackhawk frame. More precisely ours is built on the fixed-sighted Vaquero frame. The gun comes with the Vaquero size and shape grip, so it has the feel of a Colt. The frame, unlike a Colt percussion revolver, has a strong, solid top-strap similar to the 1858 Remington revolvers. Also similar to the Remington, the Ruger uses a base pin, but in this case the head of the base pin acts as a fulcrum for the loading lever.

I have to give Ruger a lot of credit, from a mechanical standpoint they have really put some thought into this revolver. For instance, they have added a gas ring to the face of cylinder to help keep hot powder gases from fouling the cylinder axis pin and they have set the rear of the barrel well back into the cylinder opening in the frame. By doing the latter, they have kept the barrel-to-cylinder gap behind and away from the front of the gas ring. This aids greatly in keeping black powder fouling out of the base pin area. The percussion nipples are equipped with little hex facets for turning and Ruger supplies a neat little hex nipple wrench screwdriver combination tool that is very effective. They have also machined neat, precise pockets around the nipples that serve to provide excellent support to the nipple wrench. The nipples, by the way, are stainless steel. A nice touch.

Its hard to see the seams where the grip frame fits up to the receiver, the polish work is that good.

Taken apart for cleaning, all it takes to remove the cylinder is a half turn of that base pin lockscrew in front of the cylinder and the loading lever and base pin comes out as an assembly.

Left; the front of the Old Army cylinder sports a gas ring, an old S&W invention that keeps black-powder from fouling cylinder rotation. Right; from the rear of the cylinder we can see the stainless steel nipples. In between the nipples are the machined slots for the hammer nose (firing pin) to fit into, these act as a safety device.

Our Old Army is the blued steel version with fixed sights and has a 7 1/2-inch round barrel. The blue finish was, I thought, exceptionally well polished to a medium luster before it was blued. The edges and corners were crisp and sharp. Overall the gun makes a very professional-looking appearance. Even the grip frame had been polished to fit the frame almost perfectly with no unsightly seams. The grips were made of rosewood and of the typical Ruger pattern with the factory logo at the tops. We were not as impressed with the wood-to-metal fit-up. In fact, the grips were not well fitted at all. There were large gaps at the tops, between the metal and wood, overhanging areas and other areas where the

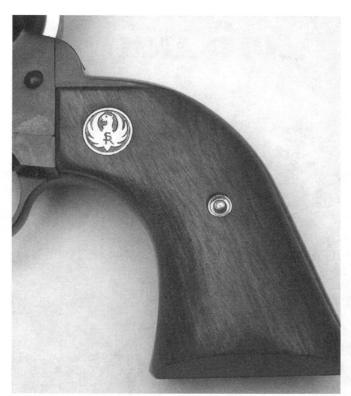

Ruger uses rosewood for its grip panels. This particular set of grips was not fitted very well to the grip frame.

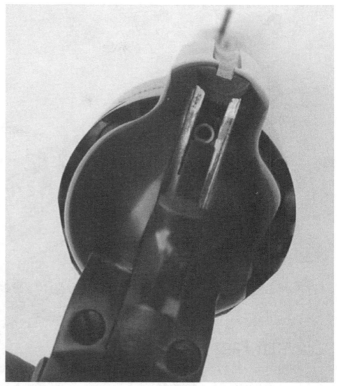

A sharply machined, square notch forms the rear sight. This gun has a very clear sight picture.

Ruger's hammer has very sharp, deep serrations that offer the shooter a firm grasp on the spur. Notice the huge hammer nose, that's for bashing caps!

grip frame wasn't covered by the wood. The grips were an attractive red-orange with a light oiled finish and in spite of the fit-up problems, they offered a comfortable hold. Personally, I find these grips a little fat and would prefer to have grip panels made a little thinner, ala; the Colt percussion revolvers and very early SAA grips that were so comfortable and easy to wrap your fingers around.

The Old Army's action does not use a transfer bar like all of Ruger's New Model single-actions. Nope, this is a two-clicker like the percussion revolvers of old, and the only safety devices are the machined notches in between the cylinder chambers, where the hammer nose is meant to be rested. Sights consist of a cleanly machined, square notch in the rear of the frame's top-strap and a barrel-mounted front blade

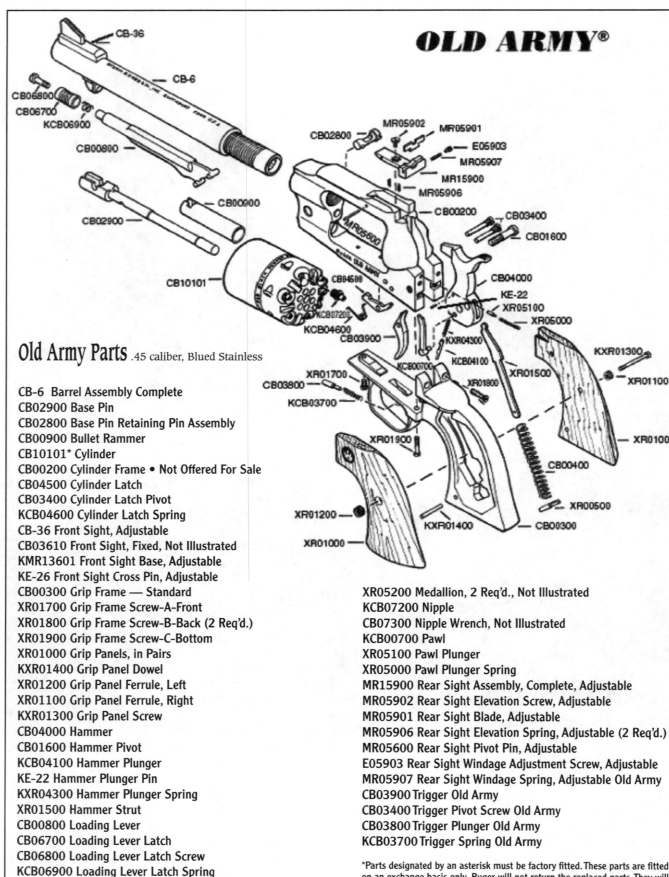

OLD ARMY®

Old Army Parts .45 caliber, Blued Stainless

CB-6 Barrel Assembly Complete
CB02900 Base Pin
CB02800 Base Pin Retaining Pin Assembly
CB00900 Bullet Rammer
CB10101* Cylinder
CB00200 Cylinder Frame • Not Offered For Sale
CB04500 Cylinder Latch
CB03400 Cylinder Latch Pivot
KCB04600 Cylinder Latch Spring
CB-36 Front Sight, Adjustable
CB03610 Front Sight, Fixed, Not Illustrated
KMR13601 Front Sight Base, Adjustable
KE-26 Front Sight Cross Pin, Adjustable
CB00300 Grip Frame — Standard
XR01700 Grip Frame Screw-A-Front
XR01800 Grip Frame Screw-B-Back (2 Req'd.)
XR01900 Grip Frame Screw-C-Bottom
XR01000 Grip Panels, in Pairs
KXR01400 Grip Panel Dowel
XR01200 Grip Panel Ferrule, Left
XR01100 Grip Panel Ferrule, Right
KXR01300 Grip Panel Screw
CB04000 Hammer
CB01600 Hammer Pivot
KCB04100 Hammer Plunger
KE-22 Hammer Plunger Pin
KXR04300 Hammer Plunger Spring
XR01500 Hammer Strut
CB00800 Loading Lever
CB06700 Loading Lever Latch
CB06800 Loading Lever Latch Screw
KCB06900 Loading Lever Latch Spring
CB00400 Mainspring
XR00500 Mainspring Seat

XR05200 Medallion, 2 Req'd., Not Illustrated
KCB07200 Nipple
CB07300 Nipple Wrench, Not Illustrated
KCB00700 Pawl
XR05100 Pawl Plunger
XR05000 Pawl Plunger Spring
MR15900 Rear Sight Assembly, Complete, Adjustable
MR05902 Rear Sight Elevation Screw, Adjustable
MR05901 Rear Sight Blade, Adjustable
MR05906 Rear Sight Elevation Spring, Adjustable (2 Req'd.)
MR05600 Rear Sight Pivot Pin, Adjustable
E05903 Rear Sight Windage Adjustment Screw, Adjustable
MR05907 Rear Sight Windage Spring, Adjustable Old Army
CB03900 Trigger Old Army
CB03400 Trigger Pivot Screw Old Army
CB03800 Trigger Plunger Old Army
KCB03700 Trigger Spring Old Army

*Parts designated by an asterisk must be factory fitted. These parts are fitted on an exchange basis only. Ruger will not return the replaced parts. They will not return any part that is broken, malfunctioning, badly worn or has been modified.

that is shaped like a later Single Action Army. The combination works and presents a very clear, easy-to-find sight picture. The Old Army's hammer spur is serrated, similar to the spur on their Vaquero models, only the serrations on this one were very sharp and easy to grab. The action operation was very smooth. That coil mainspring offers Ruger's usual, easy hammer operation. With the hammer placed in the half-cock or loading position, the nipples were not sitting anywhere near the center of the capping port, requiring manual rotation of the cylinder to place the nipple where it could be capped. Timing was not bad but we did take notice of the fact that the hammer came into full cock a bit early, before the cylinder had been mechanically rotated, or indexed, by the hand. Pulling the hammer slightly farther to the rear did bring the cylinder around to the point where the bolt locked it, but we always like to see this operation done mechanically at the same moment the hammer reaches full cock. Our gun's trigger pull was not bad at all. After a minimal amount of creep the hammer fell away at just about 3 3/4 pounds. While it's not a competition-grade trigger, that's still pretty darn good for an out-of-the-box single-action revolver. Other than that slight under-timing we mentioned, the only complaint one could make about the action is when dry fired the mainspring vibrates and makes the eeriest ringing noise.

We did not test fire this revolver for the simple reason that we ran out of time before the deadline. However, I can give you the benefit of my experience with an Old Army adjustable-sighted version I owned for several years. When fired with .457-inch round balls over 35 grains of FFFg GOEX powder, that revolver would always shoot 1-inch groups at 7 yards and quite often, even smaller. My Ruger Old Army was not susceptible to powder fouling in the degree that Colt or Remington percussion guns are and it always worked dependably.

Old Army® Black Powder Revolver · BP-7	
Caliber:	45
Capacity:	6 Rounds
Finish:	Blued
Stock / Grip:	Rosewood
Barrel Length:	7 1/2"
Grooves:	6
Twist:	1:16" RH
Overall Length:	13 1/2"
Weight:	51 oz
Front Sight(s):	Ramp
Rear Sight(s):	Adjustable
Suggested Retail Price:	$ 525

Based on what we saw here, the fixed-sighted Ruger Old Army is one honey of a black powder revolver and I have absolutely no doubts that it will make a wonderful shooter. With this revolver, Ruger has stuck with the same formula that they have for half a century. They use a proven, basic design to start with and then they tailor it to fit the specialized need. When they get finished they offer the public a mechanically superior revolver, built with what I like to call "over-kill." Over-kill translates into over-design, over-built, stronger than it needs to be, built like a tank, etc. Call it what you will, it's something I wish more American companies would practice. Based on this, I am confident that the Old Army is one of those guns that will last a lifetime and deliver thousands of shots without a hitch. . .just as every Ruger I have ever owned has.

Cimarron Richards-Mason
cartridge conversion revolver

A. Uberti manufactures Cimarron's fine replica of the Colt Richards-Mason conversion revolvers, which were based on the 1860 Army percussion revolver. The Cimarron is chambered in .44 Colt caliber (the modern version that uses .430-inch bullets) but it accepts and shoots .44 S&W Russian as well. Author photo.

From the right side we get a good look at the ejector assembly. In use, the ejector head is turned almost straight down, then pushed rearward to eject the fired cartridges. As you can see Uberti has paid very close attention to details, fit and finish. Author photo.

After the Civil War, Colt had countless thousands of percussion revolvers left over from the conflict. These guns were at least partially obsolete by the advent of the metallic cartridge revolver and the company dearly wanted to find ways of salvaging these otherwise perfectly functional weapons. One sensible solution seemed to be to devise ways of converting them so they could accept metallic cartridges. The fly in the ointment for Colt and others was that another company already held the rights to a patent covering the concept of loading a rimmed cartridge into a cylinder from the rear. That company was Smith & Wesson and the patent's legal protection would not expire until 1869. One way Colt found to go around this was by adopting the invention of Alexander Thuer, a conversion for percussion Colts that enabled them to accept an unconventional, front-loaded, tapered metallic cartridge. The Thuer system wasn't the greatest idea, but it did provide Colt with a stopgap measure and allowed them to sell about 5,000 revolvers that they otherwise may not have sold.

Colt employee Charles Richards patented a better method of converting Colt percussion models into, metallic cartridge revolvers in 1871. Richards's cartridge conversions of the 1860 Army were breech-loading and they chambered a rimmed, centerfire .44-caliber cartridge (the .44 Colt.) A loading gate was added to the revolver by virtue of a conversion ring which was attached to the revolver frame after some intricate machine work was performed. Contained within the conversion ring were a fixed rear sight and a ring-mounted, spring-loaded firing pin. Part of Richards' conversion was the addition of a barrel-mounted ejector rod assembly that attached by fitting up into the recess were the percussion rammer once lived. The next step up in conversions for Colt came with the Richards-Mason, which was a combination of the efforts of the former and the patents of William Mason, who in 1872 contributed among other things, a simpler, neater ejector assembly that was also less expensive to manufacture. Richards-Mason conversions differed from the Richards by retaining the rear sight on the hammer nose, just like the earlier percussion models. They also used a fixed,

The Richards-Mason close-up, giving you a good look at the patent dates and cylinder details. The screw to the front of the wedge is what holds the ejector tube on the opposite side of the barrel. Author photo.

With the hammer placed in the loading position and the gate opened, you can see how the R-M placed the chambers nicely in the center of the loading port, this makes for unencumbered loading and unloading. Author photo.

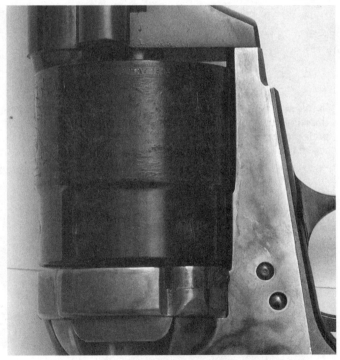

In this view we can see some of the intricate cylinder scene, originally engraved for Colt by Wm. Ormsby. It has been replicated nicely by Uberti. Notice the rebated cylinder reminiscent of the 1860 Army .44. Author photo.

hammer-mounted firing pin. For Colt, this helped the bottom line since both these features shaved their expenses. As we can see, the R-M was a more refined, easier to manufacture (read that; more cost effective) conversion than the Richards.

Cimarron Firearms Richards-Mason conversion revolvers are faithful copies of the originals that are produced in Italy by the Aldo Uberti. Co. The gun we tested is an 1860 Army conversion in .44 Colt caliber with a 5 1/2-inch barrel in blue and color case

In this side view of the R-M with the loading gate opened we can see the screw on the hammer side that is used to operate the Uberti hammer block safety. An interesting idea and an effective safety device, but the author found it clumsy and slow to use. I prefer to leave it in the "off" position. Like the early Colt percussion revolvers, the rear sight on this model is a notch formed on top of the hammer. Author photo.

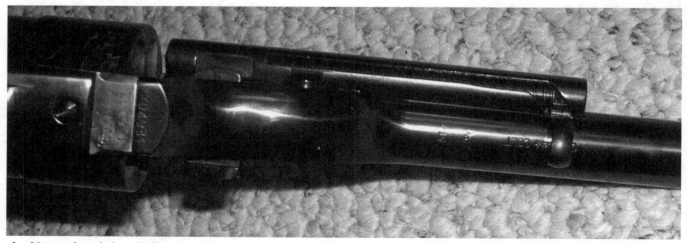

Looking up from below the barrel, we can get a good look at William Mason's patented ejector system. Author photo.

hardened finish. We soon found that this revolver would safely chamber and fire .44 S&W Russian ammunition, so later in the day we proceeded to test the gun with both calibers. The frame of the new R-M has been machined to accept a conversion ring that mounts a loading gate, and the Mason patent ejector rod is mounted as it should be, with a screw passing through the barrel lug exactly like the original revolvers.

Uberti has done a very fine job with this replica, this is a sharp-looking gun, the finishes on the metal parts are professional looking, and give the revolver a real 19th century look. We could see right away that the preparation of the metal surfaces was done correctly, with nice, sharp edges and distinct, clear markings. Just like the original R-M revolvers, the replica has "44 CAL" stamped on the left side of the trigger guard and the rebated cylinder is rolled with a lightly stamped version of the well-known Ormsby naval scene. The Uberti factory did a superb job with the way metal fits to metal, leaving nearly invisible seams and the one-piece walnut grips are mated to the frame and grip straps very nearly as well, with only paper-thin wood overhangs in a few, hard-to-spot areas. The only real criticism we have of the finishes is the color of the case coloring, which is bright, light, and indistinct, suggesting it was accomplished by a method other than the traditional bone and charcoal quench. Not that the colors are bad looking, they are attractive, but just not as faithful to the originals as we expected them to be.

Richards-Mason Parts

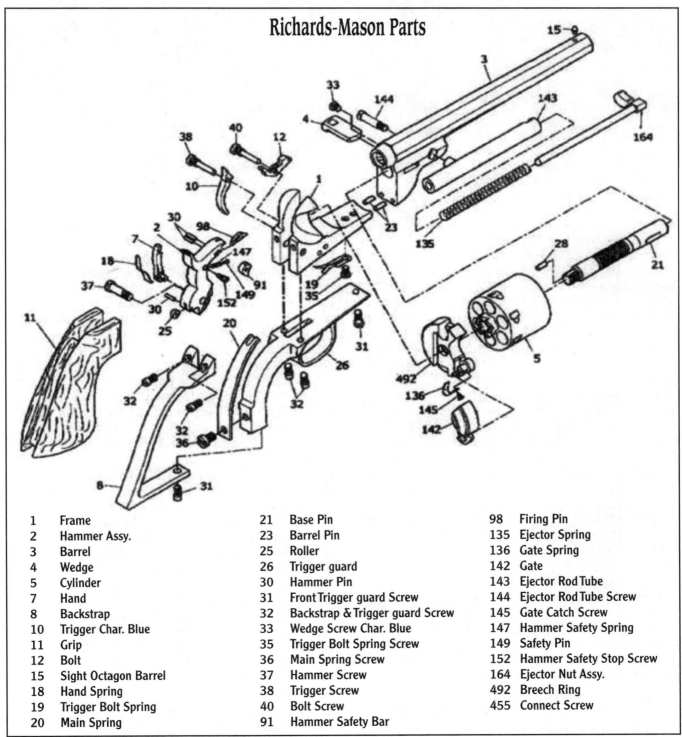

1	Frame	21	Base Pin	98	Firing Pin
2	Hammer Assy.	23	Barrel Pin	135	Ejector Spring
3	Barrel	25	Roller	136	Gate Spring
4	Wedge	26	Trigger guard	142	Gate
5	Cylinder	30	Hammer Pin	143	Ejector Rod Tube
7	Hand	31	Front Trigger guard Screw	144	Ejector Rod Tube Screw
8	Backstrap	32	Backstrap & Trigger guard Screw	145	Gate Catch Screw
10	Trigger Char. Blue	33	Wedge Screw Char. Blue	147	Hammer Safety Spring
11	Grip	35	Trigger Bolt Spring Screw	149	Safety Pin
12	Bolt	36	Main Spring Screw	152	Hammer Safety Stop Screw
15	Sight Octagon Barrel	37	Hammer Screw	164	Ejector Nut Assy.
18	Hand Spring	38	Trigger Screw	492	Breech Ring
19	Trigger Bolt Spring	40	Bolt Screw	455	Connect Screw
20	Main Spring	91	Hammer Safety Bar		

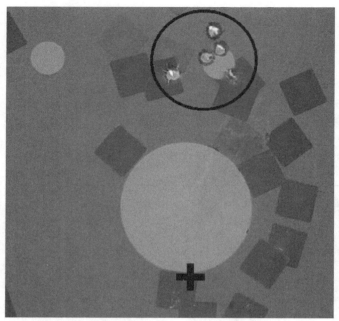

This is typical of the groups fired using Black Hills .44 Colt ammunition, they averaged 2 to 2 1/2 inches and printed 3 1/2 inches high and half an inch right. Author photo.

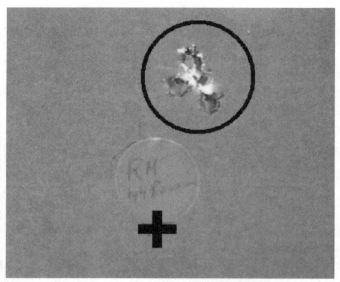

This replica was a fine-shooting gun all around. When we switched to Black Hills .44 Russian ammunition, the Richards-Mason conversion started giving us groups averaging just 3/4 of an inch, with a few as that could be covered with a 25-cent piece, in one ragged hole! Notice the point of impact drifted down to just an inch or so above the aiming point. Author photo.

Cylinder and action timing were very good; with the hammer reaching the cocked position the same time the cylinder bolt was locking the cylinder. We noticed when the hammer was in the half-cock/loading position that the cylinder chambers did not park exactly in the center of the loading port, although the problem wasn't near as serious as we experienced on other revolvers and it did not manage to slow us down much at all during the reloading process. Operation of the conversion ring-mounted loading gate was smooth and very positive, giving you the impression that it was a very well fitted part. The factory did leave some sharp edges on the underside of the lip of the gate. This is the area where you open the gate with your thumb and both shooters had raw, nearly cut open thumbs after using that gate just a few times. The hammer is equipped with a unique safety device. It is manually operated by turning a screw on the hammer side to rotate a solid steel block forward. When the safety is placed in the "on" position, it prevents the hammer from falling all the way forward so the firing pin cannot reach the cartridge primer. I am in favor of this kind of safety because it is well hidden and doesn't detract from the gun's looks. Plus, we have the option of never using it, and most likely, I never would. As much as I dislike adding devises like this to replicas of old gun designs, I did try the safety and it is, in practice, the safest device of its kind that I have seen on a replica revolver.

Because it is different from the "norm" and because it is a replica of one of the author's personal all-time favorite Old West guns, we checked this gun over closely before shooting it to see what we actually had here. Right out of the box this new revolver had a barrel-to-cylinder gap that measured a nice tight .004 inches. Both the barrel groove diameter and cylinder chamber mouths were measured at exactly .430 inches. This is a very nice combination, and it was an early indication to me that this gun was probably going to shoot very well. The wedge is secured by a screw on the left barrel side whose large diameter head fits into a notch on the wedge. This "smart screw" also has a flat ground on one side of the head, so a quick, partial turn with a screwdriver is all that is required to free the wedge for removal. I did notice when reassembling the barrel to the frame that it was possible to drive the wedge in too far, thereby binding the barrel against the cylinder, tying up the cylinder so it refused to move. Applying a few careful taps on the wedge in the opposite direction with a plastic hammer allowed the barrel to move back away from the cylinder, thus its operation along with the original gap was restored. The problem described is an indication that this cylinder arbor pin was never properly fitted to the barrel by the factory and, in fact, the cylinder arbor, as Colt called it, is actually too short [1]. This condition allows the wedge to force the barrel back until it pushes too hard on the frame and being unsupported at the front of the arbor, the barrel begins to move upwards until the forcing cone area at the rear of the barrel comes into direct contact with the cylinder face, binding up the whole works.

Trigger pull on the R-M was a good, light 2 3/4 pounds and the sear finally let go only after a long,

Caliber:	44 Colt BHA, 45 Schofield, 38 Special, 38 Colt
Barrel Lengths:	8", 7 1/2" & 5 1/2"
Frame:	Forged steel
Stocks:	One-piece walnut
Finishes:	Modern blue, charcoal blue, Cimarron Original Finish, or custom nickel
Backstrap:	Navy grip - brass or optional silver, Army grip - blue steel
Suggested Retail:	Starting at $529

slow creeping period. Interestingly enough, the grip was so comfortable and the trigger break was so good that both shooters quickly found themselves ignoring the creep. The sights on the R-M consist of a simple "V" notch in the hammer, just like the old Colt Percussion revolvers, mated with an inverted "V" shaped front. Surprisingly, that crude combination on this particular gun was very easy for both shooters to pick up and the fact that it worked is graphically illustrated in the accompanying photos. We fired the Richards-Mason first using Black Hills .44 Colt ammunition and we were delighted with its performance. Ten cylinders of .44 Colt gave us several five-shot groups that averaged just about 2 to 2 1/4 inches in diameter that hit the paper roughly 3 1/2 inches high and an inch right. Switching to Black Hills .44 Russian ammo, we fired six five-shot groups that, on the average, measured right around 3/4 of an inch, with one group producing what was basically one very small, ragged hole. With .44 Russian, the point of impact was much closer to the point of aim, perhaps only an inch high.

We liked the way this gun shot so much that we took it to another range a week later for further shooting tests with yet another shooter. With the new shooter, my son Dave, and this time at an indoor range, the gun performed exactly as it had before, delivering wonderful accuracy. Throughout a total of just over 300 rounds fired, the revolver never balked and the accuracy remained as excellent as it did in the first test sequence. As far as dependability, aside from the wedge/cylinder arbor problem mentioned earlier, which by the way, was never an issue during

Cimarron Open Top, as tested	
Model	Cimarron CA931
Name	Richards-Mason
Finish(s)	Blue & color case hardened
Barrel length	5 1/2"
Overall length	11 1/2"
Caliber	.44 Colt
Capacity	6 shots
Action	Single
Front sight	Fixed blade
Rear sight	Fixed notch
Grips	1-piece walnut, smooth
Chamber mouth	.430" (actual)
Barrel groove	.430" (actual)
Retail as tested	$529
Available from	Cimarron Firearms, P.O. Box 906, Fredericksburg, TX 78624-0906 (830) 997-9090

the tests since the wedge was not disturbed again, this new gun is an outstanding performer in every way. No balks. No misfires. The revolver ran like a Swiss watch. The Cimarron Richards-Mason has a wonderful, classic appearance, it balances and feels great and man, this baby shoots!

Endnotes

[1] See David Chicoine's article relating to this in *American Gunsmith, Volume XV, Number 5,* May 2000, "Unlocking the Colt Open-Top Barrel Mystery."

Cimarron 1872 Open-Top

3-1872-left.jpg: Cimarron's beautiful replica of Colt's first official cartridge revolver, the 1871-1872 Open-Top, sports a 7 1/2-inch barrel and makes use of the 1860 Army grip frame. The original Colt was available chambered in .44 rimfire. The Cimarron version is available in .44 Colt, .44 Special or .45 S&W Schofield. Author photo.

The Cimarron Open-top viewed from the right, notice the ejector tube arrangement, this is Mason's patent as used on the Richards-Mason conversion revolvers. Author photo.

The revolver we call the Open-Top was Colt's first real made-for-cartridges revolver. As such it was the immediate predecessor of the Single Action Army. Unlike their other contemporary converted percussion revolvers, Colt's Open-Top used a frame that was specifically intended to fire metallic cartridges, in that the frame of the Open-Top was machined to accept a loading gate which was held on with a screw and it did not have to use a separate conversion plate like converted cap-and-ball pistols did. Still, it remained a throw-back, retaining the open-top type of frame along with the barrel held in place by a wedge like Colt's former percussion pistols. Colt's Richards and Richards Mason conversion revolvers were chambered to fire the .44 Colt centerfire but all 7,000 of the original Open-Tops were chambered for the .44 Rimfire cartridge. Like the Richards-Mason conversion revolver, William Mason's patented ejector was also used on the Open-Top, fastened through the barrel's under-lug exactly as with the former.

"The graceful lines created by nineteenth century artisans have been captured fully in this late 20th century work of art in steel. The CIMARRON 1872 Open Top is without a doubt the finest replica to come forth in the last decade." Texas Jack Harvey, President, Cimarron Firearms.

After looking over and using the Aldo Uberti-manufactured Cimarron Open-Top, I am left with little choice but to agree with Mr. Harvey. This is indeed one beautiful revolver with the graceful lines of the original kept largely intact. One really encouraging change from the original is that the Cimarron version is available to us in off-the-shelf calibers like .44 Russian, .44 Colt, .38 Special and .45 S&W Schofield. The revolver we tested had a 7 1/2-inch barrel and was chambered in .44 Colt caliber. Open-Tops, like their percussion grandfathers, have only two cock notches on the hammer; the half-cock or loading position and full-cock, not three like the later Single Action Army.

Outwardly, Cimarron's Open-Top is a thing to behold. The blue and case color finishes are nicely executed, the metal is polished sharply, cleanly, the lines are intact and crisp, very much like a 19th century Colt would have been. All the little details are there too, the precise Colt-Ormsby naval battle cylinder scene, a two-line patent on the frame and a one-line address on the barrel (albeit, Cimarron's address in Texas!) All the parts fit together really well, too. Metal-to-metal fits are precise and almost invisible and the wood-to-metal fit are nearly as good. Overall, some great craftsmanship has been

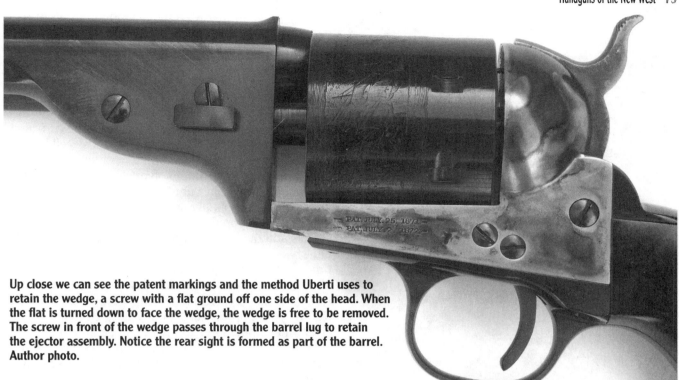

Up close we can see the patent markings and the method Uberti uses to retain the wedge, a screw with a flat ground off one side of the head. When the flat is turned down to face the wedge, the wedge is free to be removed. The screw in front of the wedge passes through the barrel lug to retain the ejector assembly. Notice the rear sight is formed as part of the barrel. Author photo.

The Open-Top can be purchased with the Navy grip (Single Action Army size) or the 1860 Army grip (shown here) which is a bit longer. Either way the standard grips are well fitted one-piece walnut. Author photo.

The rear sight is a notch machined into the barrel top, making the sight picture far more stable than that of the Open-Top's parent percussion Colts which had a sighting notch cut into the top of the hammer. Author photo.

displayed in the finish work on this gun. The grips are made from nicely figured, oil-finished walnut. They are one-piece of course and are furnished in the large 1860 Army size, with the shape pared down to nearly perfect Colt dimensions. I normally find the 1860 grip size to be just a bit awkward and large for my liking, but there is something about the feel and look of this gun as a whole that gives an almost indescribable sense of comfort and surprisingly good balance. If you have never held one, I would encourage you to pick one up and heft it on your next trip to the local gun shop.

This view of the 1872 with its hammer cocked shows the screw in the side of the hammer that is turned to help rotate the safety bar forward preventing the hammer from falling. This is a feature found only on some Uberti revolvers. Take a look at the perfect metal-to-metal fit where the grip straps fit to the frame. Author photo.

Uberti's hammer is equipped with a unique safety device. This safety is manually operated. After placing the hammer at half-cock turning a screw on the hammer side causes a solid steel block to rotate down (see photo) so the block actually protrudes from the hammer face. With the safety thus placed in the "on" position, the hammer is prevented from falling all the way down so the firing pin cannot reach the cartridge primer. I like the safety because it is fairly well hidden. It can't be seen when the hammer is down, so it doesn't detract from the revolver's gorgeous lines. I also like the fact that I am left with the option of never using it, and I probably never will since I prefer to load five and drop the hammer on the empty chamber. This is still the only really safe way to carry a loaded, old-style single-action. In the interest of these tests I did try the safety and I have to say it is the most effective and the safest safety device I have seen on a foreign-made revolver. Requiring a tool to be operated, the safety is impractical for daily use, it's just too slow and cumbersome to operate to be an effective everyday safety devise. Because most people would not know it was there it would be great for use as a storage safety devise. The hammer is fitted with a very small diameter fixed firing pin that is fastened with a cross-pin. We measured the firing pin's protrusion through the frame and came up with .074"; that's a lot of firing pin to leave sticking out (optimal is about .055-.060"). In the tests ignition was, as you might guess, flawless, but there was a tendency toward piercing primers. We thought it best to polish the

We found that at times, operation of the ejector rod was difficult since the rod ran into the front of the cylinder, missing the chambers. You can see how the rod is actually in contact with the inside wall of the chamber. Author photo.

Just below the firing pin you can see the steel block that is the safety device on this revolver. Here the safety is shown in the "on" position. Turning a screw on the right side of the operates it. Author photo.

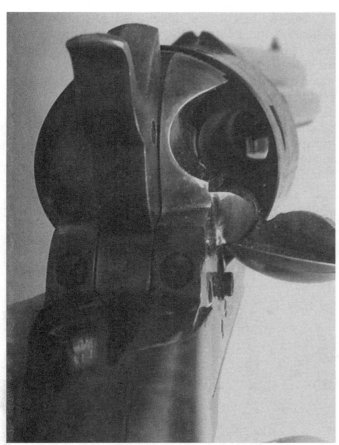

When the hammer is placed in the loading position, the chamber was being held in a position that was more advanced in the loading port than we would like, but this didn't seem to interfere much with loading and unloading. Author photo.

firing pin tip slightly. In the process we removed about 10 thousandths of an inch and this cured the piercing problem and still left excellent ignition.

Open-Tops are taken apart for cleaning in the same manner as percussion Colts are, by removing the barrel wedge and pulling the barrel, then the cylinder, forward and off the frame. Uberti has supplied the Open-Top and their late manufacture conversion revolvers with a notched-head wedge screw. That is, the screw head has a flat ground in it. When the screw is turned so this flat faces away from the wedge, the round portion of the screw head is rolled into a notch in the wedge, locking the wedge in place and preventing it from coming out. When you want to remove the wedge, the screw is turned so its flat faces the wedge. This unlocks the wedge for removal. Neat, simple. I like it.

Our revolver's cylinder timing was truly excellent, with the cylinder bolt dropping into the bolt notch on the cylinder at the precise moment the hammer reached the full-cock position. You really can't do better'n that! Trigger pull was very good and crisp. Sear let off occurred at about 3 3/4 pounds with some creep, but you expect that from this type of action. When the hammer was placed in the half-cock setting, in other words, in the loading position, the cylinder chambers were located a bit over to the right side of the loading port but not so much that it interfered with cartridge loading. With .44 Special cartridges there was some rim dragging on the right side of the port, but nothing that seriously slowed

Here is Ed Wade about to touch off the Cimarron Open-Top for the first time. The Open-top had a nice action and performed quite well. Author photo.

us down. We did notice that the ejector rod diameter was large enough that it actually hit the front of the cylinder between the chambers unless we manually rolled the cylinder back slightly. Even then, after entering the chamber, the rod was in contact with the inside of the chamber wall during ejection. As I recommended to Cimarron, they might try tapering the first quarter inch or so of the ejector rod slightly. It wouldn't take much, just enough so it doesn't run into the cylinder face. That would speed up ejection by helping to ease the rod into the chambers.

The sight picture on this gun amounted to a small "U" shaped notch that was nearly filled by an inverted "V" front. This made for what was, at best, an indistinct sight picture that, unfortunately, was made even worse by the strong sunlight reflecting off the bright top of the brass front sight. Still, the Cimarron Open-Top performed better than either of us shooters imagined it would, planting five-shot groups about on center and just about 2 1/2 inches higher than the point of aim at 25 feet. We used Winchester .44 Special Cowboy Loads for the tests

1872 Open Top Parts

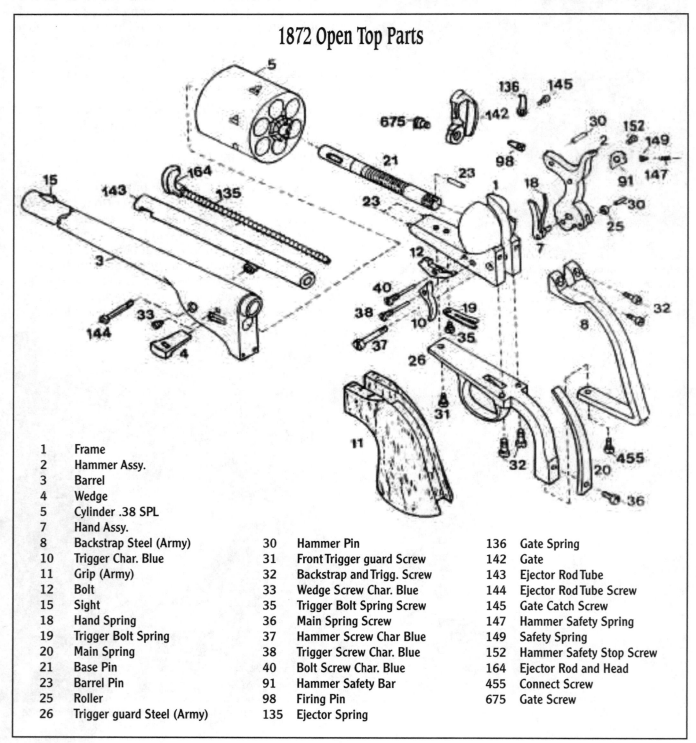

1	Frame
2	Hammer Assy.
3	Barrel
4	Wedge
5	Cylinder .38 SPL
7	Hand Assy.

8	Backstrap Steel (Army)	30	Hammer Pin	136	Gate Spring
10	Trigger Char. Blue	31	Front Trigger guard Screw	142	Gate
11	Grip (Army)	32	Backstrap and Trigg. Screw	143	Ejector Rod Tube
12	Bolt	33	Wedge Screw Char. Blue	144	Ejector Rod Tube Screw
15	Sight	35	Trigger Bolt Spring Screw	145	Gate Catch Screw
18	Hand Spring	36	Main Spring Screw	147	Hammer Safety Spring
19	Trigger Bolt Spring	37	Hammer Screw Char Blue	149	Safety Spring
20	Main Spring	38	Trigger Screw Char. Blue	152	Hammer Safety Stop Screw
21	Base Pin	40	Bolt Screw Char. Blue	164	Ejector Rod and Head
23	Barrel Pin	91	Hammer Safety Bar	455	Connect Screw
25	Roller	98	Firing Pin	675	Gate Screw
26	Trigger guard Steel (Army)	135	Ejector Spring		

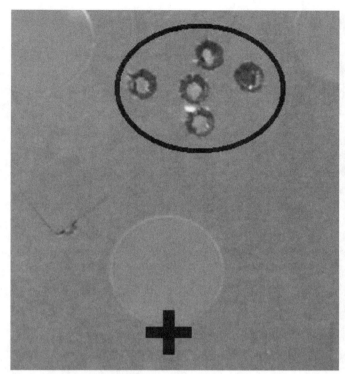

With Winchester .44 Special Cowboy ammunition, the Uberti-made 1872 replica delivered fine accuracy and produced consistent groups similar to this one. Author photo.

Cimarron Open Top, as tested	
Model	Cimarron CA900
Name	1872 Open Top
Finish(s)	Blue & color case hardened
Barrel length	7 1/2"
Overall length	13 1/2"
Calibers	.44 Special
Capacity	6 shots
Action	Single
Front sight	Fixed blade
Rear sight	Fixed notch
Grips	1-piece walnut, smooth
Chamber mouth	.4305" (actual)
Barrel groove	.4295" (actual)
Retail as tested	$529
Available from	Cimarron Firearms, P.O. Box 906, Fredericksburg, TX 78624-0906 (830) 997-9090

Caliber:	45 Schofield, 44 Russian, 44 Colt BHA, 38 Special, 38 Colt
Barrel Lengths:	7 ½" & 5 ½"
Frame:	Forged steel, color case hardened
Stocks:	One piece walnut
Finishes:	Modern blue, charcoal blue, Cimarron Original Finish, or custom nickel
Backstrap:	Navy grip - brass or optional silver, Army grip - blue steel
Suggested Retail:	$529

and the ammunition performed very well indeed. The average five-shot group size at 7 yards was just 1 ¼ inches and the smallest group (fired with Black Hills .44 Russian ammo) could be covered by a quarter with all the shots touching. We measured the barrel to cylinder gap at .005" and there was very little perceptible cylinder end-shake. The barrel's groove diameter measured out at a nice, tight .4295" and the cylinder's chamber mouths came in at .4305". This is a good mechanical combination for a revolver. Just how good was reflected on the target range in the excellent accuracy of this gun.

This particular revolver caused quite a stir whenever we took it out to the range. Its distinctive appearance made people raise their eye brows and ask questions. Indeed, everyone who shot and handled this Cimarron Open-Top liked it very much. What do we think? This Open-Top looks great. It shoots even better. Except for having to alter the firing pin, our test revolver operated basically without any hitches throughout the 200 rounds of ammunition we fired. The only small trouble we had was that, because of its placement and rod diameter, the ejector rod sometimes runs into the front face of the cylinder and that slowed down the ejection process a bit for us. This is a small and easily corrected flaw. Overall, the Open-Top is a classy looking and extremely well balanced revolver that is a joy to shoot and to handle.

The 1873 Colt Single Action and its modern look-a-likes.

An original 7 1/2-inch barreled Colt cavalry revolver from the 1873 contract . Author collection and photo.

We are all familiar with the famous Colt Peacemaker. This is the revolver officially called the Model of 1873, Model "P" or Single Action Army. Whatever name you know it by, the silhouette of the famous Colt is easily recognized worldwide. Indeed, wherever there is the slightest mention of the American West, or the American cowboy, an image of the Colt Peacemaker will be present as the foremost icon of that much-admired era in our history.

Today's cowboy action shooter has more choices than ever in single-action Colt-type revolvers. These range from expensive American-made antiques to modern foreign- and domestic-made revolvers in varying price ranges. He may opt to use an original Colt and in this line he has much to choose from. Choices include high-dollar pre-World War II (first-generation) production guns made from 1873 through 1940; the so-called second-generation guns made starting in 1955 through about 1976 and the newest or third-generation, manufactured from about 1976

to date. Colts are good guns; even those that have been made in recent years that might have been made with flaws are still very fine platforms for building a good competition revolver. Colts are also known for being pricy, especially when they are compared to replicas. On the up side, Colts will normally not require as much gunsmithing work and new parts to make them into a full-fledged competition gun as some of the replicas might. However, even that statement is not cut in stone, as you will see later.

There are Peacemaker replicas on the market today from several very good Italian arms makers and one that has not always been so consistent about making very good revolvers. In addition, we have the American-made Colt and a new kid on the block, United States Fire Arms Mfg. Co. These two American companies make single-actions in competing price ranges and generally, of very fine quality. Then, there are new kinds of 1873-based

This is a modern, third-generation Colt Model P with custom one-piece ivory stocks by Jerry Meacham of Charlotte, NC. From the Ed Wade collection. Author photo.

The Cimarron Firearms Model P is made in Italy by Uberti and it is a beautiful replica. Revolver courtesy Cimarron Firearms. Author photo.

Ruger's Vaquero is a truly modern single-action, its actually safe to carry with all six chambers loaded. Revolver courtesy Sturm Ruger. Author photo.

This replica of the Colt Open-Top is sold by Cimarron and made by Uberti, it shoots as well as it looks! Revolver courtesy Cimarron Firearms. Author photo.

single-actions available today in configurations that were never made originally but which might have been if only someone had thought about marrying the birds-head double-action grip with the single-action frame. New to the market, but a very welcome sight, are stainless steel versions that are made as very faithful copies of the original 1873.

Then we have the Sturm, Ruger single-actions, which are available today in many configurations and in blue or stainless steel. As you may already know, the Ruger New Model™ is the only single-action being made which is really safe to carry with all six chambers of the cylinder loaded. Ruger's single-actions are not exactly what you would call completely faithful copies of the old Colt, but they

are the only truly modern single-action revolvers available. Running a tad larger in most dimensions than the 1873, they offer the shooter a revolver that is rugged in the extreme.

Let's go ahead and have a look at a few of the more popular 1873-type revolvers being used in Cowboy Action Shooting today and see how they stack up. We've included a look at a conversion Colt-type revolver as well as the immediate forerunner of the Peacemaker, the 1872 Open-Top since they are not only historically important, they are becoming very popular. This review by no means covers all of these types of revolvers. It is however a good representative sampling of those currently available.

Colt Single Action Army Revolver

Colt's new P1850, with a 5 1/2-inch barrel in .45 Colt caliber pictured along with the ammo that performed the best in our tests, Black Hills .45 Colt Cowboy loads. Author photo.

History

Colt's Single Action Army, the revolver that many folks reverently call "The Peacemaker," was first introduced in 1873. The SAA is a simple, tried and true single-action revolver design that uses a solid frame and with a cylinder capacity of six cartridges. As many readers already know, in 1873 the Colt was after a series of tests chosen over other revolvers by the U.S. Army and was consequently adopted in .45 Colt caliber as the official U.S. service revolver. A close look at how the SAA operates will betray that its lineage dates back to Colt's percussion revolvers of the 1840s. In fact, the .36 caliber Model 1851 Navy percussion revolver is where the SAA grip and frame size and shape came from. In the place of an open frame with a removable barrel held on with a wedge, the SAA used

a solid frame with a barrel that was firmly screwed in place. The great Sam Colt passed away in 1862 and he was followed in 1865 by his famous chief engineer, Elisha K. Root, but neither of those famous firearms designers had a hand in the Single Action Army's final design. This drastic makeover of the Colt percussion revolver into a true metallic cartridge handgun was the result of work by William Mason, a firearms inventor, designer and engineer who had been hired to work on this and other important projects at Colt. The Peacemaker soon became, and has remained, one of the most popular handguns ever produced and it has since grown into a much-copied international icon. It is the gun that many consider to be the classic symbol of the Old West.

A close-up of the new P1850 showing the beautiful Colt blue and case colors. Author photo.

The design and how it worked

Colt's SAA was slow to load and unload when compared to other guns of its time, such as the fast-loading S&W top-break revolvers. However, early on the Colt developed a good reputation for dependability. The Colt is what we call a "three-

This close-up of the grips shows the fancy "Eagle" pattern which proved to be rather uncomfortable to two out of three shooters. Author photo.

clicker" because you will hear three audible clicks as you pull the hammer back. In order to unload the Colt you first had to pull the hammer back to the rear two clicks, this places the hammer in the loading or half-cock position. The shooter then opened the loading gate and inserted the cartridges into the chambers while he manually revolved the cylinder. All this happened at the rate of one cartridge at a time. The same slow procedure was used for unloading. In addition, a barrel-mounted rod ejector was operated to manually eject the cartridge case from each chamber while the cylinder was rotated by hand. Like loading, this operation also occurred at the rate of one chamber at a time. Colt's hammer had a so-called safety notch that was reached by pulling the hammer back to the first click. But the truth is, the safety wasn't really safe because it could be overcome and broken rather easily just by pulling a bit too hard on the trigger. This means that the only safe way to carry an SAA was, and is, to load only five of the six chambers, then carefully let the hammer down to rest on the empty chamber. Sluggish though it might have been to load and unload, after handling one, most folks seem to agree that there is just something about the classic look, its balance, and the overall feel of the Colt Single Action Army that gives the holder a sense of confidence. Most folks agree that the famous Peacemaker is somehow comparable to nothing else.

Three generations of revolvers

Collectors identify three generations of the Colt Single Action Army. The first-generation guns are the originals, produced from 1873 through 1940 and beginning with serial number 1 on up through serial number 357,859. The greatest share of these revolvers, about 310,000 guns, was manufactured as the standard version of the Single Action Army with fixed sights. From 1888 through 1896 Colt also made a limited number (just over 900) of a flat-topped target version to cater to target shooters. Likewise with the target shooter in mind, starting in 1894, a new variation of SAA called the Bisley Model was introduced. Bisley Models had an unusual and fairly radical grip shape, a low, wide-spur hammer and wide trigger. The Bisley was made with standard fixed sights and in a flat-topped target version and was discontinued about 1915. Over its 67-year production, Colt chambered the SAA in .45 Colt, .44-40, .38-40, .32-20 and to about 30 other calibers. Standard barrel lengths were 4 3/4 inches, 5 1/2 inches and 7 1/2 inches but they may be encountered with barrels from 2 1/2 inches to 16 inches in length. Standard SAA finishes were blue and case color or full nickel plate.

After a lull of 16 years a second-generation SAA appeared when, in 1956, the Colt factory re-introduced this famous revolver. Made available in 4 3/4 inches, 5 1/2 inches and 7 1/2 inches, these second-generation revolvers were offered in .38 Special, .357 Magnum, .44 Special and .45 Colt. Second-generation SAA revolvers were nearly identical in outward appearance to the first-generation Colts and had only minor internal changes. The suffix "SA" was added after the serial number and Colt produced approximately 80,000 revolvers up to 1975 in standard configuration, as a short-barreled (3 inches, and made without an ejector) "Sheriff's Model", a "Buntline Special" with

To remove the cylinder the hammer is placed at half-cock with the loading gate open. Next, depress the base pin lock and pull the base pin forward. Once the base pin is out, the cylinder is rolled out the right side of the frame. Author photo.

It's a pretty easy procedure to break open one of these Colt-designed, open-topped percussion revolvers for cleaning.

a 12-inch barrel, as well as a target-sighted version with a flat-top frame named the "New Frontier".

The so-called third-generation Colt SAA came along in 1976 at around serial number 80,000SA. This version of the single-action, although the same in external appearance, had internal changes that included a fixed, non-removable base pin bushing and a new barrel thread pitch. When serial number 99,999 was reached in 1978, the serial number suffix was changed to a pre-fix and a new serial range began with serial number SA01001. Since 1982 the venerable Colt has been available only as a special-order model produced by the Colt Custom Shop. They are presently available in .357 Magnum, .38-40, .44 Special, .44-40 and .45 Colt calibers.

How do the newest SAA revolvers look and perform?

For the cowboy shooter, Colt's Model P is the most expensive of the variety of available 1873 look-a-like sixguns. We would like to be able to assume that since they are more expensive, the original Colt SAA would work flawlessly right out of the box and need no further attention or fine-tuning, but sadly, that is often not the case. To be fair, almost all brand new revolvers require some custom work to make them into super-dependable sixguns. Of all the available, new single-actions, the Colt Model P usually makes the best starting platform for you to hand over to your gunsmith and have the fine-tuning done that will

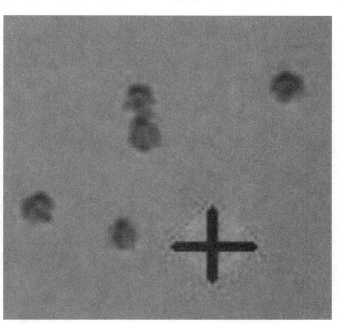

Always make sure your single-action is unloaded by opening the loading gate, placing the hammer at the loading position and spinning the cylinder at least two full rotations so you can observe each chamber. Author photo.

The SAA delivered 3 1/2- to 4 1/2-inch groups with Winchester Cowboy ammo, shown here is one of the larger groups fired at 7 yards. Author photo.

The P1850, with its hard trigger pull, delivered its best accuracy for Ed Wade, who fires hundreds of rounds in practice each week. Author photo.

make it into a strong competition revolver. As a basis for comparison, we selected a first-generation Single Action Army to shoot along side the P1850. This revolver is regularly used in cowboy competitions, also in .45 Colt caliber but with a 7 1/2-inch barrel. Our control revolver had a crisp 3-pound trigger pull and delivered consistent 1 1/2- to 2-inch, five-shot groups at 7 yards with Black Hills ammunition. With Winchester Cowboy ammo the same gun produced 2 1/2- to 3 1/2-inch group sizes.

The revolver we tested is a factory-fresh, 2003 production Model P1850 with a 5 1/2-inch barrel in .45 Colt caliber. The fit and finish of this revolver was very good. While it was not up to pre-WWII Colt quality, it was definitely much nicer than many revolvers similar to it being produced in the today. We were all a bit surprised to see that the grips

Gen. John Pickett (USAF ret.) is about to touch off the Colt P1850 with Black Hills ammo. Author photo.

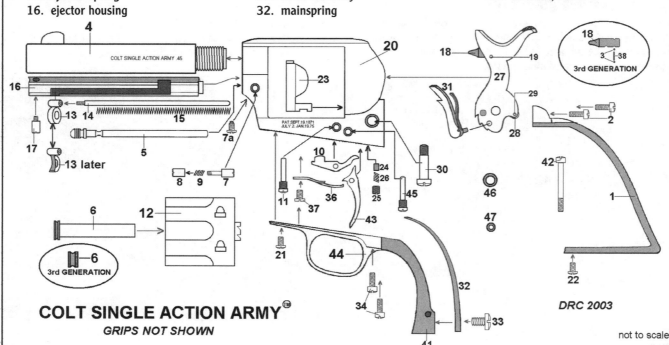

Colt Single Action Army Parts

1. backstrap
2. backstrap screw, upper (2)
3. detent ball (2)
4. barrel
5. base pin
6. base pin bushing
7. base pin lock screw
8. base pin lock nut
9. base pin lock spring
10. bolt
11. bolt screw
12. cylinder
13. ejector rod head
14. ejector rod
15. ejector spring
16. ejector housing

17. ejector housing screw
18. firing pin
19. firing pin rivet
20. frame
21. trigger guard screw, front
22. backstrap screw, lower
23. loading gate
24. loading gate detent
25. loading gate detent screw
26. loading gate detent spring
27. hammer
28. hammer roll
29. hammer roll pin
30. hammer screw
31. hand assembly
32. mainspring

33. mainspring screw
34. trigger guard screw, rear (2)
35. recoil plate (not shown)
36. sear and bolt spring
37. sear and bolt spring screw
38. firing pin detent spring
39. grip, left (not shown)
40. grip, right (not shown)
41. grip locating pin
42. grip screw
43. trigger
44. trigger guard
45. trigger screw
46. washer, hammer screw
47. washers, No. 8

COLT SINGLE ACTION ARMY™
GRIPS NOT SHOWN

DRC 2003

not to scale

A first-generation SAA in .45 Colt with a 7 1/2-inch barrel during recoil, this is Ed Wade firing a personal revolver that has been worked over for use in Cowboy competition. The gun had no trouble producing 1 1/2- to 2-inch groups at 7 yards with Black Hills Cowboy ammunition. Author photo.

Colt Single Action Army Specifications, as tested	
Model	P1850
Name	Single Action Army
Finish(s)	Blue and color case hardened
Barrel lengths	5 1/2 "
Overall lengths	11 "
Calibers	.45 Colt
Capacity	6 shots
Action	Single
Front sight	Fixed blade
Rear sight	Fixed notch
Grips	Black, eagle checkered
Chamber mouth	.454" (actual)
Barrel groove	.451" (actual)
Suggested Retail	$1375

were not very well fitted to the grip frame, a fact that stood out dramatically against the beautiful blue and case colors of the steel parts. Ed Wade, Gen. John Pickett (USAF Ret.) and I all test fired this revolver one chilly morning in February 2004. We fired approximately 125 rounds of factory ammunition and about 20 rounds of Ed's handloaded ammunition. This revolver was tested exactly as sold, brand new, right out of the box and with no alterations whatever.

The trigger pull on this new revolver was hard and somewhat creepy. When the trigger finally broke, the hammer fell at just over 11 pounds. This white-knuckle combination made it difficult for any of the three shooters to obtain good groups on target. Moreover, the hard rubber grips were not fitted well to the grip frame, they overhung the grip straps in several locations and the sharp edges of the grips gave the shooters an uncomfortable time during recoil. Toward the end of the session, these edges actually did cut open one shooter's hand. In spite of those built-in handicaps, the revolver did perform well and gave us no operational problems. The timing was good. At half-cock the cylinder chambers were parked almost at the center of the loading cut in the frame and the cylinder indexed smartly into place just as the

hammer reached full cock. At 7 yards the new Model P1850 Colt SAA delivered groups that measured 2 1/2 to 3 inches with the Black Hills .45 Colt Cowboy ammunition and with Ed Wade's .45 Colt handloads. Groups with Winchester's 255-grain Cowboy loads averaged from 3 1/2 to 4 1/2 inches. The point of impact for all the groups was just slightly to the left of center and averaged about 1 inch high. When the range was increased to 50 feet, the point of impact settled down to the sights. As a matter of interest, on disassembly we were happy to see that the factory has changed the base pin bushing back to the old type removable bushing that was formerly used in its first- and second-generation single-actions.

In the end, in spite of its relatively high retail price, the new Colt Model P would need some careful gunsmith smoothing and adjusting to make it a suitable revolver for serious competition. Colt's Single Action Army is still an extremely well made gun and truth be told, the workhorse Peacemaker is still the best basic platform of all available modern single-actions. The one replica single-action we found that came closest to the Colt in quality, in fact actually surpassing it in some areas, was the new EMF Great Western II made by Pietta. But of the two, the Colt does offer the best surface fit and finish.

Colt Cowboy

The Colt Cowboy, this one is a CB1850 in .45 Colt with a 5 1/2-inch barrel. Notice the lack of patent dates on the frame. Author photo.

Seen from the right side, the Cowboy really appears to be a clone of the Model P. The case coloring may not be up to the usual Colt Single Action Army quality, however, the Cowboy is still a handsome gun. Author photo.

Colt introduced the single-action Cowboy model in 1999 in an attempt to fill what was seen as a public demand for a less expensive version of the famous Single Action Army. That is, to offer the public a genuine Colt but at a price that was in the range of the imported copies. The obvious intended specific market for the Cowboy Model was to be cowboy action shooters.

Colt's Cowboy models have a different finish than the standard blue and case-hardened Single Action Army Model P in that they are not as highly polished. The color case hardening was also done using a different process that did not leave the familiar Colt bone and charcoal colors. In fact, the Cowboy case colors have a look that is more reminiscent of some of the older Italian imports than of Colt case coloring. Hand fitting in areas like the fit of the grip

Even though the safety notch is gone the hammer must still be placed in the half-cock position for loading. Note the chamber is not perfectly aligned with the loading port in the frame. Author photo.

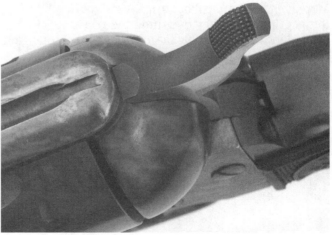

The Cowboy model hammer spur turned out to be the best single-action hammer the author has ever used. It has excellent, sharp checkering and offers a really positive grip. Author photo.

straps to the frame and grips to the grip straps were obviously not given the usual careful attention to detail and we noticed several areas where gaps were present between the mating surfaces of two metal parts. Other areas were not finished as completely, including the front edges of the cylinder where the flutes used to be cleanly chamfered. For all those reasons, some of the Cowboy models may be found with sharp edges protruding around certain places.

Colt's factory model designation numbers for the Cowboy models were CB1840 for 4 3/4-inch, CB1850 for 5 1/2-inch and CB1870 for the 7 1/2-inch barrel length. Official factory terminology for the Cowboy's standard finish was "case hardened." In actuality the guns were furnished with a color case hardened frame and with a blued barrel, cylinder and grip straps, in a fashion similar to the Model P. The hammer appears to be parkerized.

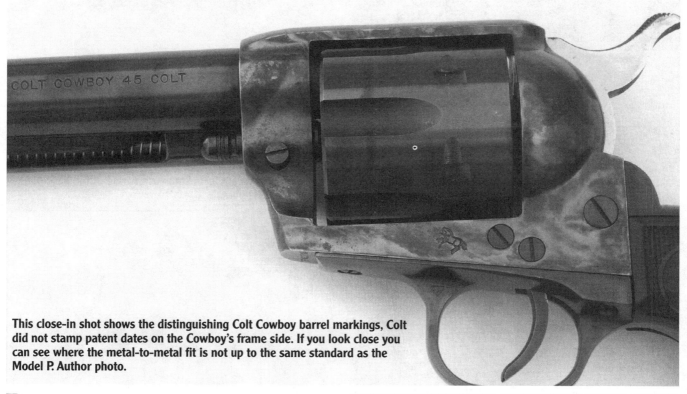

This close-in shot shows the distinguishing Colt Cowboy barrel markings, Colt did not stamp patent dates on the Cowboy's frame side. If you look close you can see where the metal-to-metal fit is not up to the same standard as the Model P. Author photo.

When the trigger is pulled the transfer bar rises up to cover the firing pin. This allows the hammer to drive the pin forward. When the trigger is released the transfer bar moves downward out of the way so the hammer can no longer contact the firing pin. Author photo.

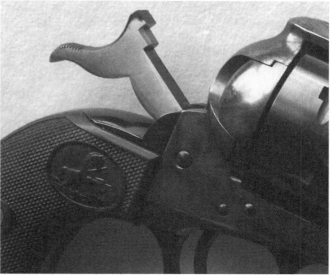

This doesn't look like an SAA hammer does it? The large, hammer-mounted firing pin is gone from the Cowboy model. Instead it uses a frame-mounted rebounding firing pin. Those odd-looking cut-outs on the hammer face are to accommodate the new trigger-actuated transfer bar. Author photo.

With the cylinder removed the Cowboy looks like most other single-actions. That little knob sticking out the rear of the base pin is a spring-loaded plunger which provides rearward tension to the transfer bar. Author photo.

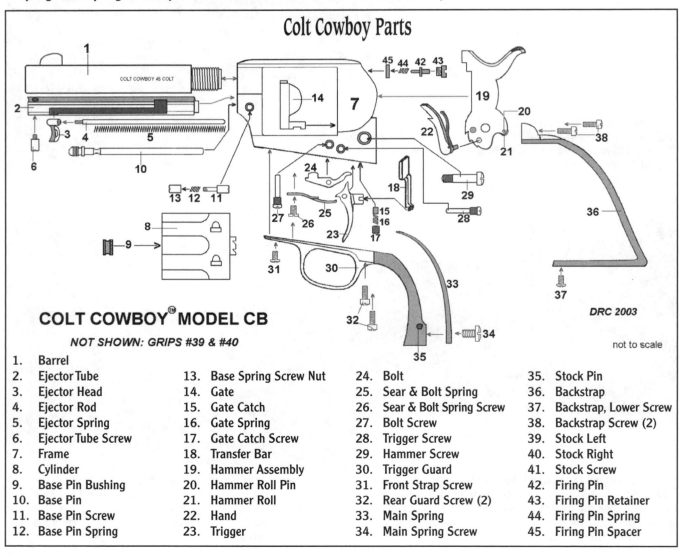

Colt Cowboy Parts

COLT COWBOY™ MODEL CB

NOT SHOWN: GRIPS #39 & #40

DRC 2003

not to scale

1. Barrel
2. Ejector Tube
3. Ejector Head
4. Ejector Rod
5. Ejector Spring
6. Ejector Tube Screw
7. Frame
8. Cylinder
9. Base Pin Bushing
10. Base Pin
11. Base Pin Screw
12. Base Pin Spring
13. Base Spring Screw Nut
14. Gate
15. Gate Catch
16. Gate Spring
17. Gate Catch Screw
18. Transfer Bar
19. Hammer Assembly
20. Hammer Roll Pin
21. Hammer Roll
22. Hand
23. Trigger
24. Bolt
25. Sear & Bolt Spring
26. Sear & Bolt Spring Screw
27. Bolt Screw
28. Trigger Screw
29. Hammer Screw
30. Trigger Guard
31. Front Strap Screw
32. Rear Guard Screw (2)
33. Main Spring
34. Main Spring Screw
35. Stock Pin
36. Backstrap
37. Backstrap, Lower Screw
38. Backstrap Screw (2)
39. Stock Left
40. Stock Right
41. Stock Screw
42. Firing Pin
43. Firing Pin Retainer
44. Firing Pin Spring
45. Firing Pin Spacer

The first cock notch, the so-called safety notch, is missing from the Cowboy hammer. Gone with it are the hammer-mounted firing pin we are so used to seeing on Colt Single Actions. A more modern transfer-bar ignition using a frame-mounted floating firing pin was also designed into the Cowboy model. The hammer still has to be pulled back into the half-cock position for loading and unloading operations, making the Cowboy officially a "two-clicker." Barrels are stamped on their tops with the Colt factory name and address and the barrel sides are marked "COLT COWBOY .45 COLT" but there are no patent dates on the left frame side. The very practical hammer spur is equipped with some of the most positive, non-slip checkering on its spur that we have ever seen on a Colt single-action revolver.

Amy Navitsky of Colt has told the author that the Colt Custom Shop also did work on some Cowboy models, and that the Custom Shop assigned a "Z" model number designation, denoting custom work, on a few of the Cowboys. There was also a Cowboy Buntline manufactured, as well as a few Cowboys chambered in .38 Special caliber. Navitsky says, "I have seen Nickel Cowboys and engraved Cowboys, and Cowboys with wood grips. All of these deviations of the standard models were done through the custom shop."

It seems the American cowboy action shooter did not respond as well to the lower-priced Cowboy model as Colt would have hoped, so in 2003 the Colt factory made the decision to discontinue the Cowboy. As some sharp Colt collectors are already aware, Colt actually made and sold 140 Cowboys prior to the official beginning of production in 1998 and the advertising and sales began in earnest by 1999. A total of 13,984 CCB models were manufactured. [1]

Our test Cowboy model was a brand new, 5 1/2-inch barreled version in .45 Colt and we tested the revolver in early March 2004 using a combination of Black Hills Cowboy and Winchester Cowboy ammunition. This off-the-shelf, factory-fresh revolver came with a trigger pull that broke at about 4 pounds. The trigger did have a fair amount of creep. Nevertheless the Cowboy's trigger was much easier to control than that of its more upscale cousin, the P1850, which we had tested earlier that same day. On target, the Cowboy not only shot to the sights, it shot very well, giving us consistent 2-inch to 2 1/2-inch groups with Black Hills ammo and 2 1/2-inch to 3-inch groups with Winchester Cowboy loads at 7 yards.

Throughout more than 100 rounds of test firing, this Colt Cowboy performed remarkably well for us. We did notice the chambers were not as cleanly reamed as the P1850, having been left with more roughness, as a consequence, the shells did not drop out as easily as we might have liked, almost always requiring a shove from the ejector rod to get them moving. We also noticed that the Cowboy did not park the chambers exactly in the center of the

Colt Cowboy Specifications, as tested	
Model	CB1850
Name	Cowboy
Finish(s)	Blued and color case hardened
Barrel lengths	5 1/2"
Overall lengths	11"
Caliber	.45 Colt
Capacity	6 shots
Action	Single, transfer bar ignition
Front sight	Fixed blade
Rear sight	Fixed notch
Grips	Black checkered
Chamber mouth	.456" (actual)
Barrel groove	.451" (actual)

loading port opening in the frame when the hammer was placed in the loading position. This minor glitch made loading and unloading even slower than usual, and necessitated the shooter having to manually nudge the cylinder around to remove or insert cartridges. It is a complaint I hear frequently from owners of newer third-generation Colt Single Actions. However, the only real complaint about the Cowboy from both shooters was the poor fit of the grips to the grip frame at the back side. There were sharp plastic edges sticking out to the rear that dug into and cut the hands of the shooters. Because of this the author resorted to a shooting glove after the first few shots. To make it into a competition shooter's gun our Cowboy would have needed only minor help from a gunsmith. That might have involved getting the cylinder to index at the loading position, which would make loading and unloading much faster, maybe some careful internal polishing to clean up the roughness in those chambers which would allow the shells to fall out more readily and a good-fitting pair of grips. During the course of the shooting, we experimented with a slightly lighter mainspring but, probably due to the transfer bar ignition, we quickly found that anything less than factory mainspring tension left us with a misfiring revolver. All in all, we liked the Colt Cowboy and we thought it had real potential for a gun in this price range. Perhaps if enough shooters will say something positive about the Cowboy to the Colt factory, they will change their minds someday and bring it back?

Footnotes

[1] Source: Colt's Manufacturing Company, LLC

Cimarron Firearms Bisley Model

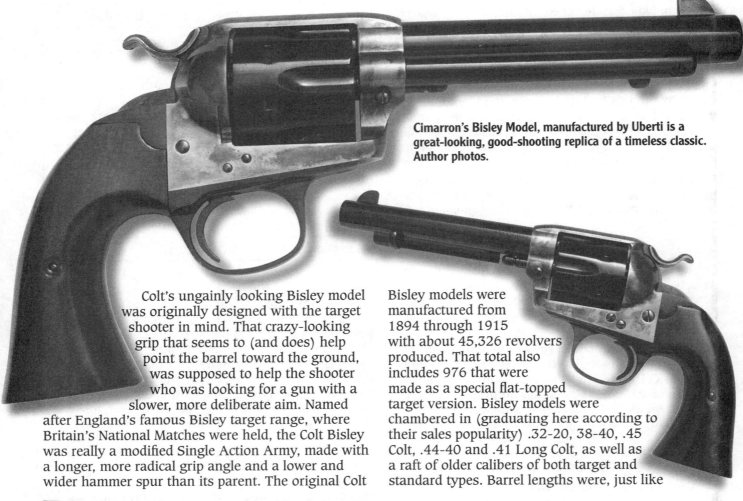

Cimarron's Bisley Model, manufactured by Uberti is a great-looking, good-shooting replica of a timeless classic. Author photos.

Colt's ungainly looking Bisley model was originally designed with the target shooter in mind. That crazy-looking grip that seems to (and does) help point the barrel toward the ground, was supposed to help the shooter who was looking for a gun with a slower, more deliberate aim. Named after England's famous Bisley target range, where Britain's National Matches were held, the Colt Bisley was really a modified Single Action Army, made with a longer, more radical grip angle and a lower and wider hammer spur than its parent. The original Colt

Bisley models were manufactured from 1894 through 1915 with about 45,326 revolvers produced. That total also includes 976 that were made as a special flat-topped target version. Bisley models were chambered in (graduating here according to their sales popularity) .32-20, 38-40, .45 Colt, .44-40 and .41 Long Colt, as well as a raft of older calibers of both target and standard types. Barrel lengths were, just like

This close-in view gives you a good look at the frame and barrel caliber markings, notice how nicely the screws are fitted. Look closely, and you can see some gaps between the walnut grips and the grip straps. Author photo.

the regular Colt Single Action Army, offered in 4 3/4-, 5 1/2- and 7 1/2-inch versions, in addition to the much rarer 3-, 3 1/2- and 4-inch lengths, that were made without ejector systems. Despite its unusual look and for many, its uncomfortable grip shape and angle, the Bisley, has right up to this day, always attracted a strong following among certain shooters who seem to prefer the odd grip.

Cimarron Fireram's modern-made Bisley model revolver is manufactured in Italy by the Aldo Uberti company. Our test gun is chambered in .45 Colt caliber with a 5 1/2-inch barrel. The new Bisley has, like many of the modern replica single-actions, a double-notched base pin/safety device. In these, the base pin acts like a normal cylinder axis pin until the hammer is placed at half-cock, from there the shooter can depress the base pin latch screw and then push the base pin farther into the frame, until it locks into its rear notch. Once the base pin has been locked into its rear-most position, the back end of it protrudes slightly into the hammer opening of the

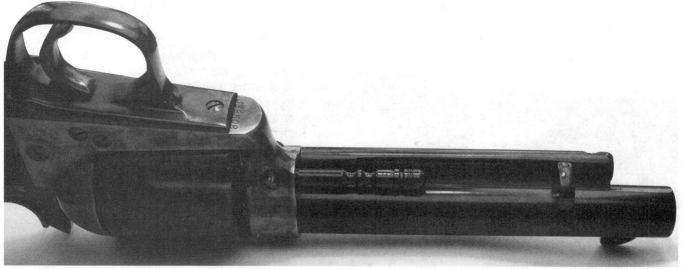

Here, the base pin has been withdrawn slightly to give you a look at the two notches, the forward notch being the "safe" notch. Author photo.

In this shot you can get a good look at the Bisley bottom side, note the base pin sticking farther out than you may be used to seeing, that's the "fire" position for this two-notch base pin/safety. Author photo.

The only real glitch we found was that the cylinder chambers were not parked in the middle of the loading port at half-cock. This slowed down unloading. Author photo.

frame and prevents the hammer from falling all the way forward. In addition, we noticed this Bisley still has the familiar Uberti hammer-block safety, thereby having the unusual combination of two additional hammer-block safety devises the original revolvers did not have. Nevertheless, the only way the Bisley, like all old-style single-actions, can be considered safe to carry when loaded is to load only five of the chambers and then carefully rest the hammer down on the empty chamber.

Our Bisley Model came furnished in blue and case color finishes. The case colors on the frame and hammer were pleasing to look at although they did seem unusually subdued, mainly very subtle shades of gray mixed with smaller splotches of light blue

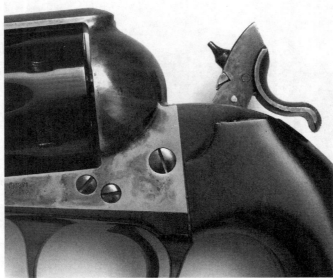

This Bisley has the unusual feature of having two safety devices. It retains the Uberti hammer block safety along with the two-notch base pin/safety. Author photo.

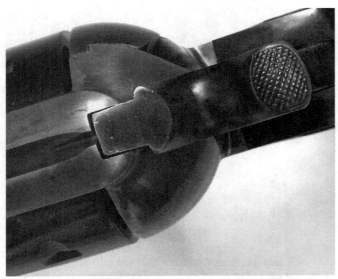

Very well executed checkering, similar to the originals, decorates the top of this functional hammer spur. Author photo.

and darker grays. They were not the dramatic older colors we are used to seeing on 19th century Colts. The barrel, cylinder and grip straps were very well finished in modern blue and nicely polished. Metal-to-metal fit was excellent all over and the overall presentation is that of an excellently finished weapon. The hammer's spur has checkering that is very much like the original Bisley. It is sharp and well defined with a neat border. Stocks were two-piece and made from smooth, finely finished walnut. The wood-to-metal fit was not quite as good as we have seen on most of the current Uberti-made revolvers, but it was still much better than the new Colts we tested, and there were no sharp edges sticking out to cut the shooter's hand.

Action operation on this out-of-the-box revolver was good. When the hammer was pulled to the rear, the cylinder was revolved into position smartly and it locked tightly in place at exactly the moment the hammer reached full cock. Cylinder lock-up on this Bisley was very tight and positive and the gap between the barrel and cylinder was measured at .005 inches with automotive feeler gauges, that is right within proper specs, in fact, .005 inches is considered to be just about the ideal gap. The cylinder on this revolver was incredibly well fitted, with no perceptible end-shake or radial play. We did notice that when the hammer was placed at half-

Here is the base pin/safety in the "on" position, notice how the base pin is sticking back into the hammer opening just slightly. This is enough to prevent the hammer from falling forward all the way, keeping the firing pin away from the primer. Author photo.

cock, the cylinder's chambers were not perfectly centered with the loading gate opening in the frame, this slowed down the loading and unloading process for both shooters and is an indication that the top of the hand was made too short by the factory. The Bisley's trigger pull was not heavy, however it was definitely on the "mushy" side, and only after a considerable amount of trigger movement (creep) did the hammer at last fall at about 3 1/2 pounds.

We test fired the Cimarron Bisley Model with .45 Colt Winchester Cowboy and Black Hills Cowboy ammunition. Although the Bisley did not deliver the desirable small groups of the Model P, it nevertheless

printed about 20 very consistent five-shot groups that afternoon. We found the gun capable of shooting 3-inch groups with Winchester Cowboy ammunition and somewhat smaller 2 1/2-inch groups with the Black Hills Cowboy ammo at the 7-yard range. All the groups fired were right on for windage but uniformly printed about 1 to 2 inches below the point of aim. The sight picture, for replica sights, was not bad. The maker left enough of a rear notch so we had plenty of daylight around the front sight, enabling a better-defined sight picture than some we have tested. We both noticed the Bisley's front sight was leaning off to the left

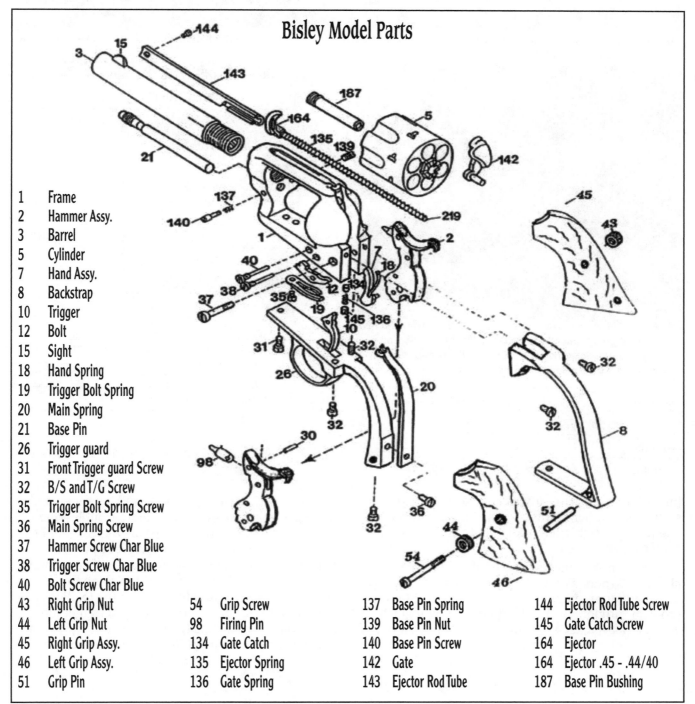

Bisley Model Parts

1	Frame
2	Hammer Assy.
3	Barrel
5	Cylinder
7	Hand Assy.
8	Backstrap
10	Trigger
12	Bolt
15	Sight
18	Hand Spring
19	Trigger Bolt Spring
20	Main Spring
21	Base Pin
26	Trigger guard
31	Front Trigger guard Screw
32	B/S and T/G Screw
35	Trigger Bolt Spring Screw
36	Main Spring Screw
37	Hammer Screw Char Blue
38	Trigger Screw Char Blue
40	Bolt Screw Char Blue

43	Right Grip Nut	54	Grip Screw	137	Base Pin Spring	144	Ejector Rod Tube Screw
44	Left Grip Nut	98	Firing Pin	139	Base Pin Nut	145	Gate Catch Screw
45	Right Grip Assy.	134	Gate Catch	140	Base Pin Screw	164	Ejector
46	Left Grip Assy.	135	Ejector Spring	142	Gate	164	Ejector .45 - .44/40
51	Grip Pin	136	Gate Spring	143	Ejector Rod Tube	187	Base Pin Bushing

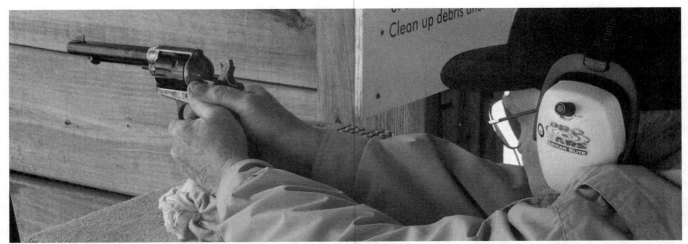

Our old friend Ed Wade didn't like the Bisley grip shape at all, nevertheless he suffered through the test firing and delivered some great shooting. Author photo.

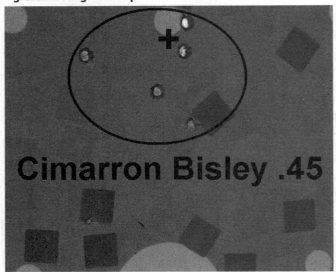

A five-shot group that was fired using Winchester .45 Colt Cowboy ammo, this group was typical of the results we obtained and measures about 3 inches. Author photo.

Caliber:	.357, .45LC, .44SPL, and .44WCF
Barrel Length:	4 3/4", 5 1/2" & 7 12"
Stocks:	1-piece walnut
Finish:	Standard Blue

Bisley Model Specifications, as tested	
Model	Cimarron CA613
Name	Bisley
Finish(s)	Blue and color case hardened
Barrel length	5 1/2"
Overall length	10 1/2"
Caliber	.45 Colt
Capacity	6 shots
Action	Single
Front sight	Fixed blade
Rear sight	Fixed notch
Grips	2-pc walnut, smooth
Chamber mouth	.454" (actual)
Barrel groove	.4505" (actual)
Retail as tested	$525
Available from	Cimarron Firearms, P.O. Box 906, Fredericksburg, TX 78624-0906 (830) 997-9090

just a bit, in this case it was easy to see that the sight was not bent, however the barrel had been slightly over tightened, probably to correct an off-center bullet impact.

At the end of the day, we fired the Bisley with about 150 rounds of both Black Hills and Winchester brand ammunition and the gun operated without a problem throughout the shooting. The only glitch we experienced, as we pointed out earlier was the fact that the cylinder chambers were not lining up

very well with the loading port, making the reloading process somewhat slower and more troublesome. All in all, this Cimarron Bisley was a great-looking, good-shooting, off-the-shelf revolver that gave us very good, but not great performance. If some minor gunsmithing work were invested to bring those cylinder chambers up into line with the loading port at half-cock, and perhaps a good trigger job, this revolver would easily make a fine competition shooter for those who prefer this classic design.

Cimarron Firearms Lightning Single Action

Cimarron's Lightning model is a great-looking little revolver. This one is in 32-20 with a spare cylinder chambered in .32 H&R Magnum. Author photo.

This photo of the Lightning's right side shows the flush ejector rod on the 3 1/2-inch barrel. The rod is so short that to get the base pin out the ejector head has to be pivoted down so the base pin can pass over it. Author photo.

Mike "Texas Jack" Harvey, the president and founder of Cimarron Firearms originally came up with the idea for the .38 Special caliber Cimarron Lightning Single Action in order to offer a revolver with a smaller grip frame and milder recoil for shooters with smaller hands. The Cimarron Lightning is a medium-sized revolver that is very close in size to the 1877 Colt double-action. The grip shape and size are nearly a perfect copy of that 19th century double-action Colt. The actual frame size of the Cimarron Lightning is very much like the older Colt Scout series of .22 single-action revolvers or the Ruger Single Six.

The Aldo Uberti Company manufactures the Lightning in Italy and it is based on their Stallion revolver series. The factory modified both the angle of the grip and the hammer slightly from the 1877 double-action in order to offer better handling qualities and, in our opinion, they have succeeded. For the shooter with medium to small hands, the Lightning is just about perfect. This six-shot revolver is now S. A. S. S.-approved and is chambered in the popular .38 S&W Special caliber. It will, of course, also safely fire .38 Colt cartridges. The other caliber offering is our old favorite .32-20 Winchester chambering that can be purchased with an interchangeable .32 H&R Magnum cylinder that will also accept .32 S&W or .32 S&W Long cartridges.

One modern, practical feature of the Lightning is that it makes use of a spring-loaded, frame-mounted, floating firing pin that has been thoughtfully designed so it can be easily replaced. Unlike many modern replica revolvers, a hammer-block safety is not used in this design. Instead a double-notched

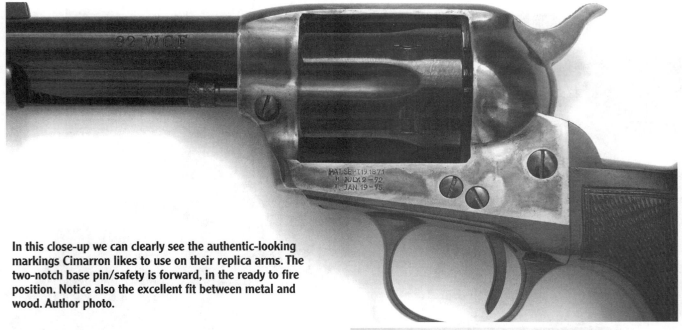

In this close-up we can clearly see the authentic-looking markings Cimarron likes to use on their replica arms. The two-notch base pin/safety is forward, in the ready to fire position. Notice also the excellent fit between metal and wood. Author photo.

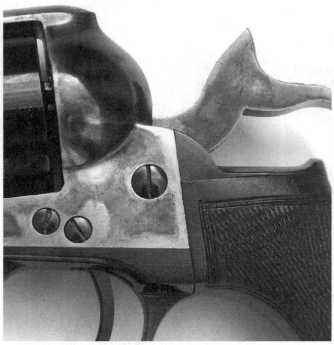

Here the hammer is shown at full cock. As you can see it has no firing pin mounted on its face like most single-actions. The firing pin is frame mounted on the Lightning and Model P Jr. Author photo.

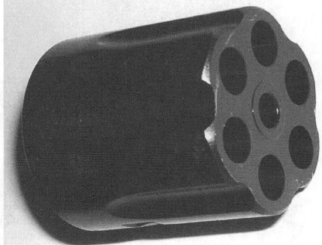

Look at the front of the Lightning cylinder and you will discover it does not have a removable base pin bushing like its full-size cousins. The author feels it should be equipped with a bushing. Author photo.

base pin safety device is offered. In order to operate the safety, the hammer is placed at half-cock and the base pin catch is depressed, then the base pin is pushed into the frame farther than normal and when the base pin catch is released, it engages the front notch on the base pin. All this causes the base pin to protrude back into the hammer opening in the frame so it will prevent the hammer from moving all the way forward. Internally, the Cimarron Lightning is essentially a scaled-down version of the Colt Single Action Army revolver with only a very few noted alterations made to the original Colt design.

Cimarron's Lightning is offered with barrels in 3 1/2-inch, 4 3/4-inch and 5 1/2-inch lengths and like its larger brothers, it is available in full nickel plate or blue and case colored finishes. One-piece walnut grips are supplied either smooth, or handsomely checkered. For those with smaller hands who prefer a more traditional Single Action grip shape, Cimarron Firearms also offers this same model with the same options, but with a standard SAA style grip shape, this model is called the Model P Jr. Just like the original 1877 Colt and the Colt Scout models, the cylinders in the Lightning and Model P Jr. do not use

There isn't much room between that sight and the frame for markings on top of the barrel but Cimarron has placed them in two lines, reminiscent of the early Colts. Author photo.

Uberti has done a remarkably nice job on these checkered grips. They fit well and are shaped perfectly. The checkering pattern is very much like an 1877-1878 Colt. Author photo.

removable base pin bushings. That is an omission the author would like to encourage the factory to seriously reconsider. The addition of a removable, replaceable cylinder or base pin bushing to these revolvers would allow a gunsmith to refit the cylinder when too much end shake occurs, as it surely will after considerable shooting. In fact, the .32-20 cylinder supplied with our nearly new Lightning was already displaying too much cylinder end shake.

With this short barrel, the ejector rod head will prevent the base pin from being removed in the usual fashion, so we have to get creative here. In order to remove the base pin, the revolver is placed at half-cock and as always, the chambers are carefully checked to be sure the gun is empty. After that, the ejector rod is first pushed back just far enough to cause the head to

rotate down, in this position there is enough clearance for the base pin to be removed completely. Now the base pin latch screw is depressed and the base pin is withdrawn all the way out of the frame, passing under the ejector rod head, at which point the ejector rod head can be released and the cylinder may be removed in the conventional way.

For our tests we selected a Cimarron Lightning model with the 3 1/2-inch barrel in .32-20 caliber, this revolver was also fitted with an interchangeable cylinder in .32 H&R Magnum. Because of its reduced size, this seemingly short barrel length is very well balanced on this gun. Proportionately it has the approximate look of a full sized, 4 3/4-inch barreled single-action. Our Lightning was the blue and case colored version and the fit and finish overall were excellent. Uberti's case colors were not quite 19th century Colt quality as to their color, nevertheless, they are very good quality. The metal was certainly well-prepared and nice to look at, while the blue on the barrel, cylinder and grip straps was well polished, all in all making a smart-looking combination. The bird's-head shaped, one-piece grips were of nicely finished walnut, with neatly bordered checkering in the Colt style, and the grips are impressively well-fitted to the steel grip straps, with no "proud" wood or metal edges sticking up anywhere. As small in size as this grip appears to be most shooters are able to get more of a substantial hold than you might think possible. Both shooters who tested the gun, one with large and one with rather small hands, found the grip size and shape comfortable, although recovery was a bit slower than with the conventional single-action grip shape.

The revolver's maker, A. Uberti Company of Italy, is obviously paying careful attention to the internal mechanical details these days. This fact was in evidence from the moment we took the gun out of its box. As the hammer was being operated

Ed Wade is about to touch off the Lightning to see how well it will group. This gun averaged 2-inch, five-shot groups at 7 yards and one excellent 10-shot volley went into a group just a tad over 2 inches in diameter. Both shooters found firing the Lightning Model fun. The gun performed well, was easy to control and it proved to be quite accurate for its size and barrel length. Author photo.

Cimarron Lightning and Model P jr. Parts

1	Frame
2	Hammer Assembly
3	Barrel
5	Cylinder
7	Hand Assembly
8	Backstrap
10	Trigger
11	Grips
12	Bolt
15	Front Sight
18	Hand Spring
19	Trigger Blot Spring
20	Main Spring
21	Base Pin
25	Hammer Roll
26	Trigger guard
30	Hammer Pin
31	Trigger guard Screw
32	Trigger guard and Backstrap Screw
35	Bolt Spring Screw
36	Main Spring screw
37	Hammer Screw
38	Trigger Screw
40	Bolt Screw
95	Firing Pin Spring
98	Firing Pin
129	Firing Pin Bearing
134	Gate Catch
135	Ejector Spring
136	Gate Spring
139	Base Pin Nut
140	Base Pin Screw
142	Gate
143	Ejector Rod Tube
143	Ejector Rod Tube
144	Ejector Rod Tube Screw
145	Gate Catch Screw
164	Ejector Rod Assembly

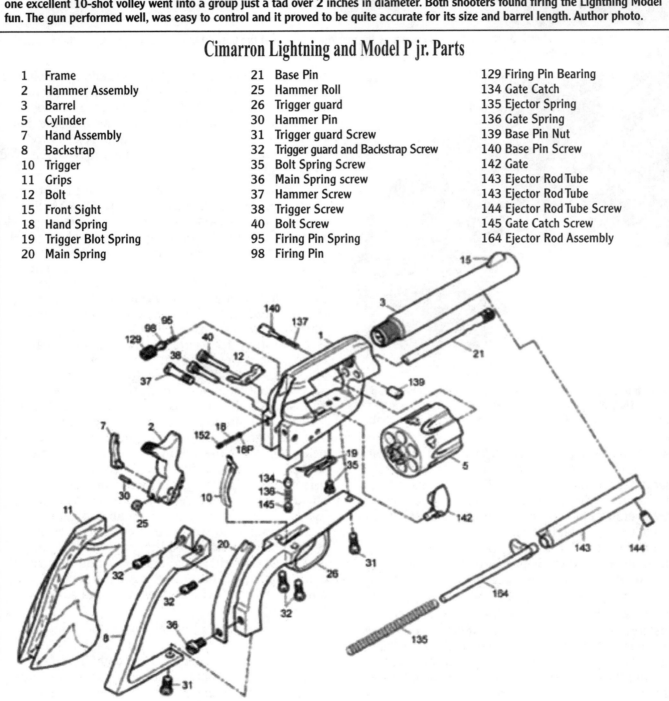

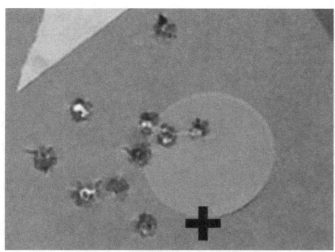

One 10-shot group went into just over 2 inches at 7 yards. Not bad for a pocket-sized pistol! Author photo.

Cimarron Lightning .32 caliber Dual Cylinder specifications and available options	
Calibers:	32-20 and 32 H&R
Barrel Lengths:	3 1/2", 4 3/4", 5 1/2"
Frames:	Color Case Hardened Steel
Stocks:	Smooth Walnut or Checkered Walnut
Finish:	Standard blue

Cimarron Lightning .38 caliber specifications and available options	
Calibers:	38 Colt and .38 Special
Barrel Lengths:	3 1/2", 4 3/4", 5 1/2"
Frames:	Color Case Hardened Steel
Stocks:	Smooth Walnut or Checkered Walnut
Finish:	Standard blue

Cimarron Lightning Specifications, as tested	
Model	Cimarron CA3000
Name	Lightning SA
Finish	Blue & color case hardened
Barrel length	3 1/2"
Overall length	8 1/2"
Calibers	.32-20 & .32 H&R (2 cyls)
Capacity	6 shots
Action	Single
Front sight	Fixed blade
Rear sight	Fixed notch
Grips	1-piece walnut, checkered
Chamber mouth	.315" (actual)
Barrel groove	.311" (actual)
Retail as tested	$604
Available from	Cimarron Firearms, P.O. Box 906, Fredericksburg, TX 78624-0906 (830) 997-9090

we noticed that when it was placed at the half-cock (loading) position the cylinder chambers were centered nicely in the frame's loading port, as they should be. Continuing along with the hammer cycle, the cylinder came into index and the bolt fell into place locking the cylinder at exactly the moment the hammer reached full cock; this is perfect timing, seldom seen any more on out-of-the-box revolvers. On squeezing the trigger, there was some noticeable trigger creep but we honestly were not prepared when the diminutive revolver's hammer fell off at a surprisingly clean 2.75 pounds.

On the outdoor target range the cute little Lightning revolver really raised some eyebrows not only because it's such a handsome little gun, although shooters always seem to remark on how attractive it is. That day the Lightning delivered a solid, on-target performance. Lacking .32-20 ammunition on the day we test fired the gun, we decided to fire it with .32 H&R Magnum and some Remington .32 S&W Long ammunition. The first five shots from the .32 S&W grouped just under 1 1/2 inches. The second five shots, combined in the same group open it to just under 2 inches for 10 shots. Not bad for a little runt! Because of the much lower velocity, the .32 S&W Long ammunition printed about 5 inches lower than the point of aim at 7 yards. The overall average group size for both calibers fired was about 2 inches and the .32 H&R Magnum printed about 1 inch low and slightly to the left at 7 yards. Cimarron's Lightning revolver performed perfectly throughout all aspects of the test firing for both shooters. This revolver's mild recoil, good accuracy and excellent handling qualities quickly made it a favorite of everyone present.

Cimarron Firearms Model "P" Single Action

The new Cimarron Model P in .45 Colt is remarkably close to an original first-generation Colt in almost all the important details. Notice the "bull's-eye" ejector rod head. This one shoots real well too! Author photo.

Cimarron's new Model P single-action is, with very few exceptions, a very accurate replica of the original, first-generation Colt Single Action Army revolver. As Cimarron says in their own advertising: *The Cimarron new Model 'P' is the ultimate Single Action Army revolver. There are none other that have the authentic features of the Model 'P'. Our new Model 'P' is not a copy of a 3rd or 4th generation but an exact copy of early 1st generation SAAs. As with most of our line of firearms we have purchased tooling, or paid extra, to make the Cimarron the most authentic and highest quality SAA on the market. . .The Cimarron Model 'P' features an early Colt style hammer with early heavy knurling for a better thumb grip, no safety is visible in the hammer, grip frame is sized to fit actual Colt hard rubber replacement grips. Features include early 2-line patent dates on frame. Serial number placement as on early Colts, parts interchange with the originals, barrel markings are sized to look like Colt, and more. No others go to the trouble to bring you this degree of detailed authenticity. Internal parts in the Cimarron Model 'P' are properly hardened and hand fit by gunmakers that have worked on guns all their lives. Actions are tuned to 3lb trigger pull; internal working surfaces of parts are polished."*

Getting in a bit closer, you can clearly see the knurled thumb screw used to hold the base pin and the two-line frame patent marks. Author photo.

From the right side we can see how well the 4 3/4-inch barrel mates with the ejector tube length. Note the close metal-to-metal fit at the grip straps and frame and how nicely the grips fit to the metal. Author photo.

Look closely and you can see that the base pin seems to protrude more than a Colt, this is a two-notch pin for the safety system and it is in the "off" position. Pushing the pin all the way in would put the safety "on." The base pin thumb screw should also be slotted for a screwdriver. Author photo.

Those statements from Cimarron are included here because, for the most part, what they are saying above is actually true. The fact is, we decided on using several Uberti-made Cimarron revolvers to evaluate for this book in lieu of Uberti replicas that are marketed by other makers because of Cimarron's reputation for paying attention to details, and Mike Harvey's (the owner) reputation for standing behind what he sells.

The revolver selected for this test series was a standard blue and case colored version of the 4 3/4-inch barreled Model P, with the Old-Model frame in .45 Colt caliber. This gun has the two-notch base pin safety, where the base pin may be pushed in to the rear and while in that position it bars the hammer from falling all the way forward. It was also equipped with the old-style screw type retainer for the base pin. This new version is furnished with a nicely knurled thumb-operated base pin retaining screw. The knurled screw makes setting the safety or removing the base pin an easy job that requires no tools, however, because it is only finger-tightened, the screw does have a tendency to back out during firing. During the second round of shooting tests, I replaced the screw with a standard slotted screw that could be adequately tightened. My suggestion to the factory is that they might consider adding a screw slot to this thumb screw, that would help avoid embarrassing costly base pin jump-outs during a match. This new Model P has no hammer-block safety at all but instead of seeing the old large, fixed

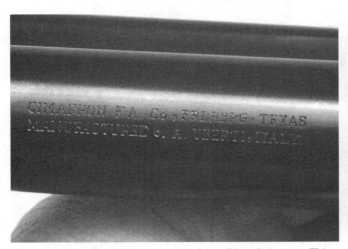

Cimarron has always done a neat job marking their guns. This is what importer's and manufacturer's marks look like on the barrel top. Author photo.

This new model uses a firing pin that is reminiscent of the second- and third-generation Colts. It is slightly smaller in diameter than a first-generation firing pin and it floats in the hammer. Author photo.

firing pin, the hammer is equipped with a smaller, semi-floating pin, much like the ones used in second- and third-generation Colts. Like the first-generation Colt, the hammer is equipped with excellent and sharp knurling with a nice early-type border on its spur, but its top does not quite protrude up above the top edge of the frame. The ejector is also equipped with the large round "bull's-eye," or first type SAA ejector rod head.

Fit and finish are very good, with wood-to-metal fits nearly perfect and metal-to-metal seams tight and well matched. The large blued parts (barrel, cylinder and grip straps) have been professionally polished and blued with modern caustic blueing methods while the smaller parts and screws are nicely nitre blued. Case colors on the frame and hammer are good-looking. They exhibit mostly light tans with brown splotches and small patches of blue. These are different from 19th century, or even more

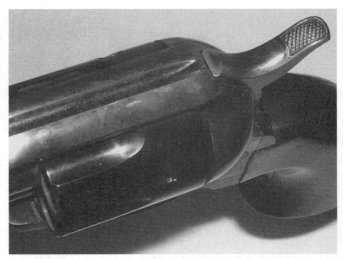

The hammer spur is nicely knurled with an authentic-looking first-generation type border. This knurling is deeper than it looks, providing an excellent purchase for the thumb. Author photo.

We did all the accuracy testing for this book from a sand bag rest. Here, Ed Wade is test firing the Cimarron Model P with the Black Hills .45 Colt Cowboy ammunition, the revolver is at the height of recoil. Author photo.

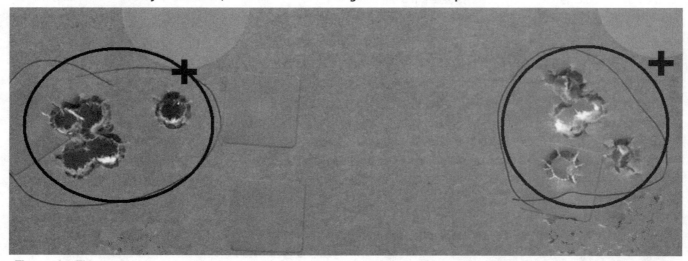

The results: This revolver was a terrific shooter with both Winchester and Black Hills ammunition and these two groups are typical of our test results on paper. Notice the left group. Except for that flyer caused by the shooter it would have been one ragged hole. The smallest five-shot group fired was actually just a bit under 3/4 of an inch using Black Hills ammo with Ed Wade on the trigger. Author photo.

modern guns with case colors achieved using the old bone and charcoal process but, in all honesty, they are quite attractive for a modern gun in this price range. Standard grips are one-piece walnut, finished in a pleasing dark red-brown color. These grips are perfectly shaped and closely match the early, Colt SAA shape and style, that is, slim and minimalistic. Our overall impressions of this revolver are that it is handsomely finished and marked to very closely match a period 1870s piece. It was nicely fitted and, all in all, makes a very smart-looking revolver that I would be proud to own.

Cimarron Model "P" Parts

1	Frame	19	Sear & Bolt Spring	135	Ejector Spring
2	Hammer Assy.	20	Main Spring - Cimarron	136	Gate Spring
3	Barrel 3	21	Base Pin	137	P/W Base Pin Spring
5	Cylinder	25	Hammer Roll	139	P/W Base Pin Nut
7	Hand Old Style W/Spring	26	Trigger guard (steel)	140	P/W Base Pin Screw
7C	Hand for Coil Spring	30	Hammer Pin	142	Gate
8	Backstrap (Steel)	31	Trigger guard Screw	143	Ejector Rod Tube
10	Trigger	32	Trigger guard and Backstrap	144	Ejector Rod Tube Screw
11	Grips SAA Smooth	32H	Hollow Backstrap Screw	145	Gate Catch Screw
12	Bolt	35	Bolt Spring Screw	152	Coil Hand Spring Set Screw
15	Front Sight	36	Main Spring screw	164	Ejector
18	Hand Spring	37	Hammer Screw Char. Blue	187	Base Pin Bushing
18C	Coil Hand Spring	38	Trigger Screw Char. Blue	354	Base Pin Screw
18P	Coil Handspring Plunger	40	Bolt Screw Char. Blue	354	Base Pin Screw Old Style
18PR	Coil Handspring Plunger Rod	98	Firing Pin	354	Base Pin Screw Knurled
	Type - Old Style	134	Gate Catch		

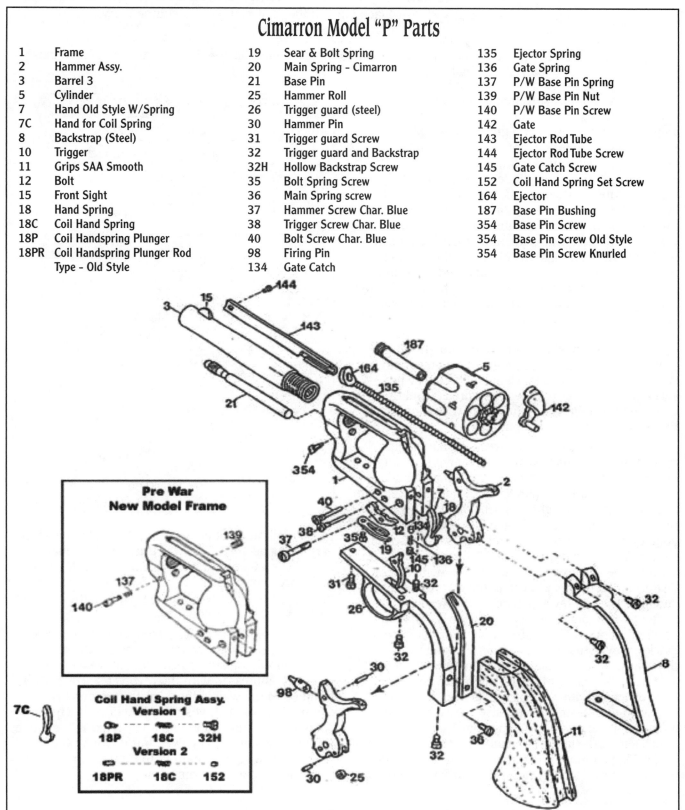

Pre War New Model Frame

Coil Hand Spring Assy.
Version 1
18P   18C   32H
Version 2
18PR   18C   152

Cimarron Model P specifications and available options	
Calibers:	45 Colt, 45 ACP, 45 Schofield, 44 WCF, 44 Spec.,357 Magnum, 38 WCF, 32 WCF
Barrel Lengths:	Sheriffs, 3 1/2", 4 3/4", 5 1/2", 7 1/2"
Frames:	Forged Steel, Pre war and Old Model Color Case Hardened
Stocks:	1-piece walnut (standard), Black hard rubber, Izit real Ivory, Genuine Ivory, Mother of Pearl
Finish:	Old Style Charcoal Blue, High Polish Modern Blue, Custom Nickel, Custom USA finish, Cimarron Original finish

But. . .the proof is in the puddin', as they say. No matter how pretty a gun is, if it doesn't perform well, it's just not much of a gun. Our test Model P had a good, smooth action operation with very positive and well-timed cylinder lock-up. By that I mean to say that the cylinder was mechanically turned to the point where the bolt dropped into the cylinder bolt notch, locking the cylinder at exactly the same point when the hammer reached the full-cock position; that's about as perfect as it can be. When the hammer was placed in the loading position and the gate opened, we noted the cylinder chamber was parked just a bit shy of being perfectly centered in the loading port. This small flaw was not enough to cause any inconvenience during loading and unloading and is the result of a hand whose top is just slightly short. Out-of-the-box trigger pull and let-off was surprisingly short and crisp. Remembering the seller's claims of a factory pre-set 3-pound trigger pull, we measured it and the actual pull weight was right in line with that boast, breaking at around 3 1/2 pounds.

The gap we measured between the barrel and cylinder was .006 inches and the cylinder itself had very little noticeable end-shake. My shooting buddy, the notorious Ed Wade (AKA, Jake Slade), noticed right away that the front sight was bent slightly over to the right, an obvious attempt by the factory to move the point of impact. Even though the sights on these guns were made to duplicate the early Colt tapered blade and V notch, the apparent sight picture was nonetheless distinct and easy to see, even in the glare of bright sunlight. The real revelation about this revolver was on the target. It shot so well that when we saw that first group we thought it must be a fluke. Further shooting quickly proved that nothing about this gun was a fluke; as it gave us group after group ranging from 1- to 1 1/2-inches with Black Hills and Winchester Cowboy loads, with one Black Hills five-shot group measuring just a smidgeon under three quarters of an inch. All the groups printed about 1 inch low and 1 inch left on the target at 7 yards. After firing, the shells dropped from the chambers about 95 percent of the time with absolutely no assistance from the ejector

Cimarron Model P, as tested	
Model	Cimarron MP512
Name	Model P, old model
Finish(s)	Blue & color case hardened
Barrel lengths	4 3/4"
Overall lengths	10 3/4"
Calibers	.45 Colt
Capacity	6 shots
Action	Single
Front sight	Fixed blade
Rear sight	Fixed notch
Grips	1-piece walnut, smooth
Chamber mouth	.454" (actual)
Barrel groove	.451" (actual)
Retail as tested	$499
Available from	Cimarron Firearms, P.O. Box 906, Fredericksburg, TX 78624-0906 (830) 997-9090

rod, an indication of perfectly sized chambers that are very well machined. This was true with both makes of ammunition we tested. In all, we fired over 250 rounds of factory ammunition. For all of that there was not one misfire nor a failure to rotate the cylinder, the revolver's performance was without flaw.

All in all, both shooters enjoyed the chance to look over and shoot the new Cimarron Model P. It's a good-looking pistol to be sure, but we were both uniquely impressed with the revolver's action, the timing and the way it shot. For the serious CAS competition shooter, yes, the Model P will require some fine tuning and gunsmith "tweaking" to make it into a competitive revolver, but it won't take much. From what we saw, we think that right out of the box this is a lot of gun for the money.

Cimarron Firearms Model "P" Stainless Single Action

The new Stainless Steel Model P from Cimarron firearms was a lot of fun to shoot and man this gun performs! Author photo.

We had the opportunity to examine and test the new Cimarron Firearms Model P Stainless revolver in April of 2004. Since we had plenty of time, we fired the revolver on three separate occasions, first at the outdoor range at Charlotte Rifle and Pistol Club, later that week we shot it again on the indoor range at the local Shooter's Express. Then a few weeks later, at another outdoor range. Outwardly, the new revolver is, in most respects, a stainless steel version of the Cimarron Model P or Uberti Cattleman, but there are some subtle differences, notably the sights, which are very good, certainly an improvement over most fixed-sights on replica guns. The gun's barrel markings are authentic-looking, as you would expect from Cimarron, presented in a Victorian style with the frame carrying the familiar two-line patent marking. Like the new Cimarron Model P, which is also made by Uberti, the Model P-SS uses a semi-floating firing

This view of Cimarron's Stainless Model P reveals the nice details they have put into little things like markings and screw heads. Author photo.

pin mounted in the hammer. It is similar to later generations of Colt's Single Action Army revolvers. Cimarron's Model P Stainless also uses the cross-bolt type of base pin release like the 20th century, or so-called smokeless version of the Colt SAA, to retain the modern two-notch base pin that also serves as a safety device. Ejection is accomplished by means of the later type, crescent-shaped ejector rod head and operation was flawless with the rod head returning smartly back up to fit tightly against the barrel side when it was released.

We noticed right away that the factory fitting work on our test revolver was really quite excellent, showing nearly perfect metal-to-metal joint work and very tight wood-to-metal seams. The screw heads are nicely domed, and they have narrow slots

Here's what the markings look like on top of the barrel, even though Cimarron is a modern-day company, the lettering is very authentic-looking. Author photo.

We were happy to find that the Cimarron SS Model P came with very nice sights. They were easy to get and to keep a sight picture with. The gun shot about an inch and a half high, but dead on the money at 7 yards. Author photo.

like the originals. The screw heads are set into the frame just a bit deeper than we would have liked, going below the edge of the frame sides. Our Model P stainless was finished in low to medium luster polish with all the edges kept perfectly square and sharp, as it should be. The factory polish work was of such good quality, we could see right away that it probably would not have taken much to bring the gun into a beautiful, high-gloss nickel-like state, if that was what a person wanted. Personally, I enjoyed the fact that the Model P stainless was finished in this not-so-bright luster. At the outdoor range we were shooting on a bright, sunny day and I am sure it helped to keep the glare down.

Sights on the stainless Model P are fixed of course, but the rear is a squared notch in the frame while the front sight is a fairly wide blade with a round side profile like an original Peacemaker. Its edges were thoughtfully left reasonably square so (unlike the original Colt,) the combination gave the shooters a delightfully clear sight picture.

The cylinder timing on the Model P-SS was very good, but it was not perfect, with the trigger dropping into the full cock notch just a smidgeon before the cylinder bolt had locked the cylinder into battery. Pulling the hammer just a tad farther past full cock point did rotate the cylinder until it locked. We suspect the factory may have removed just a bit too much from the lower hand tooth during final fitting.

When the hammer was cocked smartly, just as if you would during a match, the cylinder was pushed into battery every time; the only time it gave us trouble was when the hammer was deliberately cocked slowly. Another small flaw in the timing showed up when the hammer was placed at half-cock. Then the cylinder chambers were not parked at the center of the loading gate opening. Instead the chambers tended to lay over to the left just enough to shade a bit of the chamber. This little flaw slowed the reloading process a bit by forcing the shooter to manually roll the cylinder into a position where the cartridge cases could be removed and inserted. Once again, this is just an annoying little hitch, but it is one that could easily have been corrected if the factory had left just a tad more material on the top leg of the hand.

Looking up from underneath you can see the two-notch base pin/safety, shown here in the forward or "off" position. Author photo.

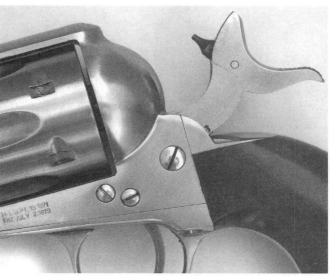

Another close look, this one at the side of the hammer and the second-generation Colt-type firing pin. The hammer spur had excellent knurling very much like the kind used on 1880s Colt hammers. Author photo.

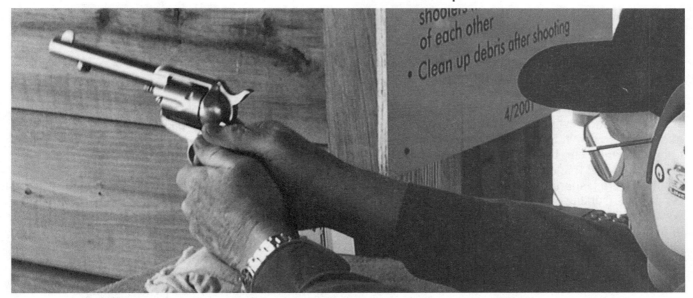

We see here Ed Wade, AKA; Jake Slade, champeen cowboy action shooter and generally an extraordinarily reprehensible character, putting the Model P-SS through its paces. I must confess, we whupped on this gun pretty hard and it came through with its colors flying. Author photo.

We took some measurements, and the barrel-to-cylinder gap was a loose .007 inches; that is a tad on the large side, but in this case it had absolutely no effect on the accuracy of this fine-shooting sixgun. The cylinder had almost no perceptible end shake and rotational play was at a minimum. Firing pin protrusion was a smart .070 inches, so make no mistake, this baby will light the primers every time! Smooth is the word we both used to describe the overall action operation. The hammer was a bit hard on the draw on account of a strong mainspring but it cycled very smoothly. She had a nice trigger, too. It broke at a surprisingly clean 3 1/4 pounds with very little creep. The gun had really good sights and these

proved out for us as soon as we started the shooting. Winchester Cowboy ammo went into consistent 2-inch to 2 1/2-inch, five-shot groups, while with the Black Hills Cowboy ammunition the groups stayed right around 1 1/2 inches. The best group of the day was fired by Jake Slade, he put five shots into about three quarters of an inch with those Black Hills .45 Colt cowboy loads.

Throughout all the testing, which amounted to roughly 350 shots fired, the new stainless Model P operated perfectly. The only troubles any of us experienced with this revolver were a somewhat slow, cumbersome unloading process. This was caused by that timing problem we mentioned above. Yeah, so

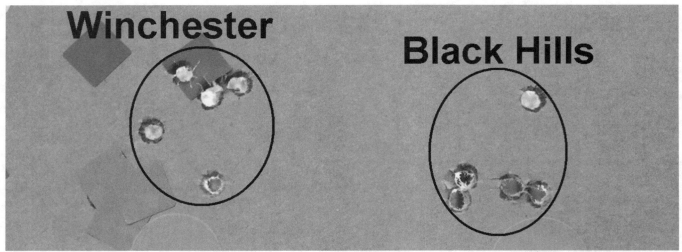

These two groups are nowhere near the best groups we fired all day, but they are quite typical of the average size groups that this gun gave us. Author photo.

Cimarron Model "P" Stainless	
Calibers	45 Colt, .357 Magnum
Barrel Lengths:	4 3/4", 5 1/2", 7 1/2"
Stocks:	1-piece walnut (standard), Black hard rubber, Izit real Ivory, Genuine Ivory, Mother of Pearl
Finish:	Polished Stainless Steel

what's the bottom line. What did we really think? Well, we all think this is a great gun, I mean, it is after all a brand new product (our test gun was serial number 89) so we might expect some teething pains to become apparent, but all-in-all, I thought the new Cimarron Model P Stainless performed very well indeed. Overall, shooting the gun was a very pleasant experience. Outside of a few small timing problems, which can be corrected with a new part and some light gunsmithing work, this revolver impressed all three shooters who test fired it as being accurate, well-made and fitted, well-sighted and well-finished. We all think Cimarron has a winner on its hands.

(Please refer to the Cimarron Model P parts list, the parts are identical, simply add the words Stainless Steel when inquiring about parts for this model)

Cimarron Model P Stainless Single Action, as tested	
Model	Cimarron MP411-SS
Name	Model P Stainless
Finish(s)	Polished stainless steel
Barrel length	5 1/2"
Overall length	11"
Calibers	.45 Colt
Capacity	6 shots
Action	Single
Front sight	Fixed blade
Rear sight	Fixed notch
Grips	1-piece walnut, smooth
Chamber mouth	.452" (actual)
Barrel groove	.450" (actual)
Retail as tested	$599.95
Available from	Cimarron Firearms, P.O. Box 906, Fredericksburg, TX 78624-0906 (830) 997-9090

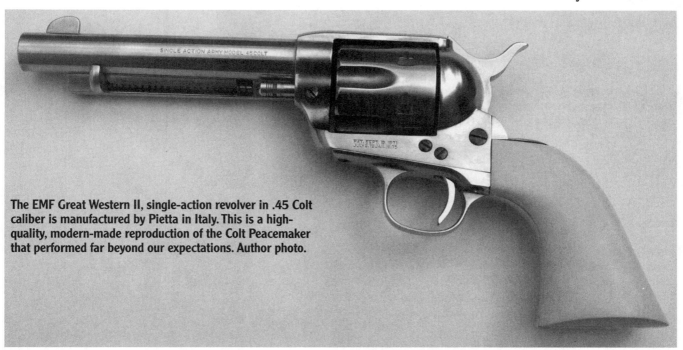

The EMF Great Western II, single-action revolver in .45 Colt caliber is manufactured by Pietta in Italy. This is a high-quality, modern-made reproduction of the Colt Peacemaker that performed far beyond our expectations. Author photo.

E.M.F. Great Western II

An excerpt From the EMF Web site: *In the late 1950s, the Great Western Single Action revolver was manufactured by Great Western Arms Company, a separate company formed by the then principals of E.M.F. Company to buy the assets of the original Great Western Company. At that time, the Great Western was the only production single-action revolver on the market. . . Over 50,000 of these guns were produced by Great Western, and its successor companies. Today, many are still in use at SASS shootouts... E.M.F. Company, Inc. is now proud to announce our latest innovation. The all-new Great Western II has been developed over the past three years in collaboration with F. LLI Pietta of Italy. We have incorporated the knowledge and experience gained in continuously marketing single-action revolvers over the past 45 years. We understand the value and importance of authenticity and attention to details concerning contours, overall cosmetics and interchangeability of parts. E.M.F. Company Inc., based on its close relationship with SASS and Cowboy Action Shooting, has developed this single-action to satisfy the demands of this sport. The Great Western II has been designed to offer authenticity, durability and affordability to satisfy the needs of the most demanding connoisseurs of single-action revolvers. Boyd A. Davis, CEO*

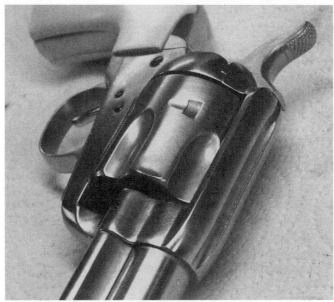

The hammer top is slightly higher than the frame, blocking the view of the sights when the hammer is down; just like a first-generation SAA. Author photo.

This new revolver is a fairly recent entry into the world of SAA look-alikes. F. LLI Pietta in Italy is manufacturing the revolver. Because of that, the author admits to being skeptical of the quality I would find in these new Great Western II single-action revolvers. After all, many of us remember the early Italian replicas, and how long the teething process took before most of the bugs got worked out of the internals. And then there was the hit-and-miss quality of those ASM single-actions that ranged all the way from excellent to truly awful. Nevertheless, from our first examination it became apparent that Pietta was manufacturing a very high-quality

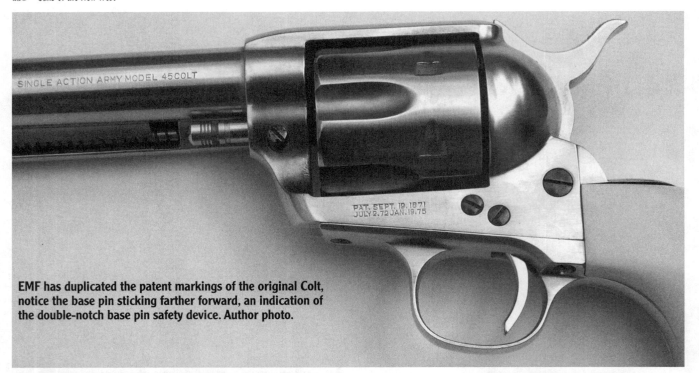

EMF has duplicated the patent markings of the original Colt, notice the base pin sticking farther forward, an indication of the double-notch base pin safety device. Author photo.

In the loading position the Great Western II parked the chambers exactly in the center of the frame's loading port, just exactly like it oughta'. Author photo.

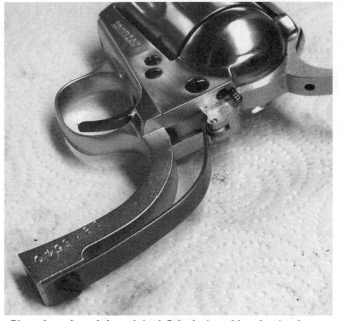

Pietta has altered the original Colt-designed handspring by mounting a small plunger and coil spring in the frame to take the place of the commonly broken leaf spring. This works well and the operation is perfectly smooth. Author photo.

firearm, perhaps, as it would turn out, much higher than anyone expected.

For these tests, we acquired a 5 1/2-inch Great Western II in .45 Colt caliber and finished in satin nickel. This is a handsome finish that has the look and feel of a stainless revolver. For some reason Pietta has nitre blued all the screws, this unusually happy combination leaves a striking contrast and offers a very pleasing look. Externally, the GWII is a very close copy of the Colt first-generation Peacemaker. Even the hammer's top is left slightly higher than the frame so it partially obscures the sights, just like the originals. The hammer is equipped with a loose-fitting firing pin, similar to the second- and third-generation Colts. Our revolver came equipped with one-piece simulated ivory stocks as well as a spare set of one-piece walnuts. The

grips were not fitted perfectly to the grips straps and gaps were apparent in several places. On the plus side, there were no uncomfortable edges sticking out that might cut the shooter's hand; like there were with some other makes of revolvers we tested. We should also note that although the grips were not fitted as closely as they might have been, they were better fitted than the grips on its American-made counterparts. Metal-to-metal fit left nothing to be

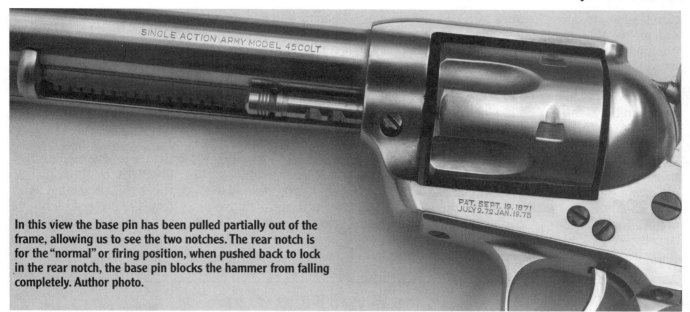

In this view the base pin has been pulled partially out of the frame, allowing us to see the two notches. The rear notch is for the "normal" or firing position, when pushed back to lock in the rear notch, the base pin blocks the hammer from falling completely. Author photo.

desired. Where the grip straps meet the frame and the ejector tube fits on the barrel all the fitting was excellent, at least as good as an American-made single-action.

I have to say that the action in our GWII was one of the most perfect out-of-the-box actions I have ever seen on a modern-made single-action. That statement is made regardless of the country of origin because even the new American SA's are not usually this good. Except for a slight over-timing at full-cock (the result of the lower leg of the hand being left too long), this Pietta single-action was indexed to perfection; parking the chambers at the exact center of the loading port at half-cock and the hammer reaching full cock at just the instant the bolt locks the cylinder in battery. We noticed that the factory even took the time to lightly round off and hand-polish the bolt top to prevent cylinder scratching. All in all, this is one of those rare, excellently fitted actions that has a feel of operation like that of a Swiss bank vault. In spite of full-tensioned factory springs, our revolver's trigger broke at 3 1/2 pounds with only a mild amount of creep. Pietta's internal parts appear to be well hardened and properly heat-treated. The action operation and trigger pull remained consistent throughout the entire test session and for three different shooters. All three of the shooters test firing revolvers that day remarked they were struck by the quality and ease of operation this gun displayed, especially in comparison with the two new Colts that we were firing along with it. When we measured the bore and chambers, we learned the barrel had a good, tight .450-inch groove diameter with .4515-inch chamber mouths, a nice combination to have in anyone's .45 Colt. The gap between the barrel and the cylinder was .006 inches and the cylinder displayed only minimal end shake; these measurements were taken after 300 rounds of shooting.

Because the GWII uses a coil spring and plunger to supply hand tension, the hand is manufactured without the normal machined cut-out for the leaf spring that we are used to seeing. Author photo.

Our next pleasant surprise came during the firing tests. This gun delivered consistent five-shot groups of 1 inch to 1 1/2 inches at 7 yards with Black Hills Cowboy ammunition. Winchester's Cowboy ammunition gave groupings nearly as good, ranging from 1 1/2 to 2 inches. We think the sights bear some notice, although they are at a glance, standard, fixed sights with nothing extraordinary to offer. One pet peeve of mine has been the lack of attention replica arms makers, and in some cases, American arms makers, have given to fixed revolver sights. When was the last time you bought a new replica revolver that shot to the sights or that had sights that gave a clear sight picture? The GWII is the exception to what seems to have become a bad habit. When compared to almost any other factory single-action, the fixed sights on this GWII give the shooter a truly superior sight picture, sharp and well defined, with plenty of room on either side of the blade. Moreover, they were just about right on the money for windage at 21 feet with all the ammo we tested that day, and impacted about an inch high. When the distance was increased to 50 feet, the gun shot exactly to the sights for both windage and elevation. This increased distance opened group sizes only moderately and both brands of factory ammunition and one handload all still printed from 2 inches to just under 3 inches.

To appease some overly cautious North Americans, the new Pietta revolver comes with one of those double-notch base pin safety devices. That is, the base pin acts like a normal axis pin until you place the hammer at half-cock, from that position the shooter may depress the base pin screw and push the base pin farther into the frame until it locks at its rear notch. With the base pin locked in the rear position, its back end protrudes into the hammer opening, preventing the hammer from falling all the way forward. Is this safety effective? In terms of preventing accidental discharge this type of safety is effective. On the practical side, the safety is slow and clumsy to engage and even clumsier to disengage. No matter how you slice it, the action is a copy of the Colt SAA and it really isn't safe to carry with all six chambers loaded; with or without the base-pin safety. We prefer to forego the safety idea altogether and carry the gun with only five rounds loaded and the hammer down on the empty chamber. Now, that is safe.

Great Western II Parts single-action revolver manufactured by Pietta

1. Frame	15. Front sight	29. Hand spring and plunger
2. Base pin	16. Ejector housing	30. Hammer screw
3. Base pin latch screw	17. Ejector housing screw	31. Trigger
4. Base pin latch nut	18. Ejector housing screw bushing	32. Bolt
5. Base pin latch spring	19. Ejector head	33. Trigger and bolt spring
6. Base pin bushing	20. Ejector rod	34. Trigger screw
7. Cylinder	21. Ejector spring	35. Bolt screw
8. Trigger guard	22. Hammer	36. Trigger spring screw
9. Backstrap	23. Firing pin rivet	37. Mainspring
10. Gate	24. Firing pin	38. Mainspring screw
11. Gate catch	25. Hammer roller pin	39. Backstrap rear screw
12. Gate spring	26. Hammer roller	40. Hammer pin
13. Gate catch screw	27. Hand pin	41. Backstrap front screw
14. Barrel	28. Hand	42. Grip

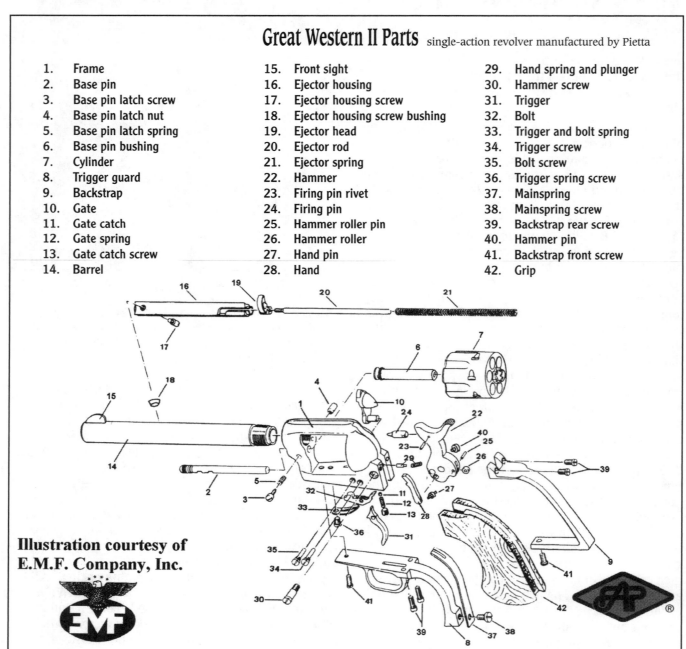

Illustration courtesy of E.M.F. Company, Inc.

This is Ed Wade (Jack Slade) on a cold March morning shooting a tight group with the Great Western II using .45 Colt caliber Black Hills Cowboy ammunition. Ed liked shooting this gun so much that we had trouble getting it back from him at the end of the day! Author photo.

Since this revolver performed so well during our short tests we decided to see how the GWII would perform in a real competition and set out to slick its action up just a bit. Only minimal tuning was done to the GWII. We started by correcting the over-timing problem mentioned earlier, to do that we removed approximately .004 of an inch from the shelf of the lower hand leg. That did the trick, and the action timing was now flawless. Next, the trigger leg of the bolt and sear spring was "tweaked" just a little in order to reduce its tension. Then a mainspring from a Colt Model P that had been previously reduced in width and thickness was installed. We did no trigger and sear work at all. However as a result of repairing the over-time problem and then reducing the spring tension on those two springs, we found the revolver had turned into a very easy-cocking single-action that offered us a 2 3/4-pound trigger pull. After about 300 rounds more ammunition had been fired, the general consensus from shooters was that the new Great Western II is definitely a winner, fully capable of withstanding the rigors of stiff competition. Furthermore, the gist of unsolicited comments we heard were that the gun was, overall, a delight to handle and to shoot. This was apparently a surprise for some, who we heard comparing the GWII favorably to revolvers costing almost three times the price.

How do I rate the Pietta Colt clone? That's easy. This is a top-notch single-action revolver. All three shooters agreed, EMF did everything right

EMF Great Western II Specifications, as tested	
Model/Name	Great Western II
Finish(s)	Satin Nickel
Barrel lengths	5 1/2"
Overall length	11"
Caliber	.45 Colt
Capacity	6 shots
Action	Single
Front sight	Fixed blade
Rear sight	Fixed notch
Grips	1-piecec walnut & sim. Ivory
Chamber mouth	.4515" (actual)
Barrel groove	.450" (actual)
Retail as tested	$625

with the GWII. It's a winner all the way around. Mechanically, the gun was very well fitted and it was one of the best shooting single-action sixguns we tested for this book, and it has the best sights. Based on the experiences we had we would rate the EMF Great Western II along with the Cimarron Model P, among the best of the modern single-actions. This revolver is a very fine basis for building a serious competition revolver.

Ruger New Model Vaquero®

These two photos show both sides of the Vaquero in blue and color case finish. Author photos.

The stainless steel Vaquero is nicely polished so that it closely resembles nickel plating. This is a handsome revolver, especially with the contrasting rosewood grip panels. Author photos.

Most shooters are familiar with the Ruger Blackhawk, the revolver that was Sturm, Ruger's entry into the centerfire revolver market back in the 1950s. The Blackhawk was a strong, modernized, coil spring-powered single-action, that came with adjustable sights. It became an instant success among single-action fans. Some years ago the Blackhawk was revamped and re-introduced as the New Model Blackhawk with an entirely new and radical action that was readied for loading not by moving the hammer, but by simply opening the gate. This radical New Model action broke with tradition but at the same time became the only single-action revolver that was truly safe to carry when the cylinder was fully loaded. A few years later, in 1993, the New Model Vaquero was introduced in order to fill a need for those desiring a single action with a more traditional look and fixed sights. As such it became a great choice for the cowboy shooter. We tested two New Model Vaquero's for this book, a

blue and case color version alongside a stainless steel Vaquero. Both had 5 1/2-inch barrels and were chambered in .45 Colt caliber.

Sturm, Ruger's New Model single-actions are quite different from most of the single-action revolvers you may be used to handling. This is because from their inception, these guns were designed with user safety in mind. The New Model revolvers have no half cock or safety positions. The hammer is either fully cocked, or else it is all the way down. There are no "clicks" in between. The idea of safety goes beyond the mechanism and you can see this graphically if you lay one alongside a standard Colt-type single-action, where one can't help but note the Ruger is a more robust revolver, larger and heavier in almost all aspects than the parent 1873 design.

The blued Vaquero has a blued barrel, cylinder and grip frame with a color case hardened receiver. The bluing is typical modern black oxide or hot blue

Looking in close we can see the Vaquero name stamped into the side of the frame. The case colors are not 19ᵗʰ century, but they look very good. Author photo.

The Vaquero in stainless is generally very well polished by the factory. If you look closely, you can spot some of the gaps between the top of the grip and the steel.

Looking down on both guns, we can see the Vaquero's nicely squared rear sight notch and the sharp serrations provided on the Ruger hammer spur. Author photo.

The only objection we had to the Ruger New Model is from a practical standpoint, that is, the inability of the mechanism to park the chambers in the center of the loading port. This slows up loading and unloading and takes some getting used to. Notice how nice and thick those Ruger chamber walls are, compared to a Colt type SAA. Author photo.

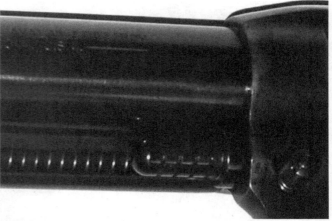

The Vaquero uses a shouldered base pin which is notched to fit the barrel contours, this prevents the pin from rotating with the cylinder. That's a good thing because it helps prevent the holes in the frame from wearing. Author photo.

Here is the Vaquero's ejector rod head. Ruger single-actions use a smaller ejector rod head than the Colt types, and a larger head would be preferable. Nevertheless, ejection is still manageable. Author photo.

finish. The steel was obviously professionally polished before this finish was applied, leaving the exterior with nice, sharp edges and well-defined lettering. The color case hardening on the frame does not look like your typical old bone and charcoal 19th century Colt type finish. Instead, the case colors are uniformly lighter and we found it to be more reminiscent of some of the modern Italian replica colors. Lock-up was tight and positive, but there was a slight under-time; the hammer reached full cock just a tad before the cylinder could be locked by the bolt. By pulling the hammer slightly farther to the rear the cylinder was rotated mechanically into battery. Trigger pull was crisp but on the hard side. Let-off occurred at just over 6 pounds. We measured the barrel groove diameter and diameters of the cylinder chamber throats at an identical .452 inches.

The stainless Vaquero was polished with equal care. Only it did not require a separate final finish; the stainless revolver was taken to a high polish that closely resembles a nickel-plated finish by the factory. We noticed the factory polishers did get a bit carried away when they polished the front sight, the edges of which were rounded off. That did not help the sight picture. This revolver also had a nice, tight cylinder lock-up but it did have somewhat the same problem with under-timing as the blued Vaquero did on four out of the six chambers. In other words, the hammer reached the cocked position before the cylinder rotated

far enough to be locked four out of six times. In every case, pulling the hammer back a bit more caused the cylinder to rotate into lock. The trigger pull on the stainless revolver was much longer and creepier than that of the blued Vaquero but the sear finally let go at an easier-to-live-with 4 pounds. Our Brown & Sharpe dial calipers told us the barrel's groove diameter and the diameters of the cylinder's chamber throats were .452 inches, very consistent, and just the same as its carbon steel brother

Both Vaqueros came equipped with smooth rosewood grips that have Ruger medallions at their tops. These were fitted to the grip frames fairly well, although there were some areas of overhang and a few others where the wood did not quite make it to the edges of the metal. There were also small, but noticeable gaps at the tops of the grips between the wood and metal on both revolvers. Nevertheless, the overall appearance of both revolvers is very good. They are well finished and present a very pleasing look.

Ruger® Vaquero® Parts List

* Barrel, MR20604
Base Pin Assembly, MR02900D
Base Pin Latch Body, XR02700
Base Pin Latch Nut, XR02800
Base Pin Latch Spring, XR04700
* Cylinder, MR-1
Cylinder Latch Assembly, KXR04500
Cylinder Latch Spring, XR04600
Cylinder Latch Spring Plunger, XR07700
Ejector Housing, MR02208
Ejector Housing Screw, XR03300
Ejector Housing Spring, XR04400
Ejector Rod Assembly, XR-55
Firing Pin, MR02100
Firing Pin Rebound Spring, KE-48
Front sight Blade, MR03617
Gate, MR02400
Gate Detent Spring, MR07300
Grip Frame, BR00300

Grip Frame Screw Front, XR01700
Back (2 Req'd.) Grip Frame Screw, BR01801
Grip frame screw, rear, bottom, XR01900
Grip frame screw, and pivot lock, XR01901
Grip Panel Dowel, KXR01400
Grip Panel Ferrule - Left, XR01200
Grip Panel Ferrule – Right, XR01100
Panel Screw, KXR01300
Grip Panels, Sold in Pairs Only, XR01000
Hammer Assembly, MR04000B
Hammer Pivot Pin, XR01601S
Hammer Plunger, KXR04100
Hammer Plunger Cross Pin, KXR04200
Hammer Plunger Spring, KXR04300
Hammer Strut, XR01500
Mainspring, XR00400
Mainspring Seat, XR00500

Medallion, 2 Req'd., XR05200
Pawl, KMR00700
Pawl Spring, XR05000
Pawl Spring Plunger, XR05100
Recoil Plate, MR02000
Recoil Plate Cross Pin, XR04900
Transfer Bar, KMR07200
Trigger, XR03901
Trigger Pivot Pin, XR03400
Trigger Spring, XR03700
Trigger Spring Pivot Pin, KE02800
Trigger Spring Retaining Pin, KXR06300

* PARTS SO MARKED MUST BE FACTORY FITTED

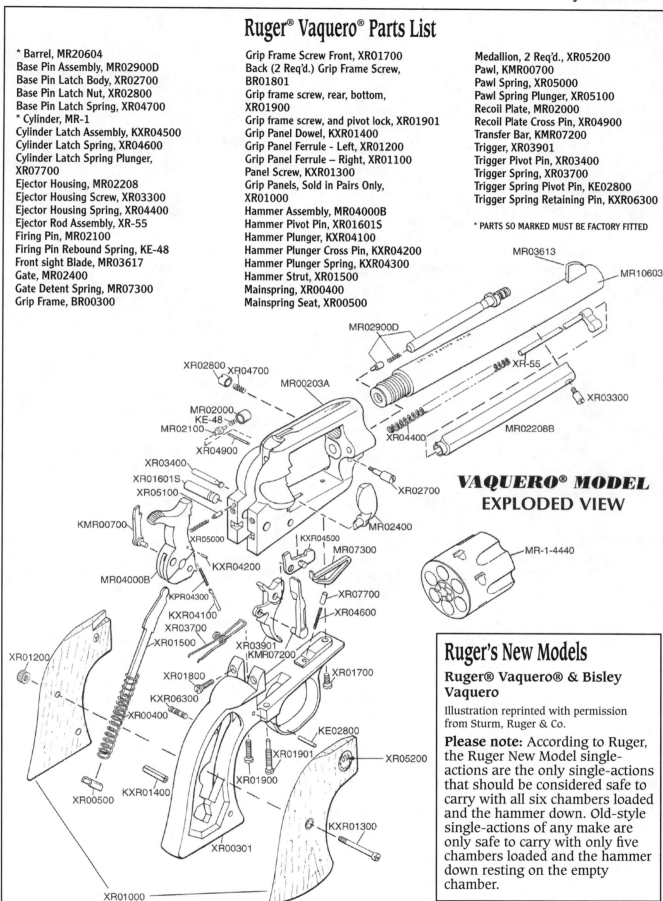

VAQUERO® MODEL EXPLODED VIEW

Ruger's New Models

Ruger® Vaquero® & Bisley Vaquero

Illustration reprinted with permission from Sturm, Ruger & Co.

Please note: According to Ruger, the Ruger New Model single-actions are the only single-actions that should be considered safe to carry with all six chambers loaded and the hammer down. Old-style single-actions of any make are only safe to carry with only five chambers loaded and the hammer down resting on the empty chamber.

The blued Ruger Vaquero is shown here in Ed Wade's capable hands at the height of recoil with Winchester .45 Colt ammunition. Both shooters agreed the 6-pound plus trigger pull on this revolver had an effect on the group sizes. Author photo.

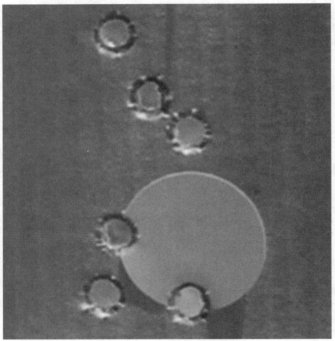

Although we did obtain several groups that were better, this is actually quite typical of the average six-shot group from the blue Vaquero when fired with the Winchester .45 Colt Cowboy loads. Author photo.

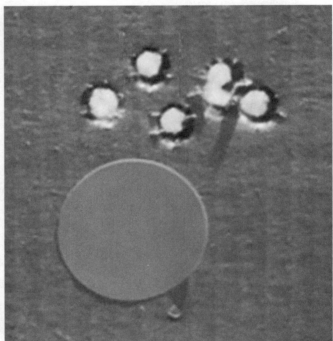

Black Hills .45 Colt Cowboy ammo gave us this six-shot group, which was about average size for the stainless Vaquero. This brand of ammunition with the stainless Vaquero produced several groups that measured under 1 inch. Author photo.

Both revolvers had very good, but not great, sight pictures with nicely machined, wide square notches in the frames. The only problem with the sight pictures came from the rear edges of the front sights, especially on the stainless gun, the rear edges of which had been over-polished. This left us with a less distinct picture than we would have liked. In our opinion both guns might have performed better on target had the front sights been more distinct. Still, the sight pictures on the Vaqueros were far better than many of the original Colts and replicas we have fired.

Operation of both revolvers was perfectly flawless through the duration of several shooting tests that involved the firing of more than 200 shots per gun at both outdoor and indoor target ranges over the span

of three months. The actions on both guns worked without a hitch and the only real complaint I have is the same one that many shooters have. With the gate open to place the revolver in the loading position, the cylinder chambers do not park anywhere near the center of the loading port in the frame. This makes for a slow unload and reload since the shooter has to manually place and hold the chambers so they line up with the loading port.

On average, the Black Hills .45 Colt Cowboy ammo gave us five-shot groups that consistently went into 1 1/4-inch groups at 7 yards. Winchester's .45 Colt Cowboy Loads would put five shots into 1 1/2 inches at 7 yards. The stainless steel Vaquero did give us groups that were, proportionately, very

Ruger New Model Vaquero	
Calibers	.357 Magnum, 44-40, .44 Magnum, 45 Colt
Barrel Lengths:	4 3/4", 5 1/2", 7 1/2"
Stocks:	2-piece rosewood (standard), simulated ivory optional
Finish:	Polished Stainless Steel
Suggested retail:	$535

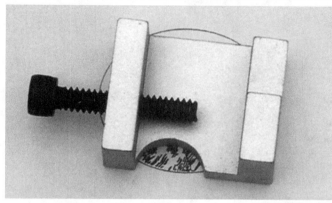

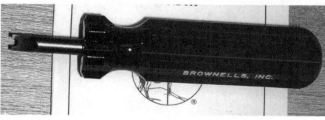

These two specialty tools are just a few of many available from Brownells that can help immensely with the Ruger New Model takedown procedures. Author photo.

Ruger Vaquero Specifications, as tested	
Model	BNV-455, KBNV-455X-C
Name	Color Case Blued Vaquero, Stainless Vaquero
Finish(s)	Blue and color case hardened, gloss stainless
Barrel length	5 1/2"
Twist	1:16" RH
Grooves	6
Weight	43 ounces
Overall lengths	11 1/2"
Caliber	.45 Colt
Capacity	6 shots
Action	Single, transfer bar ignition
Front sight	Fixed blade
Rear sight	Fixed notch
Grips	2-piece, rosewood
Chamber mouth	.452" (both, actual)
Barrel groove	.452" (both, actual)

slightly smaller with either brand of ammunition, but not significantly smaller. For instance, where the blued Vaquero shot 1 1/4-inch groups, as a rule we found the stainless Vaquero would shoot a 1 1/8-inch group with the identical ammo. However, this blued Vaquero put one 10-shot spread into a 1 3/4-inch group at 7 yards using Black Hills .45 Colt Cowboy ammunition. That's not too shabby.

The New Model Ruger is a very different animal from the standard Colt 1873 type single-action and I found it took me some time to get used to its operation, and then again, to get un-used to it so I could get back into shooting conventional single-actions. Now, that doesn't make the New Model Ruger bad, but there are some practical differences between the two that the shooter has to learn to adjust for.

The Vaquero is also a slightly larger and heavier gun than a Colt SAA and the Ruger's grip is somewhat wider. As far as dependability goes, the Ruger is an incredibly rugged design and as we mentioned earlier, the Ruger New Model is the safest of all single-actions to carry loaded. It is, in fact, the only single-action that can be safely carried with all six of its chambers loaded. If all these features appeal to you, as they do to a great many shooters, then right out of the box, the Vaquero is a lot of gun for the money and as these tests proved, the new Rugers are certainly capable of shooting along side the best of them.

United States Fire Arms Mfg. Co., Cowboy Action Rodeo® revolver.

The USFA Rodeo is finished in matte blue and uses a color case hardened hammer. The revolver is intended as a practical alternative for the budget-conscious cowboy action shooter. Author photos

United States Fire Arms Mfg. Co. or USFA located in Hartford, Conn., is a relative newcomer to the arms industry. Nevertheless, this company is manufacturing some very fine single-action revolvers built on the Colt Single Action Army pattern, as well as some intriguing variations thereof. All USFA revolvers are manufactured entirely inside the U.S., at their plant in Hartford. We selected a Cowboy Action Rodeo® model for testing in this book since the model is being specifically manufactured with the cowboy action shooter in mind and in that respect it is in many ways compatible with Colt's Cowboy model.

Except for its color case hardened hammer, a finish which USFA calls Bone Case™, the Rodeo comes finished entirely in a flat, non-glare, Cowboy Action Matte Blue™. The external finish is well executed and pleasing to look at, but I must say this is an unusual finish to see on a classic single-action revolver and we are left with the impression of a high-quality single-action revolver, but one that could have been built for the modern military. We noticed the front sight is firmly secured into a slot in

At half-cock the chambers were parked very close to the center of the loading port. This makes for easy loading and unloading, an important feature to a competition shooter. Author photo.

the barrel using silver solder, exactly like they did in bygone days. We also noticed the thin, gold-colored "seam" from the silver solder stands out in stark contrast with the matt black barrel. The Cowboy Action Rodeo® model is available in .45 Colt, .44-40 or .38 Special calibers, and with 4 3/4-inch, 5 1/2-inch or 7 1/2-inch barrel lengths. "US" logo,

The Rodeo's hammer is very reminiscent of the first-generation Colt SAA with its large diameter, fixed firing pin. Author photo.

This is the only area of the Rodeo that both shooters thought could use more attention; the knurling on the hammer spur could have been deeper and sharper to provide a better purchase on the hammer. Author photo.

checkered hard rubber grips are standard. Our test revolver was chambered in .45 Colt caliber with the 5 1/2-inch-long barrel. USFA machines these revolvers the old-fashioned way; from solid bar-stock, using a combination of modern state-of-the-art CNC equipment but with traditional hand fitting playing a large part in production.

The Cowboy Action Rodeo is being built on the smokeless-type frame, which uses the spring-loaded cross pin to hold the base pin in place and the base pin bushing is the easily removable, Colt type, just like the ones used on the latter's first and second-generation guns. Externally, the metal-to-metal fits

are really excellent with no gaps or voids at any of the seams. In fact, as you run your fingertips over the areas where seams are, you cannot detect a junction. This is metal-to-metal fitting in the tradition of pre-World War II Hartford-built revolvers. The screws are brightly polished and blued with narrow slots and the screws that pass through the frame are nicely domed on both ends. The hammer is a look-a-like of the early first-generation Colt, with its large, fixed firing pin. The knurling on the hammer spur was very neatly done but rather faint. The sharply checkered hard rubber grips are thin. In this respect they are very reminiscent of the early Colt hard rubber grips, however these panels sport a large US logo near their tops. A word about the way the grips fit to the gun. Both shooters noticed right away that these grips were mated to the metal grip straps about as close to perfection as I have ever seen on a modern-made revolver. There were no overhanging sharp edges on which to cut yourself. Actually we found you had to look to find the seams, because they were so closely mated that they couldn't be felt.

Everyone thought the sights on our Rodeo test revolver were a nice surprise. At first glance, they appeared to be similar to the run-of-the-mill fixed sights we see on many single-actions, but when we took a closer look we could see these sights were anything but run-of-the-mill. The Rodeo's rear sight notch is a nicely cut, wide square that is machined into the rear of the frame-top with sharp, and well-defined edges. The front blade, while it is shaped to look like a standard fixed sight when viewed from the side, also has "using" edges that are nice and sharp and it is not tapered. The resulting combination leaves the impression of classic single-action sights that in reality give the shooter a sight picture that is excellent. Just like the early Colt single-actions, the sight picture is obscured when the hammer is all the way forward.

How well does it work? Well, in a word, prettydarngood! The action on this Rodeo was as good as its looks, with the hammer reaching full cock at the same moment the bolt locks the cylinder into battery and at the rearmost point in the hammer's travel. Cylinder lock-up was positive and very tight. It locked up like a bank vault and was the tightest lock-up of any single-action revolver we tested. The ranging, which is the alignment of the cylinder chambers to the barrel bore, was perfect. At the half-cock position, the chambers were parked very nearly on exact center in the loading port and this gun gave us no trouble during the loading or unloading processes. Indeed, the cylinder's chambers were so perfectly polished that most of the fired cartridge cases from factory ammunition dropped out without help from the ejector rod. Even with some of the heavier handloads we tried, most cases fell out of their own accord, needing little, if any, assistance from the ejector. Ejector operation was positive and crisp, with ejector rod return helped along by a rather aggressive spring. The trigger let-off was reasonably crisp. We actually expected a lot of creep but there was less than we thought. The hammer fell at about 4 pounds, and it did this with a fully tensioned, rather stiff main spring. Because the Rodeo is built in the U.S.A. there is no requirement for added safety devises and so it has none, thus, this revolver is a genuine "load five chambers and drop the hammer on the empty one", old-style six-shooter.

We measured the flash gap between the barrel and cylinder at a tight .005 inches (about perfect) with some noticeable cylinder end shake present,

but there was not enough end shake to allow the cylinder to hit the rear of the barrel. All six of the cylinder's chamber mouth diameters were a remarkably consistent .454 inches and the barrel's groove diameter measured on the tight side of .452. Looking inside the gun with the grips and grip straps removed, the folks at USFA seem to have done an equally nice job with the internals. Tool marks are at a minimum and like the older Colts, USFA uses fitter's (or assembly) numbers on mated parts like the frame, gate, straps and grips, while the cylinder is serial numbered to match the frame.

On the shooting range the Rodeo performed very well. We fired just under 100 rounds using Black Hills .45 Colt Cowboy and Winchester .45 Colt Cowboy loads. At 7 yards the Black Hills struck the target

USFA Cowboy Action Rodeo, parts list

Numbered parts
1. barrel
2. ejector rod housing
3. ejector rod and spring
4. cylinder bushing
5. cylinder
6. base pin
7. frame
8. gate
9. bolt
10. hammer screw
11. bolt and trigger spring
12. firing pin and pin
13. hammer
14. trigger guard
15. main spring
16. trigger
17. hand and hand spring
18. roller and pin
19. grips
20. back-strap

lettered parts
A. Ejector tube screw
B. Base pin lock screw, black powder frame only
C. Cross pin (3 pcs)
D. Recoil bushing
E. Bolt screw
F. Trigger screw
G. Front guard screw
H. Bolt and trigger spring screw
I. Gate detent
J. Gate detent spring
K. Gate detent screw
L. Rear guard screw (2)
M. Lower back-strap screw
N. Main spring screw
O. Grip screw
P. Upper back-strap screw (2)

Black Powder frame only B

Cross Pin frame only (3 pieces) C

**Model 1873
Single Action
Center Fire Revolver**

Exploded view

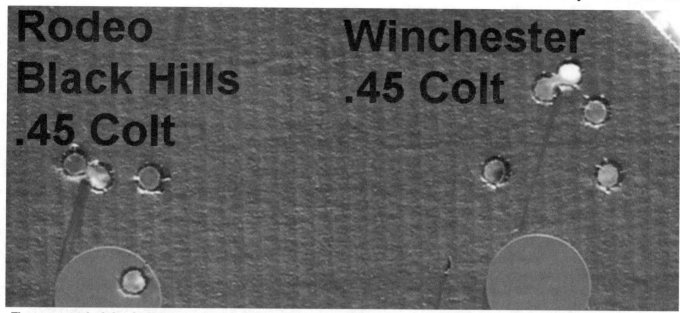

The target on the left, which seems to have only four holes is actually five shots (two went through the center-top hole), fired with Black Hills Cowboy ammo, the group on the right is typical of the groups we fired with Winchester Cowboy loads. Author photo.

USFA Cowboy Action Rodeo	
Caliber:	.38 Special, 44 WCF, .45 Colt
Barrel Lengths:	4 3/4", 5 1/2", 7 1/2"
Frame:	Machined steel
Stocks:	2-piece, checkered hard rubber
Finishes:	Cowboy Action Matte Blue™
Suggested Retail:	$658

United States Firearms Mfg. Co., Cowboy Action Rodeo®, as tested	
Model	Cowboy Action Rodeo
Finish(s)	Cowboy Action Matte Blue
Barrel length	5 1/2"
Overall length	11"
Calibers	.45 Colt
Capacity	6 shots
Action	Single
Front sight	Fixed blade
Rear sight	Square, fixed notch
Grips	2-pc. checkered hard rubber
Chamber mouth	.454 (actual)
Barrel groove	.452 (actual)
Retail as tested	$658
Available from	United States Firearms Mfg Co., P.O. Box 1901, Hartford, CT 06144 1-877 227-6901

on center and about 1 inch high, giving us average groups of about 1 1/2 inches. The Winchester ammo hit the paper about 2 inches high and averaged 1 1/2-inch groups. The Rodeo went through the entire shooting test without any malfunctions. Loading and unloading was easy with no slow-downs.

This Cowboy Action Rodeo is obviously a cut above average and in every way a very nicely made firearm. This was an opinion shared by everyone who handled this gun. If this gun had one fault, I would have to say it would be the hammer knurling, which could have been deeper and sharper, but that is a relatively minor complaint. For use in serious cowboy competition this gun would not require any mechanical alterations since timing and overall performance were excellent. But the revolver would require some gunsmithing to lighten the springs and perhaps to slick things up a bit. You would expect that from any out-of-the-box factory new revolver. Overall, if this revolver is any indication of what is normal for USFA, the Rodeo is a high-

quality, cowboy revolver that can be put into immediate use with a strong expectancy of excellent results. Chalk one up for the U.S.A. This is a classy, very well built revolver, everyone who handled it was duly impressed.

Smith & Wesson
top breaks and modern copies

The mainstay of S&W revolver production before the Model 3 was invented were guns like this Model 1 third Issue, a .22 rimfire that held seven shots. The barrel tipped-up for loading and unloading. Author photo.

The Colt Richards conversion for metallic cartridges (top) was based on the 1860 Army percussion revolver. Notice the difference in size between it and the S&W Model No. 2. (below) The Model 2 was the largest S&W tip-up and it held six, .32 rimefire cartridges. Author photo.

Back in 1870, Smith & Wesson introduced a revolutionary new revolver they called the Model Number 3. All the signs were that this new .44 caliber revolver was going to be a great success. This gun appeared less than a year after the famous Rollin White patent (the one which protected an idea that allowed metallic cartridges to be loaded into open cylinder chambers from the rear) expired in 1869. Up until that point S&W had built their fortunes on that idea, having had exclusive rights to that patent. They manufactured a line of popular rimfire revolvers whose barrels tipped-up for loading. Now, with that patent out of the way, we might expect that the major American revolver manufacturers of the day would be introducing new revolvers made specifically to fire those new metallic cartridges that were causing such a stir, but actually; they didn't. They hesitated, and instead began selling altered versions of their old percussion revolvers that they converted to use metallic cartridges. Although they had years to prepare for this and the field was now cleared for all competition, all the large gunmakers really did was offer a re-hash of their old designs. Make no mistake about it; for the most part these revolvers were well-proven designs. Once converted to fire metallic cartridges these revolvers had to have some sort of device to remove the fired shell casings. This took the form of the now very simple and familiar ejector rod system. With revolvers that use this system, the cylinder may be loaded, and the fired shells removed from the cylinder, at the rate of one shell at a time.

A short time after that important patent protection expired, S&W released a thoroughly modern .44 caliber, belt-sized, top-break cartridge revolver. This was the Model Number 3. This first large S&W single-action was roughly the size and shape of the familiar Colt and Remington Army-sized percussion revolvers, but it had a large hinge at the lower front of the frame. The Model 3 was a top-break revolver, so the barrel could be unlatched and opened from the top. Then it tilted down like a shotgun and as it did it took the cylinder along with it and all the cartridges were automatically, simultaneously ejected. With that one weapon, S&W instantly unleashed the world's fastest loading and unloading revolver; nothing like it had ever been seen.

This firearms engineering feat was immediately latched onto by a waiting public and sales quickly followed. This was helped by D.B. Wesson, who strategically sent off gift revolvers to some very well-placed people. One such well-placed person was the Russian military attaché to the United States, General Alexander Gorloff, who in 1870 was in Hartford at the Colt factory. Wesson apparently followed up the gift with a series of letters that urged the Russians to visit Smith & Wesson, just up the Connecticut river, at Springfield. Almost as soon as it was introduced, the U.S. Army tested an S&W in .44 rimfire caliber, and they had favorable results. The Army ordered 1,000 of the new Model Number 3 revolvers, but they had S&W chamber them for a new centerfire .44

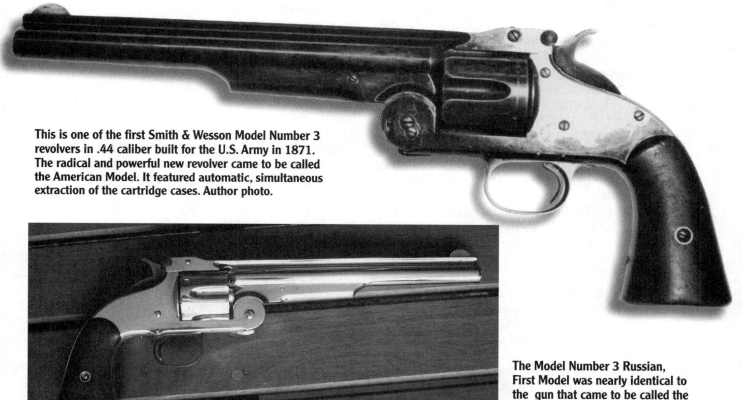

This is one of the first Smith & Wesson Model Number 3 revolvers in .44 caliber built for the U.S. Army in 1871. The radical and powerful new revolver came to be called the American Model. It featured automatic, simultaneous extraction of the cartridge cases. Author photo.

The Model Number 3 Russian, First Model was nearly identical to the gun that came to be called the Second Model American except for its chambering in .44 S&W Russian caliber. Author photo.

Here we see a good example of the New Model (Third Model) Russian .44. This particular revolver was built for the Russians in Germany by the Ludwig Lowe company. Author photo.

cartridge for the field tests, this is the cartridge that came to be called the S&W .44/100 or .44 American. Those 1,000 revolvers would be the only S&W .44s the U.S. Army would buy, at least for the near future. The Army felt the S&W was too complicated and fragile for further purchase. As it turned out that was fine, because other military organizations were already taking a close look at this amazing new revolver. This same model, with variations, continued to be manufactured until 1874 and has come to be called the Smith & Wesson Model 3 American.

The Russian General did make the short trip up river to Springfield. Soon thereafter S&W struck a deal with the government of the Czar of Russia. That was on May 20, 1871 and the first contract was signed with the Russians for Smith & Wesson's revolvers. The Czar delivered a cash advance of $50,000 in gold to cover tooling costs. Part of the negotiations caused changes to the S&W design that were specified by the Russians. One of those changes was the caliber; Gorloff had specified a cartridge using a bullet with the same outside diameter as the inside of the cartridge case. Presently, the S&W was chambered for .44/100 S&W centerfire that used a stepped or heel-type bullet, its lower diameter being the same as the inside of the cartridge case but its upper diameter was the same as the outside of the case. The new round soon became known as the "Russian." This new cartridge also used a different chamber shape. Both previous S&W .44s used a straight, bored-through cylinder with no shoulder in the chamber, the Russian used a shouldered chamber with a smaller diameter at the front.

Some important mechanical changes were also made to the Model 3 at the request of General Gorloff and his aide, Captain Kasavery Ordinetz. Their job was to alter the basic S&W into a more dependable revolver, to make it into one that would better fit the needs of the Russian military. Some of their changes included a larger diameter trigger pivot-pin with a bolster added to that area of the frame to strengthen it. They also demanded a stronger, easier to remove

cylinder retainer. They added an interlocking feature to the hammer and barrel catch that assured the barrel was locked closed at the point of firing, among other internal changes. The Russian alterations actually did make S&W's revolver into a more dependable weapon for military use and eventually, most of those improvements were incorporated by S&W into all of their Model 3 revolvers.

The arms contracts between Smith & Wesson and the Russian government continued on through 1878 and they involved more major changes, inside and out. These changes formed the three different single-action Russian Models, the final two models using a knuckle at the top of the grip, a rounded butt shape and a unique hooked trigger guard. These latter features are distinctly Russian and have been used for years to identify the second and third S&W Russian Models. The last of these models, the third model, which is also called the New Model, was introduced in 1874 and was the most improved of the Russian models. Third models share the distinct Russian grip shape with the second model but its barrel was shortened to 6 1/2 inches and the front sight was forged as part of the barrel. This model had a quick-removable cylinder system, patented by D. B. Wesson, so the cylinder could be removed without tools. Its extractor system, still a fairly complex rack and gear mechanism, was simplified over earlier versions. S&W supplied this model revolver to Russia, Turkey and Japan as well as selling them on the commercial market.

From 1877 to 1884, the firearms maker Ludwig Lowe manufactured New Model Russian revolvers for the Russian government in Germany. Lowe manufactured somewhere between 70,000 and 100,000 revolvers. The Russian military also manufactured its own New Model Russian revolvers starting about 1886 on German-made machinery at Tula Arsenal. Exact quantities of these revolvers made at Tula are not known, but manufacture

The .45 Schofield Model was basically a Model No. 3 that was redesigned by George Schofield, a U.S. Army officer, with a view to making it better for military use. This revolver is a First Model built in 1875, restored by the author in 2002. Author photo.

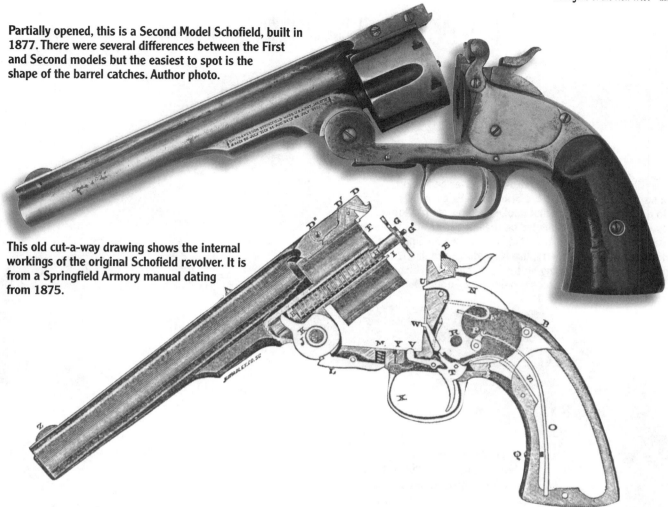

Partially opened, this is a Second Model Schofield, built in 1877. There were several differences between the First and Second models but the easiest to spot is the shape of the barrel catches. Author photo.

This old cut-a-way drawing shows the internal workings of the original Schofield revolver. It is from a Springfield Armory manual dating from 1875.

continued until at least 1892 and totals have been estimated at from 80,000 to 160,000. Unknown quantities of copies of the S&W New Model Russian were also manufactured in Spain and Belgium for both commercial and military use. A modern replica of the New Model Russian is being re-manufactured today by A. Uberti and it is being offered in its original chambering of .44 S&W Russian.

George Schofield was a U. S. Army colonel who sincerely believed the Army should have pursued the S&W top-break design, especially for cavalry use. He felt (correctly) that the S&W, with its rapid unloading and reloading capabilities, offered a very advanced design and that our troops were presently under-gunned with a single-action revolver that was much too slow to load and reload. In effect he recognized the Colt SAA as an obsolete design. In the early 1870s Schofield experimented with the Model 3 and he invented some interesting changes; changes that made it into a less complex revolver that truly was better suited for military service.

In 1875 the U.S. Army adopted the S&W Model Number 3 Schofield with its much simplified extraction system and barrel catch that was pulled to the rear instead of lifted up. That last innovation permitted one-hand operation of the barrel mechanism and the new extraction system proved to be very successful. Schofields were also equipped with a full-length sighting groove that ran the length of the barrel top rib. Many collectors and shooters today feel the Smith & Wesson Schofield was the best single-action revolver ever built. A total of about 8,900 Schofields were manufactured and just over 8,000 of these .45 caliber revolvers were purchased by the U.S. Army from 1875 through 1877. In Army service, the Schofield S&W was issued to, among others, units of the famous 9th and 10th U.S. Cavalry (the Buffalo Soldiers) who used it with success during the Indian Wars. The Aldo Uberti Company is manufacturing a modern, replica of the Schofield and the revolvers are available in 44-40 and .45 Colt calibers.

Uberti's New Model Russian .44

The Uberti Russian is a handsome revolver and bears a strong resemblance to the original S&W, especially in grip shape and with that hooked trigger guard. Notice the caliber marking stamped on the left barrel side, just over the maker's name. On the right side, we see the importer's (Stoeger) marking. The replica New Model Russian is also fitted with a lanyard ring on the butt, much like the originals. Revolver courtesy of Stoeger Industries. Author photos.

Originally released by Navy Arms, the Italian-made New Model Russian is being produced by Aldo Uberti. We obtained our test revolver directly from Uberti's new U.S. representative, Stoeger Industries in Maryland. This unique revolver gives the outward appearance of the Smith & Wesson New Model Russian .44 single-action revolver. It comes with a Russian-style hooked trigger guard, and there is even a knurled thumb screw in the barrel's top strap for cylinder removal. The Uberti Russian is chambered to accept the .44 S&W Russian cartridge, but it has a 7-inch barrel like a Second Model Russian instead of the 6 1/2-inch barrel of the S&W Third Model Russian. A lanyard ring fixed to the revolver butt is much like that used on the original. The Uberti New Model Russian appears a bit top-heavy. The barrel rib seems to be wider than it should be, but a closer examination reveals the factory chose not chamfer the edges of the barrel rib at an angle like the original Russian, thus giving this modern Russian's barrel a broader and higher appearance. We measured the dimensions of this barrel and they are actually very close to an original S&W. In an attempt to gain more strength in that thin area at the junction of the barrel with its top strap Uberti extended the wider portion of the top strap even farther forward out into the rounded area near the rear of the barrel. This is similar to what they did with their Schofield

Russ-close Up-close you can see the knurled thumbscrew on the barrel's top-strap that is used for cylinder removal, you can also get a good look at the hammer/barrel catch interlock feature. The barrel catch sides are nicely checkered and easy to grasp when opening the barrel.

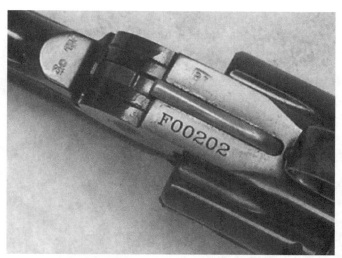

The serial number is now stamped on the bottom flat of the frame just forward of the trigger guard. Originals and earlier Uberti imports had their serials on the butt. The rectangular piece you can see just above the serial number is the extractor pawl.

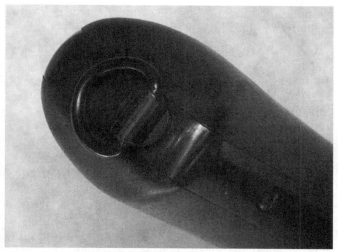

Here is a good look at the butt showing the lanyard ring or what some call the butt-swivel.

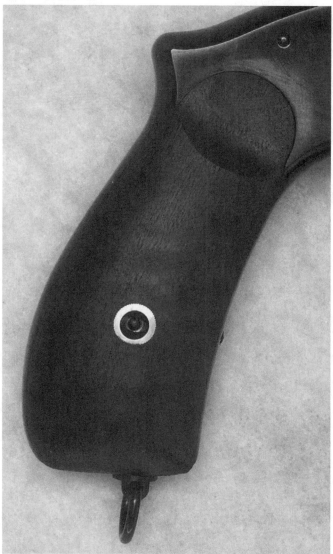

The two-piece grips are nicely finished walnut and they are perfectly fitted to the steel grip frame.

replica. This alteration adds strength to an originally weak area; however unfortunately, it also furthers the revolver's top-heavy appearance. Still, the New Model Russian points very naturally downrange, just as its older relatives always have.

Although they have pretty well kept the original look and feel of the S&W, the new-New Model Russian (NMR) has been heavily re-engineered by Uberti. What this means is that this new revolver's component parts are dimensionally different from original S&W's in almost all respects. Perhaps the only exceptions to this are parts that might be easily altered to work in an original S&W Russian model. They would be the cylinder stop spring, the extractor spring, and with some serious alteration, the hand.

The S&W Russians used a rack and gear extraction mechanism but Uberti's New Model Russian does not, instead Uberti makes use of the much simpler hook and pawl extractor cam, like the system in use on their Schofields. This is an internal change that is not readily apparent unless you disassemble the revolver. Also, like on their Schofields, Uberti has increased the diameter of the joint pivot (the barrel hinge) and its screw. Unlike some Italian replica revolvers we have seen, both the Russian revolver I used for the tests in this book and several others tested more than three years ago had a good combination of barrel groove diameter at .429 inches and cylinder's chamber mouths measured in at a consistent .430 inches. The barrel-to-cylinder gap was a tight .004 inches with very little noticeable cylinder end shake. The cylinder is actually easier to remove for cleaning than the original S&W was. You first open the barrel and loosen the knurled thumb screw on the barrel a few turns, then you pull off the cylinder to the rear. By moving to the rear, the cylinder pulls the cylinder catch back just enough to allow it to snap out of the way, enabling the cylinder to be removed completely. For reassembly, the shooter reinstalls the cylinder and then presses the cylinder catch back into the barrel and retightens the thumb screw.

Our replica is finished in a modern, bright blue-black (caustic, hot blue) finish and the prep work put into this is top-drawer, really presenting a very fine finish with sharp edges and crisp lettering. In contrast, the hooked trigger guard, the hammer and barrel catch are all color case hardened, as are the extractor cam, the pawl and the joint pivot assembly. The barrel's top-rib is marked in Cyrillic Russian with the name and address of the Uberti factory while the left barrel side, on the round, is roll stamped with "CAL. 44 S&W RUSSIAN." The grips are walnut, stained a dark orange-brown and they are exceptionally well fitted to the metal with no air gaps or overhang all the way around. Sights on this revolver consist of a half-moon shaped front blade set into the barrel top rib, the edges of which are left square. The rear sight is formed of

two posts machined out of the barrel catch and when you put the front and rear together the shooter sees three vertical, rectangular posts of nearly identical size that together form a surprisingly sharp picture. Indeed, this revolver presents the best sight picture we have seen on any fixed-sighted revolver, replica or original.

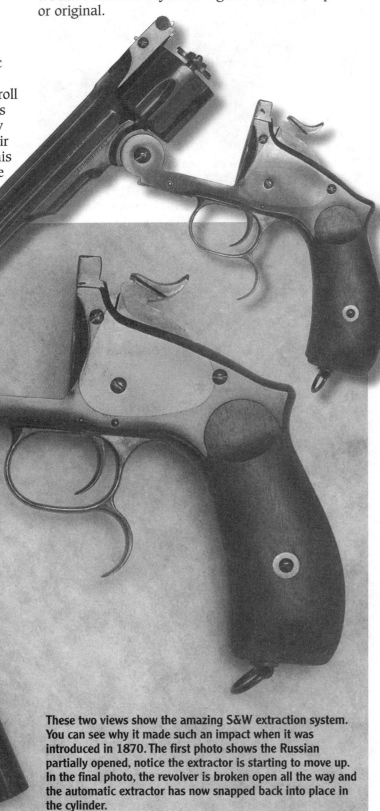

These two views show the amazing S&W extraction system. You can see why it made such an impact when it was introduced in 1870. The first photo shows the Russian partially opened, notice the extractor is starting to move up. In the final photo, the revolver is broken open all the way and the automatic extractor has now snapped back into place in the cylinder.

This view of the top of the barrel offers a good look at the the large, knurled takedown screw in the center of the barrel top strap.

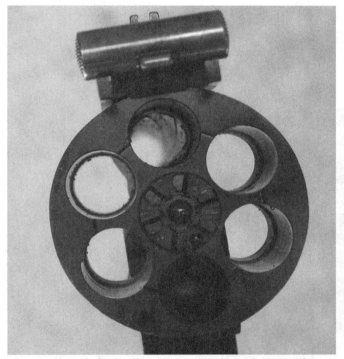

Open and ready for loading, the top-break revolvers are the fastest of all to reload.

This is champion shooter, Tommy Abernathy about to touch off the Uberti New Model Russian. The revolver delivered wonderful accuracy in spite of a horrendous trigger pull. Author photo.

In full recoil, Ed Wade is in the middle of shooting a five-shot group that measured only about 5/8 of an inch! Author photo.

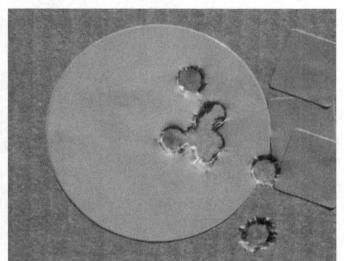

Believe it or not, this group consists of 10 shots, fired with Black Hills .44 Russian ammo at 7 yards. Author photo.

We found the action operation to be a bit sticky. This was obviously from a balky cylinder rotation and it occurred on several chambers and was only overcome by placing still greater thumb pressure on the hammer spur. Throughout the tests, the cylinder never failed to rotate, but as we just hinted, its operation was at times difficult. The Russian hammer spur, by the way, is sharply but simply checkered and while it is not exactly like the original S&W checkering, I have to say the checkering is done in a practical fashion leaving the shooter with a very useable hammer. Cylinder timing was perfect with the cylinder being pushed into its locked position

at the same moment the hammer reached full cock on every chamber. The Russian's trigger pull left something to be desired. It had lots of creep and the duration of the pull was almost unbelievably long. The pull actually occurred in three stages, but the sear let-off itself, when it finally happened at the end of the build-up, was crisp, with the trigger breaking at almost 7 pounds. A hammer block safety is fitted to these revolvers but other than an extra-noisy click at half-cock, its operation never seemed to interfere in any way with the action. Since I have previously handled hundreds of original Russian models, I can honestly say that I could "feel" those extra hammer

Uberti Russian Parts

1	Frame	B	Pawl pin	H	Stirrup Pin	
2	Barrel	18	Extractor pawl spring	35	Hand	
3	Front sight	19	Extractor cam	36	Hand spring	
F	Front sight pin	21	Joint pivot	E	Hand spring pin	
6	Cylinder catch thumb-screw	21a	Joint pivot screw	38	Mainspring	
7	Cylinder catch	23	Trigger guard screw	39	Sideplate	
8	Barrel catch	24	Cylinder stop (bolt) spring	40	Plate screw, center	
9	Barrel catch cam spring	27	Strain screw	41	Plate screw, front or rear (2)	
9a	Barrel catch cam	28	Cylinder stop (bolt)	42	Hammer stud	
11	Extractor spring	A	Cylinder stop pin	43	Trigger guard	
13	Extractor rod	30	Trigger	D	Grip pin	
14	Cylinder	30a	Trigger spring	45L &	Grips left and right	
15	Extractor	C	Trigger pin	45R		
16	Barrel catch screw	32	Hammer	46	Grip screw	
17	Extractor pawl	33	Stirrup	47	Base pin	

DRC 2004

not to scale

block safety parts in motion as the action was operated, but they didn't bother anything. When the barrel was opened for extraction the extractor mechanism worked perfectly although we did notice the barrel catch had an annoying habit of sticking in the up position. Very often we would have to manually push it back down after the barrel closed when it would not fall of its own accord.

On the target range in the actual shooting tests the Russian performed without a hitch. It delivered the best accuracy of any replica handgun we tested for this book. We fired this revolver using exclusively Black Hills .44 Russian caliber Cowboy ammunition. Three shooters were involved in the test firing including the author, Ed Wade and Tommy Abernathy of Mt. Holly, N.C. The Russian was a very accurate revolver. We all found that the average five-shot group size at 7 yards was just about 1 inch. The truth is many of the groups were actually one-holer's that measured under three quarters of an inch. The Uberti-Russian printed all of its groups very near the center of the target at this distance, perhaps averaging a half inch high and slightly to the right when using a six-o'clock hold. This gun's exceptional accuracy was remarkable, I think, especially when you consider that this was done with factory ammunition and that we were hampered by such a long and difficult trigger pull.

What were our overall impressions of the Uberti-Russian model? Just out of the factory box with no modifications whatever, the New Model Russian revolver is very nicely finished. Its overall appearance is, in all respects, quite beautiful. When you consider the ability of a revolver to deliver such outstanding accuracy when it has such a terrible trigger pull,

Uberti New Model Russian .44, as tested	
Bbl. Length:	6 1/2"
O.A.L.:	12"
Weight:	2 lbs. 8 oz.
Caliber:	.44 S&W Russian
Finish	Blue
Chamber mouths	.430"
Bbl groove diam	.429"
Retail	$825
From	Stoeger Industries, 17603 Indian Head Hwy., Ste 200, Accokeek, MD 20607 (301 283-6300

honestly, it really has us all curious as to how well this revolver might perform if it were given a good tune-up and trigger job by a competent gunsmith! Having said that, all the Uberti top-break revolvers, including this one, could have stood some trigger work. The sights in actual use, were obviously very effective. The only objection which both Ed Wade and I had to them was the inability to acquire the sight picture as quickly as we would have liked. Once the picture was acquired, we both found it easy to maintain. The Uberti New Model Russian is a very nice looking gun and it was extremely accurate right out of the box, our test gun worked well throughout the tests, all it needed to make things perfect were some small adjustments (re: the sticky barrel catch and balky cylinder rotation) and a good trigger.

Uberti Schofield .45

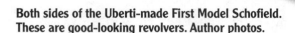

Both sides of the Uberti-made First Model Schofield. These are good-looking revolvers. Author photos.

The Aldo Uberti company's replica of Smith & Wesson's famous top-break Schofield .45 U.S. Army revolver is actually one of the most complicated revolvers ever to be reproduced in modern times. This S&W design, at more than 125 years old, relied heavily on very tight machine tolerances, so this was surely one of the most intricate machine projects ever attempted by a modern firearms manufacturer.

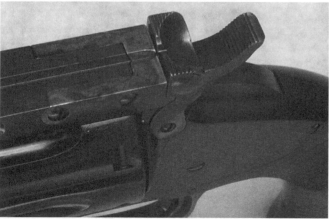

The top shot shows the First Model Schofield close-up and the bottom shows the Second Model.

On the top is the First Model and on the bottom is the Second Model Schofield barrel catch. These illustrate the easy-to-spot differences between the barrel catches.

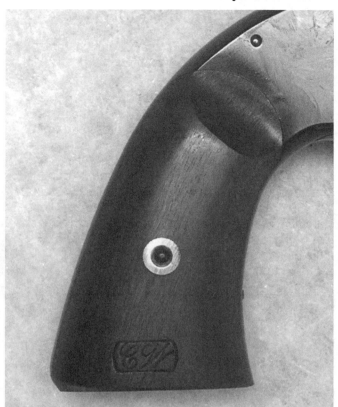

Bottoms up. The First Model butt markings (top) vs. the Second Model (bottom).

The right grip on both Schofield models.

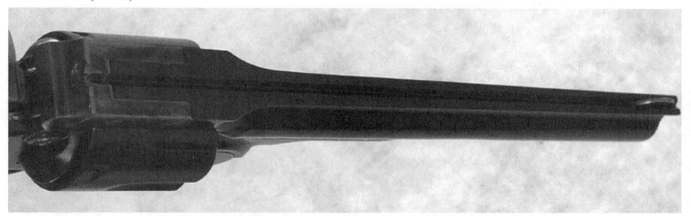

All Schofields, original and repro, have a full-length sighting groove that runs the length of the barrel top rib.

The Schofield was originally manufactured by Smith & Wesson in Springfield, Mass., and they made almost 9,000 Model Number 3, Schofield revolvers between 1875 and 1877. Most of those revolvers went to the United States Army. All of them were chambered in .45 S&W caliber. Val Forgett first introduced the Uberti Schofield in this country through his company, Navy Arms. In more recent years other importers have offered it. Since Uberti U.S.A. closed its doors, American distribution for A. Uberti Co. products is being handled by Stoeger Industries in Maryland. Uberti's replica of the Schofield has been re-engineered in many aspects by its manufacturer. Some of this reworking is not such a great idea. On the other hand, it is not entirely negative. For instance,

this replica is machined from modern steel and it can be safely fired with smokeless powder ammunition. That alone is a good thing because it provides an alternative to firing a valuable, original Schofield. The Italians have also altered the original S&W design a bit so it could be more easily manufactured using modern machine tools. That is both good and bad. The degree of bad is going to be measured by how much of a purist you think you are.

There was interest in replica revolvers like this for years but the real demand for them that made the replica companies take notice was created by the sport of cowboy action shooting. Talking about it and actually moving such a gun from the drawing boards onto the gun case of your local dealer often involves concessions. In this case, the concessions were mechanical alterations to the Smith & Wesson design, along with the addition of a new hammer-block safety device in order to allow the revolver to enter the U.S.A.

Some of the new revolvers initially experienced teething problems, but the factory has made great strides toward eliminating many of those and these revolvers have been proving themselves, with many now receiving regular hard use in CAS events. The Model No. 3 revolver design uses a jointed-frame, and after considerable shooting you will see increases in tolerances as a result of wear and hard use. That statement is true of both the original and the reproduction. Some gun writers and shooters have questioned the ability of the Uberti product to stand up under continued hard knocks. It is

often compared with the original Smith & Wesson and many assume the S&W would have stood up better than the replica. The truth is, I have personally

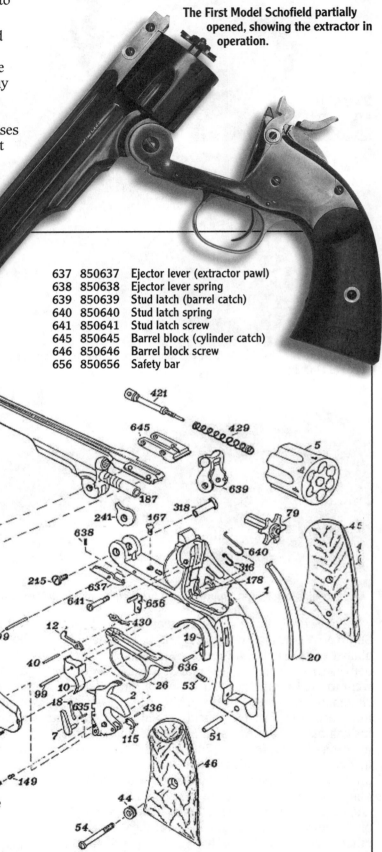

The First Model Schofield partially opened, showing the extractor in operation.

Uberti Schofield .45 Parts

1	850001	Frame assembly
2	850002	Hammer
3	850003	Barrel .45-7"
5	850005	Cylinder .45
7	850007	Hand
10	850010	Trigger
12	850012	Bolt
15	850015	Front Sight
18	850018	Handspring
19	850019	Bolt spring (trigger spring)
20	850020	Mainspring
26	850026	Trigger Guard
37	850037	Hammer pin screw (center sideplate)
40	850040	Bolt Pin (Cylinder Stop Pin)
43	850043	Right grip nut
44	850044	Left grip nut
45	850045	Right grip
46	850046	Left grip
51	850051	Grip pin
53	850053	Mainspring screw (strain)
54	850054	Grip screw
79	850079	Ejector (extractor) .45
99	850099	Sight pin
11	850115	Stirrup
147	850147	Hammer safety spring
149	850149	Hammer safety pin
152	850152	Hammer safety stop screw
167	850167	Trigger guard screw
178	850178	Hammer pin (hammer stud)
187	850187	Base pin bushing (base pin)
215	850125	Hinge pin screw (joint pivot screw)
241	850241	Ejector cam (extractor cam)
316	850316	Safety spring
318	850318	Hinge pin (joint pivot)
421	850421	Ejector rod
429	850429	Ejector spring
430	850430	Bolt spring
436	850436	Stirrup pin
453	850453	Sideplate screw (rear)
574	850574	Sight pin
635	850635	Handspring pin

637	850637	Ejector lever (extractor pawl)
638	850638	Ejector lever spring
639	850639	Stud latch (barrel catch)
640	850640	Stud latch spring
641	850641	Stud latch screw
645	850645	Barrel block (cylinder catch)
646	850646	Barrel block screw
656	850656	Safety bar

repaired at the least a couple hundred original S&W Schofields. I've also fired thousands of black powder cartridges from original S&W Schofield revolvers. After also firing and repairing quite a few Uberti-made Schofields that have fired in excess of 5,000 rounds with smokeless powder ammunition. These were all guns that had been put into good operating condition by a gunsmith beforehand. I know this may seem hard to believe, but the Uberti Schofields actually show less overall effects of wear and tear, and they are definitely breaking fewer springs than original revolvers would during that kind of use.

Uberti is now making two versions of their Schofield replica, a First and a Second Model. The main difference being in the style of barrel catch used. Original S&W First Model Schofields had a catch with a sort of pointed top. Second Models had flat-topped catches with checkering. Uberti has followed suit although they use serrations instead of checkering on the Second Model barrel catch and on hammer spurs for both models. Unfortunately, the serrated hammer spurs more closely resemble something you would see on $100 shotgun, not on a top-of-the-line revolver. This is one area that Uberti has ignored and that I have complained about in print before. It would not take much to reshape that hammer spur and properly checker it like an S&W. It would be a simple change really, but one that would add a great deal to the appearance of these guns. There were other subtle differences between First and Second Model Schofields that Uberti has not touched on. Some, such as the shoulder around the screw on the First Model's barrel catch have been detailed.

Both Schofields were very nicely finished in a well-executed, very nicely polished, modern blue, with hammers, guards and some small parts finished in color case hardening. The hammer spurs are furnished with deep serrations that, as I mentioned above, are

not very attractive, but they are effective and provide a good, solid gripping surface for the shooter's thumb. The fit of the grips to the metal on both guns was very good; not quite as good as the Russian but both were much better than many replicas. Grips were plain walnut, finished minimally in oil and they were shaped to be very close representatives of the original S&W military grip. Both models carry the CW (Charles Woodman) cartouche on the right grip. In actuality CW should only appear on the right grip of second models. Both guns also carry a DAL (David A. Lisle) stamp on the left grip and the second model bears the date 1877 above that cartouche. The butts of these revolvers are also stamped US but both have the stamps located at the heel.

Mechanically, the First Model had a barrel-to-cylinder gap of .005 inches with very little cylinder end shake. The Second Model also had about a .005-inch barrel-to-cylinder gap, and this could be opened to .010 inches if the cylinder was shoved rearward, thus indicating a good bit of cylinder end shake. Both guns indexed well, that is the hand mechanically rotated the cylinders into the locked position at about the moment the hammer reached full cock. They both also had a tendency to overtime, that is, the hand forced the cylinder locked tightly when the hammer was cocked but let go when the hammer dropped, leaving a fair amount of radial play in the cylinders at the point of firing. Cylinder rotation on each gun was balky as the hammer was being cocked, just as the Russian model had been. Each gun had differences in the trigger pulls, however, both broke at approximately 4 1/2 pounds and only after pulling the triggers through considerable creep.

Sights consist of a simple half-moon-shaped front blade that is pinned into the barrel rib and a rear sight that is formed on the barrel catch. This is a wide U-shaped opening with a smaller U-shaped

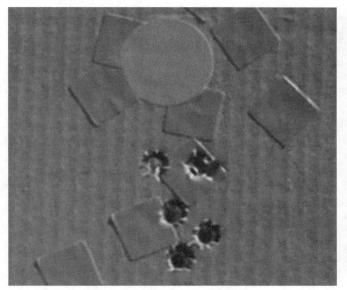 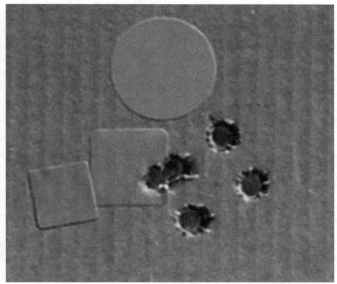

Black Hills .45 Colt cowboy loads produced consistent groups on about 1 1/2 inches from both First (left) and Second Models at 7 yards.

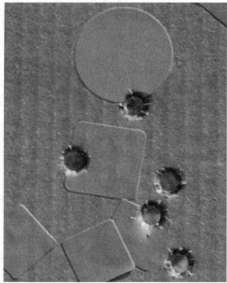
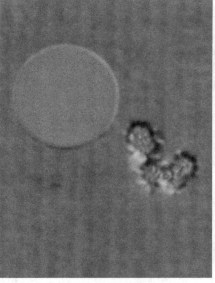
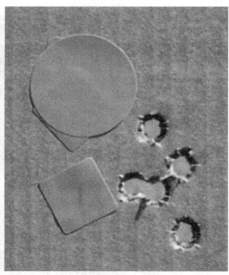

Hornady Cowboy loads produced very different results with the First Model (left) with which it did not agree, and the Second Model which it loved.

Winchester .45 Colt cowboy loads performed well in both guns. This 1 1/2-inch group was fired with the Second Model.

notch at its center. The sight picture was very easy and fast to acquire but if the rear notch had been just a bit wider it would have made for a clearer picture. Of the two revolvers, the First Model offered the clearest sight picture.

In spite of balky cylinder rotation, both guns worked very well throughout the tests, which consisted of a total of slightly more than 100 round each from a variety of three brands of .45 Colt cowboy ammunition: Black Hills, Hornady and Winchester. Both guns shot groups at 7 yards that consistently averaged about 1 1/2 inches with Black Hills to about 2 inches with Winchester ammunition. The First Model Schofield gave us several 2 1/2- to 3-inch groups with the Hornady ammo. On the other hand, the Second Model really seemed to love Hornady's Cowboy loads and that revolver cut several groups that measured just 1 inch, or slightly under using that ammo. We found the First Model printed all its groups about 1 inch low and to the right, while the Second Model printed about 1/2 inch low and slightly right, using a six o'clock hold in all cases. All in all, both guns showed very good to excellent accuracy with all brands of ammunition, but most consistently with Black Hills and Winchester.

What did we think of these newest Uberti Schofields? Well, they are very nicely finished revolvers. They both are really good-looking and good-handling guns no matter how you slice it. To me, of the two, the First Model looks a bit classier, but that's just my opinion. The revolvers were certainly accurate enough to be used as is and showed us

Uberti Schofield specifications	
Bbl. Length:	3 1/2", 5" or 7"
O.A.L.:	3 1/2"- 9 1/4", 5"- 10 3/4", 7"- 12 3/4"
Weight:	3 1/2"- 2 lbs. 2 oz., 5"- 2 lbs. 3 oz., 7"- 2 lbs. 5 oz
Caliber:	.38 Spl. (5" and 7" only), .44-40 or .45 Colt
Chamber mouths	Both guns, average .455"
Bbl. groove diam.	Both guns, average .452"
Retail	$775
From	Stoeger Industries, 17603 Indian Head Hwy., Ste 200, Accokeek, MD 20607 (301 283-6300

the potential of being able to do even better if some gunsmithing work was devoted to the triggers and generally tuning the guns up. This is work that probably should have been done at the factory. In comparing them to originals, there is absolutely no question that the quality of machine work, the degree of hand fitting and finishing were literally world's better on the original than they are on these replicas. Nonetheless, these are good, serviceable revolvers made from modern steels. So if you like the big S&W top-break revolvers and would like one to shoot in cowboy events, give these modern Uberti's a look.

Chapter 4

Rifles of the New West; What's being shot today and where it came from.

From slow-to-load single-shots in various configurations, on through the myriad lever-operated guns and up into the slick Colt Lightning slide-actions, the rifles being used in cowboy events today closely follow the kinds of rifles available to the folks who settled the American west a century or more ago. Some of the rifles being fired in competition are originals manufactured 75 to 125 years ago. The majority, however are of modern manufacture. A large number of these modern rifles are new reproductions of original Winchester, Colt, Sharps and other famous makes, but there are some newly made originals available as well, such as the rugged Marlin lever guns.

It wasn't that many years ago when few replica rifles other than single-shots were available. Thanks to our popular new sport of cowboy action shooting, all that has changed and today we have an ever-expanding line-up of modern-made rifles that are close copies of the originals. The Italians replica arms makers, who are producing the clear majority of these reproduction rifles, are doing a great job. No only are the Europeans producing some fine-looking guns but they are turning out some of the most dependable rifles of their type that have ever been manufactured. That last statement may raise some objections, and more than a few eyebrows. To cite a quick example of this, many years

> ### SIXTY SHOTS PER MINUTE
> # HENRY'S PATENT
> ### REPEATING
> # RIFLE
> ## The Most Effective Weapon in the World.
>
> This Rifle can be discharged 16 times without loading or taking down from the shoulder, or even loosing aim. It is also slung in such a manner, that either on horse or on foot, it can be **Instantly Used**, without taking the strap from the shoulder.
>
> ## For a House or Sporting Arm, it has no Equal;
> #### IT IS ALWAYS LOADED AND ALWAYS READY.
>
> The size now made is 44-100 inch bore, 24 inch barrel, and carries a conical ball 32 to the pound. The penetration at 100 yards is 8 inches; at 400 yards 5 inches; and it carries with force sufficient to kill at 1,000 yards.
>
> A resolute man, armed with one of these Rifles, particularly if on horseback, **CANNOT BE CAPTURED.**
>
> "We particularly commend it for Army Uses, as the most effective arm for picket and vidette duty, and to all our citizens in secluded places, as a protection against guerilla attacks and robberies. A man armed with one of these Rifles, can load and discharge one shot every second, so that he is equal to a company every minute, a regiment every ten minutes, a brigade every half hour, and a division every hour."—*Louisville Journal.*
>
> **Address**   **JNO. W. BROWN,**
>   Gen'l Ag't., Columbus, Ohio,
>   At Rail Road Building, near the Depot.

19th century advertising was wonderfully colorful. Much of it was designed with the gullible in mind. This early advertisement for Henry's rifle makes the bold claim that *"A resolute man, armed with one of these Rifles, particularly if on horseback, CANNOT BE CAPTURED"*

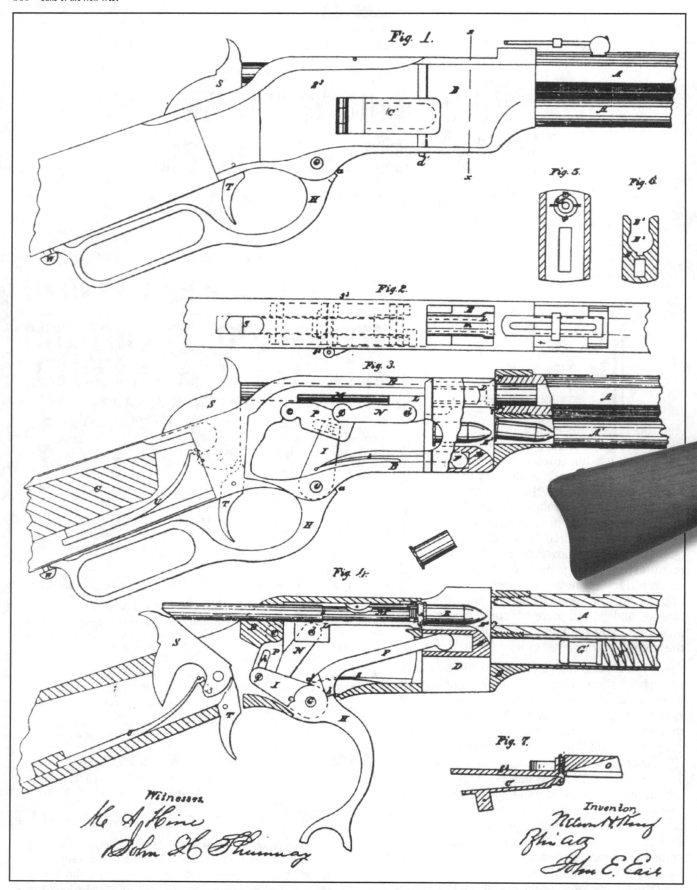

A copy of the King patent for the 1866 Winchester feed system that allowed the rifle's magazine tube to be charged through the sideplate.

ago I used to practice with a Model 1873 Winchester in .44-40 caliber and I can vividly recall that this gun never got through more than about 300 rounds before a spring would break, or the extractor would shear off. Looking back now, it seemed like some part of this classic rifle was almost always in some state of disrepair. That Winchester '73 was a beautiful gun with over 90 percent original finish and a perfect bore, but the truth is it was often broken and did not stand up as well as I would have liked to hard use. Having been a gunsmith for many years, I know that breaking springs and small parts is a fairly normal event, even for these great, 100-year-old rifles. I am not saying these wonderful old Winchesters lack stamina, but in all fairness the world has learned a lot about making springs in the last 100 years.

By way of comparison to the above, I have a good friend who regularly shoots a Uberti replica 1866 in Cowboy events and in well over 25,000 shots he has only had one part fail. That was the spring cover (loading gate) when it lost its spring tension and began to interfere with the smooth loading operation. We also have American companies, such as Marlin, who have been producing rifles of this sort since the 19th century and whose products are of incredibly high quality. Guns like this are also proving to be ultra-dependable, even when put to the steady, heavy use of Cowboy competitions. More to the point, they are standing up to the unbelievably grueling use we all know these guns see during the long practices that lead up to those weekend events.

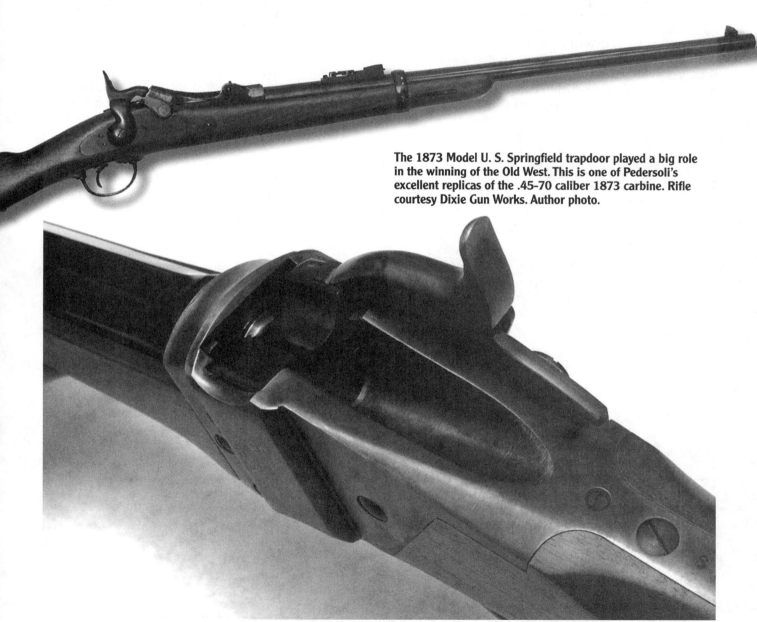

The 1873 Model U. S. Springfield trapdoor played a big role in the winning of the Old West. This is one of Pedersoli's excellent replicas of the .45-70 caliber 1873 carbine. Rifle courtesy Dixie Gun Works. Author photo.

Looking down on the massive action of the Sharps. This rifle is a modern replica made by Pedersoli in Italy, caliber .45-70. Rifle courtesy of Cimarron Firearms. Author photo.

Single-shot rifles just never die

In the Old West a large variety of single-shot, metallic cartridge rifles were available. The design encompasses some of the most accurate and powerful rifles of the day, as well as some of the most simple and trouble-free breech mechanisms ever produced. That last point kept the single-shot rifle popular well after the introduction of powerful, rapid-loading, high-capacity magazine-fed repeating rifles.

We'll start here with the rifle that was not necessarily the first, but is nonetheless always a favorite, the "trapdoor" Springfield. Trapdoor Springfield rifles were actually quite popular on the frontier since the U.S. Army adopted the system, beginning in 1865. That powerful virtue of having been accepted by the Army put the design into use gave it exposure by setting it out quickly into plain sight of people all over the continent. This series of rifles and carbines all stemmed from the Allin conversion of 1866 that was applied to the 1863 Springfield musket. The Allin conversion was a method of making a muzzleloader into a breech-loader by applying a swinging breech-block to the rear of the

muzzle-loading musket barrel. These were initially offered in .50 Government (.50-70) but this was later reduced to .45 caliber. No, it wasn't the strongest of single-shot actions by a far cry, nor was the system noted for excellent extraction. Nevertheless, it's a good-looking design that worked well and it remains popular to this day. There are some fine replica's of the trapdoor Springfield on today's market, such as the carbine replica featured in these pages manufactured by Davide Pedersoli of Italy.

Another very popular, indeed, legendary single-shot rifle was the amazing Sharps rifle. The action design was originally conceived by Christian Sharps in the 1840s and brought to a state of perfection during the 1850s by Richard Lawrence of the Robbins & Lawrence Armory in Vermont. Sharps' rifle was an extremely strong, breech-loading percussion weapon whose breech was closed by a massive falling breech block, which was operated by an under-lever. Sharps rifles and carbines were battle-proven and used extensively by both sides in the American Civil War. As metallic cartridges began to appear, gunsmiths, and the U.S. government arsenals found the Sharps breech-loader could be easily converted and adopted

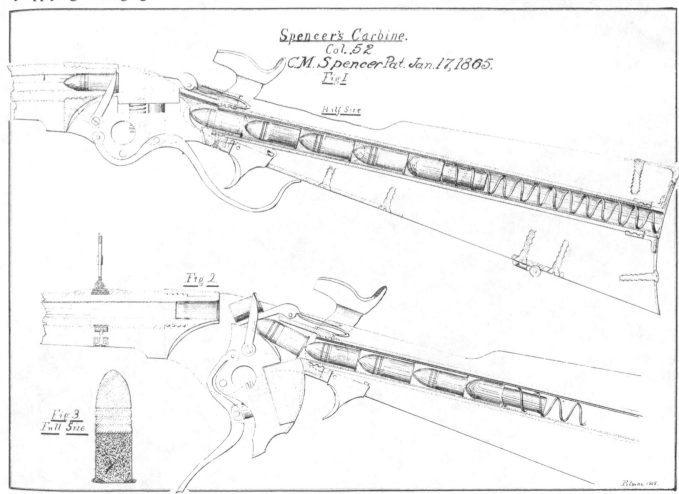

The Spencer carbine and rifle was a metallic-cartridge repeater that saw much use in the Civil War. This great old drawing is one of Brig. General John Pitman's from the 1890s.

The Winchester Model 1885 High-Wall was from a design by John M. Browning. The gun shown here is a high-quality, modern replica in .45-70 caliber made in Italy by Uberti. Photo by Maria Uberti. With permission from Bullet 'N Press.

to this new-fangled metallic cartridge system. By the late 1860s the Sharps factory was producing rifles specifically intended for metallic cartridge use. Even though Sharps went out of business around 1880 the design is one of the most famous and surely one of the most robust single-shot actions ever designed. Today's shooter has a wonderful selection of replica Sharps single-shot rifles to chose from. Some of excellent quality are being made right here in the U.S.A. Others, also of very fine quality, are produced in Italy.

During the latter half of the 19th century Remington also produced many single-shot rifles, undeniably the most famous of those being their incredible rolling-block rifles. This design uses a breech block that literally rolls back to expose the rear of the barrel for loading. It dates from a rolling breech patented by Leonard Geiger in 1863 and later perfected in the late 1860s by Joseph Rider at Remington. Rolling-block rifles are noted for their utter simplicity. While not as strong as the falling-block Sharps, they are certainly much stronger than the trap-door types and they have a somewhat better extraction system. Remington made rolling-blocks in a large array of configurations (rifle, pistol and shotgun) from 1867 right up until 1934. In terms of military rifles alone, they manufactured more than a million. It has been said that in years past recordkeeping was not a high priority. As a result, so many rolling-blocks were produced that to this day nobody is really sure how many Remington may have manufactured. The rolling-block is today being reproduced by Remington here in the U.S.A., and many variations of replica rolling-block rifles are also available from importers.

Winchester purchased John M. Browning's patent for a new single-shot rifle in 1883 and after some refinement the gun hit the streets as the Model 1885 Winchester single-shot. Browning's unique design used a strong falling breech block like the Sharps, but with advanced features like a firing pin

retractor and a lever-cocking, centrally mounted hammer. Browning's nifty new design would also fit into a narrower receiver than the Sharps, all this together made into a very strong, lightweight, even streamlined rifle that was popular from the day it came out until about 1920. Over the years the Winchester 1885 was produced as a "high-wall" or high breech side, chambered in large, powerful rifle calibers as well as in a so-called" low-wall" or low breech side which was chambered for shorter, lower-powered, pistol-size cartridges. Original Winchesters, for the most part, are still quite shootable today and at this time a strong, high-quality modern, American-made replica of the 1885 is available from C. Sharps Arms. An Italian-made replica, also of high quality, is available from Aldo Uberti of Italy. Both weapons use receivers that are forged from 8620 tool steel.

Quite a few other single-shot rifles were available in the 19th century, but they are really too numerous to go deeply into here and it would be of limited value since their rarity, and/or strength would preclude use in modern competition events. Of note were the tilt-barrel single-shot rifles produced by Frank Wesson (one of Daniel's brothers) from about 1859 through 1888. Wesson's tilt-barreled rifles, which were almost all chambered for rimfire calibers, used two triggers, one to open the barrel for loading and a normal, rear trigger to release the hammer. Frank Wesson also produced some extremely strong, very high quality falling-block single-shot rifles from about the mid-1870s through the 1890s, although they are hardly ever encountered. These beautiful rifles were built mainly for long-range target shooting and hunting.

Among the more popular "other" single-shot rifles are the Marlin-Ballard. This interesting single-shot action was the invention of Charles Ballard and it began life as a breech-loading percussion weapon in 1861. By 1864 a convertible, dual-ignition breechblock was invented that enabled it to be fired as a percussion or rimfire metallic cartridge rifle. The rifle was produced by several companies and with only limited success until John M. Marlin, who made the rifle part of his regular line of sporting arms, purchased it. It was at that point the Ballard got "noticed" and became a very popular sporting arm. Marlin produced the Ballard single-shot in a great many forms and calibers both rim-and centerfire, until about 1891.

The famous 1873 Winchester is a rifle whose profile is recognized worldwide. The short rifle version shown here is a modern Uberti-made replica in .44-40 caliber with a color case hardened receiver. Rifle courtesy Stoeger Industries. Author photo.

The famous lever guns

Lever-action repeating rifles that fired metallic cartridges really began in 1860 with B. Tyler Henry's famous repeating rifle and Christian Spencer's repeating rifle. The Spencer was used extensively by the Union during the Civil War, and was available as a carbine or rifle. It was lever-operated and held seven cartridges, that   fed through a tubular magazine concealed

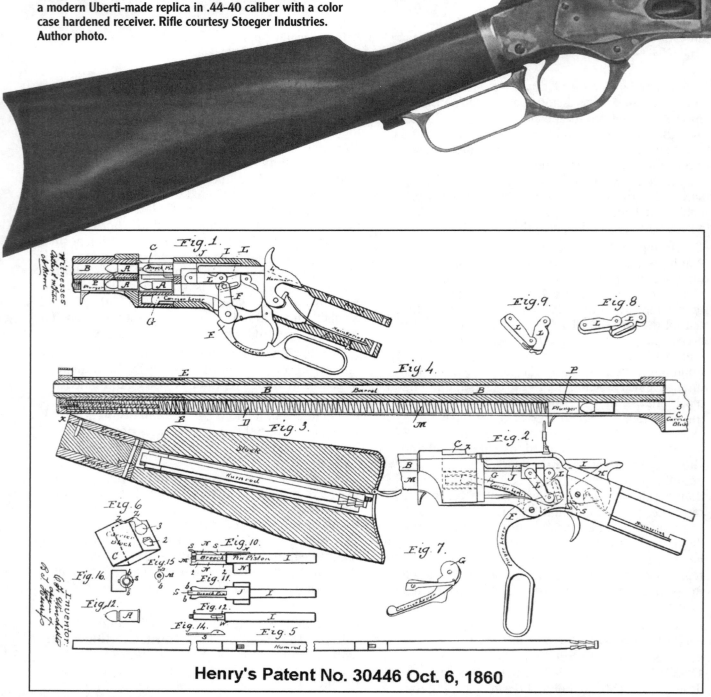

Henry's Patent No. 30446 Oct. 6, 1860

The Henry is the rifle that really started the ball rolling for Winchester. This is a copy of B. T. Henry's original patent filed in 1860.

within the buttstock. Although it proved itself a very rugged and reliable weapon during the war, it did not manage to stay popular in the public eye for very long after the war. Civil War Spencer rifles and carbines were chambered for .52 caliber rimfire cartridges and the government converted many of these after the war to .50 caliber rimfire. Even after being superceded and made obsolete by more modern repeating rifles, the Spencer

Henry, as well as the basic Henry toggle-link action. Coupled with a new brand new loading system invented by King the 1866 allowed the cartridges to be fed in from the side of the receiver through a spring-loaded loading port. King's improvements did away with the handle on the cartridge follower and allowed the magazine tube to be sealed all the way around. A neat wooden forearm was also added to this design, giving the shooter a convenient place to

remained a staple firearm of the American West by virtue of the shear quantities left over from the conflict, about 144,000 in all.

Henry's lever-action was an alteration of an earlier Smith & Wesson design that used a toggle-link action. The S&W had been designed to fire a form of caseless ammunition and because it was very underpowered, the design was altered by Henry to accept metallic cartridges. Henry's rifle was chambered to fire a .44 rimfire cartridge of revolver size and power. It offered the shooter a large magazine capacity; the cartridges being stored and fed from a tube under the barrel. Henry rifles actually saw some service in the civil war where, legend has it, confederate soldiers referred to the Henry as that "Darned Yankee rifle, you could load on Sunday and shoot all week." Although the Henry's wartime use was limited, it fast developed a reputation for murderous firepower and excellent reliability. The Henry had its drawbacks. One of which was the lack of a forearm. When the barrel got hot, the gun became difficult to hold onto. Another inconvenience was the magazine follower whose handle stuck out through a slot in the bottom of the magazine and followed the cartridges rearward as the magazine was emptied. The slot often allowed the entrance of dirt and foreign matter into the magazine, and if the shooter forgot to move his hand out of the way, the follower would be stopped. Then, of course, so would cartridge feeding. The Henry was produced from 1860 through 1866 with about 14,000 manufactured. Finely made replicas of the Henry are made today by A. Uberti. Many are imported by Dixie Gun Works. Uberti's modern replicas are chambered in calibers which are easy to obtain off the shelf such as .44 S&W Special, .44 WCF and .45 Colt.

Oliver Winchester, the major investor in Henry's rifle company, took full control of the venture in 1866. He introduced the first of the now world-famous line of repeating rifles, the model 1866 Winchester. Sometimes called the "Yellow Boy," Winchester's 1866 used a brass action like the

grasp the front of the rifle without the chance of being burned.

The new Winchester rifle was an instant success around the world and immigrating settlers heading off to discover a new frontier carried countless thousands into the American West. The 1866 was offered in carbine, sporting rifle and musket configurations. In all about 170,000 of the Model 1866 Winchester lever-actions were manufactured from 1866 up through 1898. A. Uberti of Italy also produces a very popular replica of the 1866 Winchester and these are available in a carbine, short rifle or a full-length sporting rifle. The original 1866 was only available in .44 Rimfire Henry caliber, with a very few made in .44 CF. The modern-made counterpart offers a much wider variety and is available in calibers .32 WCF, .38 S&W Special, .38 WCF, .44 S&W Special, .44 WCF and .45 Colt.

Winchester followed up the success of the 1866 with a new rifle in 1873. This was really a refined 1866, and it retained the famous toggle-link action operation of the Henry. However the receiver of the Model '73 was made from iron and was also slightly larger to accept a more powerful new centerfire cartridge, the .44 WCF or as it has come to be known, the .44-40 Winchester. Not long after the introduction of the 1873 model, Winchester introduced the calibers .32 WCF and .38 WCF for the 1873 model and in 1884 they even offered a .22 rimfire version. Like the previous model, the 1873 was also manufactured as a carbine, sporting rifle and as a musket. The '73 was a very popular model for the Winchester company with about 720,000 Model 1873s manufactured from 1873 to well up into the 20th century in 1919. Today we are fortunate to have a fine replica 1873 manufactured in Italy by A. Uberti that is sold in the United States by several importers including Stoeger Industries. The Uberti '73 is available in carbine, short rifle and sporting rifle configurations and comes in calibers .32 WCF, .38 S&W Special, .38 WCF, .44 S&W Special, .44 WCF and .45 Colt.

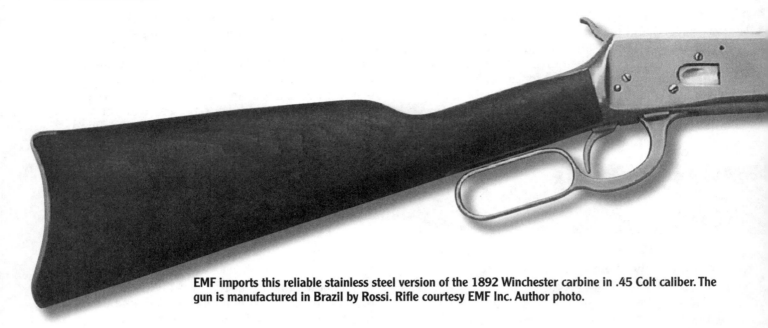

EMF imports this reliable stainless steel version of the 1892 Winchester carbine in .45 Colt caliber. The gun is manufactured in Brazil by Rossi. Rifle courtesy EMF Inc. Author photo.

Introduced during our nation's centennial year, the Model 1876 Winchester lever-action rifle was based on the 1873 design, however it was made proportionately larger in order for it to handle powerful big-game cartridges. These cartridges were physically much larger than the handgun rounds chambered in the 1873 model. The '76 was chambered for .40-60, .45-60, .45-75 and .50-95 Winchester calibers. This model was manufactured up to 1897 and about 63,800 were manufactured in carbine, rifle and musket form. The famous Canadian Northwest Mounted Police used 1876 carbines in caliber .45-75. These are highly prized by collectors today.

In 1886 Winchester adopted yet another, much more modern lever-action by purchasing another patent from John M. Browning. After altering the original design somewhat, Winchester introduced their newest large-caliber big-game rifle as their Model 1886. Preserving the Winchester "look" by still using a tube magazine and two-piece stocks, Browning's action was far stronger than the toggle-link pattern used in all Winchester's earlier models. Having a horizontal sliding breech bolt that was locked by two vertical steel bolts, the rifle, although having a large frame, was sleek and streamlined. The '86 was offered in a variety of powerful calibers that ranged from .33 Winchester up to the huge .50-110 Express and including the popular .45-70 Government. Winchester manufactured this model from 1886 through 1935, producing almost 160,000 rifles, carbines and a few muskets. An interesting and rare version of the 1886 is the take-down variation, also introduced with this model. Until recently, Browning and later Winchester (the two now wear the same hat) offered an excellent Japanese-made replica of the 1886 Winchester.

In 1892 Winchester was the successor to the incredible model 1873. This rifle was a simplified and scaled down version of the model 1886 that was built to handle the familiar Winchester handgun sized cartridges such as the .44-40, .32-20 etc. The model of 1892 was destined to be an instant success. This new rifle was streamlined, simple, lightweight and handy, with the carbine version weighing in at just 6 pounds. The 1892's action was also substantially stronger than the 1873 and as with the parent model 1886, its breech bolt was locked closed firmly by two sliding, vertical-locking bolts made from solid steel. Winchester produced over a million model 1892s, right up until 1941, in calibers .44-40, .38-40, .32-20, .25-20, and even a few chambered for the .218 Bee. With so many of this model manufactured, the 1892 was popular all over the world and had a habit of turning up everywhere. Astute western historians will often find model 1892s were used in early cowboy movies, sometimes they even turned up in movies which were supposed to be set in a time frame before the 1892 was made. Bottom line, the Winchester 1892 was a rugged, dependable rifle and it remains so to this day. Rossi of Brazil is manufacturing an excellent replica of the 1892 that is sold by several U.S. importers, including a stainless steel version from EMF featured in this book.

Winchester was certainly not the only manufacturer of lever-action rifles used in the Old West. Marlin Firearms Co., is still very alive and well today. Marlin was always an innovative gun company. The fact is, if you follow the chronology of Marlin's rifles and when they were introduced, it may start to look like the big guys, namely Winchester, were constantly trying to play a game of catch-up. Marlin started making lever-action rifles in 1881 with the model named after the same year. Andrew

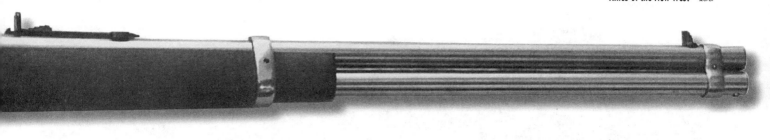

The Marlin 1894 was a competitor of the 1892 Winchester and a very fine gun in its own right. This is an original in .38 WCF caliber, restored by the author in the 1990s. Author photo.

Burgess, John Marlin and other firearms inventors contributed elements of this rifle's design. The 1881 was a big lever-action, chambered for big-game cartridges like the .38-55, .40-60 and .45-70, so it was a direct competitor of the 1876 Winchester, which was not as modern nor as strong as the Marlin.

A series of other rifles followed, most notably the model 1888 which the famous arms inventor Lewis Hepburn had a central role in designing. The Model 1888 was chambered for pistol cartridges like the .44-40, so it was at once in direct competition with the Winchester 1873. Actually, the Model 1888 Marlin was a much stronger and lighter weight gun than the Model 1873. Indeed, it was more modern in every way. This Marlin rifle may well have been what urged Winchester into producing the 1892 Winchester. The 1888 formed the basis for all future center-fire Marlin lever-actions, even the ones they make to this day. Hepburn's action was carried forward into the Marlin line with the introduction of the 1893, a medium-sized lever-action chambered for hunting cartridges like the .30-30, .32-40 and .38-55. Winchester followed suit with Browning's design for the 1894 just a year later. Marlin's successor to the big-bore model 1881 was their own Model 1895, itself an enlarged version of the 1893 but chambered to accept calibers ranging from .33 WCF and .38-56 on up through the powerful .45-90.

Marlin's lever-actions today, as we mentioned above, are all direct descendents of that basic, excellent Lewis Hepburn design stemming from the 1888 Marlin. The modern Marlin Firearms Company makes lever-action rifles and carbines in pistol cartridge size, which today includes the .45 Colt in the revised model 1894, in medium-sized game cartridges like .30-30 and .38-55 as the Model 336 and on the big-bore model 1895 frame, in the time tried .45-70 caliber. Many of us think of Marlin's modern rifles as being not finished as high as some of their competition, but for years they have built a well-deserved reputation for being dependable, accurate hunting rifles and they remain every bit of that. The Marlin is an excellent platform to build on and we have seen, and built, a good many custom Marlin rifles that look, and work every bit as good as any lever-action ever made.

And pumps . . .

We'll end this introduction with what might seem an unlikely rifle maker: Colt Firearms. Now, the Colt Patent Firearms Company was not a stranger to longarms. Colt started with the Paterson rifles, on up to the Model 1855 Revolving Rifle, not to forget about the 100,000 Model 1861 muskets they made for the Union during the Civil War. However, since Colt's primary focus was handguns, and lots of them, that is what the world associates with when

United States Fire Arms in Hartford, Conn. is manufacturing this beautiful replica of the Colt Lightning medium-framed rifle right here in the U.S.A. USFA photo.

the name Colt is mentioned. From the mid-1880s on up through just after the turn of the last century, Colt produced a line of pump-, or slide-action, rifles known as the Lightning. Lightning rifles were made in three distinct frame sizes; small for .22 rimfire caliber, medium for pistol-sized cartridges and the large, or express frame that was built to accept really big-bore cartridges that ranged from .38-56 up through .50-95 Express. Colt made about 90,000 of the small frames, roughly 84,000 medium-framed

rifles and nearly 6,500 of the large-framed guns. These were very well made rifles and they were in every way excellent competition for Winchester. A high quality, modern, American-made replica of the medium-framed Colt Lightning rifle is now being introduced by United States Fire Arms Company of Hartford, Conn. It will be made in both carbine and rifle form. The USFA version will be available chambered for .38-40 Winchester, .44-40 Winchester or .45 Colt calibers.

Cimarron Sharps 1874

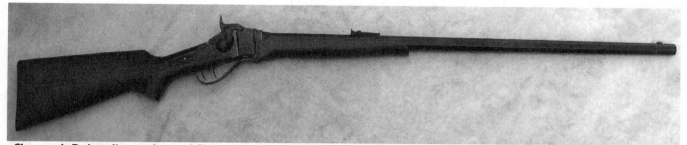

Cimarron's Pedersoli-manufactured Sharps is a very good-looking and close replica of the original, but what is more important, it shoots! Rifle courtesy of Cimmaron Firearms. Author photos.

Of all the rifle names in the world, probably the most easily recognized, next to Kalashnikov or Winchester, is the amazing Sharps rifle. It is truly the stuff that legends were made of. Christian Sharps originally designed the single-shot Sharps action in the 1840s. Richard Lawrence took the action to perfection during the 1850s. The Sharps rifle was an extremely strong, breech-loading action that started life as a percussion weapon. Its breech was shut by a huge falling breechblock that was operated by a finger lever. Sharps rifles and carbines were used extensively and proved in battle by both sides in the American Civil War. As metallic cartridges appeared, gunsmiths, and U.S. government arsenals saw that Sharps' breech-loader was easy to convert to accept metallic cartridges. The Sharps factory in Bridgeport, Conn. was manufacturing rifles specifically intended for metallic cartridge use shortly after the Civil War ended. The great Sharps company went out of business about 1880, but the design is one of the most famous ever built, certainly it is one of the strongest single-shot actions ever designed. Today, the cowboy shooter has a good selection of replica single-shot rifles built on the Sharps-designed action. Some are being made right here in America; others also of very high quality, are being manufactured in Italy.

We had the opportunity to test one of Cimarron's Model 1874 Sharps No. 1 Sporting Rifles; what they call the Silhouette model. This model is a more basic rifle than many. It comes from the factory furnished with plain, unchecked walnut stocks and barrel-mounted, open hunting sights. Our rifle is in .45-70 caliber and has a 32-inch tapered octagon barrel that measures .885" across the flats at the muzzle. The Silhouette model receiver, lever and hammer are finished in color case hardening, while the barrel, butt plate, breech bolt and sights are finished in blue. The two-piece, dark walnut stocks are finished in oil. It may interest the reader that other than the maker's and importer's name and address and the caliber, which are located on the lower barrel flat forward of the forearm wood, there are no apparent markings on the barrel. The receiver is marked with the Italian governments proofs on the left side on the barrel ring area. Other than this there are no other markings on the receiver except the serial number, which is on the upper tang like an original Sharps.

The right side of the Cimarron Sharps action showing off the nice case colors and double-set triggers.

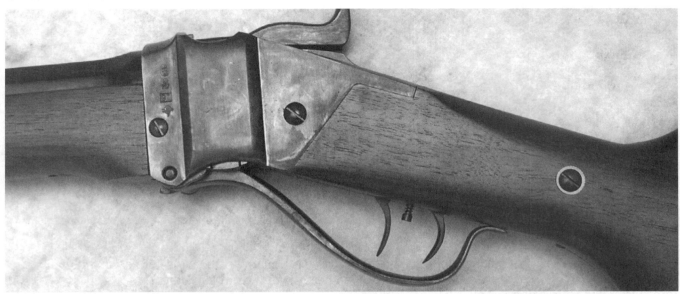

Looking closely at the left side we see the Italian government proof markings, these are the only external marks on the action other than the serial numbers on the upper tang. Notice the nice wood-to-metal fit-up.

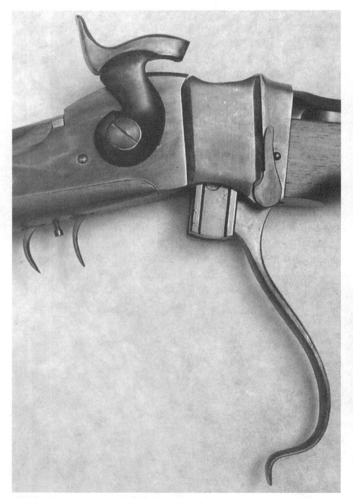

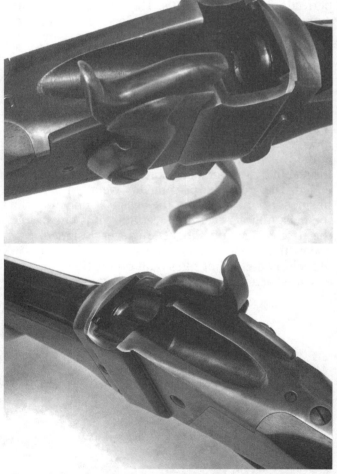

With the action opened the bottom of that massive breech block can be seen. One of the original Sharps features is a quick and simple take down. That small lever on the front of the action, just above the finger lever is for take down, when that one piece is removed, all the action guts may be taken out the bottom of the frame.

These photos show the Sharps action in open and closed poses. Viewed from the top, they give you an idea of how massive that Sharps breech block really is. The large U-shaped cutout you see in the action top is the cartridge loading tray.

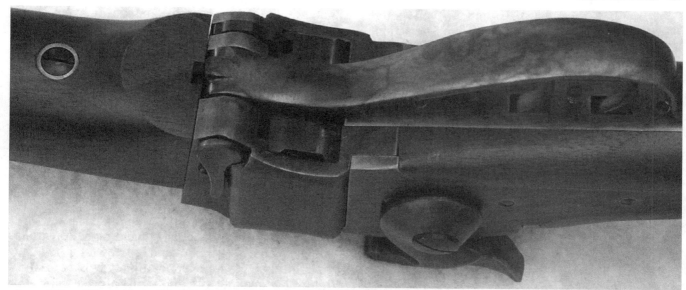

A good view of the bottom of the Sharps action with the breech shut. The darker part, just above the lever and in the hinge, is the bottom of the extractor. The hinge pin (lower center) is the pivot point for every internal moving part in the action itself.

This is a close-up view of the take down lever on the right side of the Sharps action. One of the original, excellent Sharps features is easy disassembly.

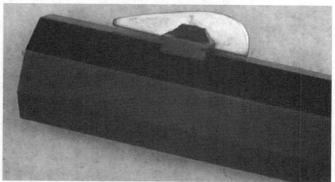

This is the Rocky Mountain style front sight, a nice touch and very traditional.

A ladder sight, graduated to 800 yards, is mounted in a barrel dovetail. The lower sight offered the shooters an excellent sight picture. The sight had good, firm detents and it did not flop around during the test firing.

The quality of the finish work is excellent, with good professional-looking prep work going into the barrel before it was blued, leaving sharp octagon flats and smooth, flat surfaces. The color case hardening is likewise excellent, and although I cannot say for sure if it was done using the old bone and charcoal method, it could have been; the colors look that good. All the screws in the action and stock are nitre blued (that lovely old translucent blue-of-blues). They have nice narrow old-time screwdriver slots and they are correctly shaped; domed. The butt stock is equipped with a pistol grip and the butt is shotgun style with a steel butt-plate with an inletted top-tang. Double-set triggers cap off this rig and the length of pull from the center of the front trigger to the center of the buttplate is 14 1/2 inches. The plain walnut forearm is about 10 1/2 inches long with a semi-Schnabel shaped tip. It is fastened to the barrel with two machine screws. Wood-to-metal fit-up is all around very good, not perfect but for the most part they have about 95 percent contact with some tiny gaps. The wood has also been left a bit "proud" (higher than the metal).

Action operation was very smooth even though this rifle has a very heavy lever spring. The action was positive. It opened and closed readily and paused in both positions correctly. One has to overcam the lever slightly, that is, open it more than is required to open the bolt, in order to fully operate the extractor. The double set triggers worked out very well. When un-set, the front trigger had a heap-'o-creep and a very long, double stage pull that finally cracked at almost 8 pounds. When the rear trigger was set, that big Sharps hammer fell off at a very crisp and quick 1 pound with absolutely no creep. Neither shooter liked this very much, and for safety's

Here is what the double set triggers look like, the screw at the center adjusts the amount of sear contact with the hammer, governing the amount of creep and to some extent, the weight of the trigger pull.

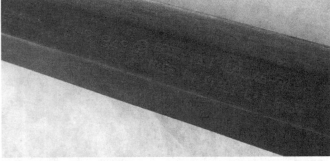

These markings, located on the lower barrel flat just forward of the forearm, are the only markings on the barrel.

sake we decided to reset the adjustment screw so the trigger would have just a little bit of creep. Doing this increased the let off to about 2 pounds for the shooting tests. We thought that would be a more practical weight and that idea proved itself out. This Pedersoli version of the Sharps also has a spring-loaded firing pin that retracts as the hammer is pulled back away from it. The hammer was nicely checkered in the original pattern although it was not quite as sharp as we would have expected. Not that this would bother things much, the upward angle of that big Sharps hammer spur would probably give the shooter ample purchase, even with no checkering.

I enjoy looking over guns that Mike Harvey (Cimarron's owner) has had something to do with. Mike has an eye for detail and is known for being thoughtful about not overlooking really important things; like making sure the sights are useable. Sights on the Cimarron Sharps Silhouette model are open and barrel-mounted and the upper receiver tang is pre-drilled and tapped so it can quickly accept a tang-mounted rear sight. The front sight is a typical Rocky Mountain-style, mounted on the barrel in a dovetail with a long, brass blade. The rear is a barrel-mounted ladder type sight, also in a dovetail and graduated out to 800 yards. The rear sight notch (folded down) is an easy-to-acquire ultra-wide U with a sharply cut smaller U at and below its center. This combination offered what turns out to be an excellent sight picture, even in the very bright sunlight and one that is very quick for the eye to pickup when the gun is fired offhand. When the ladder was lifted up, the sight picture was similar, but not nearly as sharp. We decided to use the sight in the down position for our shooting and the sights were left where the factory set them.

We test fired the Cimarron Sharps using Black Hills .45-70 ammo. These are 405-grain lead bullets with flat noses. We also tried out some of Winchester's 300-grain soft-point hunting ammunition with surprisingly good results.

The shooter is Ed Wade and he's just finished shooting a tiny, 5/8-inch group with the Winchester 300-grain soft points.

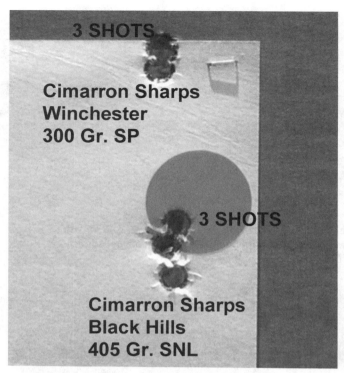

The small upper group was fired with the Winchester 300-grain soft-point .45-70 ammo. The lower group is typical of the good groups we got with Black Hills 405-grain loads.

Cimarron Sharps specs	
Model	**1874 No. 1 Sporting Rifle,** Silhouette Model
Caliber:	.45-70, .50/70
Barrel Length:	32" heavy octagon
Weight:	10.57 Lbs (45-70)
Frames:	Forged steel, color case hardened
Stocks:	Straight grip, semi-crescent butt plate, deluxe walnut with hand checkered grip and fore end, silver Hartford style nose cap, hand rubbed oil finish, extra fancy wood available at extra cost.
Finish:	Standard blue barrel with case hardened frame, lever, and butt plate.
Retail:	Starting at: $1350
From:	Cimarron Firearms, 105 Winding Oak, Fredericksburg, TX 78624 (830) 997-9090 fax (830) 997-0802 on the Internet at www.cimarron-firearms.com

Cimarron says *"Our barrel features cut rifling, lapped and polished for maximum accuracy."* Well, the targets will tell the rest of the story. At 10 1/2 pounds this rifle was heavy enough that even with the Winchester ammo, which was considerably warmer than the Black Hills ammunition, the shooter-sensed recoil was actually rather mild. We fired three-shot groups at 25 yards. Exactly the range we used for all the rifles in this book. Interestingly, the target results we got in this test were very, very similar to the results we got with the Uberti Model 1885, also in .45-70 caliber. With Black Hills ammunition, the groups were very consistent at around 1 inch, with a few going into 3/4 inch center-to-center. The rifle shot almost perfectly to the sights with this 405-grain lead bullet, placing the groups uniformly about 1/2 inch to the left.

We discovered that the rifle loved the hotter Winchester 300-grain soft-point ammunition. It kept dumping three-shots into one hole that was about 5/8 of an inch center-to-center. Using the same six o'clock hold, the Winchester ammo groups printed about 2 1/2 inches high and slightly to the left of center. The test target shown is after firing about 40 shots with each brand and this target was shot with a very hot, dirty barrel. We also fired a few rounds offhand and much more casually, at a 4-inch steel gong which we had set out at the 100-yard marker.

In this informal test we were able to hit the gong near its center 14 out of 15 times. The final shot also hit the gong, but the hit was up near its top edge.

Here is what we really think. Cimarron Firearms, in its Internet advertising, tells us, *"You could spend hundreds more and would not have a better shooting long-range rifle than the Cimarron."* This is truth in advertising; they are giving you the real skinny. This rifle has what Cimarron is describing as a basic, shooter's finish, yet we found it to be better finished than many higher-end factory rifles. The gun's manufacturer, Pedersoli, has done a really great job here, and I am referring to the work done both on the inside and the outside. The action operated perfectly throughout the tests and the rifle shot two different brands (and types) of factory ammunition extremely well. The "basic" open sights offered with the rifle gave us excellent results and show a darned good sight picture. Again, like the 1885 Uberti we tested, this is obviously a rifle that has greater potential. It makes us curious as to what it might be able to do with a set of really high-precision vernier tang and globe front sights. This Sharps replica was an excellent, useable, working rifle, that impressed everyone at the range who saw and handled it. It was all of that right out of the box, with no additional work required; other than to swab the barrel clean before we shot it.

Trapdoor Springfield, Model 1873 Carbine

The Pedersoli replica of the 1873 U. S. Springfield .45 caliber carbine is amazingly well-made and faithful to the original in almost all respects. Rifle courtesy of Dixie Gun Works. Author photos.

Springfield Trapdoor rifles and carbines started with something called the Allin conversion of 1866. This was a conversion of the Civil War Springfield .58 caliber rifle-musket into a single-shot, breech-loading, metallic cartridge rifle. This feat was accomplished by cutting away a section from the top rear portion of the muzzle-loading musket barrel, then adding a hinge and a cam-locked swinging breech block. These conversion rifles were initially chambered for a cartridge called the .50 Government (.50-70) caliber by sleeving the original .58 caliber rifle-musket barrels.

The U.S. Army adopted the system in 1866 and by 1873 the caliber was reduced to .45 with 70 grains of powder. Also by 1873 the rifles were being produced with new receivers made for this purpose and that used screwed on barrels instead of being converted from percussion rifles. Acceptance by the Army assured that the trapdoor design was exposed to people all over the American West, where it soon became a familiar and popular rifle. It was the Springfield Model 1873 carbine that most of 7th Cavalry carried at the battle of the Little Big Horn. The 7th had received their first model 1873 carbines

With the action open you can see how this design came from the early efforts to find an inexpensive way to convert existing Civil War muzzleloaders into metallic cartridge breech-loaders.

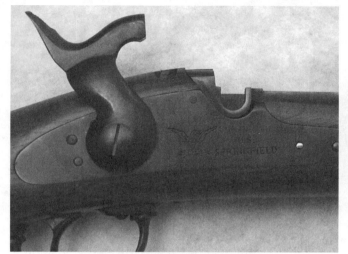

The Pedersoli lock-plate displays the Eagle and U.S. Springfield markings that are quite similar to the originals.

Looking down at the bolt in the closed position we also get a good look at the saddle ring and bar.

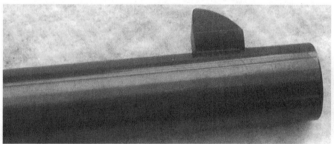

The replica front sight is one piece, apparently a casting. Original fronts were a separate blade that was pinned in place on the sight base.

The rear sight looks very similar to an original but it is a casting, finished in matte blue, the sight picture it presents is, much like the originals, not very practical. What the photo does not show is that the leaf is graduated on its right leg.

in June, 1874 as replacements for their Civil War-vintage Sharps and Spencer carbines. The U. S. Army continued to use this single-shot design until 1892 when it adopted the .30 caliber bolt-action Krag. Even then many thousands of trapdoor Springfields were carried to Cuba in 1898 and used in the Spanish-American war. Something over half a million rifles, carbines and even some shotguns were produced by Springfield Armory using the trapdoor system during the period from 1865 through 1890.

The trapdoor action was far from being the strongest of the available single-shot actions. In the 1860s through the 1880s the Sharps held that title. Erskine Allin's trapdoor action was not noted for its excellent extraction either. But after its bugs were worked out, the design worked well, looked good and it remains popular to this day. Springfield Armory manufactured approximately 73,000 of the

Model 1873 as rifles with barrels 32 5/8 inches long, as carbines with 22-inch barrels and half-length forearms and as cadet rifles which used a 29 1/2-inch barrel.

Our replica 1873 Springfield carbine is chambered in .45-70 Government caliber. It came to us from Dixie Gun Works and Davide Pedersoli of Italy manufactured the gun. This good-looking replica has a blued barrel and lock, a case hardened breechblock, walnut stock equipped with a saddle bar and ring. We had the opportunity to compare this replica to an original Springfield 1873 carbine that was in the shop at the time and I have to say the Pedersoli replica is in almost all respects a very faithful duplication of the real deal. The only blatantly obvious difference is the front sight, which is made as one piece on the replica where the original used a separate blade pinned unto a base on the barrel.

Here the bolt is flopped all the way open, the lever at the top is the opening lever that operates the locking cam in the rear of the bolt.

The buttplate, like the breech bolt, is very nicely color case hardened with pleasing, original looking colors. Notice the excellent wood-to-metal fit-up.

Pedersoli's trapdoor is blue all over, except for the breech block and butt plate. The blueing itself is of a modern, hot-caustic type but the quality of the preparatory polish work was truly excellent, leaving sharp, crisp corners and lettering. The work is so good that the overall appearance of the metal is truly excellent. The factory did a very professional job. Color case hardening on the breech block and butt plate is also quite lovely and appears as though it was done with the old bone and charcoal process. The left side of the receiver is stamped with Italian government proof markings and the importer's name and address (Dixie Gun Works), while the barrel's left side, just under the rear sight, is stamped with the manufacturer's name and country of origin, and the caliber .45-70. The stock is one-piece walnut, which is relatively straight-grained and appears to be American walnut finished in linseed oil. The wood itself is dark and apparently without any stain. A carbine-style steel buttplate, beautifully color case hardened, caps off the stock. Metal parts are fitted into the wood with great precision, leaving wood-to-metal fit-ups that are about perfect. In most areas, Pedersoli has left the wood a bit "proud," that is, standing higher than the metal, as they did with the original rifles. In my opinion, this is impressively good woodwork for a production-line rifle made in this day and age.

Sights on the trapdoor carbine are of the original pattern but aren't precisely like the originals. For one thing, the front sight on originals was a separate blade pinned into a base fixed onto the barrel. The replica uses a one-piece front sight that is apparently a casting. The rear sight fits the original pattern but also appears to be a casting, or assembled from castings. Both sights were finished in a flat, matte blue. The sight picture, while very quickly acquired, was very indistinct. The rear sight is a very wide angled V with a rounded bottom, the front is an inverted V with a flattened top and neither was sharply defined.

The action on the trapdoor was typical of the type. Like an original, cocking the hammer with that massive mainspring requires considerable effort on the part of the shooter. These hammers have three "clicks" or positions. The first is the safety position (Of course, this is not actually a safe way to carry these guns if they are loaded. The only truly safe method to carry a trapdoor Springfield is to unload it first and carry it empty.) The second click is the loading position. This leaves the hammer far enough back so the breech bolt can be opened but not quite far enough to be the fully cocked position; which would be the third click. Operation of the breech bolt was smooth and positive even if the bolt seemed a bit on the loose-wobbly side while it was open. It did lock shut tightly. Extraction was good, with the shells being "sprung" back into the feed tray as the bolt reached it farthest open position. Original Springfield rifles used a one-piece firing pin. The Pedersoli uses a two-piece firing pin. The front firing pin section is spring-loaded so it retracts when the hammer is pulled back, but it is not a rebounding pin. Trigger pull was in two stages. The first one included a long period of creep that ended in a slight bump and abruptly finishing in a relatively crisp break at just a hair over 4 1/2 pounds. The lock time seemed a bit slow, in spite of the aggressive mainspring tension. This is because the arc that big hammer has to fall through is quite a long one. Remember, it's a leftover from the musket days.

We fired about 40 rounds through the trapdoor, this consisted of about 35 shots with Black Hills .45-70 and only five of the Winchester 300-grain soft-point ammo. The latter were showing us some pressure signs that made us wonder if it wasn't a bit on the hot side for this rifle, so we discontinued its use. The Black Hills ammo was milder and we ran the accuracy tests with it exclusively. Recoil from the little carbine was moderately heavy with the mild

Trapdoor parts, 1873 Pedersoli carbine Illustration used with permission from VTI Gun Parts

2	Hammer	58	Butt plate	95	Firing pin spring	357	Tang
3	Barrel	60	Trigger guard	97	Breech block	362	Hammer screw
10	Trigger	63	Tang screw	98	Firing pin	363	Sear screw
15	Front sight	64	Trigger plate screw	109	Cam latch screw	365	Bridle screw
19	Sear spring	66	Saddle ring bar	112	Stirrup screw	421	Extractor-retractor pin
20	Mainspring	66a	Saddle ring	115	Stirrup	429	Extractor pin spring
26	Trigger plate	67	Rear firing pin	122	Band spring	502	Front lock plate screw
30	Rear firing pin screw	72	Cam latch	174	Sear	504	Butt plate screw
35	Sear spring screw	72a	Cam latch spring	176	Ejector stud	609	Rear sight screw
36	Mainspring catch	73	Lock plate	215	Ejector screw	632	Trigger screw
36a	Mainspring catch pin	79	Extractor	239	Trigger guard screw	639	Thumb piece
55	Rear sight	80	Front band	296	Tumbler		
57	Stock	83	Hinge pin	352	Bridle		

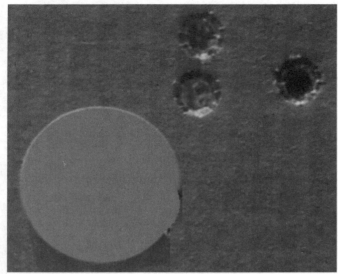

This is typical of the three-shot groups, averaging about 1 inch with Black Hills ammunition.

1873 Trapdoor carbine specs	
Model	CRO750
Barrel Length	22"
Overall length	40 1/2"
Weight	7 lbs.
Finish	Blue and color case hardened
Stocks	One-piece walnut
Caliber	.45-70 Government
Retail	$799
From	Dixie Gun Works, Gunpowder lane, Union City, TN 38271 (800) 238-6785 fax (731) 884-0440

Black Hills ammunition, but it was almost punishing with the hotter Winchester shells. Fired from a sand bag rest at 25 yards, the Winchester ammo put one three-shot group into about an inch and a quarter. We did not fire a second group owing to our concerns about this ammo possibly being a bit too hot for the rifle. Black Hills 405-grain lead ammunition turned in several groups that averaged at just about 1 inch. This is saying something because, in practice, the sight picture on this carbine was terrible and made even worse by the glare of a bright, sunny day. Both of us had serious doubts about being able to shoot a consistent group because of that. All the groups printed about 1 inch high and 1 inch to the right at this distance. The overall performance of this gun was very good. All areas of its action performed without any difficulties through the test process.

Our thoughts on the Pedersoli replica 1873 Trapdoor are that it is a strikingly good-looking replica in almost every respect. It performed very well during our tests and showed potential for good accuracy. Except for the hard recoil we got from the Winchester ammo, the gun was a pleasure to shoot. One thing the gun does need if it is to be seriously shot, are good sights. The sights that come with the gun could, and should be improved upon. The trapdoor design was never a particularly strong action, the strength factor is certainly improved by the fact that the replica is built from modern, heat-treated steels, but it still has it weaknesses. In all fairness then, the limitations of the trapdoor action may have been showing themselves when fired with the more modern Winchester jacketed soft-point ammunition and I think my recommendation would be to stick with milder factory (like Black Hills) or handloaded ammunition in a load that is easier on the action. And finally, this is a well-built and exceptionally nicely crafted replica that, within limitations and with some improved sights, would make a wonderful shooter. As for appearance, right out of the box this is one gun that you won't have to be ashamed to show off at the range.

The 1885 Single Shot

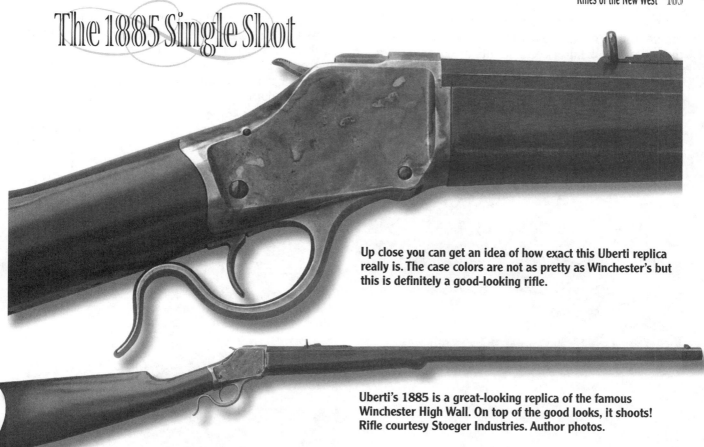

Up close you can get an idea of how exact this Uberti replica really is. The case colors are not as pretty as Winchester's but this is definitely a good-looking rifle.

Uberti's 1885 is a great-looking replica of the famous Winchester High Wall. On top of the good looks, it shoots! Rifle courtesy Stoeger Industries. Author photos.

The original Model 1885 Winchester single-shot rifle was designed in 1878 and sold by John M. Browning at the Browning Brothers shop in Utah. In the early 1880s it was "discovered" by a Winchester sales representative. In 1883 Winchester bought the Browning patent and soon began manufacturing the rifle as their Model 1885 single-shot. This excellent rifle action was, like the famous Sharps single-shot, an ultra-strong falling-block action. The differences between the Sharps and the Browning designs were very easy to spot, the Browning was sleek and slimmed down. It had no separate sideplate and its hammer, mounted in the center of the action, was cocked automatically as the action was closed.

Winchester continued its production through 1920, offering a wide array of variants and options. The rifle was made in High Wall configuration for large, powerful calibers and as the Low Wall, suitable for pistol calibers. It was also offered in a huge selection of calibers that ranged from .22 short rimfire up to a massive .50 caliber centerfire cartridge. There was even a 20-gauge shotgun offering. Winchester produced something over 100,000 single-shot rifles, carbines, muskets and a few shotguns on this classic Browning action design. The excellent 1885 action, especially the High Wall, has been a favorite of single-shot rifle builders for many years.

The Italian arms manufacturer Aldo Uberti introduced a version of the Model 1885 High Wall and Low Wall rifles several years ago and I have been fortunate enough to have several examples in my hands over the last few years. Our test 1885 is from Stoeger Industries and is the 30-inch barreled sporting rifle in .45-70 caliber. The 1885 is finished

Looking at the underside of the action, everything here is color case hardened. The maker has done a good job. We did notice the wood-to-metal fit, while very good, was not perfect.

with color case hardened receiver, breech block, hammer, trigger, and lever. Uberti is proud of the fact that all of those latter components are forged from super-tough No. 8620 steel alloy. The barrel, sights and buttplate are blued by modern methods and with what is obviously good metal preparation. Although the barrel flats were just a tad over-polished, the fairly heavy, tapered octagon barrel still retains a very pleasing appearance. Color case hardening on the receiver and small parts is quite attractive and offers a great contrast between the blued barrel and red-brown wood. It's not the traditional bone and charcoal type, being much more subdued and having more of a gray tone than the original Winchester rainbow colors.

Our 1885 is stocked in walnut and the patterns of the original rifles have been closely adhered to. Wood-to-metal fit is very good. It might be better but

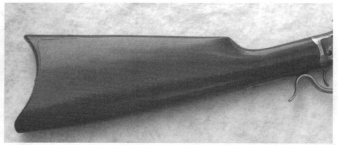

The buttstock on Uberti's 1885 is very pleasingly shaped and nicely finished to look like the original.

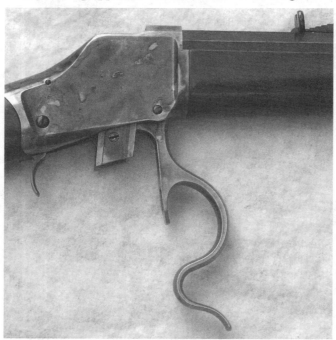

Opened up, the 1885 action is simplicity itself. This sporting rifle is equipped with standard, hunting type open sights but options are available.

Here is a look at the coil-type main spring that powers the hammer. This is a copy of the late model Winchester High Wall main spring.

The patent markings on the lower tang are a duplicate of the original Browning dates.

In the buttplate you will find this great Winchester-type sliding trapdoor to conceal the cleaning rod in the butt.

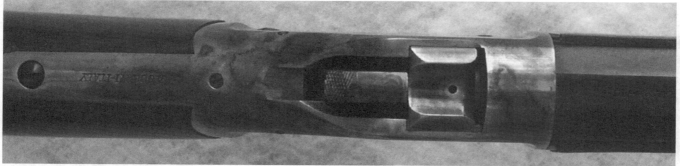

The view from the top shows the nicely cut checkering on the hammer spur. Notice the gas vent hole in the top of the breech block.

Uberti Model 1885 Single Shot Parts

1	Frame	79	Extractor	177	Block pin	363	Sear spring screw
2	Hammer	89	Lever	178	Hammer pin	449	Link pin
3	Barrel	92	Right lever spring	199	Sear pin	617	Link
10	Trigger	95	Firing pin spring	182	Tenon	661	Firing pin bearing
15	Sight	97	Breech block	183	Forend screw		screw
19	Trigger spring	98	Firing pin	217	Butt plate gate	662	Lever spring tenon
20	Mainspring	99	Trigger pin		assembly		
26	Triggerguard	101	Lever screw	231	Butt plate gate spring		
35	Trigger spring screw	107	Lever pin	232	Butt plate gate screw		
55	Rear assembly	119	Rear screw	245	Bushing		
57	Buttstock	124	Lever spring screw	294	Knock-off		
58	Butt plate	129	Firing pin bearing				
61	Rear sight windage	167	Trigger guard screw				
62	Butt plate screw	172	Fore end cap				
63	Tang screw	174	Sear				
68	Fore end	175	Sear spring				

Two very careful and well known shooters, Ed Wade (top) and Tommy Abernathy tried out the Uberti 1885; both men walked away from the range wanting to buy the rifle!

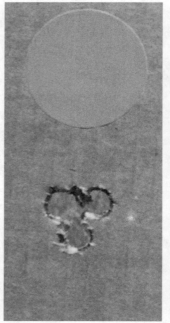

▲ With the very tame Black Hills 405-grain lead bullet loads, we obtained several three-shot groups at 25 yards that looked like this. It seems that no matter how many groups we fired, nor how hot the barrel became, the pattern would not grow any bigger, though a few were smaller!

▲▲ Winchester's 300-grain soft-point ammunition, noticeably a hotter load than the Black Hills, performed exceptionally well in this rifle, giving each shooter tiny three-shot groups almost just like this one.

I may be too fussy. My complaints come from paper-thin gaps in only a couple of spots at the tangs. For the most part the fit-up is excellent. For some reason this rifle had a longer length of pull than most production rifles. At 14 1/2 inches the stock fit me, and one of the other tall shooters, perfectly. On its back, the buttstock is nicely capped with a crescent rifle-style buttplate that has a nice reverse curve at the toe, making for a very comfortable fit on the shoulder. The buttplate is also equipped with a neat Winchester-style sliding trapdoor, in which one might store a multi-piece cleaning rod. A rounded, modified Schnabel forend is held in place with one screw and by the inletting at the face of the action, like the original 1885. The wood was well filled and finished in a stained, varnish-like clear finish. My guess is its some sort of sanded-in varnish or polyurethane. At any rate, it presents a darned good appearance and the color looks like the original Winchesters.

This is the Sporting Rifle model, so it comes equipped with basic sporting or hunting-type open sights, which are also very close duplications of earlier Winchester sights. The rear copying the 3-C type open sight, adjustable for elevation with a sliding, stepped elevator, while the front sight is a close copy of the Winchester Type 21, a plain post with a set-screw in its base to hold it from sliding side to side.

Uberti has altered the firing pin to a more modern, small diameter, free-floating type and the face of the breech block is fitted with a removable firing pin bushing that contains the new pin and its return spring. Winchester's firing pin retractor is still on the link, but its only remaining function is to lift the hammer up slightly off the firing pin as the action is opened. The only objection I had to that is when the lever is closed it leaves the hammer at the half cock position, rather than fully cocking the arm. This won't bother hunters. It's actually a safety feature but it may be a waste of time for competition shooters who are used to the Winchester's self-cocking feature.

The internal parts of this Uberti replica (other than the exceptions noted) look remarkably like Winchester might have made them, and that is a compliment. There is one other variation from Winchester. Uberti is using the late High Wall-type coiled main spring to tension the hammer, but strangely, they have retained the early 1885 leaf spring mounted under the barrel to tension the lever. An unusual combination, but it obviously works, as the photos of those wonderfully small groups show.

Action operation was excellent. The lever worked the breech block smoothly and positively with the extractor pulling the case out just enough into the

1885 specs	
Type:	Breech Loading, single shot
Caliber:	.30/30, .45/70
Barrel Length:	30", 32"
Total Length:	47" (bbl 30")
Weight:	9.92 lbs. (bbl 30")
Barrel:	Octagonal tapered
Frame/Lever:	Forged steel, color case-hardened
Stock/Forend:	English style, walnut (Sporting) Pistol grip, checkered, walnut (Special Sporting)
Optional Sights:	Mid-range Vernier adjustable Creedmore or Lyman adjustable Creedmore
348800 - 1885 High-Wall Single Shot Sporting Rifle 30" $850 348918 - 1885 High-Wall Single Shot Special Sporting Rifle 32" - $1,035	
From:	Stoeger Industries, 17603 Indian Head Hwy., Ste 200, Accokeek, MD 20607 (301 283-6300

feed tray when the lever was opened slowly. Since the action does not cock the hammer, it must be manually cocked for each shot and that gave us the chance to really evaluate the checkering on the hammer spur. We found it to be sharp and easy to grab and keep hold of, as well as attractive. The trigger pull was almost a double stage, the long pull occurring in two separate degrees until finally the sear let go of the hammer at about 4 1/2 pounds. All in all, for a hunting rifle, it has a pretty fair and average trigger pull. Hammer operation was snappy and the lock time was fast.

In the interest of conformity we test fired the 1885 at 25 yards; exactly the same distance we used to test all the other rifles in this book, even though we knew full well the rifle was capable of performing at much longer ranges. To help eliminate errors, I enlisted the services of two excellent shooters to help with the test firing. We fired about 120 rounds of Black Hills and Winchester brand ammunition. The gun performed without any trouble or slow downs throughout the tests. We found the Black Hills ammunition with its 405-grain lead bullets would put out as many three-shot groups as we liked, all falling under 3/4 of an inch with shots touching. The Winchester 300-grain soft-point ammo was noticeably hotter than the Black Hills 405-grain ammo and it was felt plainly on the shoulder. But the gun loved it, delivering groups with all the shots touching, most of which were barely larger than a dime. I fired the rifle informally from the bench at 100 yards and produced several 2-inch groups, using the Winchester ammunition and one 2 1/2-inch group with the Black Hills. These sights are anything but clear and distinct at 25 yards, so at 100 yards that foggy sight picture played havoc with the eyes. Again, informally, I fired 15 shots at 100 yards at a little 4-inch gong and managed hit it solidly every time from the offhand position.

How about this Uberti model 1885? Perhaps the best compliment I could pay Uberti is that my two expert shooters, Tommy Abernathy and Ed Wade both wanted to buy this rifle after handling and firing it. All three shooters agreed this is a first-class single-shot rifle in every respect. This is not just another copy of a Winchester, but a bloody nice rifle on its own merits. Yes, we did pick out some small faults in wood-to-metal fit and I thought the factory should have taken the small amount of extra time required to hand polish the barrel before it was blued. Certainly, a trigger job would be a must for serious competition and would only help to further improve the group size. Overall, the gun performed so well, it would be nice to see what this rifle would do with a good set of vernier sights and a good trigger job. The fact that it shot so well with crude sights and a creepy, fairly-heavy trigger leaves open lots of possibilities. This is a really nice single-shot rifle, we liked it a lot.

Marlin lever-action rifles

Since the early 1880s firearms made by Marlin have been an important part of American history. This brief look at Marlin will give you an idea about the beginnings of this old American arms maker. John Mahlon Marlin (1836-1901), who apprenticed as a tool and die maker and during the Civil War was an employee of Colt at Hartford, Conn., began the company. Marlin had his own gun business on State Street in New Haven in 1870. His first firearms were of the small Derringer-type, single-shot .22 caliber pistols and other single-shot handguns. Sometime shortly after 1870, John began to manufacture revolvers that were similar to the then-popular Colt New Line and Smith & Wessons.

The Ballard patent single-shot rifle was manufactured by Brown Manufacturing Company of Newburyport, Mass., and in 1873, that company was sold under foreclosure. Charles Daly of New York, who was a large arms dealer of the day, bought Ballard's patents, along with guns and parts in various stages of assembly. Daly made an arrangement with Marlin to manufacture the Ballard rifles with Daly's firm Schoverling and Daly handling the sales and distribution at first. Apparently, Daly bought some interest in the Marlin Company about then; and later became its president. Marlin's venture began to make a profit and they reorganized in 1881, forming the new Marlin Firearms Company.

John Marlin's production of the Ballard single-shot rifle continued, and in 1881 Marlin released their very first successful repeating rifle, the lever-action, tubular magazine-fed Model 1881. Marlin discontinued Ballard single-shot production in about 1891 due to falling interest in single-shots and the increasing popularity of their expanding line of lever-action, repeating rifles. Still later, the company added a line of pump shotguns. Daly sold his interest in the company to John Marlin in 1893 and after Marlin passed on in 1901 the company was taken over by his two sons. At that time other items were added to the Marlin line. Likely the most well known of those items, added in 1910, was the Ideal Cartridge Reloading Manufacturing Company with its wide variety of bullet molds, reloading tools and accessories. Lyman purchased the Ideal Manufacturing Co. in 1921.

Marlin was sold in 1915 and then renamed the Marlin-Rockwell Corporation. During World War I all the Marlin-Rockwell's wartime production was devoted to the manufacture of machine guns. The peace of 1918 did not bring new interest sporting arms, and management apparently had little interest in this area so they only kept up the service and repair department for good will and to care for pre-war Marlin sporting arms. In 1921, the Marlin Firearms Corporation, a new corporation, was formed, but not much became of the new company and 1932 brought receivership. The company, in its entirety, was auctioned off to Frank Kenna. Kenna at once started to rejuvenate Marlin and he again took the company into the field of sporting firearms. The new company, the Marlin Firearms Company, continued the manufacture of sporting arms (with the exception 1942 to 1945 because of World War II demands) to the present. Marlin Firearms Company is still held by the Kenna family and still devotes most of its manufacturing capacity to sporting firearms.

During its 1880s and 1890s heyday, Marlin produced many fine-quality lever-action rifles and carbines both in heavy or big-game calibers and in the more familiar pistol calibers such as .44-40 and .38-40. They also produced guns in .22 rimfire. These original Marlin designs were quite beautiful and every bit as nice as their competition. It is these 1890s models that have gradually evolved into the modern versions the Models 336, 1894 and 1895. And the basic, sound concepts laid out by John Marlin are still being used today.

Often thought of as that "other lever-action," for many years the Marlin rifles have sort of taken a back seat to some of the fancier or better-known lever guns. Instead of focusing on high-polish blueing and fancy woodwork, Marlin has been making a good meat-and-potatoes hunting rifle for as long as this writer can remember. Over the years, I've owned quite a few Marlin lever guns, starting when I was only 17 years old with my first model 336 in .35 Remington. None of my Marlins were fancy rifles, but all of them worked perfectly and gave me more than adequate accuracy for the use I was putting them to at the time, which was hunting. The important thing to remember is that the basic Marlin design is strong and simple. These are very dependable lever-action repeaters that can be expected to last a lifetime and a offer very sound basis for someone wanting to build a custom lever-action. In recent years, Marlin has been closely following the public demands with their emphasis turning decidedly toward the needs of the cowboy action shooter.

Marlin Model 336 Cowboy

Up close the 336 shows off its new safety. The round button at the center-rear of the receiver.

Marlin's Model 336 Cowboy makes a very good-looking presentation and is exceptionally well balanced with its 24-inch tapered octagon barrel. Rifle courtesy Marlin Firearms Co. Author photos.

The Marlin Model 336 series of rifles is actually a continuation and improved version of the Model 36, which was introduced in 1936. The Model 36 had its origins even earlier, in the model 1893. The designation 336 came from the 1948 alteration of the Model 36, which gave the rifle a round bolt in order to provide more strength to the receiver. These are basically hunting rifles, chambered for cartridges like the .30-30, .32 Winchester Special and .35 Remington. Over the years it has also been chambered for .44 Magnum, .356 and .375 Winchester and .444 Marlin. More recently, in 1999, Marlin introduced the Cowboy version of the 336, making it available in .30-30 or .38-55 Winchester calibers.

For shooters who want a good long-range rifle with comparatively low recoil, the 336 Cowboy, or CB model in .38-55 caliber would make an excellent choice. This model features a 24-inch tapered octagon barrel (it tapers from about .840 inches at the breech to .675 at the muzzle) and it has deep-cut Ballard-type rifling, a full-length tubular magazine that holds eight shots, and a straight-grip walnut stock. Like the 1895 CB, the serial number is located on the left side of the receiver to accommodate tang sight installation, but the upper tang is not drilled and tapped for a tang sight, they have left this up to the owner. Since Marlin lever-actions have side-ejection, the top of the receiver is solid and its flat top

See for yourself. Marlin is doing a good job with the external polish work on their octagon barrels.

Shown here with its action open the 336 Cowboy lever has a longer throw than the 1894 but chances are it won't have to be operated so quickly. This rifle had the slickest action of any Marlin the author had ever fired.

is conveniently drilled and tapped for scope mounting and the screw holes are filled with plug screws. A cross-bolt safety button is provided on the rear of the receiver that may be activated once the shooter has pulled the hammer back into the safety, or half-cocked position. Using only the half-cocked position on the hammer is not considered a safe way to carry these rifles loaded, that is why Marlin has provided that cross bolt, which prevents the hammer from reaching the firing pin.

Marlin lever-actions use other safety mechanisms that are not so easy to spot. All their lever-actions make use of a lever safety; a device that prevents the trigger from being pulled until the shooter has the lever tightly closed. In addition, Marlin's lever-action firing pin is made in two pieces. The rear firing pin is short and located at the rear of the breech bolt. As the finger lever is opened, the locking bolt lets go of the bottom of the rear firing pin, allowing the rear pin to tilt down into a position where it cannot strike the front firing pin. This is the second reason the shooter is forced to close the lever all the way before the gun can fire.

Our new 336 CB is an attractive rifle. That 24-inch tapered octagon barrel sets the stage for a rifle with a real 19th century look. The 336 is a lighter gun than the big Model 1895, weighing in at 7 1/2 pounds. The 336 Cowboy is also a surprisingly well-balanced rifle. In fact, of the three different Marlin lever guns we tested for this book, this one swung up to the shoulder the fastest and the most naturally. Externally, the metal parts of 336 CB are all blued, with a bright breech bolt. The quality of the finish is about like that of the 1895 we tested, that is, the sides of the receiver are polished reasonably bright but over some deep surfacing marks. The barrel was very nicely polished showing flat, crisp corners and sharp octagon flats. The top and bottom of the receiver are finished in flat-matte blue. Sights are just like the other two Marlin Cowboy models, made by Marble. The rear sight is an adjustable Marble semi-buckhorn type with a carbine (actually a post and bead with a round brass bead) front sight. The sight picture is excellent, having a wider than usual rear U-notch and the sight picture is fast and easy to acquire. The only trouble we had with these sights is that the brass bead tended to get obscured easily in the bright sunlight.

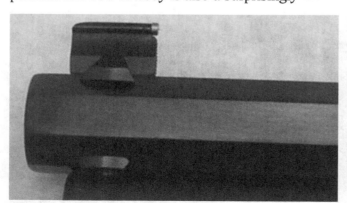

This is the Marble carbine sight. It is a nice sight but the brass bead does not do very well in bright sunlight.

Here is the Marlin signature on the hard rubber butt. It looks a bit washed out because it is. The butt plate has what is almost a modern military look.

Marlin Models 336 Parts Illustration courtesy Marlin Firearms Co.

1. Barrel
2. Breech Bolt
3. Bullseye
4. Buttplate / Buttpad
5. Buttplate Screw (2)
6. Buttstock
7. Carrier
8. Carrier Rocker
9. Carrier Rocker Pin
10. Carrier Rocker Spring
. . . . . Carrier Assembly (Consisting of above 4 parts)
11. Carrier Screw
12. Ejector
13. Ejector Spring
14. Ejector w/Spring
15. Extractor
16. Finger Lever
17. Finger Lever Plunger
18. Finger Lever Plunger Pin
19. Finger Lever Plunger Spring
20. Finger Lever Screw
21. Firing Pin, Front
22. Firing Pin, Rear
23. Firing Pin Retaining Pin (2)
24. Firing Pin Spring
25. Forearm

26. Forearm Tip
27. Forearm Tip Tenon
28. Forearm Tip Tenon Screw (2)
29. Front Band
30. Front Band Screw
31. Front Sight
32. Front Sight Base
33. Front Sight Base Screw (2)
34. Front Sight Hood
35. Front Sight Insert
36. Hammer
37. Hammer Screw
38. Hammer Spring (Mainspring)
39. Hammer Spring Adjusting Plate
40. Hammer Spur Complete (Incl. 41 & 42)
41. Hammer Spur Screw
42. Hammer Spur Wrench
43. Hammer Strut
44. Hammer Strut Pin
45. Loading Spring
46. Loading Spring Screw
47. Locking Bolt
48. Magazine Tube
49. Magazine Tube Follower
50. Magazine Tube Plug
51. Magazine Tube Plug Screw

52. Magazine Tube Spring
53. Magazine Tube Stud
54. Pistol Grip Cap
55. Pistol Grip Cap Screw
56. Rear Band
57. Rear Band Screw
58. Rear Sight Assembly
59. Rear Sight Base
60. Rear Sight Elevator
61. Rear Sight Folding Leaf
62. Receiver
63. Safety Button Assembly
64. Scope Mount Dummy Screw (4)
65. Sear
66. Swivel Stud, Rear
67. Tang Screw
68. Trigger
69. Trigger and Sear Pin
70. Trigger Guard Plate
71. Trigger Guard Plate Latch Pin
72. Trigger Guard Plate Screw
73. Trigger Guard Plate Support Screw
74. Trigger Safety Block
75. Trigger Safety Block Pin
76. Trigger Safety Block Spring

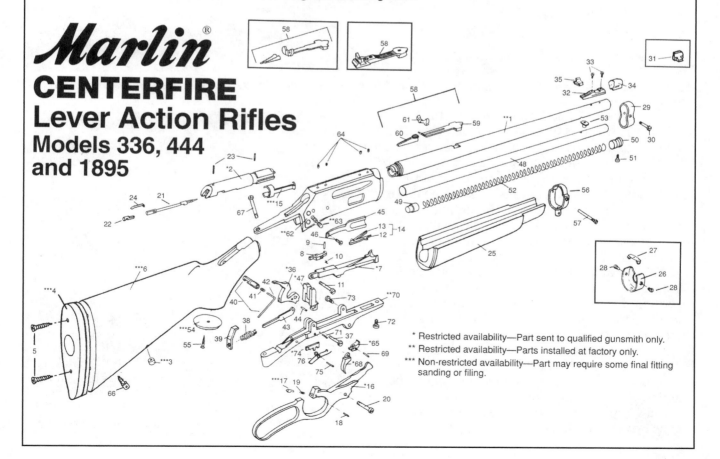

Marlin® **CENTERFIRE Lever Action Rifles Models 336, 444 and 1895**

* Restricted availability—Part sent to qualified gunsmith only.

** Restricted availability—Parts installed at factory only.

*** Non-restricted availability—Part may require some final fitting sanding or filing.

This photo shows the cross-bolt safety in the off position, notice the colored band showing, this indicates the rifle is ready to fire.

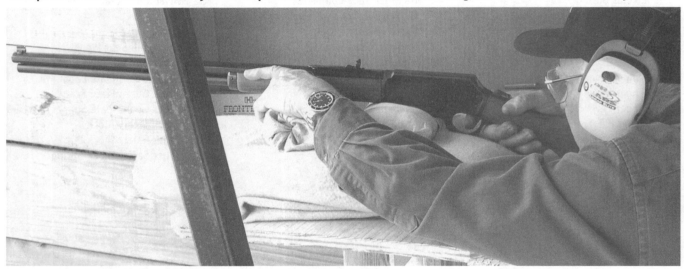

Ed Wade hunkered down shooting groups with the Marlin 336 Cowboy using the Winchester .38-55 ammunition.

The stocks are American walnut and the butt stock has a shotgun butt shape, with a black, hard-rubber buttplate. The length of pull is identical to the other two Marlin rifles at 13 3/8 inches, measured from the center of the trigger to the center of the butt. In shape, the forearm wood is slimmed down considerably from the normal 336 hunting rifle and topped off with a blued steel nose-cap so it looks more like one from an 1890s rifle and I find this look pleasing. The wood is coated with a light oil type finish that has a nice, 19th century appearance. Marlin calls this finish Mar-Shield®. I am sorry to report that the wood-to-metal fit on this particular rifle was sort of a disappointment. Not only were there fairly large air-gaps between the stock and forearm wood and the metal at the receiver, the buttstock had been sanded down below the level of the rear of the receiver, leaving an unsightly fit. There were also a couple of areas on the round of the forearm wood that had not been surfaced very well at the factory, leaving some visible flat spots.

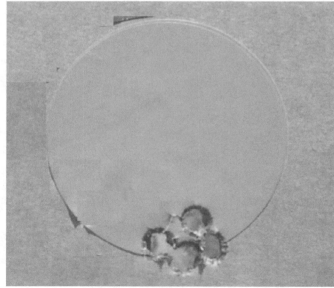

This target shows a group that was fired with Black Hills 255-grain lead, flat-point ammunition, six shots in just under 3/4 of an inch.

336 Cowboy specs	
Caliber:	.38/55 Win.
Capacity:	8-shot tubular magazine
Action:	Lever-action with squared finger lever; side ejection; blued metal surfaces; solid-top receiver; hammer block safety.
Stock:	American black walnut straight-grip stock; hard rubber butt plate; tough Mar-Shield® finish; blued steel fore-end cap.Rosewood
Barrel:	Tapered octagon with deep-cut Ballard-type rifling (6 grooves).
Twist Rate:	1:18" r.h.
Sights:	Adjustable Marble semi-buckhorn rear, Marble carbine front sight. Solid top receiver tapped for scope mount; offset hammer spur (right or left hand) for scope use. Serial number is on left side of receiver, instead of tang, allowing custom installation of a tang sight by a competent gunsmith.
Overall Length:	42.5"
Weight:	7.5 lbs.
Retail Price:	$735
From:	Marlin Firearms Co., 100 Kenna Dr., North Haven, CT 06473 (203) 239-5621

Operating the Model 336 Cowboy's action proved to be a real joy. This rifle has the smoothest Marlin action I have ever had my hands on. The lever's operation, with or without cartridges feeding through it, worked as slick as oil on water. The trigger pull on this 336 was also very good. After only a very short period of creep the hammer fell off smartly at just under 4 pounds. With two shooters, we fired about 80 shots with this rifle using both Black Hills ammunition carrying a 255-grain lead, flat-nosed bullet and Winchester 255-grain soft-point hunting ammo. Every aspect of this rifle's operation was absolutely flawless, without fault of any sort, throughout the entire test process. Winchester's excellent 255-grain soft-points gave us consistent 1-inch groups at 25 yards which were printing about an inch high. We did not adjust the sights but left them exactly as the rifle was when it came out of the factory container. Then we tried the Black Hills 255-grain flat-nose ammo and found that it hit the paper right where we were aiming. It also performed exceedingly well, putting most of the three-shot groups into little half-inch circles. The target shown in the photo was shot with this Black Hills ammo and is six shots (really!) in a group

that measured just under 3/4 of an inch. We fired the rifle informally offhand at a 4-inch steel gong at 100 yards. In this fashion we were able to hit six out of six with the Winchester ammo, using a center hold. Since we knew from the earlier targets that the Black Hills would hit lower than the Winchester, we switched to a 12 o'clock sight hold and again hit the steel with six out of six shots using the Black Hills ammunition.

We were not so pleased with the way the wood was fitted to the metal, but other than this flaw (which I am sure the factory would correct if we had complained) the 336 Cowboy is a really great performer, no doubt about it. The action was really fun to use. It was smooth and positive and fed every cartridge, every time. We loved the gun's balance and the way the rifle came up to the shoulder. Recoil was, what I would call very mild, this is a pleasant medium-large bore rifle to shoot. Marlin's 336 Cowboy is also an accurate rifle, chambered in a caliber that is well-known for its accuracy. For longer-range Cowboy matches, close to mid-range deer hunting or just plain fun shooting, this classy and well-balanced rifle would be the cat's pajamas. We liked it!

Marlin 1894 CBC

Marlin's 1894 Cowboy Competition model is a sharp-looking little carbine with a short, stiff octagon barrel and it performed very well in our tests. Rifle courtesy Marlin Firearms Co. author photo.

The Marlin Model 1894, introduced in that year, was the successor to the Model 1889, Marlin's first action using a side ejection, solid-topped frame. Like its predecessor, the 1894 was designed to use pistol-size cartridges such as the .32-20 and .44-40 Winchester. This model was made in carbine, rifle and musket configurations with octagon and round barrels that ranged in length from 14 to 32 inches. Marlin manufactured the original version from 1894 through about 1933 and during that time they sold about 250,000 of the model. During the 1960s Marlin produced the Model 336 in .44 Magnum, but this action, designed for longer, rifle-length cartridges, had trouble feeding the short pistol cartridge and so, in 1969 the old 1894 with its shorter action was re-introduced as the New Model 1894 in .44 Magnum. In more recent years, the caliber options have been expanded for the 1894 to include .357 Magnum, .22 WMRF, .41 Magnum, .25-20 and .32-20 Winchester and more recently, .45 Colt and .38 Special.

Marlin's 1894 Cowboy Competition (or CBC) model was designed specifically with cowboy action competitors in mind and it's obvious that more than a little thought went into this design. Called a carbine by the factory, the CBC offers a 20-inch octagon barrel, in the "short rifle" style, which adds just enough weight to the front end to dampen muzzle rise measurably. The gun comes chambered in .38 Special and in .45 Colt calibers and the full-length tubular magazine holds 10 shots. In order to accommodate tang sight installation, the serial number has been located on the left side of the receiver. The upper receiver tang has not been drilled and tapped to accept a tang sight, nor is the receiver's top drilled and tapped for scope mounting.

All new Marlin lever-actions are fitted with a cross-bolt type safety to positively block the hammer from reaching the firing pin when the safety is activated. To activate the cross-bolt safety, you have to first pull the hammer back into the first click. Once the user has activated it, he is provided with a real safety. There are other safety devises on Marlin lever-actions that are not so readily apparent. Marlin

(Continued on page 185)

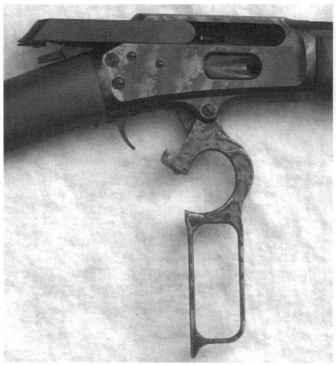

With the action opened you can see how short the stroke of the 1894's lever really is. The action can be operated very quickly.

A Look At Today's Old West

Roy Rugers (Fred Stann) looks as if he is expecting real trouble, toting his Stoeger double 12-gauge Coach Gun and a pair of Ruger Vaquero's stuffed in a Kirkpatrick Leather rig. Author photo.

Dusty (E. Stanley Coleman) is keeping his Peacemaker very handy...just in case. Floyd Oydegaard photography.

A colorfully dressed Jemison Beshears, looking pretty serious; he's obviously not decked out to be riding herd today. Floyd Oydegaard photography.

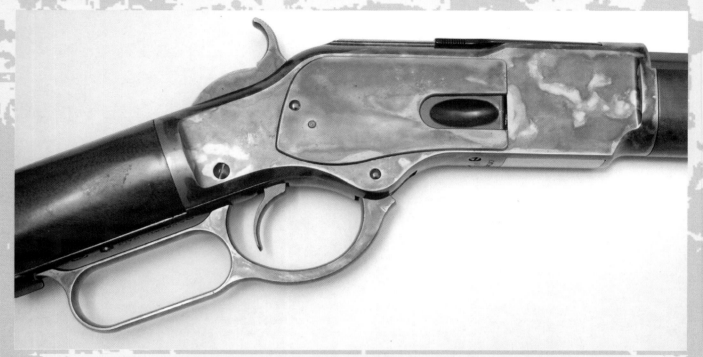

The receiver, hammer and lever on Uberti's replica of the 1873 Winchester exhibit beautiful case colors. Rifle courtesy Stoeger Industries. Author photo.

These guns will soon be test fired are shown with an array of leather from J.R. Allen, El Paso Saddlery, Kirkpatrick and Texas Jack's. Top row L-R: EMF Great Western II, Cimarron Stainless Model P, Cimarron Richards-Mason, Cimarron Open-top, Cimarron Model P, Cimarron Bisley, Ruger Vaquero. Bottom row L-R: Stoeger Coach Gun, Dixie Gun Works Trapdoor Springfield, Colt Single Action Army, EMF 1892 Hartford, Marlin 1894 Cowboy, Cimarron Lightning, Dixie Gun Works Henry Rifle, Navy Arms Uberti 1866, Cimarron Sharps Silhouette, Navy Arms Uberti 1873, Winchester 1897. Author photo.

Sturm, Ruger's very safe and rugged Vaquero models in blue/color case and in gloss stainless steel are highlighted in this series of photos. Both guns shown are in .45 Colt caliber with 5-1/2-inch barrels and rosewood grips. Revolvers courtesy Sturm, Ruger & Co. Author photo.

The Cimarron Model P looks right at home in this soft, lightweight, money-belt rig from El Paso Saddlery. Courtesy Texas Jack's. Author photo.

Um a comin' in! **Montana** (Richard Draga) isn't real sure what is on the other side of that door but the Colt Single Action Army in his hand should help even the odds. Floyd Oydegaard photography.

The notorious **Jake Slade** (Ed Wade in costume) **lookin' fer trouble** with his Colt Single Action secured in a J.R. Allen rig and a Uberti Henry rifle from Dixie Gun Works. Jake is mounted on Fred Stann's faithful horse, Rusty. Author photo.

Manufactured by Davide Pedersoli in Italy, this is an excellent replica of the U.S. 1873 Springfield Carbine in .45-70 caliber. Rifle courtesy Dixie Gun Works. Author photo.

Colt's Cowboy was introduced in 1999 and was tailored for the cowboy action shooting market. It has since been discontinued. Shown is the CB1850 in .45 Colt with a 5-1/2-inch barrel. The Cowboy model uses a transfer bar ignition. Revolver courtesy of Colt. Author photo.

This is Kip Maxwell, well armed and ready for just about anything with his big-bore Sharps carbine and a Colt Single Action Army. Floyd Oydegaard photography.

Marlin's 1894 Cowboy Competition model in .45 Colt features a 20-inch octagon barrel with color case hardened frame and lever. All the Marlins we tested were great shooters. Rifle courtesy Marlin Firearms. Author photo.

This striking 1866 is a Uberti-manufactured 1866 "Yellowboy" in .45 Colt, nicely engraved by North Carolinian Ken Hurst. It shoots as great as it looks. From the Ed Wade collection. Author photo.

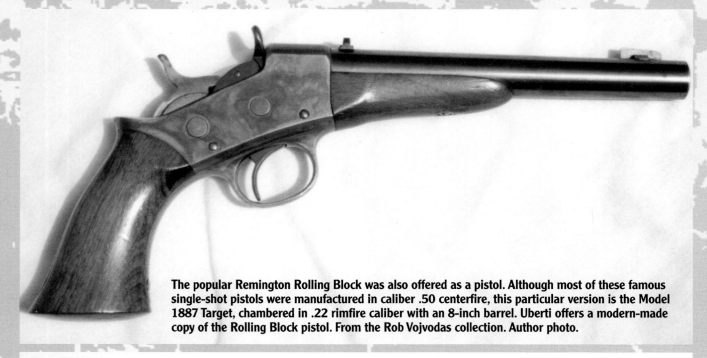

The popular Remington Rolling Block was also offered as a pistol. Although most of these famous single-shot pistols were manufactured in caliber .50 centerfire, this particular version is the Model 1887 Target, chambered in .22 rimfire caliber with an 8-inch barrel. Uberti offers a modern-made copy of the Rolling Block pistol. From the Rob Vojvodas collection. Author photo.

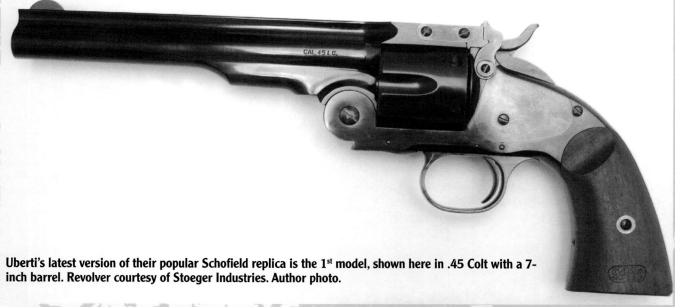

Uberti's latest version of their popular Schofield replica is the 1st model, shown here in .45 Colt with a 7-inch barrel. Revolver courtesy of Stoeger Industries. Author photo.

Cimarron's Bisley is a beautiful copy of the original, this one is in .45 Colt and was made in Italy by Uberti. Revolver courtesy Cimarron Firearms. Author photo.

EMF's Great Western II in satin nickel finish is being made in Italy by FFI Pietta. In .45 Colt caliber with a 5-1/2-inch barrel, this GWII performed wonderfully during our evaluation. Revolver courtesy EMF. Author photo.

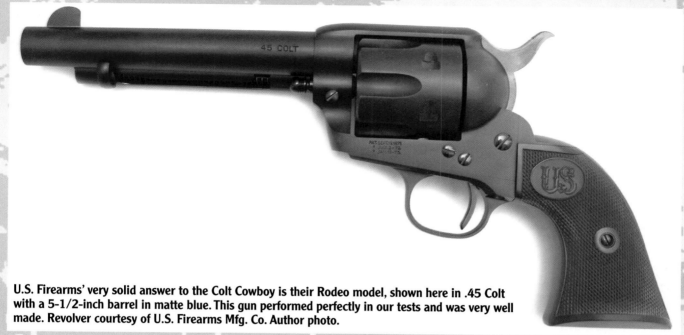

U.S. Firearms' very solid answer to the Colt Cowboy is their Rodeo model, shown here in .45 Colt with a 5-1/2-inch barrel in matte blue. This gun performed perfectly in our tests and was very well made. Revolver courtesy of U.S. Firearms Mfg. Co. Author photo.

This is the Uberti-manufactured Richards-Mason conversion offered by Cimarron Firearms in .44 Colt caliber with a 5-1/2-inch barrel. The gun proved to be extremely accurate and was very pleasant to shoot. Revolver courtesy Cimarron Firearms. Author photo.

This sweet-looking leather rig for the Cimarron Lightning is available from Texas Jack's in Fredericksburg, Texas. Author photo.

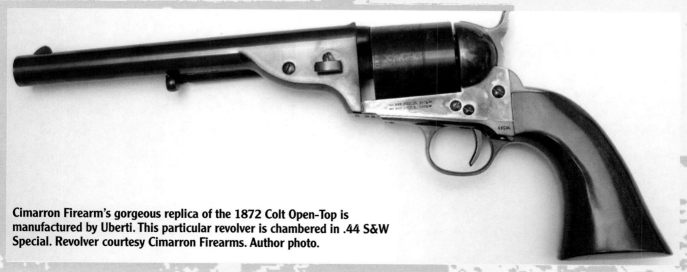

Cimarron Firearm's gorgeous replica of the 1872 Colt Open-Top is manufactured by Uberti. This particular revolver is chambered in .44 S&W Special. Revolver courtesy Cimarron Firearms. Author photo.

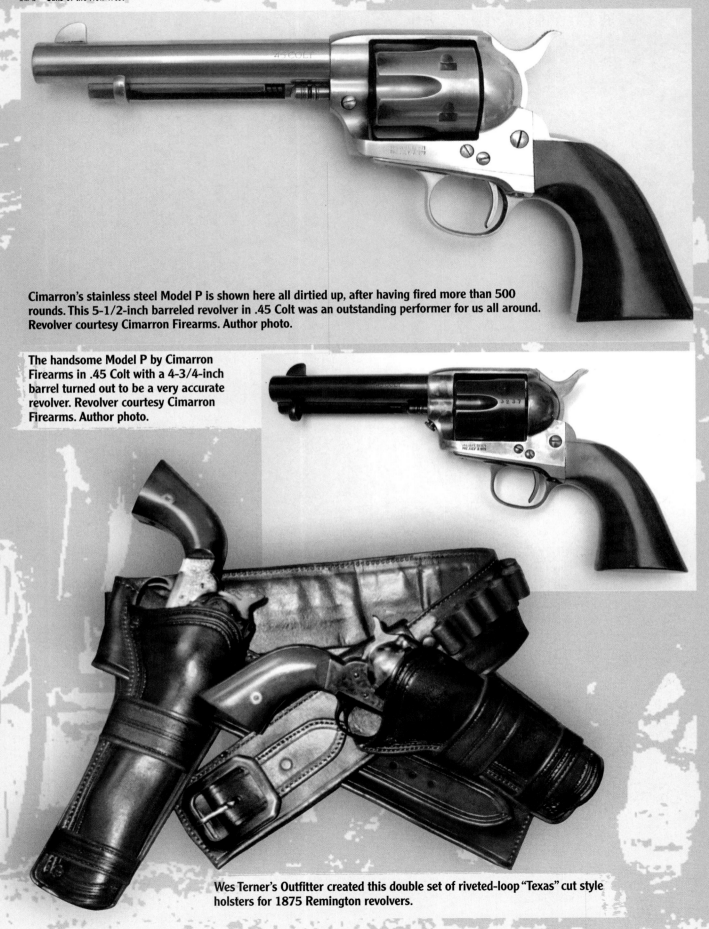

Cimarron's stainless steel Model P is shown here all dirtied up, after having fired more than 500 rounds. This 5-1/2-inch barreled revolver in .45 Colt was an outstanding performer for us all around. Revolver courtesy Cimarron Firearms. Author photo.

The handsome Model P by Cimarron Firearms in .45 Colt with a 4-3/4-inch barrel turned out to be a very accurate revolver. Revolver courtesy Cimarron Firearms. Author photo.

Wes Terner's Outfitter created this double set of riveted-loop "Texas" cut style holsters for 1875 Remington revolvers.

Marlin has recreated the original "Marlin Safety" on the receiver top, this proclaims the multiple safety devices featured on all their lever-actions.

(Continued from page 176)

also uses a lever safety. That is a device that won't allow the trigger to be pulled until the shooter holds the lever tightly closed. But wait, we aren't done yet. There is another reason the words *Marlin Safety* were inscribed in the tops of the Old Model receivers. The Marlin firing pin is made in two parts, the rear of which is very short and contained in the rear portion of the breech bolt. When the lever is opened, the bottom of the rear firing pin is released by the locking bolt, this allows the rear pin to tilt downward into a position where it cannot be made to strike the front firing pin until the lever is once again closed all the way.

Our 1894 CBC has a color case hardened receiver, trigger guard plate and lever while the barrel and breech bolt are blued. The case colors are not at all like the old bone and charcoal colors you may be used to seeing on 19th century guns, and I am quite sure they were achieved using some other method, perhaps with cyanide. The final effect is not bad looking, but it is unusual as it forms a sort of striped, splashed flame pattern. Polishing and finish blueing on the barrel, magazine tube and bolt are of high quality, with sharp edges, crisp lettering and well-defined flats on the octagon barrel. The muzzle is very neatly crowned but with a rounded crown in place of the traditional flat crown we normally see on octagon barrels and this, coupled with the magazine tube being set-back about 1/2 and inch from the muzzle, gives the front of the rifle a lighter appearance. There are cross-serrations on the hammer spur and they are deep, and enough to provide an excellent grasp on the hammer. My own preference would be to see the top of the spur rounded off, like the older rifles, and nicely checkered. That would add even more to the price but I bet most shooters would prefer it. The sights consist of a Marble's adjustable semi-buckhorn rear and Marble carbine front, which is to say, a post and bead with a brass bead. We found the sights were very easily and quickly acquired but the brass front was too easily obscured by sunlight and shooters may find it necessary to blacken the bead. The overall sight

The hammer has to be put into the half-cock position before the cross-bolt safety can be activated, here the safety is shown protruding from the right side of the right, indicating it is on safe.

The front sight is a Marble product, called a carbine sight. It's a post and bead with a bright brass bead that was easily obscured in sunlight.

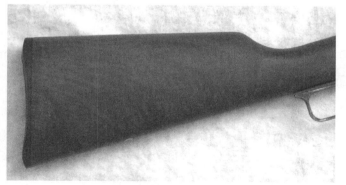

This is very nicely figured wood for a factory rifle. The CBC comes with a shotgun butt that is capped off with a black, hard rubber butt plate.

Models 1894 Parts Illustration courtesy Marlin Firearms Co.

1. Barrel
2. Breech Bolt
3. Bullseye
4. Buttplate/Buttpad
5. Buttplate/Buttpad Screw (2)
6. Buttstock
7. Carrier Assembly
8. Carrier Screw
9. Ejector w/Spring
10. Ejector Spring
11. Extractor
12. Extractor Retaining Pin
13. Extractor Spring
14. Extractor w/Spring
15. Finger Lever
16. Finger Lever Plunger
17. Finger Lever Plunger Pin
18. Finger Lever Plunger Spring
19. Finger Lever Screw
20. Firing Pin, Front
21. Firing Pin, Rear
22. Firing Pin Retaining Pin (2)
23. Firing Pin Spring
24. Forearm
25. Forearm Tip

26. Forearm Tip Tenon
27. Forearm Tip Tenon Screw (2)
28. Front Band
29. Front Band Screw
30. Front Sight
31. Front Sight Base
32. Front Sight Base Screw (2)
33. Front Sight Hood
34. Front Sight Insert
35. Hammer
36. Hammer Screw
37. Hammer Spring (Mainspring)
38. Hammer Spring Plate
39. Hammer Spur Complete
   (Includes parts 40 and 41)
40. Hammer Spur Screw
41. Hammer Spur Wrench
42. Hammer Strut
43. Hammer Strut Pin
44. Loading Spring
45. Loading Spring Screw
46. Locking Bolt
47. Magazine Tube
48. Magazine Tube Follower
49. Magazine Tube Plug

50. Magazine Tube Plug Screw
51. Magazine Tube Spring
52. Magazine Tube Stud
53. Rear Band
54. Rear Band Screw
55. Rear Sight Assembly
56. Rear Sight Base
57. Rear Sight Elevator
58. Rear Sight Folding Leaf
59. Receiver
60. Safety Button Assembly
61. Scope Mount Dummy Screw (4)
62. Sear
63. Swivel Stud, Rear
64. Tang Screw
65. Trigger
66. Trigger and Sear Pin
67. Trigger Guard Plate
68. Trigger Guard Plate Latch Pin
69. Trigger Guard Plate Screw
70. Trigger Guard Plate Support Screw
71. Trigger Safety Block
72. Trigger Safety Block Pin
73. Trigger Safety Block Spring
74. 10-Shot Plug

Marlin®
CENTERFIRE
Lever Action Rifles
Model 1894

* Restricted availability—Part sent to qualified gunsmith only.

** Restricted availability—Parts installed at factory only.

*** Non-restricted availability—Part may require some final fitting sanding or filing.

This is Ed Wade, tirelessly shooting one of those excellent groups from the rest.

picture is good, although my preference would be for a wider U notch in the rear sight, which would better define the front sight bead.

Stocks are made from American walnut, with the buttstock having a straight grip and shotgun-style butt with a hard rubber buttplate. The butt stock is a good shape and length (the length of pull is 13 3/8 inches. Both shooters found the gun could be shouldered readily and quickly without a forethought. The walnut forearm is a slim, rifle style. It's just a tad less than three-quarters the barrel's length and ending in a blued steel cap. Our rifle's buttstock was very nicely figured walnut, and the wood is finished to look like an old-style oil finish, giving the 1894 CBC a pleasing and appropriate look. Wood-to-metal fit was good, but not great, with some obvious gaps showing around most of the stock fit at the tangs as well as between the forearm wood and the front of the receiver.

The Cowboy Competition's action operation was slick and positive, and the short throw length of the 1894's lever makes everything happen comparatively quickly. This is one lever-action rifle that can be emptied very rapidly, all the while maintaining a sight picture and never moving the buttplate from your the shoulder. Here is where that short, stiff octagon barrel pays off with a very gently recoiling rifle. We were impressed with Marlin's positive, reliable feeding system. The gun was tested using approximately 250 rounds of factory ammunition and the action fed all the cartridges without a jam, a balk or failure of any sort. I will say that the inside lower edges of the lever could stand to be rounded off more than they have been by the factory. This was my only real objection to the rifle, we found that when the lever was operated vigorously, especially with the gun shouldered, the results were hard on the shooter's fingers. It didn't draw blood but it did hurt and continued use only compounded the discomfort. I think it might also help the comfort levels if the lever loop was shaped more like a

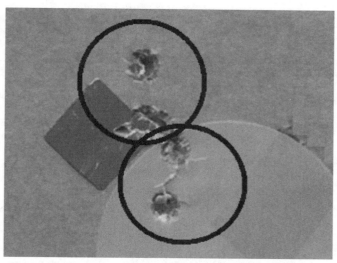

The target shows a typical set of two, three-shot groups. The top fired with Black Hills, the bottom with Winchester ammo.

Winchester, that is, with rounded corners and perhaps, another 1/4 inch more length inside the loop. This latter change would give a little more room for people with large fingers and I don't think the extra length would bother anyone else.

We test fired the 1894 CBC at 25 yards from a sand bag rest using three brands of Cowboy ammunition: .45 Colt Winchester Cowboy loads, Hornady .45 Colt Cowboy and Black Hills Cowboy loads. We tested the Hornady ammo first, and from the start it gave us groups in the 2 1/2- to 3-inch range on a consistent basis. For some reason, the 1894's barrel was just not all that happy with it. Of the other two ammunition brands, the gun preferred neither, with both maker's ammunition giving us three-shot groups that averaged just under one inch, and many that were just slightly over 3/4 of an inch with all the shots touching each other. We did not attempt to adjust the sights, so right out of the box the rifle printed about 3 inches high and a tad left using a 6 o'clock hold on the 3-inch orange paster. The photo shows two, three-shot

Marlin 1894 CBC specs	
Caliber:	.45 Colt
Capacity:	10-shot tubular magazine
Action:	Lever-action with squared finger lever; side ejection; color case hardened receiver, trigger guard plate and lever; blued bolt; solid-top receiver; hammer block safety.
Stock:	Straight-grip American black walnut; hard rubber butt plate; tough Mar-Shield, finish; blued steel fore-end cap.
Barrel:	Tapered octagon with deep-cut Ballard-type rifling (6 grooves).
Twist Rate:	1:16" r.h.
Sights:	Adjustable Marble semi-buckhorn rear, Marble carbine front sight. Offset hammer spur (right or left hand) for scope use. Serial number is on left side of receiver, instead of tang, allowing custom installation of a tang sight by a competent gunsmith.
Overall Length:	37.5"
Weight:	6.5 lbs.
Retail Price:	$986
From:	Marlin Firearms Co., 100 Kenna Dr., North Haven, CT 06473 (203) 239-5621

groups. The top group was fired with Black Hills ammunition, the lower with Winchester Cowboy loads. Notice that except for a small deviation in point of impact, both groups are quite similar in size and spread. This performance was typical of the afternoon's test firing. For an informal test, we tried the rifle on a 6-inch gong set out at 100 yards, and using a 12 o'clock sight hold, we were able to ring the gong with all 10 out of 10 shots. On a 4-inch gong at 25 yards and firing from the shoulder as fast as the sights could be acquired, we rang the gong an average of seven out of 10 shots.

In appearance, the Marlin may not be quite as classy looking as some of the toggle-action Winchester types, but in all fairness, the factory has done a credible job with both finish, and to a lesser degree, wood-to-metal fit-up. If someone wanted to, I think the rifle, like most modern Marlins, would respond beautifully to some custom, 19th century-type finish work. As to performance, the 1894 CBC is a top-drawer rifle. We were not easy on it during the tests, putting the gun through some tough paces. The little rifle worked perfectly for us. Both shooters thought it did very well in rapid firing from the shoulder. It has decent out-of-the-box sights that could be improved to be excellent without too much trouble and it displayed excellent accuracy with two out of the three brands of factory ammunition we used. The short lever stroke of the 1894's action is a plus, even with the painful lever loop. Overall, this is a nice rifle-carbine, its very strong and dependable, its also perhaps a bit pricier than most Marlins, but then, it also performed wonderfully for an off-the-shelf rifle.

Marlin Model 1895 Cowboy

Except for its large size, the side view of the 1895 is typical Marlin. The rifle is nicely finish in blue and exhibited good wood-to-metal fit.

The 1895 Marlin Cowboy Model in .45-70 caliber sports a handsome 26-inch tapered octagon barrel with a nine-shot magazine capacity and very nice sights. Rifle courtesy Marlin Firearms Co. Author photos.

The new 1895 Cowboy in .45-70 caliber is aimed directly at the Cowboy Action Shooter who wants a big-bore lever gun. Marlin is certainly no stranger to .45-70 lever rifles. They made their first .45-70 lever-action in 1881 and continued that model until 1892. In 1895 they introduced the original Model 1895, a beautiful big game rifle that was manufactured until World War I intervened in 1917 and the rifle was discontinued. Thankfully, Marlin re-introduced the 1895 in 1972 and they have kept the original caliber. The original Model 1895, in fact all of the 19th century Marlin lever rifles, used a square shaped breech bolt. The newer 1895s have a round breech bolt, which Marlin found in the 1940s offered greater strength to the action.

The newest 1895 Cowboy model has a distinctly old-fashioned flavor. It comes equipped with a 26-inch tapered octagon barrel that has deep-cut Ballard-type rifling and a full-length nine-shot tubular magazine. The barrel has a very pleasing taper, measuring .830 inches at the breech and tapering to .670 inches at the muzzle. The barrel is not too skinny. On the other hand, it is heavy enough to add what I think is the perfect amount of weight out front. Because of this the 1895 Cowboy is a very well balanced rifle and it swings into your

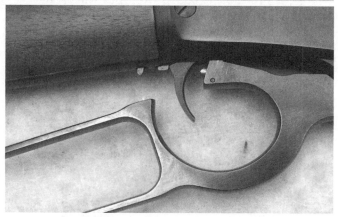

This view shows the lever safety. In order for the trigger to be pulled, the lever has to be held up closed against the action so the safety is depressed, freeing the trigger to move rearward.

shoulder almost as readily as a good shotgun. I say this despite the fact that the 1895 is actually a fairly big gun. I know the rifle was intended for cowboy shoots, but I have to say it would be absolutely dandy for hunting heavy game at close to medium ranges.

Like all new Marlin lever-actions, the 1895 is fitted with a cross-bolt type safety that will positively

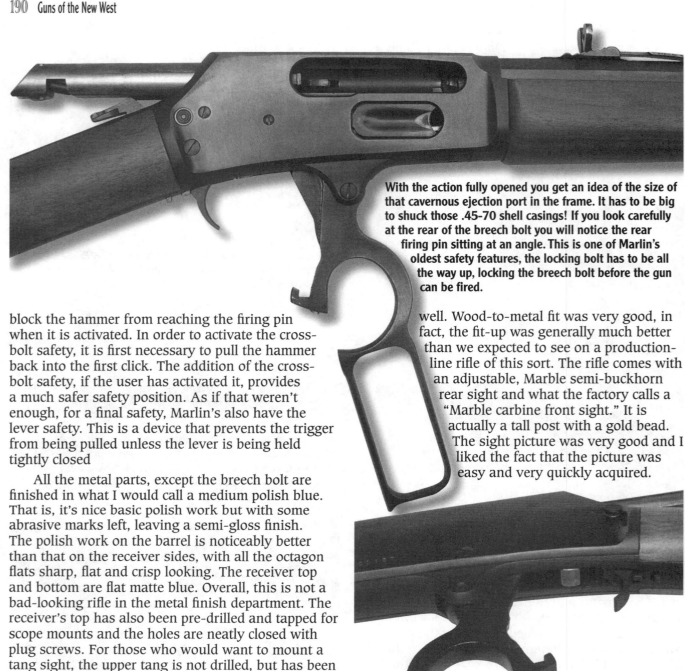

With the action fully opened you get an idea of the size of that cavernous ejection port in the frame. It has to be big to shuck those .45-70 shell casings! If you look carefully at the rear of the breech bolt you will notice the rear firing pin sitting at an angle. This is one of Marlin's oldest safety features, the locking bolt has to be all the way up, locking the breech bolt before the gun can be fired.

block the hammer from reaching the firing pin when it is activated. In order to activate the cross-bolt safety, it is first necessary to pull the hammer back into the first click. The addition of the cross-bolt safety, if the user has activated it, provides a much safer safety position. As if that weren't enough, for a final safety, Marlin's also have the lever safety. This is a device that prevents the trigger from being pulled unless the lever is being held tightly closed

All the metal parts, except the breech bolt are finished in what I would call a medium polish blue. That is, it's nice basic polish work but with some abrasive marks left, leaving a semi-gloss finish. The polish work on the barrel is noticeably better than that on the receiver sides, with all the octagon flats sharp, flat and crisp looking. The receiver top and bottom are flat matte blue. Overall, this is not a bad-looking rifle in the metal finish department. The receiver's top has also been pre-drilled and tapped for scope mounts and the holes are neatly closed with plug screws. For those who would want to mount a tang sight, the upper tang is not drilled, but has been left blank and the serial numbers have been moved to the receiver side.

The stocks are American walnut and finished with something Marlin calls a Mar-Shield® finish. From what I can see they are apparently finished with oil or some other fairly light coating resembling a linseed oil finish, it might even be a polyurethane varnish. A straight-grip, uncheckered buttstock is provided with a shotgun butt and hard-rubber buttplate with the Marlin name cast in. The length of pull, measured from the center of the trigger to the center of the butt was 13 3/8 inches. The walnut forend is also not checkered and appears to be a slimmed down version of the types used on Marlin's hunting rifles, finished off with a rounded cap held by two screws. It suits the rifle's 19th century look

well. Wood-to-metal fit was very good, in fact, the fit-up was generally much better than we expected to see on a production-line rifle of this sort. The rifle comes with an adjustable, Marble semi-buckhorn rear sight and what the factory calls a "Marble carbine front sight." It is actually a tall post with a gold bead. The sight picture was very good and I liked the fact that the picture was easy and very quickly acquired.

Looking up, we can see the cross-bolt safety button visible on the side of the receiver, here the button is in the off position as indicated by the orange band showing. The shiny part showing just in front of the trigger is the locking bolt. That part gets pushed up by the hook on the lever to lock the breech tightly shut.

Marlin Model 336, 444 and 1895 Parts Illustration courtesy Marlin Firearms Co.

1. Barrel
2. Breech Bolt
3. Bullseye
4. Buttplate / Buttpad
5. Buttplate Screw (2)
6. Buttstock
7. Carrier
8. Carrier Rocker
9. Carrier Rocker Pin
10. Carrier Rocker Spring
..... Carrier Assembly (Consisting of above 4 parts)
11. Carrier Screw
12. Ejector
13. Ejector Spring
14. Ejector w/Spring
15. Extractor
16. Finger Lever
17. Finger Lever Plunger
18. Finger Lever Plunger Pin
19. Finger Lever Plunger Spring
20. Finger Lever Screw
21. Firing Pin, Front
22. Firing Pin, Rear
23. Firing Pin Retaining Pin (2)
24. Firing Pin Spring
25. Forearm

26. Forearm Tip
27. Forearm Tip Tenon
28. Forearm Tip Tenon Screw (2)
29. Front Band
30. Front Band Screw
31. Front Sight
32. Front Sight Base
33. Front Sight Base Screw (2)
34. Front Sight Hood
35. Front Sight Insert
36. Hammer
37. Hammer Screw
38. Hammer Spring (Mainspring)
39. Hammer Spring Adjusting Plate
40. Hammer Spur Complete (Incl. 41 & 42)
41. Hammer Spur Screw
42. Hammer Spur Wrench
43. Hammer Strut
44. Hammer Strut Pin
45. Loading Spring
46. Loading Spring Screw
47. Locking Bolt
48. Magazine Tube
49. Magazine Tube Follower
50. Magazine Tube Plug
51. Magazine Tube Plug Screw

52. Magazine Tube Spring
53. Magazine Tube Stud
54. Pistol Grip Cap
55. Pistol Grip Cap Screw
56. Rear Band
57. Rear Band Screw
58. Rear Sight Assembly
59. Rear Sight Base
60. Rear Sight Elevator
61. Rear Sight Folding Leaf
62. Receiver
63. Safety Button Assembly
64. Scope Mount Dummy Screw (4)
65. Sear
66. Swivel Stud, Rear
67. Tang Screw
68. Trigger
69. Trigger and Sear Pin
70. Trigger Guard Plate
71. Trigger Guard Plate Latch Pin
72. Trigger Guard Plate Screw
73. Trigger Guard Plate Support Screw
74. Trigger Safety Block
75. Trigger Safety Block Pin
76. Trigger Safety Block Spring

Marlin®
CENTERFIRE
Lever Action Rifles
Models 336, 444 and 1895

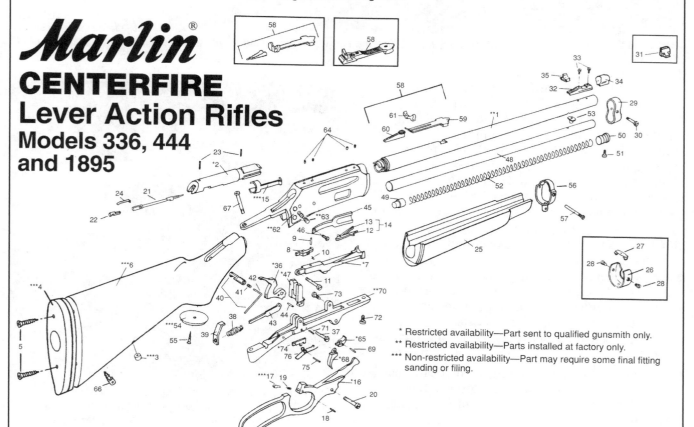

* Restricted availability—Part sent to qualified gunsmith only.

** Restricted availability—Parts installed at factory only.

*** Non-restricted availability—Part may require some final fitting sanding or filing.

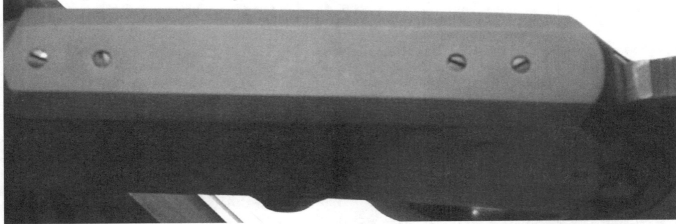

One benefit of side ejection is top-mounted scopes. Marlin's lever guns all come pre-drilled and tapped to accept scope mounts on top of the receiver.

Here is Ed Wade a moment after touching off the 1895 Cowboy. This was a fine shooting rifle that performed better than anyone thought it would.

The hammer on the 1895 is typical, with serrations on its spur that, while not particularly attractive, are very functional, providing a firm grasp on the hammer. The rifle also comes with an offset spur accessory should the owner decide to install a scope. Operation of the action on this rifle was just about as slick as grease, and I can only say that it operated through all the tests without a hitch or balk of any kind, feeding every cartridge smoothly. The edges of the lever did not cause any of the shooters grief, even when we operated the action at hyper-speed. We all found the trigger pull to be quite excellent for an off-the-shelf rifle. In what we thought was a nice surprise, the pull occurred in one stage. The sear let go at about 4 pounds and with almost no creep. But, the real surprise was in the shooting because the performance department was where the 1895 Cowboy decided to show us its heels.

We test fired the rifle sitting, from a sand-bagged rest at 25 yards using three-shot groups. Black Hills 405-grain lead-bullet loads and Winchester 300-grain soft-point ammunition were used. Neither brand of ammunition provided us with any

The lower group is typical of the groups we fired with Black Hills 405-grain ammo, the top group is three shots using Winchester 300-grain soft-points, the Winchester aiming point was 6 o'clock.

1895 Marlin specs, as tested	
Caliber:	.45/70 Gov't.
Capacity:	9-shot tubular magazine
Action:	Lever action with squared finger lever; side ejection; solid-top receiver; deeply blued metal surfaces; hammer block safety.
Stock:	Straight-grip American black walnut; hard rubber butt plate; tough Mar-Shield® finish; blued steel fore end cap.
Barrel:	Tapered octagon barrel with deep-cut Ballard-type rifling (6 grooves)
Twist Rate:	1:20" r.h.
Sights:	Adjustable Marble semi-buckhorn rear, Marble carbine front sight. Solid top receiver tapped for scope mount; offset hammer spur (right or left hand) for scope use. Serial number is on left side of receiver, instead of tang, allowing custom installation of a tang sight by a competent gunsmith.
Overall Length:	44.5"
Weight:	8 lbs
Retail Price:	$802
From:	Marlin Firearms Co., 100 Kenna Dr., North Haven, CT 06473 (203) 239-5621

disappointments, as you can see from the target. The gun did not recoil badly at all with the Black Hills 405-grain loads, though it had a good degree of muzzle rise. Recoil from the Black Hills ammo was manageable enough that successive fast, accurate shots were quite easily cranked off. On the other hand, the felt-recoil levels increased markedly with the Winchester ammunition to a point bordering on moderately heavy, but with less muzzle rise. With the Black Hills ammunition the 1895 shot an average group size of 1 inch with several groups going into 3/4 of an inch and the rifle shot almost exactly to the sights with this load. Winchester's 300-grain load performed even better, averaging 3/4-inch groups with some even smaller although its point of impact was about 2 inches above point of aim. Ed Wade fired the 3-shot group in the photo using Winchester ammo. We also tried the rifle informally on a 4-inch steel gong we set at 100 yards and using five rounds of each brand of ammunition. We hit the gong solidly with all 10 shots.

What's the verdict? I have one complaint and it's my own little pet peeve. I have never much cared for that squared off shape of the Marlin lever loop, nor do I find it comfortable, I much prefer the rounded shape of the Winchester lever and frankly, I think such a change would make the Marlin a much better looking rifle, but. . .that is a very small thing and only my opinion. Although, after reading this, perhaps Marlin would consider making an optional lever with the "Winchester" look. Of course, they wouldn't have to use *that* name. Maybe they could call it the Chicoine lever?

Seriously. Everyone who shot or even looked at the Marlin 1895 Cowboy liked it. Some liked it more than others for reasons of their own, but it was universally thought of as a classy, handsome and powerful rifle. The fit and finish of the wood and metal are what you might expect from a gun in this price range, possibly even better than I would expect. However, this rifle performed in a manner that was way out of its price range. Operation of the action was very smooth. The feed and function was perfect and with three different shooters and two brands of ammunition; the darned thing shoots, as they say, some good! A rifle like this would make a fine custom project, maybe give the metal a careful, hand-polished blue, set that off with some color case hardened small parts, niter blue screws and a nice stock finish. Heck, it wouldn't take much to make it look like an 1890s production rifle. Our bottom line, we thought this was a lot of gun for the money.

Winchester lever-action rifles The Henry, the Models of 1866, 1873 and 1876

Some of the most famous lever-action rifles we think of along with the American frontier are the Henry, and the Winchester Models 1866, 1873 and 1876. All of those rifles used the toggle-link principle to operate the action and lock the breech shut. The parent design came from a Smith & Wesson-designed magazine pistol dating from about 1854. This unique firearm actually used a form of case-less ammunition. After the design was purchased by a group of investors in the mid-1850s, the S&W design was altered by B. Tyler Henry to use a rimfire cartridge and he transformed it into the gun which became the Henry rifle of 1860. A few years later, the primary investor in this repeating rifle endeavor, a man named Oliver Winchester, took over the company and with help from other inventors, the Henry rifle quickly evolved into the Winchester Models of 1866, 1873 and 1876.

This toggle-link action principal eventually caught the attention of military organizations when it was used, in a much-modified form, by Hiram Maxim inside his first machine gun in 1884. This radical and very successful gun could, with a single pull of the trigger fire 600 shots per minute. Its introduction forever changed how future wars would be waged. Still later, a toggle-link action was used in the now famous semi-automatic pistols designed by Borchardt and Luger.

In more modern times, the demand created by the sport of cowboy action shooting has caused modern-made replicas of the Henry rifle and of the Winchester Models 1866 and 1873 rifles and carbines to be manufactured in several variations. Most of these are manufactured in Italy by the Aldo Uberti Company and these lever-action guns have become very popular. Indeed, they have become the mainstay at cowboy shooting events.

The toggle-links used in these lever-action rifles are minimal. Their components do not occupy any more space in the action than absolutely necessary for their operation and the original Winchesters with this type of action were never considered to be very strong. As such, they do not have the ability to handle high-pressure cartridges, and on account of a fixed length in their feeding and operating systems, are restricted to using short, pistol-length cartridges (the exception is the Model 1876 Winchester which was made for longer cartridges, but even then, it has limitations). One thing these older lever guns are known for is their dependability. Most people will tell you that when these rifles are in good repair, they operate beautifully. In my experience this is largely true, so except for the fact that the old originals do have a habit of breaking springs and extractors on a regular basis, most of these old workhorses are still going after 100 years or more of hard use.

Thanks to their competition's introduction of lever-action rifles with stronger actions, such as the big-framed Marlin 1881 and the smaller Colt Burgess in 1883, Winchester saw that the handwriting was on the wall. They needed a stronger, more modern lever-action. Stronger, and more modern meant Winchester needed to market a lever-action like the Marlin that was better suited to handle the big game cartridges which were being introduced for single-shot rifles, or likes of the Burgess, whose action was not only stronger, but much more compact than the 1873 Winchester. For this, Winchester turned once again to the inventor of their new 1885 single-shot, John M. Browning of Utah. The end-result was the Model 1886 Winchester. The Model 1886 was a large-framed lever-action whose breech bolt was locked shut with two large steel locking bolts. This new rifle was capable of handling most of the largest and most powerful rimmed cartridges available, up to and including the .50-110 Express. Later, it proved robust enough so that it could successfully make the transition into the era of higher-pressure smokeless powder cartridges.

Perhaps egged into creation by the Colt Burgess and by Marlin's innovative, compact 1889 model, the Winchester 1886 was followed by the Model of 1892. The '92 was a simpler, lighter, scaled down version of the '86 built to accept pistol-sized cartridges like the .44-40. Still another Browning design was implemented in 1894 with a new medium-sized rifle for .30-30 sized cartridges that has since broken many sales records. Both Marlin's and Winchester's later lever-actions were very strong, reliable, well made firearms and some of both are still in production today by the parent companies. Others are now, or have recently been, produced by other manufacturers.

The Henry: One Of The First

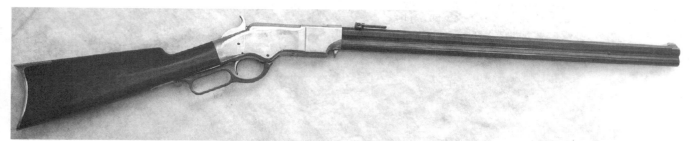

Uberti's modern Henry rifle is a fine shooting replica of the classic "Darn Yankee rifle you could load on Sunday and shoot all week". Rifle courtesy of Dixie Gun Works. Author photos.

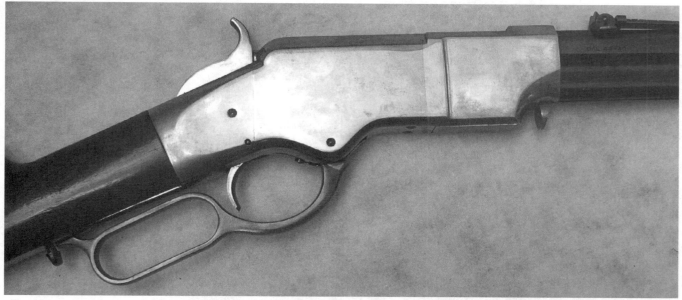

The all-brass receiver makes a striking contrast against the blued barrel and the walnut butt stock. Notice the tarnishing of the brass, that's because the rifle we used in our tests was a well-worn used gun. All new Uberti Henry rifles are furnished in brightly polished brass and are coated with a clear finish to prevent tarnishing.

Lever-action repeating rifles that fire metallic cartridges started with two rifles, both introduced just before the Civil War, around 1860. There was B. Tyler Henry's famous Henry repeating rifle and there was Christian Spencer's repeater. The Spencer was used heavily by the U. S. Army in the Civil War. It came in carbine or rifle length, was lever operated and held seven, fairly large, rimfire cartridges in a tubular magazine within the buttstock. Henry's lever-action rifle was altered from an earlier Smith & Wesson patent that was, in 1860, owned by Oliver Winchester, Henry's partner, and it used a toggle-link action. S&W's original design was altered by Henry to accept a .44 caliber rimfire cartridge, which was of handgun size and power. The Henry offered the shooter a large magazine capacity; with 14 cartridges fed from a tube under the barrel.

These rifles did see limited service in the Civil War where, as legend tells it, Confederate soldiers knew the Henry as that "Darn Yankee rifle you

loaded on Sunday and shoot all week." However small was the Henry rifle's actual contribution to the war, it's reputation for heavy fire power and reliability grew out of all proportion to the number of rifles involved. Henry rifles also had their down

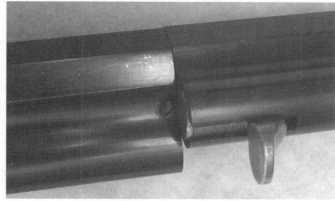

Here we see the barrel sleeve with the magazine follower tucked inside, rotated to the side for loading.

This Henry rifle is open for business. The small protrusion on the lower tang to the left is the lever lock, which may be rotated into place to lock the lever closed.

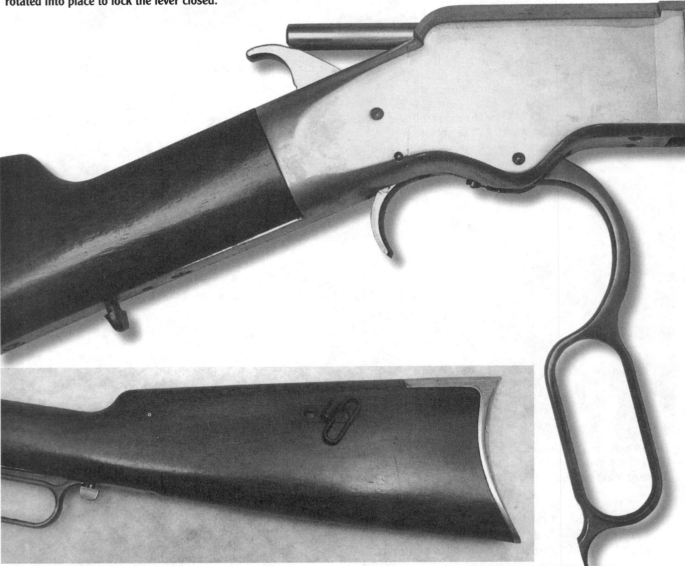

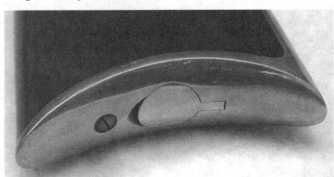

The butt stock is patterned closely, but not precisely after the original Henry. The inletted swivel is a nice touch.

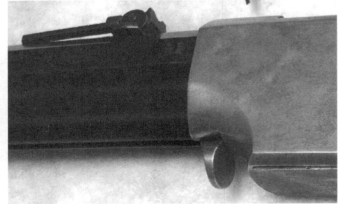

A functional trapdoor is provided in the butt that, like the real thing, is intended to hold a disassembled cleaning rod.

The brass "button" at the front of the receiver is the magazine follower that rides in a slot that is the full length of the magazine tube.

sides, one of those was that it had no forearm and as the barrel got hot the gun became difficult to hold. Another problem turned out to be the magazine follower whose little handle stuck out through a slot in the bottom of the magazine. As it followed the cartridges rearward, if the shooter wasn't observant, it would bump into the shooter's hand and stop the cartridge feed. That full-length open slot also let a lot of dirt and debris into the magazine. You loaded the Henry by pushing the magazine follower all the way forward, that caused the barrel sleeve lock to disengage, allowing the barrel sleeve to be rotated to the side, uncovering the front of the magazine

Uberti-manufactured Henry Parts Illustration with permission from VTI Gun Parts.

1	Receiver	83	Right rear link	112	Hammer link pin
2	Hammer	84	Left rear link	113	Magazine follower
3	Barrel	85	Right front link	115	Hammer link
7	Carrier block	86	Left front link	121	Band screw
15	Sight	89	Lever	124	Lever spring screw
19	Trigger spring	90	Lifter arm	217	Butt plate gate
20	Mainspring	92	Right lever spring	223	Sleeve
36	Mainspring screw	93	Left lever spring	233	Protection running screw
55	rear	95	Firing pin spring	234	Protection running spring
57	Butt stock	96	Magazine spring	237	Lever hook spring
58	Butt plate	97	Breech block	263	Trigger spring screw
62	Butt plate screw	98	Firing pin	458	Butt plate gate pin
63	Tang screw	99	Trigger pin	536	Sleeve latch
67	Firing pin extension	100	Hammer pin screw	538	Sleeve latch rod spring
69	Rear base	101	Lever screw	542	Lever hook
72	Cam lever	104	Firing pin stop	544	Rear sight pin
73	Right side plate	105	Rear link pin	546	Sleeve latch rod
74	Left side plate	106	Link pin	550	Magazine follower screw
76	Rear running	107	Lever pin	552	Lever hook spring screw
79	Extractor	108	Extractor pin	600	Rear sight spring
80	Front band	109	Cam lever pin	609	Rear running stop screw

Shooting the Henry from a rest involves being thoughtful about where the magazine follower is. This is Ed Wade firing the Uberti-Henry with Winchester ammunition.

tube. Cartridges were poured into the tube, rim facing down, until it was filled and the barrel sleeve would be rotated back into the locked position. Now the follower spring exerted pressure on the cartridges, allowing them to be fed as the action was operated. The Henry was manufactured from 1860 through 1866 and about 14,000 were manufactured, the majority of those rifles used brass receivers.

We obtained a copy of the Henry rifle manufactured by A. Uberti in Italy for our tests. I am always struck by the beauty of these rifles; the brass frame against the brightly blued barrel, that contrast is really something. Like the original, this Henry replica has a magazine tube that is actually machined integrally as one piece with the octagon barrel. Anyone who thinks he can scoff at the idea of the Italians being good machinists really needs to have a close look at one of these rifles and he will have his eyes opened. The Uberti-made copy of the Henry is chambered for modern cartridges, such as .44-40 and .45 Colt, so thankfully, finding ammunition is not a problem, the latter-day Henry rifle holds 13 rounds.

The Henry receiver and cartridge carrier are finished in bright, very cleanly machined brass that is coated with some sort of clear lacquer to help prevent tarnishing. In contrast, the barrel, barrel sleeve and finger lever are finished in a very well prepared bright blue, the hammer is also blued but with brightened sides. Our rifle was the 1860 military model, so it was equipped with sling swivels. The rear swivel base is inletted neatly into the side of the butt stock. The front swivel is fastened to the side of the barrel with screws. The metal on the rifle is finished exceedingly well. The blue is modern, caustic-type blueing but the preparatory polish was done in a professional manner, leaving sharp corners and even flats on the octagon barrel. The top flat on the barrel, forward of the rear sight is marked Henry's Patent, Oct. 16, 1860 and also carries Uberti's name and address. The caliber, .44-

This target is a group of eight shots, fired with Black Hills ammunition. Winchester ammunition performed about as well.

40 is stamped on the right barrel flat just ahead of the receiver. The lower side of the receiver, just behind the cartridge carrier and the left barrel flat ahead of the frame carry the small proof markings of the Italian government. A ladder-type rear sight is dovetailed into the barrel about an inch forward of the frame. This is graduated out to an overly ambitious 800 yards. In the down position, the rear sight presents a wide-angle U, at the center of which is filed a very tiny U for a sighting notch. The front sight is a Rocky Mountain style with a brass blade. We quickly found that with the rear sight ladder in the folded-down position, the front sight blade entirely filled up that tiny sighting notch, obliterating the sight picture. If the rear ladder is folded up, we find there is no sighting notch; only a very wide semi-circle that you have to guess at the center of. In addition, the elevating bar on the rear sight was so loose on the ladder that it would not stay in place. Worse, the ladder itself would not lock positively in the down position. Sorry, but there is not a lot of good to say about this rear sight, other than it looks something like the original. Much more attention to detail could and should have been paid to the sights on a rifle of this quality.

Henry specs	
Type:	Lever action, breech loading
Caliber:	.44/40, .45 LC
Barrel Length:	18-1/2" Henry Trapper 24-1/4" Henry Rifle
Total Length:	50-2/5" (24-1/4" bbl)
Weight:	9.04 lbs. (24-1/4" bbl)
Barrel:	Octagon, tapered, with integral magazine tube
Frame:	Brass
Buttplate:	Brass
Stock:	Walnut
Capacity:	13 rounds (bbl 24-1/4")
Retail Price:	$995
From:	Dixie Gun Works, Gunpowder Lane, Union City, TN 38271 (800) 238-6785 fax (731) 884-0440

The butt stock is made of walnut, colored a dark orange-brown and very finely finished in what appears to be varnish. A brass crescent rifle butt plate caps off the rear and it is mated to the wood of the butt stock nicely. There are some tiny gaps, no thicker than a piece of notebook paper, but they show up under close examination. The stock is fitted-up to the metal of the receiver with somewhat less care. The lower tang was a near perfect fit, however, the rear of the receiver and the upper tang displayed noticeable gaps between the wood and brass. Screws are all made with correct, narrow screwdriver slots and have nicely domed heads like the original screws. The trigger pull was. . .interesting, to say the least. It occurred in two stages. After a long period of what I would call bumpy-creeping the hammer fell off at almost 7 pounds pressure. As the trigger was being pulled, both shooters noticed the hammer slowly edging forward before it fell. Like I said, interesting.

The Uberti-Henry action operated super-smoothly and positively, as we would expect from this toggle-action design. Unlike the original Henry, Uberti's firing pin is made in two pieces and is spring-loaded. Throughout the shooting tests this rifle functioned and fed perfectly with no jams nor balks whatever, even after a fast run through where I emptied the magazine as fast as I could operate the lever. During this little rev-up, I made the mistake of holding the barrel by the two side flats, oh boy, the old reports were true, that barrel certainly does get hot. It was here that I noticed how quick the shot-to-shot recovery was with the Henry. This is a stable shooting platform, very nice and probably helped by that heavy barrel-magazine tube hanging out front. I also made the mistake, while bench resting the rifle, of forgetting about that magazine follower and we experienced a failure to feed, this was corrected just as soon as it was realized that I had allowed the magazine follower to run into the sand bag! On two separate trips to the range, we fired a total of 58 rounds through the Henry. Fifty of these shots were .44-40 Winchester brand with soft-point bullets. The remaining eight shots were from the last of a box of Black Hills ammunition with flat-nosed lead bullets. Because of the sight picture, or I should say, the lack thereof, we did not expect to be able to obtain decent groups from this rifle. In fact, on the morning before we shot the Henry, I was all set to file open that rear sight notch to make it wide enough to see through. Well, we fired a few shots from the gun as-is and discovered, to our surprise, that even with our guess-timated sight picture the Henry would easily cut consistent three-shot groups that measured about an inch at 25 yards using the Winchester ammo. The group on the target shown in the photo is comprised of the last 8 shots fired with Black Hills .44-40 ammunition.

Our impressions of the Henry are generally favorable, so lets get the bad stuff out of the way first. The sights are awful. A gun of this quality, and it is a high-quality rifle, just oughta' have sights that are useable. These sights offered a poor sight picture and were loose enough so that the rear sight ladder jumped up with each shot, I finally pasted the offender to the barrel with a strip of black electrical tape. Now having said that, from an appearance perspective the rifle is very beautiful. It is a good and almost perfectly faithful copy of the real Henry. I say this in spite of the wood-to-metal fit-up; which could have been better and, to be fair about this, on other Uberti-Henry rifles I have seen it generally is better. Overall, the Henry is a very pleasant rifle to look at and it attracted attention everywhere we took it. From a functional view, mechanically, the rifle's operation could not have been better, it did everything right, including shooting some groups that were almost unbelievably good. This is especially important when you consider the crude state of those sights. I suspect that, if the sights were improved (and the present sights could be improved without a great deal of effort), the Henry would be an incredibly satisfying rifle to shoot. As it is, it has wonderful accuracy potential.

The 1866 Yellow Boy

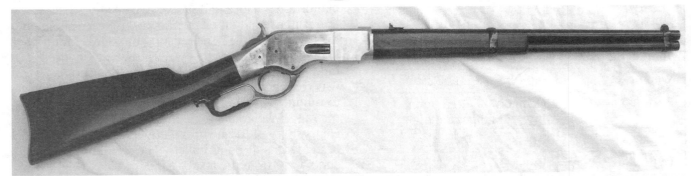

Uberti's 1866 carbine is a very well made, good-looking replica of the parent Winchester with only minor alterations to the firing pin that are actually improvements to the original design. Rifle courtesy of Ed Wade. Author photos.

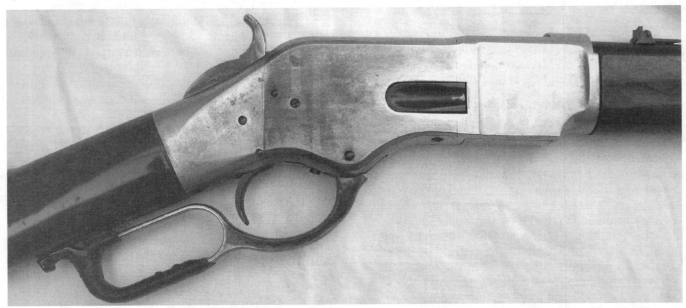

This 1866 has been fired several thousand times, much of it in cowboy competition and in heavy practice and it still works like new. Notice the brass is tarnished from being handled so much.

After the Civil War, Oliver Winchester gained control of the New Haven Arms Co. from B. Tyler Henry. One of Winchester's first steps was to try to improve the Henry rifle. The factory superintendent, Nelson King, devised a loading gate so the rifle could be loaded from the side. This eliminated the Henry's magazine and its exposed follower, allowing the addition of a wooden forearm. This improved rifle, named for the year of its introduction, 1866, and for the company's owner; Winchester, was essentially the Henry but with the objectionable features removed. The 1866 was chambered in one caliber, the .44 rimfire Henry, and offered as a round-barreled carbine, or as a rifle or musket with round or octagon barrels. Models of 1866 were quickly nicknamed the "Yellow Boy" on account of their brass frames. Roughly 170,000 Model 1866 rifles were manufactured between 1866 and 1898.

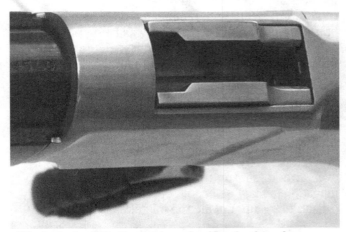

Winchester's old feed system was terrific, simple and very reliable, as is the replica. Both the receiver and cartridge carrier are brass just like the real thing.

This is the lower tang of the 1866 with the lever open. The small, dark rectangular piece just to the left of the serial number is the lever lock, when the lever is closed it can be turn 90 degrees to lock the action closed.

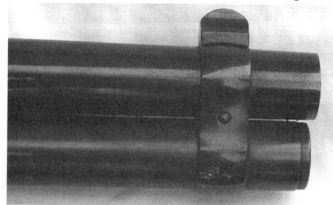

Like the original 1866 carbine, the replica has its front sight made integral with the front magazine band, thus it retains that "cool" 1866 carbine appearance.

Uberti has duplicated the early 1866 carbine rear sight. It's a good one but it needed some attention to improve the sight picture.

The 1866 carbine uses a traditional, carbine-styled butt plate made from brass. This shape is almost ideal for speed; it comes up to the shoulder fast and naturally, much faster than the crescent or "rifle" butt plate does.

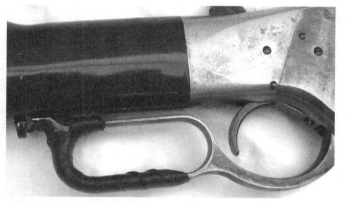

This close-up shot shows a very professional job of wrapping the lever loop. Notice that even though the top of the lever is partially wrapped, the leather does not interfere with the lever's ability to close.

This rifle is the gun that really launched the Winchester arms empire on its rise to fame and gained Winchester worldwide notice and acclaim. The model 1866 was accepted by a waiting public with open arms and was a popular weapon from the day it was introduced. It is, quite possibly the rifle most deserving of the title of the "gun that won the West." Winchester Model 1866 rifles were widely used by settlers, ranchers, lawmen, bandits and by native American warriors over the entire American frontier and well beyond our borders. Turkey took

the Model 1866 Winchester into war against the Russians, along with S&W revolvers chambered to accept the same .44 rimfire round. Introduced in 1870, Smith & Wesson's famous .44 caliber Model Number 3 revolver and the 1866 Winchester, being manufactured at the same time became, perhaps unwittingly, the first rifle and revolver to be chambered for the same cartridge. This idea of a rifle-revolver combo proved practical and popular and is a theme that gun manufacturers in America would repeat many times, even today.

We were not able to put our hands on a new Model 1866 in .45 Colt in time for these tests. However, through the generosity of a friend we were able to borrow a carbine that had already been used in competition, and that, although having been fired a few thousand times, was in excellent mechanical condition. This 1866 was in out-of-the-box condition except for a small sight alteration, a leather-wrapped finger lever and some tarnishing on the brass receiver from heavy handling. Our test 1866 replica is the 19-inch round-barreled carbine version and

was manufactured in Italy by A. Uberti Company and sold by the now-closed Uberti USA. This same basic gun is available today from several U. S. importers as a carbine with a 19-inch barrel, a short rifle using a 20-inch octagon barrel, or as a sporting rifle with a 24-inch barrel. Uberti offers the 1866 in three popular calibers; .38 Special, .44-40 and like our test gun, in .45 Colt. Just like the original Winchester, Uberti's 1866 replica comes with a solid brass frame and cartridge carrier. We had the opportunity to lay our replica alongside an original 1866 Winchester for

Uberti Model 1866 parts

1	Frame	80	Front band, carbine	112	Hammer link pin
2	Hammer	81	Fore end band, carbine	113	Magazine follower
3	Barrel	83	Right rear link	114	Magazine tube plug
7	Carrier block	84	Left rear link	115	Hammer link
10	Trigger	85	Right front link	118	Magazine tube
15	Sight	86	Left front link	119	Rear screw
19	Trigger spring	89	Lever	121	Front band screw, carbine
20	Main spring	90	Lifter arm	122	Fore end band screw, carbine
36	Mainspring screw	92	Right lever spring	123	Side plate screw
55	Rear sight assy.	93	Left lever spring	124	Lever spring screw
57	Butt stock	95	Firing pin spring	127	Ladle
58	Butt plate	96	Magazine spring	128	Ladle screw
62	Butt plate screw	97	Breech block	216	Fore end protection
63	Tang screw	98	Firing pin	224	Protection running guide
67	Firing pin extension	99	Trigger pin	225	Protection running bearing
68	Fore-end	100	Hammer pin screw	233	Protection running screw
72	Cam lever	101	Lever screw	234	Protection running spring
73	Right side plate	104	Firing pin stop	237	Lever hook spring
74	Left side plate	105	Rear link pin	239	Triggerguard screw
79	Extractor	106	Link pin	263	Trigger spring screw
		107	Lever pin	275	Magazine tube bearing
		108	Extractor pin	281	Magazine tube bearing pin
		109	Cam lever pin	283	Fore end protection screw
				284	Protection running sphere
				542	Lever hook
				542	Lever hook spring screw

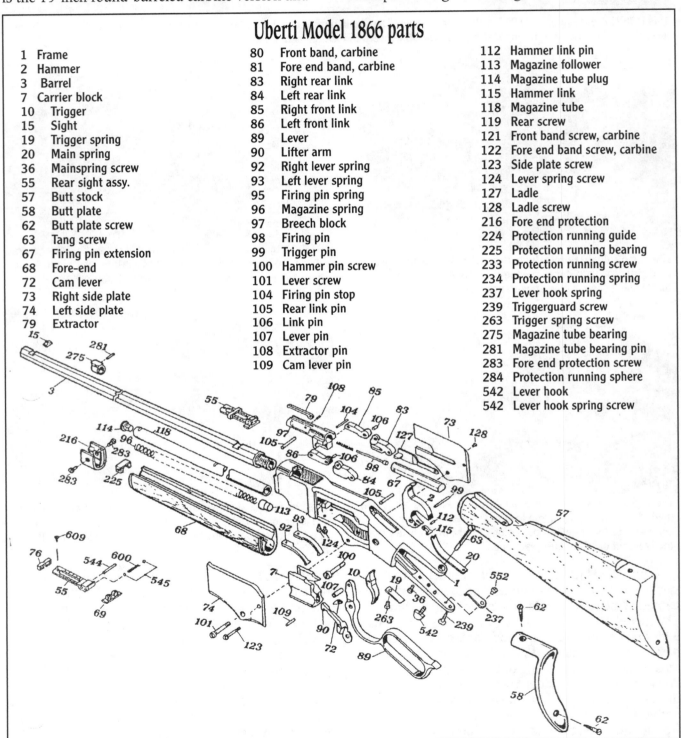

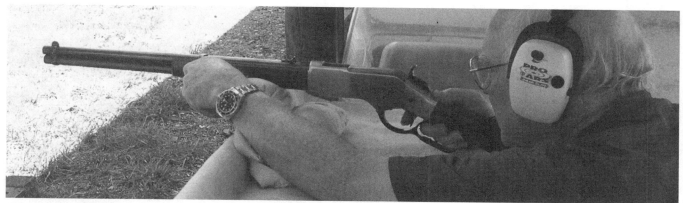

The 1866 carbine was a very pleasant rifle to shoot and operated beautifully through all the tests and with two brands of factory ammo and the owner's handloads.

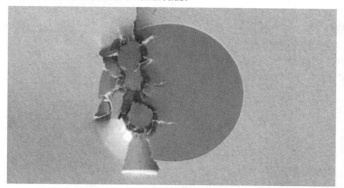

Ed's carbine liked the .45 Colt Winchester Cowboy ammunition best and gave us several groups that looked very much like this. It also shot right to the sights. The slight deviation to the left you see was caused by the angle of the morning sun on the sights, later in the day it clouded over and the gun shot to the center.

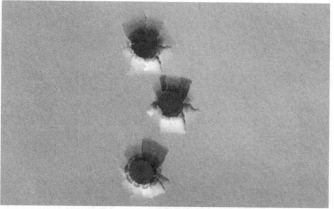

This three-shot group was typical of our experience with Black Hills .45 Colt Cowboy loads, this is about a 1 3/4-inch group that hit the paper 2 inches lower than the point of aim.

comparison and after examining and measuring the two, I have to say the Italian manufacturer has done a truly excellent job of duplication. Dimensionally, this Uberti is a very close copy, although there are subtle differences in the receiver shape, possibly on account of different polishing techniques. But by and large, the two rifles are nearly identical. The Uberti company has altered the firing pin mechanism into a two-piece pin, the front portion being spring-loaded. They had to do something. Remember, the originals used a rimfire cartridge and the modern replicas are being made in centerfire calibers. From what we have seen, the Uberti two-piece firing pins are more dependable and break less often than Winchester's one-piece firing pin as used in the original.

The brass frame exhibits very good machine work, with the seams of the side plates only just barely noticeable. The edges and corners were kept crisp by factory finishers, as they should be. Blueing on the barrel, bands and magazine tube was accomplished by modern hot-caustic means and its all-important preparatory polish was obviously first-rate, leaving a bright, highly polished surface without ripples. The hammer and lever are finished in color case hardening that is quite pleasing to look at and

reminiscent of the old bone and charcoal Winchester colors. The hammer spur is coarsely checkered and they have used a pattern which is very similar to the one used on early original 1866 models, that is, flat checkering or as the English called it; cross-checking. This carbine is stocked in walnut that is mildly figured and finished with a gloss, in what appears to be a varnish of some sort. Wood-to-metal fit-up was excellent, that is, everywhere except at the junction of the forearm wood to the front of the receiver where a gap of about 1/16 of an inch was present.

The sights on this replica carbine consisted of a plain post-type front like the originals. It is made as a part of the front magazine band. Sometimes front sights mounted on magazine bands can be a problem because, if the band gets loose and moves around, so does the sight. In this case, the band fit tightly and gave us no troubles. For a rear sight the Uberti carbine has a replica of the one used on early Winchester carbines. This is a folding sight that offers two higher elevation positions when flipped up. The sight picture was very good and it gave a much clearer picture than the sight did when the gun came from the factory. This is because the owner had previously altered the rear sight notch to give a

1866 Specs	
Type:	Lever-action, breech loading
Caliber:	.38 SP, .44/40, .45 Colt
Barrel length:	Carbine 19", sporting rifle 20", 24-1/4"
Total Length:	Carbine 38-3/10", 50" (24-1/4" bbl)
Weight:	Carbine 7.39 lbs., 8.16 lbs. (24-1/4" bbl)
Barrel:	Carbine: Round tapered, Rifle Octagonal tapered
Frame:	Brass
Buttplate:	Brass
Stock:	Walnut
Mag. Tube:	Carbine 10 rounds, 13 rounds (24-1/4" bbl)
Retail Prices:	#342280 - 1866 "Yellowboy" Carbine 19" - $755 #342290 - 1866 "Yellowboy" Sporting Rifle 24-1/4" - $800 #342340 - 1866 "Yellowboy" Short Rifle 20" - $800
From:	Stoeger Industries 17603 Indian Head Hwy., Ste 200 Accokeek, MD 20607 (301 283-6300)

clearer picture with more daylight at the sides. Action operation was very smooth, slick and positive and throughout the tests it fed and ejected cartridges perfectly. The trigger pull had just a small amount of creep with the let-off occurring at about 4 pounds. Lock time was good but I might have preferred a little more aggressive mainspring for a slightly quicker hammer fall. Readers will notice the upper portion of the finger lever loop has been tightly wrapped with a thin leather thong. Many cowboy shooters do this and it serves three purposes: 1) it reduces the amount of space in the loop and offers a quicker cycle, 2) it saves the shooter's fingers from getting torn up by sharps edges on the steel lever and 3) is offers a non-skid surface.

We test fired the 1866 carbine at 25 yards, and just as with all the rifles, the shooting was done with the rifle rested on bags off the bench. We sampled both Winchester Cowboy Loads and Black Hills Cowboy ammunition with the accuracy edge going to the Winchester loads. This is a carbine we already knew was accurate and the gun regularly shoots groups from 5/8 to 3/4 of an inch when the owner's hand-loaded ammunition is used. Black Hills .45 Colt ammunition gave us three-shot groups that hit the paper about 2 inches low and ranged from 1 1/4 to about 1 3/4 inches center-to-center. With the .45 Colt Winchester Cowboy loads the three-shot groups were consistently under an inch and the shots hit the paper

at exactly the right elevation. Operation of the 1866 was smooth, slick and totally trouble free.

How did we like the 1866 Uberti? Almost all the Uberti 1866s I have shot are more than just acceptably accurate, and this one was no exception. That great old Winchester toggle action is smooth and fast. When used in competition the guns are quick to recover shot-to-shot and they feed very reliably, although it has been my experience that when they are brand new, many of them could stand some smoothing up by a gunsmith. As for looks, there's nothing tacky about these rifles, the finishes on all of the 1866s I have seen have ranged from a low of very good to downright excellent. The sights could stand some improvement from the factory, but that would not require any expensive or complicated changes. All the factory needs to do is to supply the gun with a clear sight picture that acquires quickly. For reliability, the modern Uberti product is better than even an original Winchester. Say what? Sorry man, but its true. While the fit and finish of these replicas may not be as good as "the real deal" and in many cases the wood is not of the same quality, from a shooter's standpoint these newly manufactured guns do not break springs, firing pins and extractors on a regular basis. On the originals these parts did break, and broke often. Given all that, I guess the short answer is that we liked it a lot. This is a great gun for either cowboy competition or just plain fun plinking.

Model 1873

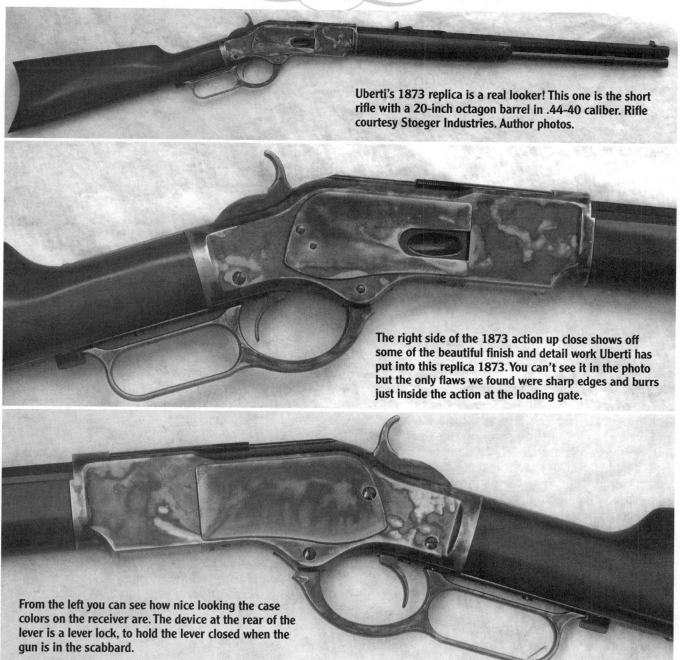

Uberti's 1873 replica is a real looker! This one is the short rifle with a 20-inch octagon barrel in .44-40 caliber. Rifle courtesy Stoeger Industries. Author photos.

The right side of the 1873 action up close shows off some of the beautiful finish and detail work Uberti has put into this replica 1873. You can't see it in the photo but the only flaws we found were sharp edges and burrs just inside the action at the loading gate.

From the left you can see how nice looking the case colors on the receiver are. The device at the rear of the lever is a lever lock, to hold the lever closed when the gun is in the scabbard.

The brass frame and the low power of the original .44 Henry rimfire cartridge limited the 1866 rifle's versatility. In 1873, continuing the process of improving the lever-action design, Winchester introduced a new steel-framed rifle that was chambered for the more potent .44-40 centerfire cartridge which they named .44 WCF (for .44 Winchester centerfire.) The Model 1873 firmly established the lever-action as an American standard, a well-known classic and one of the weapons that truly helped to "win the West." The 1873 was chambered in .32-20, .38-40 and .44-40 Winchester calibers. Almost 20,000 were also made in .22 rimfire. The 1873 was manufactured for about 50 years and Winchester produced over 720,000 of them in carbine (20-inch barrel), rifle (24-inch barrel) and musket (30-inch barrel) configurations. As was the norm of the day, Winchester also made the 1873 available in countless custom combinations of varying barrel lengths, weights, finishes, sights and wood styles.

Uberti offers several versions including the carbine with 19-inch barrel; the 20-inch octagon barrel Short Sporting Rifle; the Sporting Rifle with

This shot shows some of the beautiful workmanship on the forward end of the rifle.

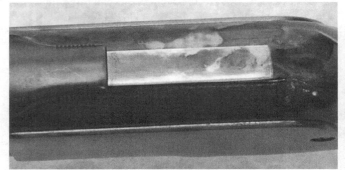

From experience gained with the Henry and the Model 1866, Winchester was concerned about dust and debris entering the action from the top so they did something about it with the 1873. In these two photos we see the 1873 action from the top with the dust cover closed (left) and opened. Operating the lever opens the dust cover automatically.

a 24 1/4-inch barrel (round or half-octagon); and the Special Sporting Rifle, with select walnut pistol-grip stock. The new Uberti 1873s are available in .357, .44/40 and .45 Colt calibers. We obtained our Uberti 1873 from Stoeger Industries. It was one of the popular short sporting rifle versions with a 20-inch octagon barrel, chambered for .44-40 caliber. We had wanted to test a short sporting rifle in .45 Colt, unfortunately one in that caliber was not going to be available in time for our deadline. The idea of the "short rifle" is a popular one with cowboy shooters. It gives the shooter a short, carbine-length rifle with the added balance of that heavy octagon barrel up front. This dampens muzzle rise for quicker successive shots. The only drawback with this idea is the short rifle is not supplied with a carbine butt, instead, it is sold with the crescent-shaped rifle butt. The carbine butt is more rounded, allowing the rifle to swing up to the shoulder much quicker.

Our Model 1873 was blued with a color case hardened receiver, lever and hammer. The overall quality of the blueing work and its preparation was first-class in every respect, showing nice, crisp flats on the octagon and polishing quality on the remaining blued parts that I would say was the equivalent to 1950s American factory work. In other words, very good. Case colors were certainly a cut above much of the color hardening we have seen on many new guns. Even the upper tang is carefully marked with a flourish in a fashion that is so much like an original it would be hard to tell them apart. While I am not convinced this is done by the bone and charcoal method, the colors are nevertheless very beautiful and somewhat reminiscent of the old

L. C. Smith colors. The two-piece stocks are walnut, stained a dark red-brown color that is quite similar to the old Winchester stain. The stocks are finished in some sort of a clear coat that looks like, and may very well be, a form of varnish. Finish work is like the metalwork, top-drawer and very, very good looking. The fit-up of wood to metal was outstanding, a cut above average in every respect.

Uberti did a very good job with all the screws in this rifle. They all had narrow screwdriver slots, the screw heads were perfectly domed and they fit into their holes well. In addition, another nice touch is the screws were nitre blued. This deep, translucent blue color really made them stand out against the color case hardened frame. Sights on the Uberti model 1873 are Winchester clones all the way, and nicely done to boot. The front sight is quite like the old Winchester Model 21. It's fitted in a dovetail and kept from sliding side to side with a set screw. The rear sight is a barrel-mounted, leaf-type buckhorn sight and adjustment for elevation is accomplished by a stepped-ramp, like the originals. I was very pleased to see that the sight picture these sights present to the shooter comes to the eyes quickly, it is clear and very distinct. In short, these are good, practical, basic sights that can actually be used.

The 1873's action operation was smooth and positive as we expected it might be, but with a lever safety spring that we found a tad too strong. The safety liked to hold the lever partially open, so unless the shooter really squeezed the lever hard, the gun would not fire. Trigger pull was crisp and it broke cleanly and fast, but it was rather on the hard side at about 7 pounds. Loading the 1873 was not especially easy, there was perfect tension on the loading gate (spring cover), however the troubles we experienced came from the fact that the factory neglected to de-burr the edge of the receiver just in front of the spring cover. It was sharp enough to cut the fingers of the shooter during the loading process. We also experienced some loading hang-ups at the front of the loading gate. This involved difficulty getting the cartridge rims past a burr and into the magazine tube. This difficulty could only be overcome by "wiggling" the rear of the cartridge with your thumb but it made for slow, sometimes painful loading. These are both problems that are likely related and probably could be cured with some quick, careful gunsmithing work, but they are faults one does not expect to find on a

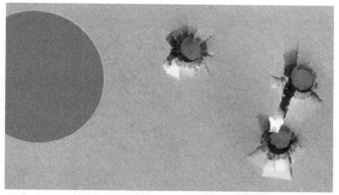

This group is typical of the three-shot groups we obtained from Hornady Frontier .44–40 Cowboy loads was about an inch and a half center to center. This load shot to the sights for elevation at 25 yards.

1873 parts

1	Frame	72	Cam lever	97	Breech block	127	Ladle
2	Hammer	73	Right side plate	98	Firing pin	128	Ladle screw
3	Barrel	74	Left side plate	99	Trigger pin	167	Trigger guard screw
7	Carrier block	79	Extractor	101	Lever screw	178	Hammer pin
15	Sight	83	Right rear link	104	Firing pin stop	216	Fore-end protection
19	Trigger spring	84	Left rear link	105	Rear link pin	218	Protection running
20	Main spring	85	Right front link	106	Link pin	224	Protection running guide
26	Triggerguard	86	Left front link	107	Lever pin	225	Protection running bearing
36	Mainspring screw	87	Trigger lower portion	108	Extractor pin	233	Protection running screw
53	Mainspring adj. screw	88	Trigger upper portion	109	Cam lever pin	234	Protection running spring
55	rear	89	Lever	111	Safety spring pin	237	Lever hook spring
57	Butt-stock	90	Lifter arm	112	Hammer link pin	238	Lever hook pin
58	Butt-plate	91	Safety bar	113	Magazine follower	240	Trigger & lever screw
61	Rear sight	92	Right lever spring	114	Magazine tube plug	275	Magazine tube bearing
62	Buttplate screw	93	Left lever spring	115	Hammer link	281	Magazine tube bearing pin
63	Tang screw	94	Safety spring	118	Magazine tube	283	Fore-end protection screw
67	Firing pin extension	95	Firing pin spring	123	Side plate screw	284	Protection running sphere
68	Fore-end	96	Magazine spring	124	Lever spring screw	542	Lever hook

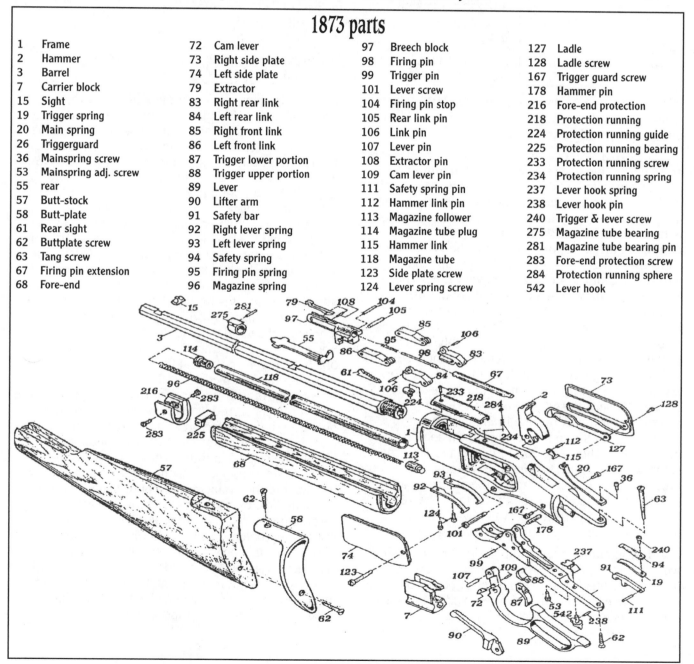

1873 Specs	
Type:	Lever action, breech Loading
Caliber:	.357 Mag., .44/40, .45 LC
Barrel length:	Carbine 19", Sptg. Rifle 20", 24-1/4"
Total Length:	Carbine 38-3/10", 50" (24-1/4" bbl)
Weight:	Carbine 7.38 lbs., 8.16 lbs. (24-1/4" bbl)
Barrel:	Carbine; round, Rifle; octagon tapered
Frame:	Forged steel, color case-hardened
Stock/Forend:	Walnut
Mag. Tube:	Carbine 10 rounds, 13 rounds (24-1/4" bbl)
Optional Sights:	Mid-range Vernier adjustable Creedmore or Lyman adjustable Creedmore
Retail Prices:	#342820-1873 Sporting Rifle 24-1/4" - MSRP $965 #342410-1873 Short Rifle 20" - MSRP $965 #342800-1873 Carbine 19-1/2" MSRP $925
From:	Stoeger Industries, 17603 Indian Head Hwy. Ste 200 Accokeek, MD 20607 (301 283-6300)

factory-new rifle. It makes one wonder if the gun was single-loaded during the factory test-fire and if the magazine operation was ever tried.

The 1873 was test fired, as per all our rifle tests, at 25 yards. We used two brands of ammunition on two separate test dates; Winchester .44-40 soft points (fired at an indoor range) and Hornady .44-40 Cowboy loads fired outdoors. The latter ammo is factory loaded to 725 fps muzzle velocity in a handgun barrel. Performance with the Winchester soft-points was very good, giving groups that measured about 3/4 of an inch every time. The Hornady Cowboy Loads also gave good, but not great accuracy, with three-shot groups averaging 1 3/4 inches. We did not touch the factory sight settings so out-of-the-box all groups hit roughly 2 inches to the right, with the higher velocity Winchester ammo striking 2 inches high and the slower Hornady hitting the paper to the point of aim for elevation. During the second set of tests, while loading the magazine for the third time I managed to cut my thumb on that sharp frame edge at the loading port I mentioned earlier. After that I decided to save myself some pain by single-loading the weapon through the breech for the rest of the tests. Despite the loading problems, all the way through the tests the 1873 action operated perfectly, it was always smooth and positive with excellent cartridge feeding.

How about an overall impression? Here is what we liked: In appearance this is a truly beautiful replica. The fit-up and the finishes of both wood and metal were excellent and attention paid to the small details was well above average. The sights are very

nice and from a practical standpoint they are very useful. The 1873's action operation was flawless and the accuracy was certainly good enough to compete. I like the concept of this short, stiff octagon barrel. It adds weight up front where you need it, helps to dampen recoil and generally, is very comfortable to point. What I don't like about many of the so-called "short rifles" is the crescent-shaped rifle butt plates that don't fit very many shooters well and are cumbersome to shoulder. It's as if the manufacturers didn't understand what the intent of a rifle like this is. The shooters don't just need milder recoil, they need a carbine-length rifle that comes up to the shoulder quickly. It is for this reason that these short-rifles ought to be supplied with carbine butts. That is just a general observation about all guns of this type, not about a flaw in this particular rifle. My only real objection involved the real flaw in this gun, and that was with the sharp edges at the loading port, also the internal burrs near this area that partially jammed the rims and kept cartridges from being easily loaded. To be fair to the manufacturer I have worked on, handled and shot a great many 1873 Uberti replicas and this is only the second gun that I have seen with this identical set of problems with in the area of loading. In addition, the problems are not difficult for a smith to repair. Yes, they are annoying on a new gun but I would not say its a deal-breaker. In fact, if we can put those problems aside, Aldo Uberti's rendition of the 1873 is, I believe, an awesome replica of the Winchester. If you like the Model 1873, don't overlook this one, even if it needs some tune-up work (and most new guns will) it will make a very reliable and good-looking cowboy competition rifle.

EMF Hartford Model 1892, stainless

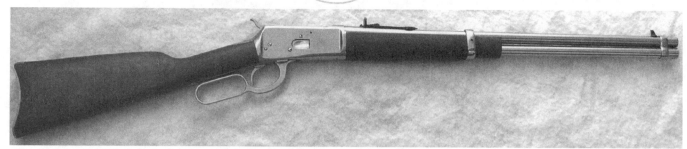

The EMF Hartford Model 1892 carbine, shown here in stainless steel is a handsome, handy little saddle gun whose practical applications extend beyond cowboy shooting. Rifle courtesy EMF Company. Author photos.

In a close-up of the right side you can see how close to the original Winchester this Brazilian-made copy is.

The famous Model 1892 Winchester was a simplified version, scaled down in size, of the Winchester Model 1886. The 1886, of course, was a full-sized rifle, originally designed by John M. Browning to handle the big, powerful hunting cartridges of its day such as the .45-70, .45-90 —and others. With fewer moving parts and of a more diminutive size than the 1886, the more compact Model 1892 was built to handle pistol-sized cartridges such as the .44-40, .38-40 and .32-20 WCF. Winchester intended that this newly design rifle would take the place of the venerable and popular Model 1873. In fact, the more modern 1892 did offer certain hard-to-miss advantages over the earlier design. In comparing the two, the 1892 action was certainly lighter and smaller than the 1873. The new action used fewer moving parts, and best of all, the 1892's breech bolt was locked shut by a pair of vertical-dropping steel bolts, thus offering a far stronger breech mechanism than the old toggle-link action of the 1873. The 1892 is an old Hollywood favorite. We recall seeing 1892 Winchesters used incorrectly in some Western movies that were supposed to be set in earlier times.

Winchester's 1892 was a beautiful rifle, however it was also a robust, simple design that has a well-known and well-deserved reputation for reliable operation. The action is actually stronger than it needed to be and at the same time is so small and lightweight that an 1892 saddle-ring carbine in .44 caliber weighs in at something just over 5 pounds, unloaded. EMF's replica 1892, called the Hartford model, is made in Brazil by Rossi. The version we obtained for our tests was the 20-inch barrel carbine in stainless steel, chambered for the .45 Colt caliber.

EMF's Hartford 1892 is all stainless steel so no separate finish is required. It is furnished polished in a medium luster. The quality of the polishing is good but not great with rougher polishing marks showing through and slight hogging near the screw holes. Still, the exterior metal presents a good appearance with sharp, well-defined lines that may not be an exact copy of the Winchester, but they have kept it very close. The screws are all properly domed with medium to narrow screwdriver slots that look very correct on this gun. We noticed that the screws were also well fitted to their holes. The exception to this was the front band screw, which was loose when the gun arrived and would

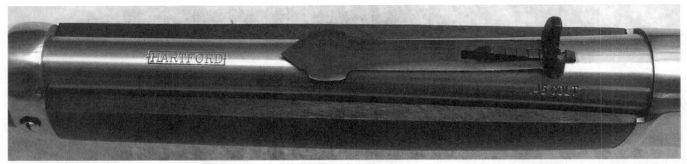

In these two shots, we can see the top of the EMF 1892 barrel. Notice the loose screw in the front band. The gun came that way. The rear band is a solid, round-shaped machined steel band similar to the original 1866 models and the rear sight is a copy of the Winchester buckhorn.

Open the lever and you will find the manufacturer's name and address neatly hidden on the lower tang behind the trigger.

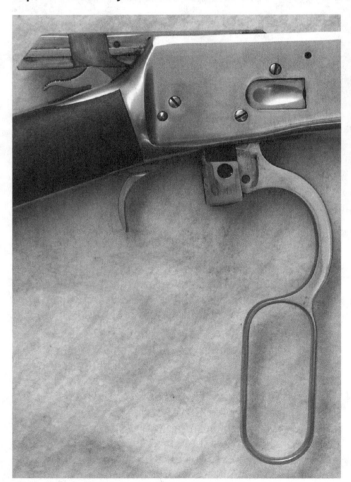

Rossi has inserted the front sight into a machined barrel dovetail, while it doesn't look exactly like an original Winchester carbine sight; this is an effective and professional method of attaching a sight.

Here is the 1892 Hartford stainless open, with the lever all the way down. This rifle has a very well designed coil mainspring and the result is a wonderfully slick action.

not go back in because the threaded end would not align with the hole on the opposite side of the band. We disassembled the forearm wood and magazine tube and relieved the notch in the bottom of the barrel just enough so the screw could pass through correctly before shooting the gun.

The Hartford stocks are two-piece, apparently some sort of straight-grained walnut, shaped in a fashion similar to, but not exactly like the 1892 Winchester. A light oil finish of some sort had been applied over a dark walnut stain. Wood-to-metal fit-up around the action faces and tangs was actually very tight and I would call it a very good fit. The fit-up of the butt plate to the stock however was another story. With large gaps on the left side and on both sides at the top curve. Up where the butt plate's top tang was inletted into the wood, here the

Parts for the Rossi EMF Model 1892

1	Barrel	26	Extractor	56-F.	Finger lever		
2-A	Receiver	27	Extractor pin	57-F.	Friction stud		
3-A	Saddle Ring Hold	28	Firing pin	58-F.	Friction stud spring		
4-A	Saddle Ring	29	Firing pin stop pin	59-F.	Friction stud stop pin		
5	Magazine tube	30	Ejector spring stop	60.	Locking bolt, left		
5-G	Magazine tube outside	31	Ejector spring stop pin	61.	Locking bolt pin		
6	Magazine follower	32	Ejector	62.	Locking bolt pin stop screw		
6-G	Magazine follower	33	Ejector spring	63.	Locking bolt, right		
7	Magazine spring	34	Ejector collar	64.	Lever & breechbolt pin		
7-G	Magazine spring	35	Lower tang	65.	Lever & breechbolt pin		
8	Magazine plug	36	Trigger		hole plug screw		
8-G	Magazine plug	37	Trigger spring	66.	Hammer		
9	Magazine plug screw	38	Trigger spring screw	67-D	Mainspring rod		
10	Magazine ring	39	Carrier	68.	Hammer screw		
13	Magazine plug screw	40	Carrier stop	69.	Main spring		
14	Forearm	41	Carrier stop spring	70-E.	Stock		
15	Forearm tip	41-G	Magazine plug slide pin spring	71-E.	Butt plate		
16	Forearm tip screw	42	Carrier stop pin	72-E.	Butt plate screw		
17-B	Complete rear sight	43	Carrier screw	73.	Upper tang screw		
18-B		44	Cartridge guide, left	77.	Strip of rawhide		
19-B		45	Cartridge stop	85.	Locking lever		
20	Elevator	46	Cartridge stop joint pin	86.	Locking pin		
20-G	Magazine tube inside	47.	Cartridge stop spring	87.	Locking spring		
21-G	Magazine plug slide pin	48.	Cartridge guide, right	88.	Locking ball		
22-G	Magazine plug screw	49.	Cartridge guide screws	89.	Firing pin spring stop		
23-G	Magazine plug slide pin	50-C.	Complete spring cover	90.	Firing pin spring		
25	Breech bolt	55.	Spring cover screw	91.	Front sight		

Illustration courtesy of E.M.F. Company, Inc.

Ed Wade is taking careful aim during a rare cloudy moment when the brass bead front sight would not be effected so much by glare.

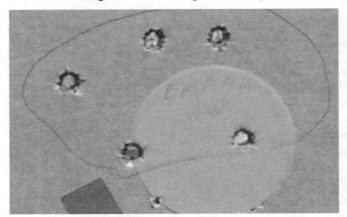

The EMF didn't care for Winchester .45 Colt ammo so much. This is two three-shot groups. In the lower group two bullets went through the left hole. Unfortunately, these are two of the better Winchester groups.

This target was shot with Black Hills .45 Colt and it is actually two three-shot groups.

Hornady .45 Colt Cowboy Loads produced several great little three-shot, one-hole groups like this one.

fit was almost perfect. This is an unusual occurrence, to see examples of both very good and fair to poor wood-to-metal fitting work on the same gun. The bands bear some mention. The rear band was of the 1866 type, solid steel, rounded in shape and nicely made. Even though it is historically out of place on an 1892, it looks rather good there. Up front, the forward band was machined steel, very much like an original 1892 Winchester band. EMF's sights are a combination of a Winchester clone leaf-buckhorn rear along with a post and gold-bead front sight that is dovetailed into the barrel just behind the front band. This latter method of mounting the front sight is a major improvement over some of the early Rossi-made 1892s, whose front sights were part of the front band and were often found loose, a situation that is destructive to accuracy. At least this way we know for sure that the front sight is fixed and stable. Looking down the sights, we are presented with a good, but unfortunately, not perfectly clear sight picture. The bottom of the buckhorn rear is a medium-sized U sight aperture and the gold bead fits but was polished off with rounded edges so the front sight was, at best, blurry. The hammer is shaped like a Winchester and has a round-edged spur, but with deep, sharp cross-serrations instead of checkering.

You should know that these serrations don't look "cheap" like the ones used on some modern guns and they are, frankly, very effective when you have to manually cock the hammer or when letting the hammer down easily from full tension.

Rossi has done something good with this 1892 and I believe they should be given credit for it. Using the EMF Hartford 1892 action was very much like operating a real 1892 Winchester with the distinct advantage of the lever feeling like it was easier to operate as the hammer is cocked by the bolt. Winchester's Model 1892 used a heavy, leaf-mainspring whose tension greatly increased as the hammer was moved rearward. Thus towards the end the amount of effort required for lever throw actually increased for a moment. The Rossi-built 1892 uses a very well-designed coil spring and strut set-up where the compression of the spring actually becomes easier as the hammer moves father back. The lever operation is slick as grease throughout the entire cycle. What is more, because that spring-strut is so well designed the hammer is very easy to cock manually but that "snap" of a fully tensioned mainspring is maintained along with a quick lock-time. Trigger pull was better than we imagined it would be. It was fast with very little in the way of creep and the let-off was quick with the hammer breaking loose at just over 4 pounds.

We test fired the 1892 with about 75 rounds of ammunition, using three brands: Black Hills, Hornady and Winchester. All were .45 Colt Cowboy Loads. The rifle performed beautifully for us all through the tests. It fed cartridges of all makes and operated perfectly from start to finish. The sights did gives us some fits in the bright sunlight, as both shooters searched for a clearer view of that elusive brass front sight. Interestingly, the bright stainless steel did not seem to cause glare or to effect the sights one little bit. Loading presented us with a small challenge, The factory did not bother to de-burr the sharp edge at the front of the loading port on the frame and this led to some cut and sore fingers, but we muddled through. All our groups were fired at 25 yards and in sets of three shots each, using a sand bag rest, exactly as we had for every rifle tested. This rifle liked the Hornady Cowboy Loads best, printing several three-shot groups with all the shots touching. The Black Hills ammo turned in average groups of about 1 1/2 inches. The normally accurate Winchester Cowboy ammo did not do quite so well in this rifle, giving us groups in the 2 to 2 1/2-inch range. As with all the rifles we tested, we did not touch the factory-set sights. This rifle shot uniformly left about an inch, but printed right to the sights for elevation with all brands of ammo. The EMF Hartford was very

Hartford 1892 Lever Action	
Model	CCR92CSS-20
Finish:	Polished Stainless steel
Stocks:	2-piece, walnut
Barrel:	20" round, carbine
Caliber:	.45 Colt
Retail:	$400
From:	EMF Company 1900 E. Warner Ave. 1D Santa Ana, CA 92705 (949) 261-6611 on the Internet at www.emf-company.com

easy to recover shot-to-shot in rapid fire from the shoulder. At 25 yards, I found I was able to ring the 6-inch steel gong with 10 out of 10 shots off-hand, shooting almost as fast as I could work the lever, using a low, three-o'clock hold for my sights.

What did we think of the EMF 1892 Hartford? Well, to be fair, the rifle has its flaws; like the wood-to-metal fit thing and the not-so-professional surface polishing on the receiver. But all-in-all, this is really a good little carbine. It showed us it can deliver very good accuracy and that it has more than a little potential to be a much better gun. For what this gun costs, one might consider putting some work into it and, in my opinion, could be made into an excellent, dependable rifle that could be competitive with the best of them. And its made of stainless steel. How cool is that? Wouldn't it make a perfect pick-up, boat or saddle gun? Both the shooters, and several of the folks who got to handle, shoot and look it over, thought the EMF 1892 Hartford was a pretty darned good gun for the money.

United States Fire Arms Mfg. Co. Lightning Pump Rifle

United States Fire Arms Mfg. Co.'s reproduction of the Colt Lightning rifle looks remarkably like the real thing. This company has paid a lot of attention to original details and the result is one very finely made rifle that is darned hard to tell apart from an original. Author photos.

In this close-up view we can see some of the beautiful craftsmanship USFA is putting into the Lightning. This is a handsome firearm, Notice the distinctively shaped loading gate, which in this instance is known as the loading trap.

The American-made reproduction of Colt's famous pump rifle has finally arrived. Originally manufactured by Colt in Hartford, Conn. from 1884 until 1904, with its lightning-fast short stroke slide action and its compact size, the Lightning Magazine Rifle was an awesome gun. In some circles the originals remain popular to this day. Colt's Lightning magazine rifle was made in three distinct frame sizes. Small was chambered for .22 rimfire. Medium was intended for pistol-sized rounds and the large or "Express" frame size that fired full-size, high-powered rifle cartridges of the day. All of these Colt pump guns were excellent rifles. They were different from the familiar Winchester pump rifles but nevertheless, extremely well made and with the sort of amazing workmanship you might expect from the late 19th century Colt factory.

USFA's modern-made version of the Lightning is offered on the medium-sized frame and is available in .38 WCF, .44 WCF and .45 Colt. They are offering the rifle in grades ranging from a 20-inch Cowboy

With the slide shoved back you can get a look at the Lightning with its action open. Like the original Lightning, the new USFA has a very short-stroke bolt operation, making for literally a "lightning-fast" action.

Action Carbine to a 26-inch barreled rifle in round, octagon (as tested) or optional half round/half octagon configurations. Stocks are available in

The rifle is finished in blue and I have to say the polish work the factory did before the blueing was very good; the lines were well maintained and

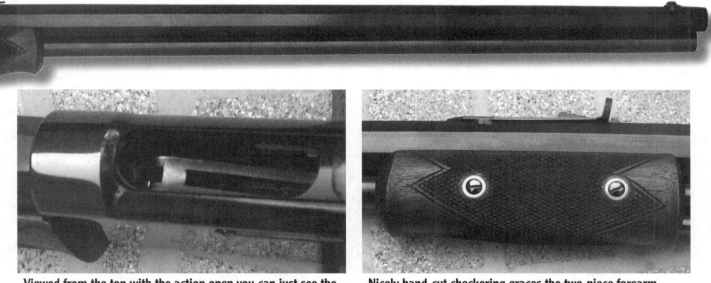

Viewed from the top with the action open you can just see the top of the cartridge carrier. To the right is the sliding top cover or dust cover that closes the top of the action nicely when the bolt is closed.

Nicely hand-cut checkering graces the two-piece forearm panels that look and act just like the real thing. The forend wood is made up of two pieces, a left and a right, just like a handgun grip.

The barrel markings on the Lightning are very similar to the original Colt marks in size and style. Also shown in this shot is the semi-buckhorn rear sight.

straight or optional pistol grip with or without checkering and several grades of walnut and blueing can also be had in the Deluxe grade (starting around $2,000.) Our test rifle is the Premium (medium) Grade version in .44-40 caliber with a 26-inch octagon barrel. Straight out of the box I could see this was one slick-looking replica and we could tell right away that this was going to be an impressive rifle. Just how faithful a replica is this new USFA Lightning? Well, aside from the fact that the type of blueing used is obviously (to me at least) a modern, hot blue and not a combination of charcoal and slow rust blue like the original Colt, this new USFA pump rifle is literally *a dead-ringer* for the medium-framed Colt Lightning. In fact, the resemblance is so good that at first glance I wondered just for a moment if I was looking at an original Colt Lightning that someone had professionally restored using modern blueing methods. As far as authenticity goes, I don't think I could find a higher compliment to pay the manufacturer.

corners and edges are kept intact and sharp. The octagon barrel is well and finely polished, leaving perfect corners and straight lines. The receiver is finished in a glossy, higher-polish blue than the barrel and I did note vertical polishing marks left in the glossy finish. But it still presented an excellent appearance. As you might expect, the large rampant Colt logo that used to be on the original receiver side has not been reproduced on the USFA version, but since it looked so much like an original, I did look for it! The hammer (like the Colt) is finished in bone and charcoal color case hardening and its appearance is just flat gorgeous. Checkering on the hammer's spur is similar to, but not exactly like the Colt. It is however, sharply cut and offers the user an effective grip. The screw heads are all nicely domed and equipped with handsome, narrow 19th century-style slots. Even the barrel address and caliber markings, which of course bear the U.S. Fire Arms Mfg. name and address, are styled to look like 1880s vintage Colt lettering.

The wood-to-metal fit-up is generally very good to excellent, with only the barest gaps showing between the two substances, and true to form, the wood has been left just a bit "proud" (in other words, standing a bit higher than the metal). The stocks are an orange-brown color, made of vintage appropriate, straight-grained American walnut, finished in Tru-Oil™ and they present a good-looking, traditional oil-finished appearance. Like the original Lightning, the forearm wood is made from two pieces of walnut, mated together and covered with very well executed, hand-checkering in a bordered pattern that is also a darned good copy of

the original. In further keeping with the original Colt style, the crescent-shaped steel butt-plate is thicker than the ones used on Winchesters, this was also very well finished in bright blue.

Sights are open, with a semi-buckhorn barrel or middle sight, adjustable for elevation and a Rocky Mountain-style front, with both dovetailed into the top barrel flat. The sight picture presents the shooter with a skinny, flat post set into a small semi-circle and although I've certainly used sights with better definition, frankly, in practice it wasn't bad. In off-hand shooting the rifle shouldered wonderfully for a gun with a crescent butt (one shooter remarked

Lightning parts

1	receiver	18	trigger spring	36	locking brace
2	left ejector	19	trigger spring screw	37	locking brace pin
3	right ejector	20	main spring	40	barrel, octagon
4	ejector screws	21	main spring screw	41	magazine tube
5	loading trap	22	magazine stop spring	42	magazine tube spring
6	loading trap spring	23	magazine stop	43	magazine spring
7	loading trap spring screw	24	magazine stop spring screw	44	follower
8	loading trap srop screw	25	bolt	45	magazine lug
9	sideplate screw	26	top-cover	46	rifle tube screw
10	hammer	27	top cover screw	47	forend stock wood, right
11	hammer roller	28	extractor	48	forend stock wood, left
12	hammer roller pin	29	extractor pin	49	grip escutcheon
13	hammer safety pin	30	firing pin	50	grip screw
14	hammer pin	31	firing pin lever	51	butt stock
15	tang	32	firing pin lever pin	52	butt plate
16	tang screw	33	slide	53	buttplate screw
17	trigger	34	carrier	55	trigger and stop pin
		35	carrier screws		

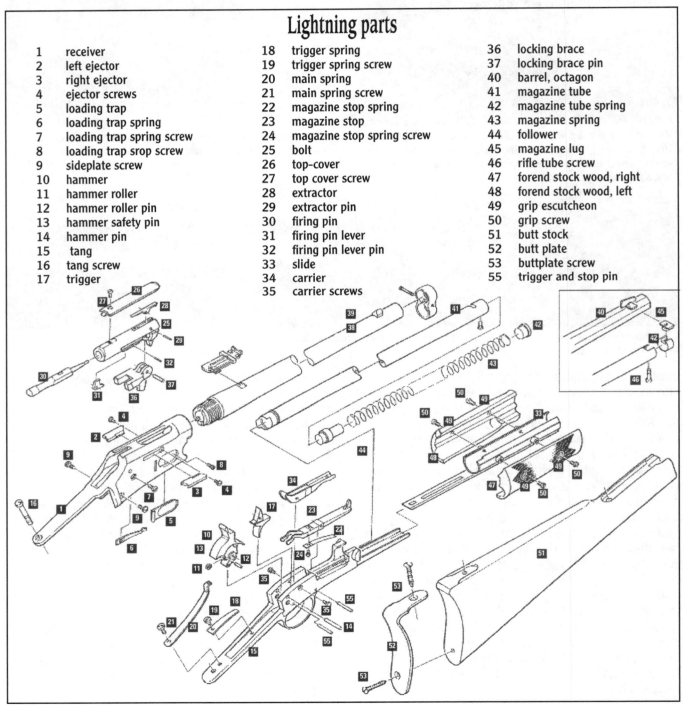

USFA Lightning Magazine Rifle ~ Specifications as tested	
Caliber:	44 WCF
Barrel Length:	26" octagon
Magazine Capacity:	15 rounds
Finish:	High-polish blue, case hardened hammer
Stocks:	Oil finished American walnut, straight grip, crescent butt plate
Sights:	Semi-buckhorn rear, Rocky Mountain front
Retail:	$1295
From:	U. S. Fire Arms Mfg. Co. 445-453 Ledyard St. Hartford, CT 06114 (860) 296-7441 Fax (860) 296-7688 www.usfirearms.com

that it shouldered uncannily fast) and that 26-inch octagon barrel offers enough up-front weight so that the piece is surprisingly well balanced on the shoulder. The pump-action operation was very smooth from start to finish. After using the slide just once the shooter comes away with a very positive feeling. I couldn't help but think this must be what an original Colt must have felt like when it was brand new, before it had been subjected to any wear and tear. The gun has no disconnector, again just like the original, so it is possible, although not recommended, to hold the trigger back and just work the slide and the rifle will continue to fire. Not to worry, the good safety feature from the Colt design; the one that keeps the hammer from falling until the bolt has locked closed, has been retained in the USFA Lightning rifle. Our gun's trigger pull was both very long and very creepy, and after what seemed an eternity, the hammer finally fell off when a "heavy" 6 1/2 pounds pressure on the trigger face was reached.

I regret that, due to a shortage of time (this was the last firearm we shot for this book) and good ammunition, we were only able to run the quickest of shooting tests on the Lightning. From a rest at 25 yards the gun gave us a three-shot groups that averaged around 2 inches center-to-center. (The one factory group was just over 2 inches, my old slow-moving handloads grouped about 1 1/2 inches.) I had purchased some Hornady Frontier .44-40 Cowboy ammunition for the tests, but those cartridges refused to chamber fully in this rifle

thanks to what were apparently slightly oversized case necks. It also appeared that the Lightning has a nice tight factory chamber and it simply did not like the way the Hornady cartridges were formed. In any event, we discovered that some of my old mild black-powder equivalent hand-loads and Winchester's factory .44-40 loads would chamber perfectly. The one "official" group we were able to fire with factory ammo was shot using my last three rounds of factory Winchester .44-40 jacketed soft-points. The groups with handloads and factory were all well within the range of what would be considered acceptable accuracy from a gun like this with iron sights, but I am quite certain that with some ammunition "tuning" this fine rifle is capable of delivering still better accuracy.

Our overall impression of the USFA Lightning is, in a word. . .WOW! As impressed as I have been with some of the newer replica arms, I don't ever recall being this excited about any modern-made reproduction firearm. This is one incredible rifle. We were delighted with its performance but disappointed that we did not have more suitable ammo on hand for the tests. There was a line of people nearby who would have loved to shoot this gun. Our rifle's trigger certainly could have used some help but that's something any competent gunsmith should be able to handle and it's really the only complaint we had about the rifle. Outwardly, the gun literally looks and feels like the real deal. It shoots well and on top of that this short-stroke slide action really is greased lightning to operate. No kiddin' man, this thing is fast, and as you push the slide forward to close the action this actually tends to help throw the muzzle back down onto the target, making re-acquisition time that much quicker. Our opinion is that the Lightning is, in all respects, an excellent rifle, one that is probably a better gun than the original if only because of superior metallurgy.

We're not quite done yet, I have just a bit more to say. When you consider the fact that the rifle is manufactured entirely right here in the United States (this is a major plus for many of us) with such a high degree of quality, and the fact that it needs so little work to make it competition-ready right out of the box, heck, I think the pricing is very fair. Think about that, if you are spending in the $900 to $1000 range for a new replica 1866 or 1873 lever gun, then you spend another $300 to $500 with the gunsmith to have it slicked up, you are already paying the price of one of these Lightnings. My prediction is once people get the chance to handle and shoot the new USFA Lightning Magazine Rifle, I think it will quickly start taking away a chunk of the niché presently filled by reproduction lever-actions.

Chapter 5

The Shotgun

A Short History And Some Mechanical Background.

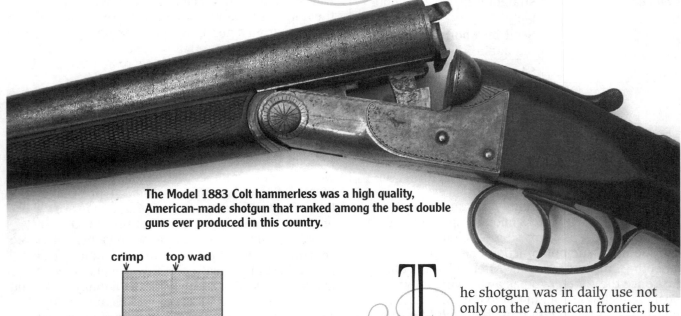

The Model 1883 Colt hammerless was a high quality, American-made shotgun that ranked among the best double guns ever produced in this country.

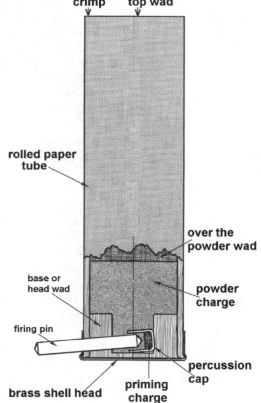

PINFIRE SHOTSHELL

The pinfire was one of the earliest metallic cartridges. This partial cut-a-way shows the pinfire shotgun cartridge, you can see the pin protruding into the shell and how it contacts the primer.

The shotgun was in daily use not only on the American frontier, but on farms and game fields all over the world. It perhaps has seen more peacetime use than any other kind of firearm. Many of these frontier weapons were muzzleloaders that used percussion or flintlock ignition. Soon after the Civil War, the breech-loading variety we know today began showing up in greater numbers. In the last quarter of the 1800s likely the most common varieties of breech-loading shotguns in America were single-barrel and side-by-side double-barreled shotguns of break-open types. By the end of the 19th century, single-barreled repeating shotguns were being manufactured with several different action mechanisms. Until the turn of the 19th century, shotgun designs followed those of the repeating rifle as it progressed. For example, John M. Browning designed Winchester's 1887 lever-action shotgun. Before the 19th century waned, slide- or pump-action shotguns began to appear with the Spenser in 1882, then the Winchester Models 1893 and 1897 and Marlin's Model 1898. By 1903 shotgun design actually jumped slightly ahead of the civilian sporting rifle when the Browning Auto-Five, a recoil-operated semi-automatic shotgun was introduced.

There is no arguing with the fact that when we think about shotguns of the Old West, most folks will picture a sawed-off double-barreled gun,

Pinfire weapons were more popular in Europe than in this country. Here we have a very high quality French-made, pinfire double gun from the early 1870s. Notice the notches on top of the barrels where the pins from the shells stick through.

The Parker was a very high quality American double. Pictured is a 10-gauge hammer gun that has seen a lot of hard use. Author photos.

The inexpensive single-barreled shotgun with a top-break action has always been popular. It is a versatile weapon that was used for hunting and defense. This one made by J. Stevens Arms and Tool Co. at the turn of the 19th century is typical of its type.

being carried by a stagecoach guard who is "riding shotgun" over a strongbox full of valuables. The shotgun has been the most versatile of weapons from its very beginning. That's because it has always been capable of being used for multiple tasks. Not that the familiar side-by-side double was the only shotgun available on the frontier, other types were used and among the most popular would have been the single barreled, top-break shotgun. The reasons for this are not hard to understand. It was the least expensive of shotguns. It could be used to fulfill the job of providing game animals for the table. You could take flying game or four-legged animals. For self-defense the large hole in the front of the barrel made it a great intimidator, and a very effective close-range weapon that required almost no skill on the part of the user.

I have believed for some time that the easily affordable, European- and American-made, single-barrel, break-open shotgun, the kind many people used to call a "farm-gun," was probably the most-used by the majority of American settlers. The exceptions would have been settlers who came west with a Civil War vet in the family, who likely still carried his reliable Springfield rifle-musket. The low survival rate of these cheap shotguns despite the high numbers of them that were likely manufactured is easy to understand. They were very inexpensive when they were new, so they got used and badly abused and in most cases were poorly cared for, often stored in barns, where they were at least partially exposed to the elements. Having such little value, they could be replaced cheaper than they could be repaired so when they broke they were thrown out or used as a fence post.

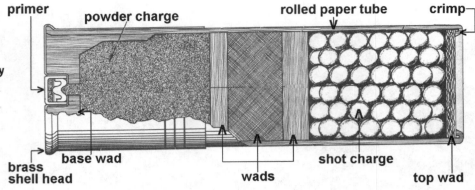

primer   powder charge   rolled paper tube   crimp

brass shell head   base wad   wads   shot charge   top wad

Breech-loading cartridge guns revolutionized how quickly a gun could be loaded. Here is a cut-away drawing of a factory shotgun shell from the 1880s.

There were plenty of double-barrel shotguns in 19th century America. Countless inexpensive doubles were manufactured abroad as well as here in the U.S.A. by a long list of companies, most long since gone. There were a good number of English-made shotguns imported as well. These came in grades ranging from very good up to some of the best guns ever produced. The hapless quest of many a modern cowboy shooter has been a short-barreled Greener 12-bore with outside hammers. The United States was also known for making good guns, like those made by Hopkins and Allen, Remington or Whitney, along with a few high-quality guns, like Colt, L.C. Smith and the Parker.

Bore sizes for shotguns

The caliber or gauge of a shotgun is described using a different terminology than rifles and handguns, and it can be confusing. The idea of calling bore size "gauge" comes from the early days of muzzle-loading when barrels were measured according to the weight of a single, round lead ball that would just fit into it. It went something like this; the 12-gauge is a gun whose barrel accepted a round ball weighing one-twelfth of a pound. Following this, the 16-gauge barrel would accept a ball that weighed one-sixteenth of a pound (that is, one ounce) and so on.

Shotgun shells used to be available in just about every gauge size you could imagine, going in increments as large as 1-gauge (That's a one-pound ball!) on down to shells as miniscule as the 32-gauge. In modern times the field of available bore sizes has shrunken considerably, shotgun shells are widely available off the shelf in 10-, 12-, 16-, 20-, and 28-gauges. And then, of course, there is the .410. A lot of people call it a gauge, but, this bore is actually .410 inches in caliber. Go figure. Somehow, this hopelessly obsolete yet time honored system for gauging shotgun barrels has held on and will likely be with us for a long while.

Chamber and shells

Just like the bore sizes, shotgun chambers exist in various lengths and shapes. Nominally, the size of the chamber does not mean that the shell is the same length. The shell is always somewhat shorter than the chamber. For instance; a 12-gauge shell is called a 2 3/4-inch shell it is actually shorter than that, until you fire it. This is because the mouths of shot-shells are crimped to hold the shot charge in place, when you fire the shell that crimp unfolds and that increases the shell's length. So, chambers are made longer than the shell so the shell crimp has room to unfold. This is an important part of shotgun chamber design.

Now that you know this. You should know that most shotguns produced during the 19th and the early 20th centuries had shorter chambers than we use today. Modern, off-the-shelf ammunition might not be safe, even if the gauge has a name that sounds similar. That's why you should pay attention to the chamber length if you are thinking about shooting one of those old guns. Okay, here is the problem: You can usually slide a modern shell for a 2 3/4-inch chamber easily into the shorter 2 1/2-inch or 2 5/8-inch chamber. Moreover, the gun will probably close and allow you to fire the shell. Here is how that happened; your 2 3/4-inch shell length is actually somewhere between 2 3/8 to 2 1/2 inches long before you fire it. Our old gun's chamber is likewise, about 2 1/2 inches or so deep; so it allows the new shell to come right in. It is when the shell is fired that we encounter the potential for danger. Here, the shell is fired and the shot charge forces open the shell's crimp, this crimped part of the shell now has nowhere to unfold into. You with me so far? The crimped portion of the shell gets partially opened and that's as far as it can go since there is no provision in the chamber for it to unfold into. In this state the shot charge is going to force its way past this constriction formed by the crimped portion of the shell. Here, we have what is called an overpressure, that is a situation with abnormally high chamber pressure being caused by this constriction and this overpressure is occurring when chamber pressure is already reaching its maximum safe levels. With this sort of situation, you will, at the least, get some shells that stick in the chambers. In the worst circumstance it is possible to explode the barrel. You could hurt yourself or some poor bystander. Whatever the result, minor or major, this is stressing the barrel steel and the action components at much greater levels than they were designed to operate under. I hope that now you can see the importance of having a gunsmith check the length of your old shotgun's chambers before attempting to shoot any shotgun made before, say, World War I or any foreign-made shotgun made before World War II.

The steels in shotgun barrels

Modern shotgun barrels are made from a piece of forged steel tube or hammer forged over a mandrel to final size. This is the way we have come to think of a shotgun barrel. There is this notion of a piece of thin-walled, seamless steel tubing, lightweight

10-gauge	Modern chambers are 2 7/8 inches standard and 3 1/2 inches magnum, but 19th century guns are liable to have shorter chambers.
12-gauge	Modern chambers are 2 3/4 inches standard, 3 inches magnum with 3 1/2 inches being a more recent addition. Early guns made before WWI are likely to be found with 2 1/2-inch or 2 5/8-inch chambers. There were even some made with 2 inch chambers.
16-gauge	Early chambers were 2 9/16 inches long; modern, standard chamber length is now 2 3/4 inches.
20-gauge	Modern chambers are 2 3/4 inches standard, 3 inches magnum. Formerly they were 2 1/2.

and very strong, an integral, homogenous piece of strong metal. But, that was not always the case. Years ago things had to be built very differently and somewhere you must have heard of the terms Damascus steel or even twist steel.

We take much of the technology of today for granted, but methods that allow us to easily make forged steel tubes have not always been available. Long ago, the only way people had to make a steel tube was literally what we would call the "hard" way. You made a steel bar first. To do that you took small strips of iron and steel, sometimes even bits and pieces from ends cut off horseshoe nails and, using a forge for heat, these small bits were hand-hammer welded into long, flat bars. Depending upon the pattern the barrel maker wanted to end up with they sometimes twisted those small strips together during the welding. This formed alternate layers of iron and steel. After that these long-flat bars were again heated and while quite hot, wrapped around a round steel bar called a mandrel. It was while they were on this mandrel that they were heated still more and the seams all hammer-welded together until the smith had made a perfect, round tube. The mandrel was removed and the inside of the tube was bored with drills and reamers to produce the inside of a finished shotgun barrel. After that, the outside of the tube was filed, polished and finish in brown or blue. That was a terrific amount of work to invest just to make a gun barrel, but they knew no other way.

Since iron and steel are known to turn different colors when they are oxidized, after the barrel was polished the finishing process, whether blue or brown produced the lovely twisted patterns that we call Damascus (named for Damascus, Syria where Damascus steel originated.) The finished pattern could be fancy or not, depending upon how much care the barrel-welding artisan put into the twisting

The top of the Colt Model 1883 shows off its strong, fancy Damascus patterns.

Here in this old drawing is illustrated an example of how Damascus barrels are constructed. The hand-welded, flat steel bars are wrapped round a steel mandrel preparatory to their being hammer-welded to make a shotgun barrel tube.

and welding of different kinds of iron and steel during the manufacture. Japanese sword-makers have practiced a process likened to this for centuries to produce the incredible steel alloys used in the blades of swords and knives.

Fine Damascus steel can be quite beautiful. By intricately interweaving the different kinds of iron and steel skilled artisans of the past produced some of the most gorgeous patterns imaginable. The only problem with this process is that no matter how skilled was the welder or how good the steel quality was, because of the literally hundreds of welded seams and the crude methods used to weld, there is a great chance that there are many flaws within the steel that might remain unseen. It is because of this that I advise people to follow this rule of thumb with twist or Damascus steel barrels: Don't shoot modern, smokeless powder ammunition. At all.

If you really want to shoot a shotgun with Damascus barrels, be careful and thoughtful to examine the barrels both on the inside and out, looking for any apparent flaws. Also, you should, as we mentioned earlier, be very certain that you measure the chamber length and then use the appropriate shell. As to ammunition for Damascus barrels, I can suggest only light charges of shot, over light to moderate charges of black powder propellant. In my experience, the heavier the side walls of the barrel, the safer it appears the barrels are. No, this doesn't mean that a great old W&C Scott 10-bore that has thick Damascus barrels can be fired with smokeless. It means that, from what I have seen, guns with thicker barrel walls don't seem to explode barrels nearly as often as the guns with thin tubes.

Dram, is that a word?

Yes, as strange as it sounds, dram is a word. Look around the outside of the shotgun shell box and you will usually find the words "dram equivalent." The word dram is from long ago when shotgun shells were loaded with black powder propellant. A dram is a unit of weight in the U.S. Customary System equaling .0625 ounce, taking it farther, there are 16 drams in one ounce and 256 drams in a pound. We know full well that if measured weight for weight, smokeless powder is way more potent than black powder. That means if modern shot shells were loaded with a weight equal to that of the black powder originally used, we would not see shotguns do much other than blow up. A smaller charge of smokeless powder has to be used, one that will make the shell equal the velocity it would have had with the same weight of shot with a measured amount of black powder. That smaller equalizing charge is called a dram equivalent.

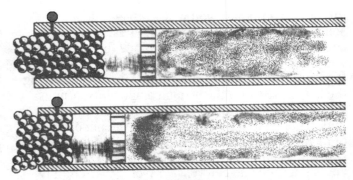

The bottom barrel in this exaggerated illustration depicts the shot charge as it leaves the muzzle of an un-choked shotgun barrel while the top shows the effect of a choke on the shot charge.

How do shotgun chokes work?

It seems pretty simple; the front part of the barrel on the inside is constricted just a little to hold the shot charge in a smaller pattern. That's about it, but there is more to a shotgun choke than you might think, heck, books have been written on them. We won't go that deep into shotgun choke science here. Lets just get hold of a good general understanding of the subject. As you know, the first shotguns were muzzleloaders. Powder was poured down the muzzle into the bore. A paper wad or a cloth patch to hold the powder in place followed that. Next came a weighed charge of round shot, that was of course, followed by another tight-fitting wad that is meant to the keep the shot from rolling out of the barrel as the gun was carried. The gun was made ready for firing by installing a percussion cap or filling the priming pan with powder. Pretty slow process, huh? That's why people loved double-barreled shotguns. They offered two fast shots. However, they were also twice the work to load. When breech-loaders came about, we had the primer, powder and shot all held in a shell made of brass and paper, the front end of which was crimped to keep the shot in place. This made the job of loading ever so much easier and infinitely faster.

As we hinted, a choke in a shotgun barrel is a constricted area at the inside of the barrel muzzle smaller in diameter than the rest of the barrel bore behind it. Its purpose is to try to control the size of the shot pattern after it has left the barrel. There are different size and shape chokes for different uses. As a general rule the smaller the choke the tighter the pattern of shot the gun will throw. Shot, being round, moves at fairly low velocity. It also sheds speed very quickly, meaning the effective range is much shorter than that of a rifle.

What is called a "full" choke is the smallest diameter choke. The "cylinder bore" on the other end of the spectrum, has absolutely no choke. Many shotguns made today come with screw-in chokes

Shotgun choke diameters

Gauge	Full	Improved Mod.	Modified	Imp. Cyl./Skeet	Cylinder
10	.739"	.748"	.757"	.765"	.775"
12	.693"	.702"	.711"	.720"	.729"
16	.636"	.642"	.649"	.655"	.662"
20	.589"	.595"	.602"	.609"	.615"
28	.530"	.535"	.540"	.545"	.550"
410	.390"	.395"	.400"	.403"	.410"

Shot diameters

Number	BB	9	8	7½	6	5	4	2
Diameter	.180"	.08"	.09"	.095"	.11"	.12"	.13"	.15"
No. per once	50	585	410	350	225	170	135	90

Buck shot sizes

Number	4 Buck	3 Buck	1 Buck	0 Buck	00 Buck
Diameter	.24"	.25"	.30"	.32"	.33"
No. per pound	340	300	175	145	130

that are replaceable, making it possible to have one gun with a variety of chokes and leaving the owner with one gun that may be suitable for different kinds of hunting. Before replaceable chokes, a shotgun barrel was bored at the factory so it had a constricted area behind the muzzle and this formed the choke. Cheaper grade shotguns had chokes that began rather abruptly, this forced the shot charge to slam into the back side of the choke where it was harshly squeezed down to size, often deforming some of the shot pellets. In the better grades of guns the barrels were reamed to have a gentle lead-in at the rear of the choked area, causing less shot deformation, lower chamber pressures and more uniform shot patterns.

How do you figure out if or how well a shotgun patterns? It's not hard at all. You can figure out how a shotgun is patterning by determining the percentage of shot that hits inside a 30-inch circle set at a fixed-measured distance, say 30 or 40 yards. The notion is very simple; the more pellets that hit toward the center, in other words; the inside of this circle, the tighter your gun is patterning. The method is easy. Open up the front of a shotshell with a razor knife, pour out all the shot in a container, and make an accurate count of the number of pellets. Let's say our count is exactly 100 pellets, okay, now fire the same kind of shotshell (preferably one from the same box) at that 30-inch circle on a clean target from 30 yards away. All you have to do is to count the number of

hits inside the circle. For example, if you count 55 holes, your gun is patterning at a rate of 55 percent and the other 45 pellets, or 45 percent of the shot, are outside the pattern circle. As an added benefit, we can also determine whether the gun is shooting to the sight by observing where on the pattern paper the bulk of your shot pattern is centered.

A 45 percent choke used to be known as an Improved-Modified. A Full choke would be patterning at around 70 percent and 55 to 60 percent was thought of as an Improved Cylinder choke. A shotgun with no choke, or what is called "cylinder bore," usually patterns at about 30 percent, but that is not cut in stone. Some shoot as tight as 35 percent or even tighter. Many, but not all, of the short-barreled "scatterguns" in cowboy shooting events are cylinder bored.

If you want to learn more about shotgun chokes and shooting, I would highly recommend you read the classic called *Shotguns* by Elmer Keith. I don't think you can do better from any single book.

Our look at shotguns here will be confined to two 12-gauge double guns, both foreign-made and of modern manufacture. The author wanted very much to be able to include the replicas of the 1887 lever-action and the 1897 pump shotguns but neither of the importers who distribute these shotgun responded to my requests in time to be included in this book.

Stoeger Coach Gun

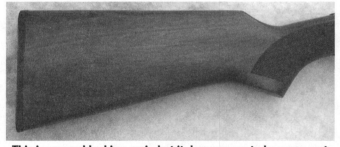

Stoeger's neat little 20-inch Coach Gun is an easy gun to handle and it performed well in our shooting tests. Shotgun courtesy Stoeger Industries. Author photos.

Short, double-barreled shotguns are a solid part of the picture of the Old West. In the mind's eye we see a stagecoach with a guard riding "shotgun" next to the hard-working driver and he is inevitably holding a mean-looking 12-bore double, usually with short barrels and outside "ears" or hammers. There is a shortage of original shotguns that fit this "criteria" from the Old West period. It is a shortage that seems to carry through into today's replicas, of which there are darned few. One, a recent entry is the Coach Gun from Stoeger Industries and it fits the bill nicely, but without the outside hammers. This little shotgun is an import, being manufactured for Stoeger in Brazil by the E.R. Amantino company.

Stoeger's Coach Gun is a 12-gauge (it also comes in 20-gauge and .410) double-barreled box-lock, of hammerless design (with internal hammers). Our test gun was equipped with a mild pistol grip, stocked in walnut (What sort of walnut it is I cannot tell you. I have been unable to identify it.) with a beaver-tail forend. The pistol grip sides and forearm wood are checkered. While this bordered checkering is stamped, I have to tell you it is much

nicer looking than the old, very hoakie, American stamped checkering of the 1960s and it actually does afford the shooter a decent grip. Length of pull, measured from the center of the front trigger to the center of the butt is a generous 14 1/2 inches, to the rear trigger it's about 13 1/2. The stocks appear to be stained to a medium-dark walnut color and are lightly finished with some sort of oiled coating. All in all, the stocks are pretty darn good looking; not excellent, but definitely a couple of cuts above "not bad looking." The butt plate is a plain-Jane black plastic affair with serrations across its back. You've probably seen many like it.

This is unusual looking grain but it does appear to be some sort of walnut finished in a light coat of oil. The gun has a nice 14 1/2-inch length of pull and that makes us tall shooters happy!

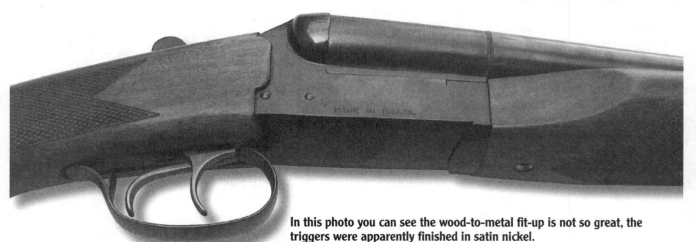

In this photo you can see the wood-to-metal fit-up is not so great, the triggers were apparently finished in satin nickel.

We'll mention the fit-up of the wood to the metal but it is honestly nothing to brag about, with fairly good-sized air gaps pretty much everywhere wood touches steel except the forearm iron, which somehow fits nicely. The forearm wood is fastened to the barrel under lug with a sliding, spring-loaded, button. This method is a much more certain way to hold the wood on the barrel than the spring tension-

The action was a bit stiff to open but once there the extractors worked perfectly and the action closed tight as a tick.

fit forearms we've seen on a lot of cheaper American and European doubles. An automatic safety is provided on the upper tang, for those who like that sort of thing. Its operation was, unfortunately, flawless. (The author is not a fan of automatic safeties, though they must have their place.)

The short, 20-inch barrels are topped with a raised rib, serrated side-to-side with sharp, semi-circular grooves that actually work. This top rib is not only good looking, it's just the right height for the stock so you pick up the sight fast and the rib does not glare back at the shooter in bright sunlight. Stoeger claims in its literature that the short barrels are actually choked M/IC. Well, guess what? We measured the chokes and the left tube measured .709", the right .720", that works out to modified and improved cylinder, just like they say. Internally, the barrels looked very good with bright shiny polishing throughout and the 3-inch chambers have long, gentle forcing cones. From the outside, the metal parts of the Coach Gun are very nicely finished. It's all in blue except for the triggers which look

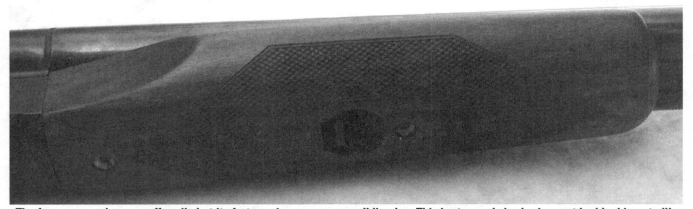

The forearm wood comes off easily but its fastener is a very secure sliding bar. This is stamped checkering, not bad looking at all!

Here's the coach gun dismantled for cleaning.

Under the barrels we found this unusual, yet attractive vented rib.

like they are finished in a satin nickel. I will tell you that the quality of the polishing-before-blue work is better than just good, it is excellent in every respect. This kind of polish work is far above the quality you would expect to find on a shotgun in this price range ($320 retail).

Action operation was just a bit stiff in both directions. We thought the top lever required a bit too much effort to open the barrels and the barrel set was kinda' stiff on the hinge operation during opening. Likewise, closing the barrels took just a little more effort than I would have liked, although they did snap shut with some authority, like a vault door. These are things that probably would "wear-in." At least, that's what a salesman would

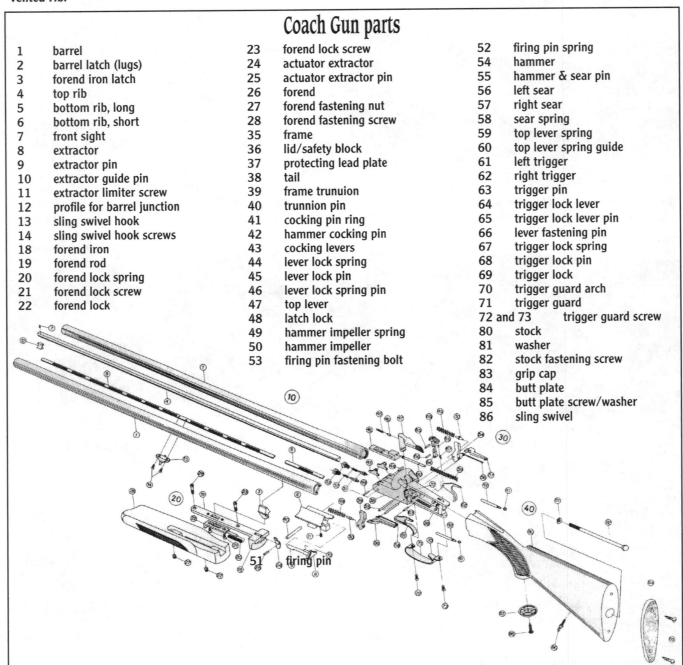

Coach Gun parts

1	barrel	23	forend lock screw	52	firing pin spring
2	barrel latch (lugs)	24	actuator extractor	54	hammer
3	forend iron latch	25	actuator extractor pin	55	hammer & sear pin
4	top rib	26	forend	56	left sear
5	bottom rib, long	27	forend fastening nut	57	right sear
6	bottom rib, short	28	forend fastening screw	58	sear spring
7	front sight	35	frame	59	top lever spring
8	extractor	36	lid/safety block	60	top lever spring guide
9	extractor pin	37	protecting lead plate	61	left trigger
10	extractor guide pin	38	tail	62	right trigger
11	extractor limiter screw	39	frame trunuion	63	trigger pin
12	profile for barrel junction	40	trunnion pin	64	trigger lock lever
13	sling swivel hook	41	cocking pin ring	65	trigger lock lever pin
14	sling swivel hook screws	42	hammer cocking pin	66	lever fastening pin
18	forend iron	43	cocking levers	67	trigger lock spring
19	forend rod	44	lever lock spring	68	trigger lock pin
20	forend lock spring	45	lever lock pin	69	trigger lock
21	forend lock screw	46	lever lock spring pin	70	trigger guard arch
22	forend lock	47	top lever	71	trigger guard
		48	latch lock	72 and 73	trigger guard screw
		49	hammer impeller spring	80	stock
		50	hammer impeller	81	washer
		53	firing pin fastening bolt	82	stock fastening screw
				83	grip cap
				84	butt plate
				85	butt plate screw/washer
				86	sling swivel

51 firing pin

Here Tommy Abernathy has only just finished firing both barrels and you can see the shells falling from the chambers of their own weight, this was a nice surprise and a feature that we were all tickled with.

Stoeger Coach Gun specs	
Model / Item#	31400
Barrel length	20 inches
Gauge	12 gauge, for 2 3/4- and 3-inch shells
Trigger	double
Chokes	IC / M, fixed
Overall length	36 1/2 inches
Weight	6.5 pounds
Length of pull	14 1/2 inches
Retail	$320
From	Stoeger Industries, 17603 Indian Head Hwy., Ste 200, Accokeek, MD 20607 (301 283-6300

probably tell you. Me. . .I suspect that "wearing-in" process would take more than just a few shots. More like a few hundred shots but as nicely as the action is made I would bet it could be slicked up and tuned by a good smith without much effort. The triggers were good and safe, the pulls were not hard at perhaps 4 1/2 pounds but the duration of the trigger pulls on both triggers was exceptionally long and mushy.

We did not target nor did we attempt to pattern this gun. Owing to the nature of the beast that seemed unnecessary. From what I saw the gun may actually pattern better than one would suspect. I noticed that it was easy to hit a 4-inch gong at 75 feet with either barrel, and that the hits were solid, indicating the gong was probably being hit with a substantial portion of the shot pattern. We test fired the gun with about 100 rounds of ammo, most of which were the light loads of Winchester AA low-brass size #7 1/2 shot, and just a few were heavy 3-inch magnum waterfowl loads charged with size #4 shot. All through the tests the shotgun performed beautifully. I say this in spite of the stiffness in the action mentioned earlier which none of us seemed to notice. What this little shotgun did do very well was to shuck its own shells clear of the barrels. With that low-brass Winchester ammo all you had to do after firing both barrels was to open the action and tilt the barrels skyward. Out they came every time via the old Gravity Express. Felt recoil at the shoulder with

the low-brass loads was very mild, really, the gun would never need a pad if its diet were restricted to these and I would be happy to shoot it all day. Slip in some of those 3-inch magnums and the picture changes dramatically. While the recoil never became what I would call "unmanageable" it certainly did get more uncomfortable and 20 rounds of magnum shells were about all I wanted that day. I will say it was noticeably more comfortable to shoot than many low-priced American-made doubles with the same loads.

Our overall impressions of this Stoeger Coach Gun were very favorable. Yeah, the wood-to-metal fit-ups were, in a word, yeck (that's yechhh if you're from New York) and opening and closing the action was somewhat stiff. But none of that is a deal-breaker because in my opinion the gun is made with good quality and it sure seems like it would be worth spending a few bucks with a gunsmith to have it loosened it up some. Maybe you could Acra-Glas the stock inletting at the action to keep the wood from splitting. Even with those flaws the metal polishing work was better than I have seen on some double guns that cost three times this much. It makes a very professional appearance. In its operation the Coach Gun just excelled and that was with exactly the sort of loads you would be using in competition. On top of that, the barrels have perfectly slick chambers, so there is this great, gravity-ejection thing going on. Man, everyone loved that!

EMF Hartford

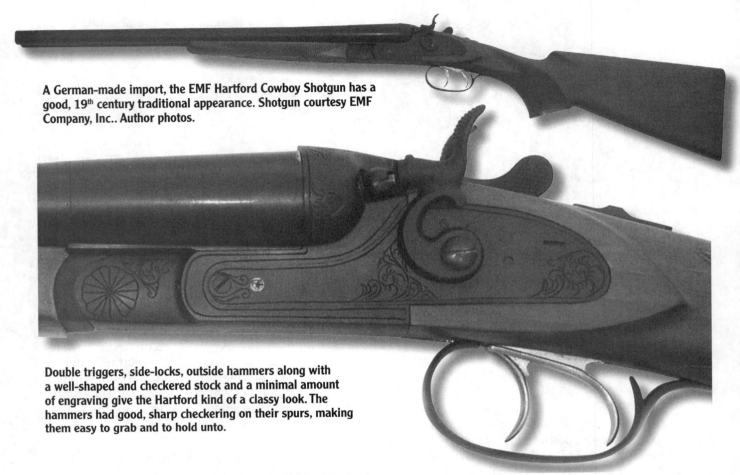

A German-made import, the EMF Hartford Cowboy Shotgun has a good, 19th century traditional appearance. Shotgun courtesy EMF Company, Inc.. Author photos.

Double triggers, side-locks, outside hammers along with a well-shaped and checkered stock and a minimal amount of engraving give the Hartford kind of a classy look. The hammers had good, sharp checkering on their spurs, making them easy to grab and to hold unto.

From EMF comes the Hartford model cowboy 12-gauge, side-lock, double shotgun with outside "ears." This shotgun is manufactured for EMF in Germany and it has an unusual feature for an outside-hammer gun. It comes with a sliding tang safety. The very traditional appearing shotgun is stocked in what appears to be tight-grained European walnut and comes with checkered panels on the sides of the pistol grip and wrap-around checkering on the forearm. Wood-to-metal fit is very good for the most part with some noticeable gaps around the fit of the lockplates to the stock. The checkering appears to be hand-cut. It's bordered and is in the old-English style with flat-topped diamonds. The stocks are finished in a dark-colored stain and apparently, a light linseed oil top finish. Length of pull for the buttstock measures 14 1/4 inches from the center of the shotgun butt to the center of the front trigger. Chambers are 12-gauge, reamed to accept either 2 3/4-inch or 3-inch magnum shells. The chambers showed more tool marks than I prefer to see but the bores themselves seemed to be nicely finished forward of the chambers.

The metal was finished in an unusual combination. Blueing methods are modern, hot-caustic blue and the entire action was bead-blasted for a flat matte black, giving it a distinctly modern military look. The barrel set was polished in a medium-luster blue. The polish on the outside of the barrels was good but not great with many abrasive lines visible through the color. The traditional double-triggers are silver colored. I am assuming apparently matte nickel-plated. Overall the gun has an unusual, yet attractive appearance.

The gun is opened with a conventional top-lever and we noticed right away that the action operation was very tight. The shooter has to actually push the barrels down after they are unlocked and it takes a bit of effort to close them as well. You won't be closing this with a flick of the wrist! I did note the action snapped tight very smartly with a nice, firm ker-thunk that echoes down the empty tubes. We measured the 20-inch barrels for chokes but they are obviously both cylinder bore, just as you would expect for an Old West scattergun. The manual extractors worked stiffly but positively. Firing pins are screwed into the action by means of removable bolsters that project rearward, rather unattractively I thought, from the rear of the action bulges. The Hartford Cowboy model hammers are rebounders, so they jump back away from the firing pins after firing. When the trigger is released the sear interferes with forward movement for safety reasons. Trigger pulls were very-y-y long and creepy, with the front sear breaking at about 8 pounds and the rear letting go at about 7 1/2 pounds.

Unfortunately, the only day we had to test fire the Hartford we ended up getting rained on soon after we started out so we didn't get to really put the gun through its paces. The original plan was for us to

Shown from the rear, the Hartford lock is very simple and reminiscent of many inexpensive American-made shotguns from earlier in the 20th century.

Parts for the EMF Hartford shotgun, German mfg.

n/i: not illustrated	16. Forearm wood	31. Lockplate retaining screw (2)	46. Tang screw, lower
	17. Forearm lever n/i		47. Tang screw, upper
1. Barrels n/i	18. Forearm release plate n/i	32. Lockplate connector screw	48. Trigger pin
2. Front sight n/i	19. Bolt spring n/i	33. Sear screw	49. Safety detent pin
3. Extractor	20. Firing pin (2) n/i	34. Mainspring (2)	50. Sear plate
4. Extractor screw	21. Firing pin bushing (2) n/i	35. Hammer, right	51. Stirrup (2)
6. Bolt n/i	22. Firing pin spring (2) n/i	36. Sear, right	52. Stirrup pin (2)
8. Top-lever	23. Safety button	37. Bridle, right	53. Trigger, left
9. Receiver	24. Safety spring	39. Hammer screw (2)	54. Trigger right
10. Forearm iron	25. Safety spring screw	40. Trigger guard	55. Top lever spring n/i
11. Forearm lever spring n/i	26. Buttplate n/i	41. Trigger guard screw	56. Top lever plate
12. Extractor actuator	27. Buttplate screw (2) n/i	42. Lockplate, left	57. Sear spring
13. Extractor actuator pin n/i	28. Trigger plate	43. Sear, left n/i	58. Sear spring screw
14. Rear forearm screw	29. Trigger plate pin	44. Bridle, left n/i	59. Sear plate
15. Front forearm screw	30. Lockplate, right	45. Hammer, left	60. Buttstock n/i

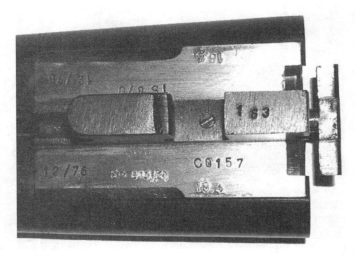

A look under the rear of the barrels shows the locking lugs, the extractor is sticking up at the top. The numbers at the bottoms of the flats 12/76 are the chamber caliber (12 gauge) the length (76) is given in mm.

EMF Hartford specs	
Model	Hartford Cowboy Shotgun
Type	Double barrel, outside hammers
Gauge	12 gauge, 2 3/4- and 3-inch magnum
Barrel length	20 inches
Choke	Cylinder/cylinder
Stocks	Walnut, pistol grip, checkered
Finish	Blued
Retail	$650
From	EMF Company, Inc. 1900 E. Warner Ave. Suite 1-D Santa Ana, CA 92705 USA (949) 261-6611 fax (949) 756-0133

shoot about five boxes of the mild stuff and then two boxes of heavier 3-inch magnum buckshot loads. In fact, we only managed about a box of 25 shots. We used those light-recoiling Winchester AA 12-gauge 2 3/4-inch, low-brass shells with size #7 1/2 shot. The gun was very easy to handle, light-recoiling of course and the comb was just the right height for me to grab a fast sight picture. Even after almost a whole box had been fired the barrel opening remained quite stiff through the tests. In fact, we had some difficulty closing the action on two occasions because of unburned powder debris getting between the barrels and the breech faces. We noticed the shells would not fall out when the barrels were tipped back a bit. In every instance they had to be urged a little by pulling them with a finger before they would fall out.

How did the Hartford shotgun fare? Although we did not have the opportunity to test this shotgun nearly as thoroughly as we would have liked, the Hartford Cowboy model performed well enough in our short-lived, live-ammo tests. Three people who fired the Hartford and two other experienced shotgun men who tried the action and looked it over, all thought the gun looked good, came up and

handled very well, but to a person, they all said that stiff barrel opening was a burden that slowed them down noticeably. It really did take some muscle to open those barrels and we find it slowed us down considerably. In our opinion the action itself is good and strong, it was just a bit too stiff and would need some slicking up to make it competition-worthy. Nobody could figure out why that sliding safety was put there, perhaps to meet a legal requirement I am not aware of. It is of no value on a gun with outside hammers. Extraction was good but we would like to see the chambers polished to a higher degree which would allow those fired shells from the light loads to drop out. That would have sped things up a little. This is a traditional, classic-looking double gun that does have a good 19th century "feel" to it and the gun's fit and finish were very good.

(Author's note: EMF representatives mentioned to the author early in 2004 that they were planning at some time in 2004 to be importing a similar shotgun from another manufacturer in another country. That model may, by the time of this printing, have superceded the model shown here.)

Chapter 6

Cowboy Ammunition

Cowboy ammunition, so-called, is really commercially available ammunition that is supposed to be tailored to match the needs and requirements of the sport, ie: *"Revolver and (main match) rifle ammunition may not be jacketed, semi-jacketed, plated, gas checked, or copper washed. It must be all lead"* (from the SASS Handbook.) Handgun ammunition must have a muzzle velocity under 1,000 feet per second and rifle muzzle velocity must be under 1,400 feet per second. Velocities are kept low for safety reasons, in an effort to keep bullet bounce-back at a bare minimum, since reactive targets, often made of steel, are used.

But there are other considerations that go into making ammunition truly suitable for cowboy action purposes. There is really more to think about than you might guess if you had taken just a superficial look at the subject. First of all, everyone wants accurate ammunition at whatever the velocity.

Another important consideration is recoil and muzzle rise. Since these are timed events, we want to do everything we can to reduce the time it takes to recover from the last shot and then to get back on target again. On top of all this, you always need to remember that you are shooting at reactive targets, that means the bullet has to have enough striking energy to belt the target and cause a reaction, if not, your scores will suffer. To quote the SASS Handbook again; *"Although the .32 caliber revolvers and .36 caliber cap-and-ball pistols are legal, they may not be powerful enough to handle all reactive targets. To the extent possible, reactive targets are set to fall when squarely hit with a standard .38 Special 158-gr. factory load."* The ammo should also be easy to chamber during tense reload situations where the shooter is "on the clock." For this reason wad-cutter type bullets that have flat faces stretching across the width of the cartridge case, while they may cut very clean holes in paper, are just not practical for this

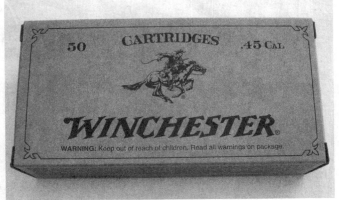

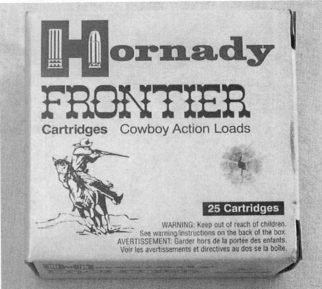

Winchester, Black Hills and Hornady are three of the major ammo makers who not only manufacture ammo specifically for cowboy action shooting, they provide attractive boxes. Author photos.

kind of shooting. There is a need to speed things up and to do everything possible to avoid balking during that critical moment at the bullet's entrance into the cylinder's chambers. For this reason the bullets used in CAS events, if not round-nosed, are at least tapered with flat faces. The rounded or tapered nose allows easy chambering and the flat face can help prevent bullet ricochet.

Cowboy ammunition is available in the calibers best suited to the shooter's guns and the events, so you will find it in .38-40, .44-40 .45 Colt and a host of other calibers that you might have guessed, like .45-70. This very specialized firearms fodder is also available in a few calibers that you might not expect, like .44 Colt, .44 Russian, .45 S&W Schofield and .38 Colt. It was not many years ago when all of these latter were considered obsolete calibers, so if you wanted to fire a gun in one of those calibers, you had to hand-roll your own ammo. In more recent times, we have seen the introduction of several replica handguns

that are being factory-chambered to accept obsolete calibers such as the .45 S&W Schofield, and the major ammunition makers are doing a very good job of stepping up to the plate by supplying what the shooter needs. Black Hills Ammunition, in particular, has come out with a nice selection of formerly obsolete, old-time calibers and their cowboy action ammo is specifically designed to fit both the requirements of cowboy shooters, and the SASS rule book.

If you shoot in cowboy matches, you have to practice for them. If you want to actually be competitive in cowboy matches, then you had better practice even more. But, if you want to win those same matches, you will have to do just about nothing but practice in your "spare" time and that last bit is a commodity that most of us have very little of. What we are getting at is that practice means having to shoot lots of ammo, we all know that the more you shoot, the better shot you will become. The down side of this is that the more you shoot, the more money it costs and many shooters have been driven to learning how to hand load their own ammunition by the costs of factory ammunition. Not that factory ammunition is outrageously expensive. Bought in small quantities or by the box I don't believe it is. But in the quantities required for competitive practice, the totals can sure add up pretty fast. We will not be going into the handloading of ammunition here, we mention it only because it is a very practical alternative for some. Indeed, loading your own is the only way that many folks can afford to do this amount of shooting.

For those shooters who don't or can't hand load, or that don't have a friend who does it for them, the ammunition factories have provided some very high-quality food for your sixguns, rifles and shotguns. They make some pretty nice stuff and it can be had right off the shelf. This chapter gives a brief overview of some of the cowboy action ammunition that is commercially available today, as stock items from local gun shops and ranges all across the country. We are not giving, by any stretch of the imagination, a list of every brand or caliber of ammunition available today. What this is, is a good look at some of the major brands and at many of the popular calibers. If you care to read deeper into the guns chapter, you will get to see how most of this ammo actually performed on target and in how it shot in specific replica cowboy guns that you might be thinking about buying, or may already own.

Black Hills Cowboy Action ammunition			
caliber	Bullet weight-type	Muzzle velocity	No. in box
.32 H&R	90-gr., FPL	750 fps	50
32-20	115-gr., FPL	800 fps	50
.38 Long Colt	158-gr., RNL	650 fps	50
.357 Magnum	158-gr., CNL	800 fps	50
.38 Special	158-gr., CNL	800 fps.	50
38-40	180-gr., FPL	800 fps	50
44-40	200-gr., RNFP	800 fps	50
.44 Colt	230-gr., FPL	730 fps	50
.44 S&W Russian	210-gr., FPL	650 fps	50
.44 S&W Special	210-gr., FPL	700 fps	50
.45 S&W Schofield	180-gr., FNL	730 fps	50
.45 S&W Schofield	230-gr., RNFP	730 fps	50
.45 Colt	250-gr., RNFP	725 fps	50
.38-55 Winchester	255-gr., FNL	1250 fps	20
.45-70	405-gr., FPL	1250 fps	20

Hornady Cowboy Ammunition			
Caliber	Bullet weight-type	Muzzle velocity	No. in box
.38 Special	140-gr., FPL	800 fps	25
.44 Special	180-gr., FPL	800 fps	20
.45 Colt	255-gr., FPL	725 fps	20

Remington ammunition			
Caliber	Bullet weight-type	Muzzle velocity	No. in box
.32 S&W	98-gr., LRN	705 fps	50
44-40	200-gr., JSP	1190 (rifle)	50
.45 Colt	250-gr, RNL	850 fps	50

Winchester Cowboy ammunition			
caliber	Bullet weight-type	Muzzle velocity	No. in box
32-20	100-gr., FPL	1210 fps (rifle)	50
.38 Special	158-gr., LFN	800 fps	50
.44 Special	240-gr., LFN	750 fps	50
.45 Colt	250-gr., LFN	750 fps	50
38-55 Winchester	255-gr., JSP	1320 fps	20
45-70 Govt.	300-gr., JHP	1880 fps*	20

Bullet sizes, bore sizes, chamber sizes, what's all that about?

If you will examine the inside of the hole down a rifled gun barrel, you will see the hole has two diameters, the diameters are called the lands and the grooves. Lands are the tops of the rifling and form the barrel's bore diameter, or the original drilled size of the hole through the barrel, a.k.a.; the bore diameter. The grooves are the rifling marks that have been cut into the bored hole. So, the groove diameter, or literally the bottom of the rifling, is the width of this hole measured side-to-side, across the groove bottoms.

In the ideal setup, a gun should use a bullet that is about the exact size of the barrel grooves, not the size of the bore. If we select a bullet of groove diameter, we can be pretty certain the bullet gets distorted as little as possible when it enters the barrel but also, we will know that it is fully engraved by the rifling. What is more, a bullet thus sized will effectively seal the hole in the barrel so no high-pressure propellant gases can leak by it. There are some exceptions to this ideal, but if you are looking for accuracy in your rifle or handgun, at some point even those exceptions will have to come into full contact with the rifling so it can spin the bullet or the gun's accuracy will never be very good.

One of the exceptions to the rule above is the famous Civil War Minie bullet. These bullets were made the same size as the barrel's bore, and were what is known as bore-riders. Minie bullets could be effortlessly pushed down the barrel of a muzzle-loading rifle without encountering the resistance from the rifling. They had a hollow base and were made of soft lead, designed so the hollow base got expanded by the high pressure powder gases when the rifle was fired. That expansion made the Minie bullet's base swell in size to fill up the rifling. This old bullet design offered fast muzzle-loading in rifled barrels as well as excellent accuracy and was a wonderful invention. Another example of an exception to a rule is the patched round balls used in a muzzle-loading rifles. The ball is made a smaller diameter than the rifling and it is the cloth patch that engages the rifling. Paper-patched bullets like the ones used in some Sharps cartridges worked in a similar fashion. With both these latter exceptions, the cloth or the paper was a sabot; it effectively encased and engaged the rifling for the bullet.

This is all pretty simple to understand and once you do, it can pay big dividends. To maintain safety, and some semblance of accuracy, the diameter of the bullets you are shooting ought to match the groove diameter of your weapon's barrel as closely as possible. Safety and accuracy, how so? If one were to

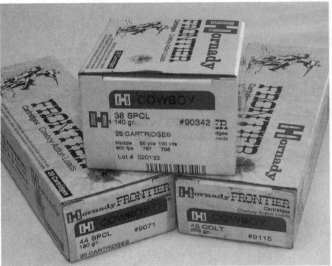

shoot say, a .38 special bullet (which is actually less than .36 caliber) down the barrel of a .38-40, which has a groove diameter of .400 inches, we could not expect any degree of accuracy since the bullet would probably never touch the barrel, let alone be get caught by the rifling. If we tried to create the opposite situation, assuming it were possible to do so; that is, to drive a .40 caliber bullet down a .36 caliber barrel, we would get an unhappy circumstance that creates what is called an overpressure. What that means is the chamber pressures would quickly rise to dangerous levels, levels no gun is designed for, as the expanding powder gases tried ever harder to force that big bullet through the tiny hole. What would be the results of such a situation? Well, in the worst case, the gun could explode causing injury or death. In the best case, and if you were very fortunate, no damage would be done to the firearm but the bullet would certainly be a total wreck and any hope of accuracy would be wrecked right along with it. Make sense so far? As far as this goes, what we are saying is the shooter should never assume anything, always be absolutely sure of the caliber of

your weapon and then be certain you are using the correct ammo.

It gets a little more complicated with revolvers because the bullet has to travel through the cylinder's chamber mouth before it can even get into the barrel. The cylinder chamber mouths should also have a diameter that is compatible with the bullet and barrel? Revolvers can be finicky about this. Let's say a revolver in .45 Colt has a barrel groove diameter of .452 inches and so do your bullets. We'll suppose for illustration that your cylinder's chamber mouths measured as large as .457 inches, that's a .005 (five one-thousandths of an inch) difference. To understand what happens here we first have to realize that when you fire this revolver the bullet will become very upset.

How does a bullet get upset? Good question, but the explanation is in the discussion of the Minie bullet mentioned earlier. When you fire the cartridge the expanding powder gases create pressure and immediately try to get out of their container (the cartridge case.) As we know, pressure will always

seek the path of least resistance. In this case the only moveable portion of the container is its head, that's the bullet. Alright, so the chamber pressure acts on the rear of the bullet and this growing chamber pressure is becoming so great that the bullet can't hold on to the cartridge case and it quickly begins to move forward out of the cartridge case and into the cylinder's chamber mouth. Now, the pressure has risen to very high levels and it is actually pushing on the bullet so hard that the bullet can't move fast enough and begins to be crushed. Being crushed causes the bullet's sides to expand, so its diameter increases or as we said, the bullet becomes "upset" into the sides of the chamber mouth, whose diameter (remember, we learned it was bigger than the bullet") it now assumes.

Right, so we have momentarily, a .452 diameter bullet which has become upset to .457 diameter and is rapidly gathering speed under the great chamber pressure from those burning powder gases that are forcing it ever forward. Next, our .457 diameter bullet runs smack into the hole in the barrel, whose groove diameter as we already know, is .452 inches. That .457-inch diameter bullet is being forced, rather violently, into the smaller barrel. Something else happened. This increased friction is offering still more resistance to the bullet, so the chamber pressure also rises to levels even higher than it normally would. The beleaguered bullet is really upset now and as it is forcibly squeezed back to its original size, its length increases somewhat. Since it is made of dense, soft, non-ferrous metal that is not particularly malleable, the tired bullet begins to deform and skid along on the tops of the rifling, which are smaller than the groove diameter, or about .446 inches. Eventually, the bullet gets upset enough by the driving force of the, now falling, chamber pressure, it grabs a bit of rifling and begins to spin.

What then, is the outcome of our little hypothetical over-sized revolver chamber mouth experiment? We have learned that such a seemingly small thing as a slightly oversized revolver chamber mouth may just lead to all sorts of problems. First, the bullet becomes severely over-worked and deformed, so accuracy from a revolver with this condition is generally not very good. We also know the condition can cause leading in the barrel's rifling and that lead (from that double-re-sized bullet) may very well be spitting out at the barrel-to-cylinder gap. Finally, but not the least, the increased bullet forcement has caused abnormally high chamber pressures that are a potential safety hazard.

Measuring barrel bore and groove diameters is not terribly difficult and as you can see, it is often well worth the effort, even if it's just to find out why a particular gun may or may not shoot with certain bullets or loads. An in-depth explanation of exactly how to measure the inside of a gun barrel is offered in my first book *Gunsmithing Guns of the Old West* also published by Krause Publications. You may also want to measure your revolver chambers to learn whether they are the same size as the barrel's rifling. This is more of a concern in revolvers than in rifle barrels because a revolver cylinder is machined as a separate piece from the barrel while the rifle's chamber is machined into the barrel. As we have seen, if the chamber mouths in your revolver are a different size than the barrel groove diameter, it might have quite an effect on your revolver's accuracy and safety. It's not at all hard to measure revolver chamber mouths by using a dial caliper you simply measure across the front of the chamber mouth. This dimension is critical on percussion revolvers and you should always measure the size of your cylinder chamber mouths to make certain you are using the correct ball size so

the chambers are effectively sealed. If they are not sealed, you may experience a chain fire (multiple chamber ignition) which would wreck your gun. Use special care to select a ball or conical bullet size that is about one-one thousandth of an inch larger than the diameter of the cylinder chamber mouths, or at least the same as chamber size, and the ball can be forced to seal the chambers by ramming it home harder. Don't forget to use either a tight fitting over-the-powder lubricated wad or over-the-ball grease lubricant, some folks use both. Either will provide the required bullet lube, offer an easier cleanup with much less powder fouling and provide greater insurance against chain fires.

Barrel Groove Diameters	
.22 Rim Fire	.222"
.22 CF	.224"
25/20 WCF	.257"
.30 caliber rifle.	.308"
.31 percussion Colt	.313"
.32/20, 32 S&W	.312"
.32/40 & Special	.321"
.33 WCF	.338"
.348 Win	.348"
.351 WSL	.352"
.38 Special/.357	.357"
.36 perc	.379"
.38/40	.400"
.38/55	.379"
.401 WSL	.406"
.405 Win	.412"
.41 Colt	.406"
.44/40	.427"
.44 perc.	.451-.457"
.44 S&W American	.434-.436"
.44 S&W Russian & Special	.430"
.444 Marlin	.430"
.45 ACP	.451"
.45 Colt	.452-.454"
.455	.457"
.45/70	.457"

Key: ACP=Automatic Colt Pistol. C.F.=Center Fire. mm=millimeter. perc=Percussion. Rem=Remington Win=Winchester. WCF=Winchester Center Fire. WSL=Winchester Self Loading

Cartridge history

A quick look at most of the calibers used in the firearms tested within this book.

.38 Special

This caliber, which has also been called the .38 Colt Special or .38 Smith & Wesson Special, was developed by Smith & Wesson just a little over 100 years ago. Properly named .38 S&W Special, the cartridge was meant to offer a more powerful alternative to the .38 Long Colt and having a longer case than the Colt, it could hold more black powder. The cartridge first appeared in S&W's .38 Hand Ejector-first model, introduced in 1899, whose barrels were often caliber marked ".38 S&W Special and U.S. Service Ctg." That marking meant the revolver would fire both the .38 Special, and that it could also fire the then-standard, U.S. service pistol cartridge, which was .38 Long Colt.

.38 S&W Special quickly grew in popularity until it became a world-class police round. Millions of revolvers of various makes chambered the .38 Special and until a few years back, more police organizations world-wide used it than any other revolver cartridge. Over the last 105 years the .38 S&W Special has acquired a great reputation for wonderful accuracy and mild recoil. This cartridge, with a 158-grain bullet, is also the minimum caliber recommended by the SASS Handbook for use on reactive steel targets.

This caliber ammunition is manufactured all over the world by countless ammunition manufacturers. Cowboy action ammunition in .38 Special is available from several makers, including Black Hills Ammunition, Hornady-Frontier and Winchester.

.44 Colt

When Colt introduced the conversion of the 1860 percussion revolver designed by C.B. Ricahrds in 1871, this was the cartridge it fired. On account of some very tight space constraints in the converted percussion cylinder, the .44 Colt had to be designed with a miniscule rim so it could fit. Even at that the rims were just about touching each other. The Army used the cartridge to some extent in some converted 1860s it had and the round would also work in the 1875 Remington that was chambered for the .44 Remington cartridge. The .44 Colt was designed to follow the .44 S&W American and like that round, the Colt used an outside lubricated bullet of .443" diameter; making it a true .44. Modern .44 Colt loadings as manufactured by Black Hills use inside lubricated bullets of .430" diameter. These smaller bullets match the barrel dimensions of the replica conversion Colts such as the Cimarron Richards-Mason.

This caliber is loaded just a bit hotter than contemporary .44 Russian ammunition. In the few Uberti Richards-Mason conversion revolvers we test fired it in, Black Hills .44 Colt was very accurate, although not quite as accurate as the .44 Russian loadings in the same guns.

Specifications shown below are for modern .44 Colt ammunition with conventional inside-lubricated bullets intended only for modern revolvers chambered in .44 Colt, not for ammunition using heel-type bullets.

.38 SPECIAL					
Case length	O/A length	Blt. diameter	Base OD	Neck OD	Rim OD
1.160"	1.550"	.357"	.379"	.379"	.440"

.44 COLT					
Case length	O/A length	Blt. diameter	Base OD	Neck OD	Rim OD
1.100"	1.500"	.430"	.456"	.456"	.483"

.44 Russian

This cartridge was one of the earliest of all metallic cartridges. It goes all the way back to 1871 when Daniel Baird Wesson designed it to conform with Russian military specifications for a cartridge that would go into a big single-action, top-break revolver he was about to sell to the Russian Army. The rest is, literally, a part of American history. S&W sold the Russian thousands and thousands of his Model Number 3 single-action revolvers. But the cartridge itself worked so well and had such designed-in accuracy, the S&W company made it their mainstay, the standard heavy caliber for commercial sale and it stayed that way until 1908. This was considered the premier target cartridge for revolver shooting in the 1880s and 1890s when world-class target shooters like Ira Paine would use the S&W revolver, chambered in .44 Russian and loaded with black powder and a bullet of his own design, to shoot incredibly long strings of very tiny groups in front of crowds of enthusiastic spectators.

Cowboy shooters today encounter this caliber in the accurate Uberti .44 New Model Russian. Cimarron offers their good-looking 1872 open-top and some of the newer Uberti-made Richards-Mason conversion revolvers will also chamber .44 Russian. Mild recoiling, but hard hitting, the .44 S&W Russian is an excellent choice for a large-bore cowboy action cartridge and Black Hills is manufacturing very good quality, modern ammunition in this caliber.

.44 Special

The .44 S&W Special was introduced in 1907 or 1908 for its then brand new .44 Hand Ejector, the famous, ground breaking double action revolver some call the Triplelock. This is actually a slightly elongated .44 S&W Russian case that originally had the same 246-grain bullet at exactly the same velocity as the Russian round. Overall, this is one of the most inherently accurate, well-balanced revolver rounds ever produced. The .44 Special has a terrific, well-deserved reputation on the target range. The cartridge is also well-known because of the pioneering efforts of Elmer Keith during the early 1950s to produce a really-powerful factory .44 handgun cartridge. The culmination of his efforts are known today as the .44 Magnum (itself an elongated .44 Special).

The .44 Special is chambered in a number of replica revolvers that we will see in cowboy matches and it is performing exceedingly well. This is not only an easy cartridge to reload, it's an easy one to make mild-recoiling, accurate big bullet loads with. An excellent choice for a big-bore cowboy revolver.

.44 RUSSIAN					
Case length	O/A length	Blt. diameter	Base OD	Neck OD	Rim OD
.970"	1.430"	.429"	.457"	.457"	.515"

.44 SPECIAL					
Case length	O/A length	Blt. diameter	Base OD	Neck OD	Rim OD
1.160"	1.620"	.429"	.457"	.457"	.514"

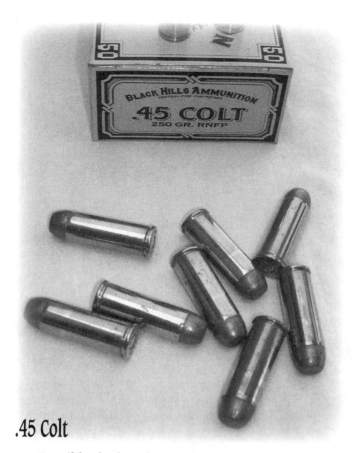

.45 Colt

Possibly the best known cartridge in the world (next to the 7.62mm Kalashnikov), the .45 Colt was introduced by Colt in 1873 and adopted, along with the gun that fired it, by the U.S. Army as its standard service cartridge. This round is often mistakenly called the .45 Long Colt. The trouble comes from the 1880s when the Army issued the 1873 .45 round to troops and then switched to a shorter .45 caliber cartridge shortly thereafter. The shorter .45 was actually the .45 S&W Schofield, which the Army adopted in place of the .45 Colt. Someone started calling the .45 Colt the .45 Long Colt to differentiate between the two and the name seems to have stuck. The truth is there never were two .45 Colt rimmed cartridges, so the caliber is correctly called .45 Colt. The Army's reasons for switching to a shorter cartridge were multifold. First, there were complaints about the heavy recoil and noise of the original .45 Colt loads, which carried 40 grains of black powder and had a muzzle velocity that was lapping at the heels of 1,000 feet per second. Also, the early cases were not of very good quality and were known for case head separation unless the charge was reduced. Further, the Army adopted another handgun, the S&W Schofield in 1875 to be used alongside the Colt

Single Action Army. The S&W used a shorter .45 cartridge. For all these reasons, the Army settled on the shorter .45 S&W caliber.

For reasons that will be obvious to most, the .45 Colt is among the most popular cartridges ever, certainly in CAS circles. This is the original cartridge Colt built for the famous Peacemaker. As such it will hold a place of endearment in many a heart for as long as there are people who appreciate fine guns. The .45 Colt is an accurate cartridge. It is capable of far greater accuracy than many modern shooters have given it credit for and I can personally attest to that fact, having cut more one-hole groups with .45 Colts than I can remember. The cartridge can be on the heavy side on recoil if you are not careful to keep the muzzle velocities down to 700 to 800 feet per second area. If you do, most folks find the recoil levels are quite manageable, even with heavier bullets. I will say this, I have noticed the quality of the factory-made ammunition being sold today is definitely a cut above what it was, even 10 years ago. Some of the store-bought cowboy action ammo we used for this book is among the most accurate ammunition in this caliber I have ever shot.

.45 COLT					
Case length	O/A length	Blt. diameter	Base OD	Neck OD	Rim OD
1.290"	1.600"	.452-.454""	.480"	.476"	.512"

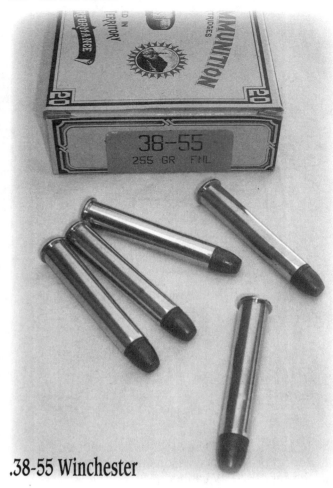

.38-55 Winchester

The .38-55 was introduced in 1884 by Ballard as a black-powder, single-shot target rifle cartridge. Like so many cartridges that were developed during the late 19th century, its name is also a technical designation. The number 38 refers to its caliber (nominally .379" bullet diameter) and the 55 indicates the number of grains of black powder the case held for optimum performance. The cartridge itself has an excellent reputation for mid-range accuracy, and on out to about 200 yards it is a hard cartridge to beat.

The .38-55 has been chambered in many single shot and lever action rifles over the last 120 years. It even shows up in European drillings. The cartridge is inherently accurate. It is also very mild shooting and easy to reload and makes a wonderful short to mid-range deer cartridge. For steel plates, the old .38-55 certainly has more knock-down power than the .30-30.

.45-70 Government

The venerable .45-70 was adopted by the U.S. military as its service rifle cartridge in 1873 where it was used in the trap-door Springfield rifle and carbines until the .30 caliber Krag bolt-action was adopted in 1892. The caliber name .45-70 stands for .45 caliber (actually, it,s almost .46 caliber with the nominal bullet diameter being .458") and 70 being the black powder charge weight in grains. Sometimes another number was added to the designation, such as .45-70-405, in this case the last number, 405, indicated the weight of the bullet.

The .45-70 Government was in use during the era of the great buffalo hunts. Even though it might be one of the shortest of the big .45 caliber cartridges used, it certainly killed more than its share of bison. This is an accurate and effective caliber. With the right loads it can be used at medium or long range with good success. Many single-shot rifles have been and are still being chambered in this caliber. Today it is the best-known and most popular .45 caliber survivor of the 19th century and ammunition has been available for it continuously. Lever-action rifles, like the 1886 Winchester, have been chambered for the .45-70 and Marlin started using the caliber even earlier in its 1881 lever-action, a tradition that is carried on today in the Marlin Model 1895. In a strong single-shot rifle, the .45-70 can be loaded up to be a shoulder-jarring hulk of a big game cartridge, it also responds equally well to being loaded-down to milder levels, as it must be to safely accommodate the old trap-door Springfield, which was not a particularly strong action. These latter are closer to the performance of modern, cowboy action loadings and are comfortable to shoot, even in the lighter weight lever-actions.

.38-55 WINCHESTER					
Case length	O/A length	Blt. diameter	Base OD	Neck OD	Rim OD
2.085"	2.510"	.379"	.421"	.392"	.506"

.45-70 GOVERNMENT					
Case length	O/A length	Blt. diameter	Base OD	Neck OD	Rim OD
2.105"	2.550"	.458"	.500"	.475"	.600"

Ammunition Sources:

Ammunition, commercially available:

*Black Hills Ammunition, Inc.
P.O. Box 3090,
Rapid City, SD 57709
(605) 348-5150 fax (605) 348-9827
www.black-hills.com

Federal Cartridge Company
900 Ehlen Drive
Anoka, MN 55303-7503
(800) 322-2342, fax: (763) 323-2506
www.federalcartridge.com

Fiocchi Ammunition USA
6930 Fremont Road
Ozark, MO 65721
(417) 725-4118, fax: (417) 725-1039
www.fiocchiusa.com

*Hornady Mfg. Co.
P.O. Box 1848
Grand Island, NE 68802
(800) 338-3220 fax (308) 382-5761
www.hornady.com

PMC - Eldorado Cartridge Corporation
P.O. Box 62508
Boulder City, NV 89006-2508
(702) 294-0025, fax (702) 294-0121
www.pmcammo.com

*Remington Arms Co., Inc.
870 Remington Drive
Madison, NC 27025
(800) 243-9700
www.remington.com

Ten-X Ammunition
4035 Guasti Road #308
Ontario, CA 91761
(909) 605-1617, fax: (909) 605-2844
www.ten-x.com

Ultramax Ammunition
2112 Elk Vale Road
Rapid City, SD 57701
(800) 345-5852 or (605) 342-4141
fax (605) 342-8727
www.ultramaxammunition.com

*Winchester Div. Olin Corp.
427 N. Shamrock
E. Alton, IL 62024
((618) 258-3566 fax (618) 258-3599
www.winchester.com

Ammunition, obsolete calibers:

Buffalo Arms Co.
660 Vermeer Court
Ponderay, ID 83852
(208) 263-6953, fax (208) 265-2096
www.buffaloarms.com

Old Western Scrounger
50 Industrial Parkway
Carson City, NV. 89706
(775) 246-2091
www.ows-ammunition.com

* - Ammunition used for test purposes within this book.

Chapter 7

Gun Leather
Featuring: The work of James Allen of Heflin, Alabama

The owner calls this unusual rig a "custom-made Texas cross-draw" holster and belt. Made by James Allen, the holster holds a Cimarron 1872 Open-Top .44 and I have to say this the lightest and most graceful cross-draw rig I have ever worn. Notice the unusual double billet straps with roller buckles. From the Bobby James collection.

For the modern-day cowboy action shooter the compound word "gunleather" means a lot more than holsters, belts, scabbards and other stuff related to the carrying of guns and ammunition. Of necessity, gunleather also includes many of the cowboy-related accessories such as boots, chaps, cuffs, spur straps and some assorted items. For a few it even includes saddles and tack. Being a book whose main focus is on the replica guns that modern cowboy shooter's are using, there was not the time,

nor the space left to include every leather product being manufactured. However, my feeling was that leather was too important a subject to be left out altogether. Thus it was that right around the time this book was begun and several times thereafter, the author contacted several of the better-known leather makers and retailers and enquired if they might like to have some of their work shown in the book. The products you will view are from the makers who responded to those contacts. We've also included some very special pieces from private collections.

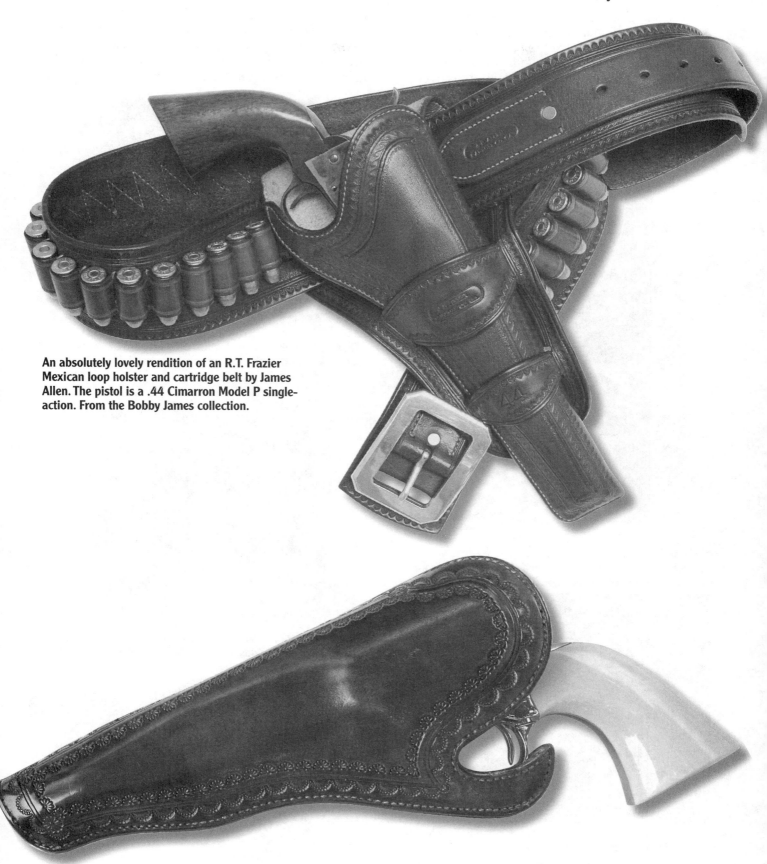

An absolutely lovely rendition of an R.T. Frazier Mexican loop holster and cartridge belt by James Allen. The pistol is a .44 Cimarron Model P single-action. From the Bobby James collection.

A beautiful border carved left-handed holster of an unknown pattern by James Allen. The gun is a 5 1/2-inch Colt SAA with one-piece ivory grips by J. Meacham. From the Ed Wade collection.

The sampling of gunleather items that follows is not, I repeat, is not, by any stretch of the imagination, a look at everything that is available today. Indeed the author would be the first to admit there is a great deal more available, but to cover it all would take and is worthy of a book in itself. Instead, what we are going to do is to take a short, mostly photographic walk through a small but rich percentage of what today's shooters have available to them. Although what you are about to see is a only

These intricately detailed leather cuffs are also the work of James Allen, I'll let the picture speak for itself. From the Ed Wade collection.

Another set of cuffs by James Allen, these feature deep relief carving and silver studs. From the Delbert Fentress collection.

This beautiful set of chaps by James Allen features very complex border patterns, fringe and silver conchos. From the Delbert Fentress collection.

Just look at the intricate details James Allen has crafted into these chaps, cross-hatch checkering on the pockets while the borders are alternating daisies and swastikas (in this case, an ancient native American religious symbol, not to be confused with the Nazi party emblem). From the Delbert Fentress collection.

A fancy set of Mexican spurs with straps by James Allen. From the Delbert Fentress collection.

small sampling of what is being made, I think you are actually being presented with a fair overview of what you might expect to find. We leave it up to the individual to find the leather maker and style that suits your own, very individual needs.

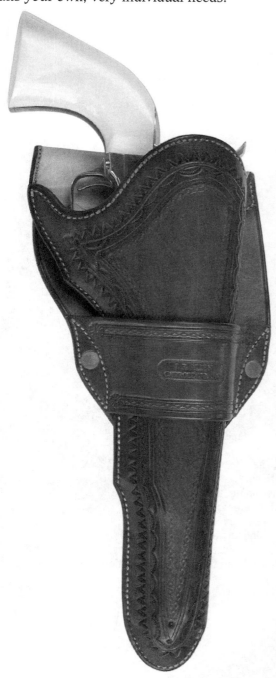

▲ James Allen made this exact duplicate of a holster made about 1880 by J.E. Rice of Dodge City, Kansas. Allen's attention to details is amazing. I believe he even counts the number of original stitches! The holster is sheathing a nickel Colt SAA with one-piece ivory grips by Jerry Meacham. From the Ed Wade collection.

Jake Slade (Ed Wade) in full cowboy dress; decked out in perfect period garb and ready for business. Everything this cowboy is wearing is correct for the 1880s era. The holster, belt, chaps and cuffs are entirely hand-made and are originals by James Allen. The hardware is a Colt SAA with one-piece ivory grips by Jerry Meacham and an engraved Uberti 1866 carbine, both in .45 Colt caliber.

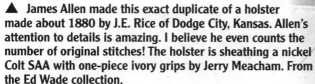

Many, but not all of the holsters and belts shown here are modern reproductions of original 19th century gunleather that was originally fabricated by such well-known leather workers as E. L. Gallatin of Denver, F.A. Meanea of Cheyenne or R. E. Rice of Dodge City, Kansas. At least one modern-old-time leather maker, El Paso Saddlery, has actually been in business for well over 100 years. Many of these modern products are hand-

I think this is the most beautiful double, California Slim-Jim rig I have ever seen. Hand-crafted by James Allen, there are more details in this leather than you can imagine. In fact it takes a few moments of studying to find them all. The decorations include deep, double-border carving with silver studs, bordered cross-hatching, silver studs, red leather lining, and yes, those decorations wrap all the way around and extend into areas you would never see, unless you looked! The 3-inch cartridge belt is also carved with borders and cross-hatching with spade-shaped billets, red-leather lining and a custom, engraved silver buckle. The guns are nickel plated .45 Colt SAA's, with one-piece ivory grips built by Jerry Meacham and checkered by Bill Hoffman. From the Ed Wade collection.

This floral carved, right hand holster is a Slim-Jim or California type by J. Allen with a 7 1/2 Colt Single Action Army, one-piece ivory stocks by Jerry Meacham and checkered by Bill Hoffman. From the Ed Wade collection. Author photos.

made, some are more or less mass-produced but styled like old-fashioned holsters. Still others are pure custom, inspired by Hollywood. The products of a very few of these modern leather makers, notably James Allen, are so good that they really can't be called reproductions, a better word was needed to indicate the level of craftsmanship in what they have done, so we have used the term "duplicate" to more accurately describe the high degree of painstaking work they put into their goods.

Another exquisite piece by James Allen; a set of deeply floral carved F. A. Meanea pattern holsters with cartridge belt. If these holsters seem to look familiar, have a look at the cover photo on the dust jacket of the book *Packing Iron*. The revolver on the left is a Cimarron .45 Model P stainless with a .45 Great Western II in satin nickel on the right. From the Delbert Fentress collection.

Another Allen holster patterned after a Meanea original, this one is for a 5 1/2-inch SAA, one-piece ivory grips by Jerry Meacham checkered by Bill Hoffman. From the Ed Wade collection.

The author owes a debt of gratitude to Ed Wade, Delbert Fentress, James Allen, Mike Harvey, Fred Stann and Bobby James for allowing me to photograph much of the beautiful leather we have been able to feature here.

For a nostalgic and far more complete look at some great original western leather, I highly recommend reading the classic book on this subject, *Packing Iron* by Richard C. Rattenbury (1993, Zon International Publishing). This book was used

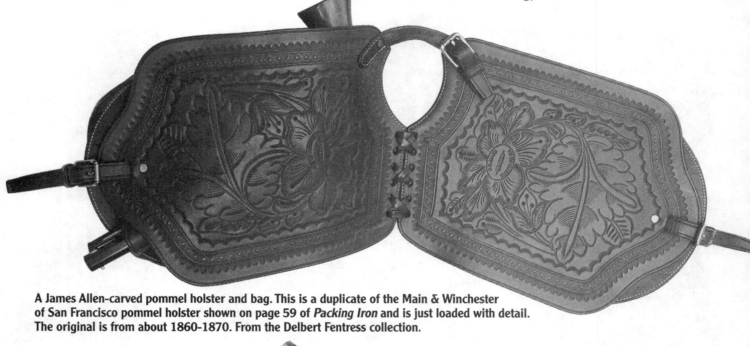

A James Allen-carved pommel holster and bag. This is a duplicate of the Main & Winchester of San Francisco pommel holster shown on page 59 of *Packing Iron* and is just loaded with detail. The original is from about 1860-1870. From the Delbert Fentress collection.

Deeply relief carved and bordered, this beautiful lined holster by J. Allen is a duplication of an original by F. A. Meanea of Cheyenne, Wyoming. It is wrapped around a blued 7 1/2-inch Colt SAA with one-piece ivory grips by Jerry Meacham. From the Ed Wade collection.

by the author as an aid in forming the core of the representative holsters shown here. Two other great reference books, although not specifically about leather, are *Metallic Cartridge Conversions* by Dennis Adler (2002, Krause Publications),which has some lovely old and new gunleather interspersed among some very cool old and new revolvers. The second is a book called *Cowboys & Trappings of the Old West* by William Manns and Elizabeth Clair Flood (1997, Zon International Publishing .)

A deeply floral and border carved, true Slim-Jim holster set cross-draw on a soft "money belt" type cartridge belt with spade billets and custom silver buckle. The gun is a Colt SAA with one-piece ivory grips by Jerry Meacham, checkering by Bill Hoffman. By J. Allen. From the Ed Wade collection.

This J. Allen holster is exactly patterned after holsters made by the Moran Brothers of Miles City, Mont., c.1890. It is carrying a Colt SAA .45 with a 7 1/2-inch barrel, blued with one-piece ivory grips by Jerry Meacham of Charlotte, N.C. From the Ed Wade collection.

Other Leather makers:

This simple, but good-looking and comfortable Mexican loop holster and belt are from El Paso Saddlery. The revolver is a Cimarron Model P in .45 Colt. Courtesy Texas Jack's.

The single Sante Fe holster from Kirkpatrick is nicely lined and has a tasteful hand-stamped border. Courtesy Roy Rugers.

A fine quality lined, California "styled" holster hand-made by Bachman, for a Smith & Wesson Schofield. From the Ed Wade collection.

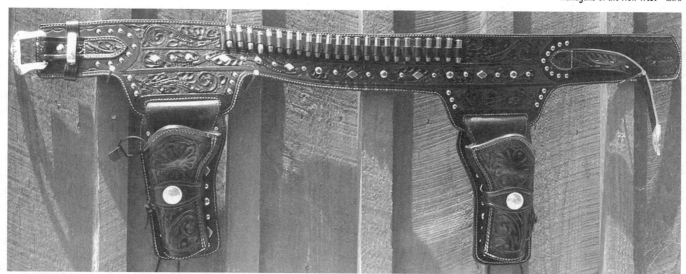

For admirers of the heroes of the Silver Screen, this hand-tooled Kirkpatrick double rig is called the "Silver King" (cat#K-59). Gene Autry would be pleased. Courtesy Roy Rugers.

From Kirkpatrick, this unusual double rig is very comfortable to wear; it's called the Graveyard. Courtesy Roy Rugers.

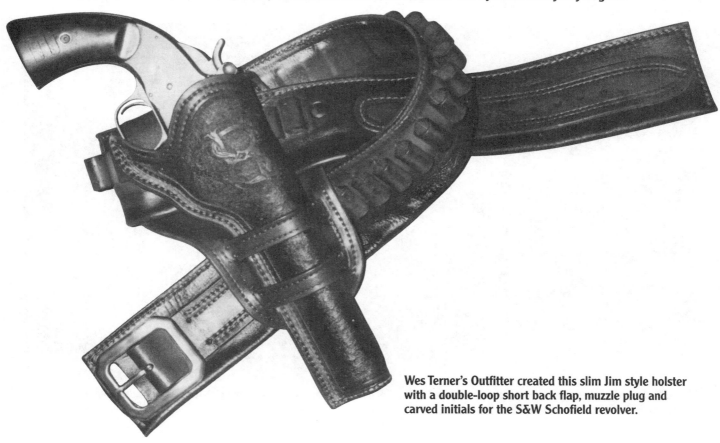

Wes Terner's Outfitter created this slim Jim style holster with a double-loop short back flap, muzzle plug and carved initials for the S&W Schofield revolver.

This double set of slim Jims by Wes Terner's Outfitter includes a matching belt, cuffs and spur straps and is done in a fishscale pattern with deer skin star inserts.

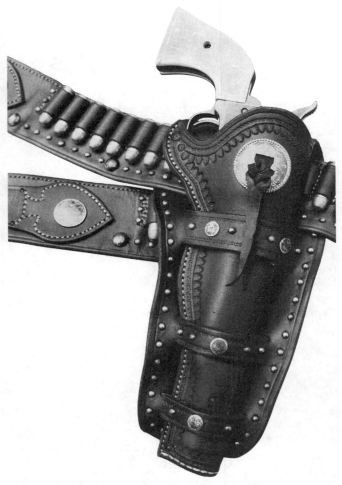

Nickel spots and conchos and nicely done edge tooling highlight this rig by Wes Terner's Outfitters.

From Texas Jack's, this handsome single-gun rig features a lined double-loop Mexican holster called the Lightning and an Uvalde cartridge belt. Courtesy Texas Jack's.

Chapter 8

Looking at the Colt Single Action Army

Here's a slick and inexpensive tool for single-action cylinder removal and replacement that came from Dave Lanara.

Getting the cylinder in and out of an 1873 pattern single-action without scratching or marring the outside surfaces can sometimes be difficult, especially if the cylinder is a good, tight fit in the frame. One good method involves the use of a removal-installation tool. The credit for this cute trick, shown in the accompanying photo, goes to the Colt master-gunsmith Dave Lanara, who shared it with the author a few years back. The cost of the removal-installation tool is a sheet of white office paper. To use the tool, place the revolver's hammer at half-cock, the loading position, open the loading gate and as you always should; check the chambers to be sure they are empty. Use a scissors to cut yourself a strip of that white office paper long-wise so its 11 inches long and about 1 1/2 inches wide. Place the gun on a soft bench top, or on a piece of cardboard on a countertop. Slide the strip under the cylinder from the loading gate side and push through about half its length. Next, tuck the front end of the paper back through the opening between the to of the cylinder and the top of the frame to make a "sling" around the cylinder, both "long legs" of the sling should be facing out the loading gate side of the frame. Remove the base pin and gently pull the legs of the paper sling. This extracts the cylinder from the frame neatly, and since its sides are covered by the paper, it can't get scratched. Reverse this ultra-simple procedure for installation.

On the left is the wrong way, an ill-fitting household screwdriver will ruin gun screws in short order, it has less than 50 percent contact with the slot and very little control. On the right, the correct way is to use a proper hollow-ground screwdriver with a blade that fills up the slot completely, giving you 100 percent slot contact and excellent purchase on the screw.

Use the right screwdriver! Everyone loves to tinker but nothing makes a beautiful gun look awful any quicker than screws with their slots all torn up from someone who used the wrong screwdriver trying to remove them. If you have not heard this before, gun screws are different from the hardware you find around the house or on an automobile. Even if they look like conventional slotted screws, I assure you, they are not. The most important difference is in the screwdriver slot, which is not tapered. But the blades of almost all conventional screwdrivers are tapered. Gun screw slots are square, all the way to the bottom. Square slots mean that a special sort of screwdriver blade should be used to remove and install them. When you use a conventional screwdriver in a gun screw slot, the only part of the slot that is in contact with the driver are its top edges. This helps explain why you see so many butched-up screw slots on guns. Gun screwdrivers are what are called "hollow-ground", that means they are factory ground with straight, square sides that are meant to slide all the way to the bottom of the square screw slot and as a consequence, to make full contact with it.

The gun screwdriver should fit the screw slot's width perfectly, but it should also fit the screw slot's length, that is from side to side. Have a look at these two photos. One shows an old wooden-handled household screwdriver in the hammer screw slot of a single-action. Notice how poorly it fits and the fact that it is much too narrow to fill the slot from side to side? This screwdriver is using less than half the available screw slot area, and that's only what we can see from the surface. Now take a look at the other photo, this is the same screw in the same gun but the driver is one of Brownell's Magna-Tip screwdrivers, a

special hollow-ground screwdriver with many sizes of replaceable driver blades. As you can see, this driver fills the slot from side to side and its width is matched much closer than the former driver. Here we have as close as we can get to having 100 percent contact with the entire screw slot and this is our best insurance against ugly, ruined screws.

How about just a few general thoughts regarding a couple of springs that are applicable to Colt SAA and many of their modern-day clones? We won't get into anything "heavy," just a few things that may help the cowboy shooter get through and hopefully, enough knowledge to know when its time to lay it all down and call the gunsmith. Many of the troubles that pop up with the early Colt designs revolve around their springs. With three exceptions, the springs in a Colt SA and many of its clones, are leaf-type designs and some of them have been around since the 1830s. You would think we are overdue for an update, so what about coil springs? Leaf springs have down sides. They can be heavy as the dickens, they are also prone to breakage. To the credit of leaf springs, on the up-side it's hard to fit a coil spring into a tiny space that will have enough "life" or power to drive the parts with the energy that a leaf spring will.

How about those mainsprings? We have seen where amateur smiths, and even some professionals, have lightened single-action mainsprings to the point where there is not enough tension left in the spring to hold the hammer all the way down after it falls. A light spring helps make for an easy action, yep, however it also slows down your lock-time. Further, if the spring has been made too light, it can actually allow the hammer to re-bound off the primer. In severe cases of this, when the spring is much too light, we have seen hammers that bounced back to the safety notch and beyond. That's too light. So is a mainspring that makes the gun prone to misfires. As big and heavy as these hammers are, it would seem that making an SAA misfire would not be easy to do, I mean, a person has to really try.

Think about it, when you are trying to hit a tiny spot on a target with an 1873 pattern, single-action revolver, you need all the help you can get just to hold the sight picture steady while that hammer drops through its long throw. Why would you want to slow down the hammer fall (increase lock-time) so much? For very practical reasons, the quicker the lock time, the less time I have on my hands to jerk the sights off target. There is a happy medium between way too light and thumb-bustin' hard and I encourage shooters to find it. However, I will share that I prefer a lively hammer fall, even if that means a slightly heavier trigger pull and maybe I have to pull back a little harder to cock the hammer. Many of the foreign arms companies that make replica Colts don't seem to have a good idea of what correct spring tension setting is, nor do their mainsprings seem as dependable as original Colt springs. In the past, I have called these Italian springs "way-too springs" because they are either way-too soft, way-too hard, they break way-too soon or all of the above. I will say right up front that some Italian springs are of very good quality, but I have been disappointed, specifically by their mainsprings. I just won't waste my time with them. If you are looking for a dependable mainspring, buy a Colt or an American-made aftermarket spring.

One old tradition is to slip a leather spacer in between the grip frame and the mainspring, this shoves the entire spring to the rear and causes it to lean forward slightly. If it's done correctly, the simple modification can lighten mainspring tension and it may leave the spring with enough whip in it to dependably fire primers. The disadvantages of using leather are that it will soak up moisture, eventually rusting the steel. Also, it shrinks and expands as moisture content in the air varies. Brownell's sells a better option, they have a factory-made neoprene spacer that is of the correct shape to help lighten mainspring tension while at the same time keeping the spring under the hammer in a manner that a good degree of whip remains so the hammer

won't bounce back off the primer. There is also the excellent option of buying mainsprings made with reduced power from aftermarket sources.

Colt's bolt and trigger spring is the small, nearly flat, split spring that you will find up under the trigger guard. This spring gives the tension to return the trigger and the locking bolt, for the trigger a moderate tension of from 3/4 to 1 1/2 pounds is what we want to see. For the bolt we would like a livelier spring, with 5 pounds tension to insure the bolt has enough tension to do its job. Most people are aware that this split-leaf spring is prone to breakage. Problems with this spring have also been seen in many replica revolvers. The Colt-made replacement is a very high-quality spring, I know it is the best one available from any arms maker and it is a good replacement to keep in your "kit box." There is not much that can be done to alter this critical spring except for some careful bending of each leg to modify the tension, however, there are a few things you can do to make it more reliable. One easy operation is to stone off any burrs that you see on and around the edges. There are also very good aftermarket springs available. In my opinion, Leroy Wisner's is the best of the bunch. There is a reliable music-wire replacement spring. I have tried them and they are just about unbreakable but wire springs never seem to offer as much liveliness as a leaf spring is capable of offering within the same physical size limitations. Both the bolt and trigger return always seem sluggish with this type of spring.

Here are some excellent reference books that you might like to read that will help you to understand better how the Colt Single Action Army works:

The Colt Single Action Revolvers; A Shop Manual, Volumes 1 & 2 by Jerry Kuhnhausen

Gunsmithing Guns of the Old West 2nd Edition, 2004, David R. Chicoine

Loading the Peacemaker by Dave Scovill

Shooting Colt Single Actions by Mike Venturino

Shooting Sixguns of the Old West by Mike Venturino

The NRA Firearms Assembly Book

Cleaning up after black powder

Many people shy away from shooting black powder simply because of the drudgery of cleaning up later. Some, though I cannot imagine why, don't seem to enjoy the great pall of blinding smoke, the smell of sulpher or getting their hands dirty. I enjoy it all. And if you are anything like me, the awful-acrid smell of brimstone, those huge clouds of billowing smoke that momentarily throw the world into fog, that great orange flash of embers that has been known to set clothing and dry grass afire, the world around you covered with soot. . .ahhh! Heavens, what could possibly be better?

The following bits regarding cleaning methods should be of interest.

Is black powder corrosive?

Yes, but perhaps not so much as you think. As black powder combusts in a gun it burns only, on average, some 43 percent[1] of its mass. That means less than half the burning powder charge is useable energy. What of the remainder, which would be the other roughly 57 percent of the powder charge? About 56 percent of the remainder is left hanging around as solid residue (fouling) and then there is a bit of water that makes up that last 1 percent[2] or so. Now we know where fouling comes from and how much of the powder charge remains in the barrel, unburned. In fact, the heat and pressure generated by firing the shot has distributed that residue, which is now a sooty mess, all over the barrel's interior. The question is, what becomes of my barrel when that messy powder residue is left in there? The belief, commonly held, is that this black powder residue is so corrosive it will eat up the steel and ruin the barrel within a day or two. There is a grain of truth in that, but, in 1880, my answer would have been different than the one I would give today. Why? Because in 1880 we had the awful, highly corrosive residue from the primer to deal with, today we do not.

After firing, black powder's residual salts, all by themselves, are only mildly corrosive. Being a salt, the residue is hygroscopic and that means it will readily attract and soak up moisture out of the air, much as a very dry soda cracker will get soft when left unsealed in the air any length of time. The result of moisture combining with these residual salts forms a slightly corrosive mixture that would cause no real harm to the barrel's steel until perhaps at least several days and probably even longer. The real reason that black powder residue was considered so corrosive, in truth, came from what happened to the residue when the that alchemic brew of a priming mixture was introduced.

Up into the early part of the 20th century, in some cases even later, the explosive mixture used in cartridge primers and percussion caps was manufactured from violently corrosive chemical compounds that were actually quite dangerous before, during and after combustion. As that very corrosive priming compound was exploded to ignite the powder charge, it was intimately mixed under heat and pressure with the much larger quantity of mildly corrosive black powder residue that has hygroscopic qualities. That, in turn, formed the compound that damaged older gun barrels. In conditions of high humidity, that corrosive priming compound/gunpowder mix soaked up and so became wet with moisture from the atmosphere. This, now highly corrosive mixture leached onto the warm-dry steel of the gun barrel where it stuck, and if left unattended, it quickly rusted and pitted the raw steel. Today the situation has changed. Almost all priming is non-corrosive so we truly do not have to worry so much about black powder residue damaging a gun barrel. Many shooters are also using modern bullet lubricants and lubricated patches that help coat the bore, further protecting it. To be sure, we still need to be thoughtful about how long we leave the residue in there. It is, after all, hygroscopic and damage will ensue if it is left there for too long, but nowhere near to the same degree as it would with corrosive priming. In most cases, except in near 100 percent humidity, you would normally be fine to leave the gun overnight before you cleaned it.

Be prepared to keep it clean, at home and on the range

It will come as no surprise to most, shooting black powder is a filthy proposition. Once it has been ignited, it quickly clogs the inside of the barrel and covers almost everything else with a powdery, crusty, foul-smelling mess. Even black powder substitutes like Pyrodex can chunk-up a gun barrel pretty well after several shots. This fouling mess does not confine itself to the gun's barrel. Under great pressure, those powder gases make their way into the axis pin that the revolver's cylinder rotates on. When that happens the cylinder may slowly start to seize and can eventually stop rotating.

The author has made the foolish mistake of driving out to the shooting range to fire a black powder firearm and forgotten to bring anything with him to clean fouling or to repair mechanical problems caused by fouling or from the debris of an exploded percussion cap. Bad move! Today, we just don't think much about it, but back in the black powder era anyone who carried a gun was aware that careful preparation was required when you traveled with a gun or went to the target range. So you brought whatever tools and equipment you thought you might need with you to keep that weapon in working order. I learned that the hard way. When you go to the range to burn charcoal, bring along sufficient cleaning supplies, including solvents, patches, brushes, and some water. Be sure you take along enough tools to disassemble and repair any of the minor glitches that can occur when firing black powder. Yes, I know, you can't bring your whole workshop with you, but you can make up a miniature version and carry it with you in a small plastic toolbox.

Various cleaning methods.

Most times, before we can begin cleaning the weapon, it will probably have to be disassembled to some degree. This fouling and dirt gets all over a gun and we have to be able to reach into any areas that have powder residue on them so it can be removed. On muzzle-loading guns, this means removing the barrel from the wood, and unscrewing the percussion nipple and or the bolster. It's also a good idea whenever it is possible to do so, to unscrew and remove the breech plug at the rear of the barrel. With cap-and-ball revolvers you remove the barrel and the cylinder and unscrew the nipples. Using black powder in metallic cartridge revolvers mandates that at the least, you should remove the cylinder. That done, we are ready to start cleaning the metal parts.

Water-based cleaning is the cheapest and I am sure the oldest method of cleaning gunpowder residue. A great many shooters still use this method and it is still today a perfectly effective means of cleaning black powder residue. Plain old clean water will dissolve and flush away most of the black powder residues, the water acts on the sulpher and the carbon, as well as residual salts. It works like this; we will first be flushing the inside of the barrel along with other effected components, like the cylinder, with clean, cold water. Your first step flushes most of the loose fouling away. At the same time it moistens and begins to loosen harder fouling that has adhered to the steel. Our next step is to flush those same areas with hot water. For this, it will be wise to devise ways to hold the barrel, cylinder or other parts so you won't get scalded, then use really hot water, as hot as possible. With this hot-water step, use a stiff bronze cleaning brush to energetically scrub the inside of that barrel, cylinder

chambers, too, then use a hard-bristled toothbrush to scrub any outsides areas that have residue deposits on them. Sometimes you have to get creative and figure out different methods to reach hard-to-get areas. You can use old-time pipe cleaners to help you reach into tight corners or odd shaped areas. By all means use a nipple pick, along with pipe cleaners when de-fouling nipples.

In a variation of the second step, parts such as revolver cylinders, sometimes barrels, nipples and like parts can be boiled in a small pot of clean water after you have given them a cold-water flush. Where it is possible, wrap the parts with short pieces of iron wire so you have something to lift them with without getting burned. Here's why, while the parts are boiling lift the parts out of the boiling water one at a time and scrub the insides with bore-cleaning brushes, also clean the outsides with a toothbrush and plunk them back in the water again.

Keep on scrubbing with the brushes and boiling water for as long as dark water runs out of the bore or off the pieces. As the scrub water starts to run clean, flush the parts again with hot water. After that scrub the bore and the cylinder chambers with clean cloth patches, then wipe the exterior clean and dry with a soft cloth. Now you can start cleaning the bore, chambers and any exterior areas using clean and dry cotton patches. Keep this up this until every nook and cranny is clean and has been dried completely. After you have the whole bunch dry, carefully look it all over for spots of powder residue. Anything that is left will normally show up clearly once dried, and then you can scrub it off with a dry toothbrush and cloths.

When you are sure that all trace of residue have been removed and the metal is completely dry, apply a light coating of metal preservative or a good light synthetic oil to the insides of the bore, the revolver chambers and all other metal surfaces. To remove powder residue that has adhered itself to a wood gunstock, wipe the area with a cloth dampened with cold water, follow it up with another clean cloth held by a clothespin and soaked with hot water. When the wood is clean and dried apply a drop or two of boiled linseed oil to the area and rub it into the wood with your fingers.

The second type of cleaning is solvent-based. Many people prefer this method as it does not use any water. The procedure is simplicity itself. You run a cleaning rod down the bore with a patch attached that is soaked with any brand of black powder cleaning solvent. In a revolver, also run the soaking wet patch through each chamber. You should let the solvent sit for a while, a few minutes to a half an hour. This way it has a chance to soften the fouling. Leaving it sit also gives the solvent time to seep into the nipple threads or into the threads of the barrel breech plug which will allow easier removal. Next remove the nipples and/or the breech plug if your gun is so equipped. Now comes the scrubbing. Do the barrel bore and the cylinder chambers, using a cleaning rod with a bronze cleaning brush soaked with the black powder solvent. Be sure to run the brush through several times, making several passes all the way through and be don't be stingy with the solvent. Scrub all the external areas of the metal parts with toothbrush wet with solvent. Use the same solvent to get after the insides of the nipples with pipe cleaners and a nipple pick and be sure to get after the threads on the nipple and the nipple threads at the rear of the percussion cylinder.

I like to let the parts sit once again for a few more minutes before going after the bore and the chambers with as many clean, dry cloth patches as it takes until they come out clean. When you have just done an abnormally large amount of shooting with your gun, you will probably find that you have to repeat the scrubbing with a brush and still more solvent to get out all the powder fouling. Whatever it takes, when your patches are finally coming out clean, just dry everything with clean cotton patches and/or cloths and as we did with the water method, check closely for any areas of residue you might have missed. Finally, I recommend you apply a light synthetic gun oil or metal preservative to all the metal parts, inside and out. Again, the wood may be wiped down clean by using a clean cotton rag dampened with the black powder solvent. Follow this with an energetic rubbing with a clean, dry cloth then daub on a couple of drops of the boiled linseed oil and rub it in well with your fingers.

Some shooters prefer to use a combination of the water and solvent clean-up. I like it because I believe it gets my guns the cleanest in the fastest amount of time. The method uses combination of both methods, the water being used only to flush away the nasty loose fouling. Then I switch over to black powder cleaning solvents. You begin, as with the cold-water method, by flushing the bore and chambers with cold tap water just like I described above. I generally follow the cold with a quick hot-water flush and then I switch over to solvents. Using a bronze bore brush soaked up with black powder solvent, scrub the bore and chambers use a toothbrush soaked with solvent on all the other external parts. For the finale', this dual cleaning method is finished by following the same final methods outlined above under solvent-based cleaning.

Hard deposits

Once in a while you will probably encounter a gun with a bore with certain areas that are really hard to clean. This is especially true where there are areas of minor pitting or surface roughness in the bore. Here powder fouling, lead deposits or copper from bullet jackets will take the opportunity to cling to the rifling. If you were to continue to fire the weapon with these deposits in the bore, the fouling will only get worse as these deposits act like a magnet for still more of their own kind. When fouling like this is close to either the muzzle or the breech end of the barrel you may be able to reach in there with sharp dental picks and carefully scrape the gunk out. Times when the deposit is not easily accessible lead you to try other means for its removal. The best remedy for such an occasion will be an abrasive of some kind. It needs to be a mild abrasive so you don't harm the rifling. One very useful product that has helped me on several occasion is called J-B Non-Embedding Bore Cleaning Compound. J-B Compound, available from Brownells, is a mild abrasive in a paste form that is used on the outside of a tight fitting cleaning cloth cleaning patch that you have wrapped around a jag. The compound may also be used as a bore lap on a cast, soft-metal slug. It has been my experience that, except in a couple of exceptional cases, with a minimum of effort this product will get out every last bit of debris that might be stuck to the inside of the gun barrel, that includes even lead and plastic debris from shotgun wads. This cleaner is an oil-based paste with abrasive in it, it is also apparently finer than jewelers rouge and I have not seen any damage to the rifling.

You can also purchase a stainless steel sponge from Brownells that is not made like steel wool, instead its like a soft, but quite coarse, steel scouring sponge. These work well when cut into patches that fit on a cleaning jag so it can be passed through the bore and it will remove surface rust and many deposits rather aggressively. It scrubs right down to the original surface but again, without removing any of the parent metal. This product will scratch finely honed bores. For badly leaded bores you can try scouring the bore with the stainless sponge patch mentioned above that you have first soaked with Shooter's Choice Lead Remover, this combination will remove just about anything in the bore that was not originally part of the barrel! One other way to get out stubborn fouling and lead deposits are the Lead Remover Cloths. These cloths are chemically treated to remove lead, plastic and other sorts of stubborn residue. They are available from Birchwood Casey and other suppliers. To use the lead remover cloth, you have to cut it into suitably sized patches for your own bore. This method will work very well in barrels with excellent bores but has not proven so effective when used in old barrels that have pitted bores.

Pyrodex fouling

Pyrodex was the first black powder substitute and it is still preferred by many shooters. Now, Pyrodex may be non-corrosive but that does not mean it will not foul a bore, quite the contrary. As anyone who has used it will tell you, Pyrodex will foul a barrel and with a residue that is apparently very dry and very adherent to steel. I know revolver shooters using Pyrodex who have loaded their cartridges with soft lead alloy revolver bullets, ones with insufficient or improper bullet lubricant, that have quickly developed a severe fouling problem. Metallic cartridge loads like this, whether they are used in a revolver or rifle have a tendency to lead rifled barrels badly and leave a messy, grey residual coating that usually has to be scraped out of the rifling so the gun's accuracy can be returned. I have found that in order to keep this residue to a minimum and prevent leading with Pyrodex, one wants to use generous amounts of good bullet lubricant intended for black powder. Lubricants such as SPG Lube will work wonders in these situations. Using generous amounts of bullet lubricant means your choice of bullets ought to be made thoughtfully, with special attention given to the size and capacity of the grease grooves and to the bullet alloy. For general use, bullet alloy should be at the ratio of about 1:20 tin to lead.

Pre-treating your gun's bore.

Another very effective method to help reduce black powder or Pyrodex residue, both of which would like to cling to your gun's bore, is to pre-treat the bore with something that resists adhering to the powder residue before a shooting session. Some time ago, we began pre-treating all our black powder barrels with a product from Brownells that is called Moly Bore Treatment Paste. Based in the incredible friction fighter called molybdenum disulfide, this paste gets applied to the clean and dry bore. If done following the makers instructions, it really does provide the interior of the bore with a microscopically thin, super-slippery surface coating, and as a side-benny, its waterproof.

After applying this stuff to my gun bores, I noticed a marked and immediate decrease in the amount of fouling and residue build-up compared to when a similar number of shots had been fired in an untreated barrel. Also, it was clear that most of the fouling in the treated bore could be easily wiped out with only a damp patch. It has also become apparent that this bore treatment has helped reduce fouling in gun barrels with pitted bores. For me, the biggest benefit of a moly-treated bore is how much it eases clean-up after shooting, and that is even true with a pitted bore. I am often asked how long this moly-treatment lasts. The best answer is, I am not sure yet. It would probably depend on how many shots you fire and how aggressive you are when you clean your barrel. I have a tendency to scrub the peewallers out of my gun's barrels and the moly paste seems to last about two

to three of these vigorous cleaning sessions before it becomes evident that the barrel needs a re-treatment. We all know that the biggest pain associated with shooting black powder is the clean-up. The moly-treated bore seems to me to be much easier to clean. Therefore, this is an idea I would recommend for any serious black powder shooter. This is one time when a very high-tech modern product works to enhance the action of a very basic old operation.

Range tips and general cleaning thoughts

With all revolvers, regardless if they are cartridge or percussion, you should remove the cylinders and disassemble them for cleaning. Don't try to leave the cylinder in the revolver, it will never get really clean. Remember to clean the center-hole in the cylinder and to clean the arbor pin or base pin on which your cylinder rotates. Give some attention to cleaning the inside of the cylinder's opening in the frame, you may use a toothbrush even a stiff bronze bore brush soaked-up good with solvent, but scrub these areas well. An area that often gets overlooked is up where the barrel is threaded into the frame. This is just loaded with little nooks and crevasses that will hold onto residue.

If you are cleaning a cartridge gun, don't forget to include the firing pin area in your cleaning chores. On revolvers or rifles with permanently screwed on barrels, try to keep the gun held upside down to avoid running water or dirty solvents into the frame when you are cleaning the barrel.

Top-break revolver barrels don't always have to be removed from the frame for cleaning, however, just as with other revolvers you should keep water or dirty solvents out of the rest of the mechanism unless it is your intent to disassemble the entire revolver. On S&W top-breaks, instead of removing the barrel, remove the cylinder catch and/or the barrel catch so that there are no more parts remaining in the barrel's top strap and keep the barrel open, upside down during the cleaning process. This way the frame is always held up over the top of the bore and it lessens the chance of nasty stuff running into the action.

To clean up percussion nipples or any other removable small parts subjected to powder fouling, drop them into a small jar containing clean, black powder cleaning solvent and leave them there to soak while you are cleaning the rest. When you are finished with the major cleaning work, you will find that these small items and parts will clean up much easier after soaking in the solvent.

Lever-action types should be disassembled up to the point where the breech bolt and firing pin are removed and then give them a good scrubbing out with solvents after they have been fired either with black powder or Pyrodex. I know it is important to clean these areas because on many occasions I have seen large amounts of powder residue that were blown back inside the bolt around the firing pin. This seems to happen more often with pistol-sized cartridges, in older guns with loose chambers, or in situations where there is not enough chamber pressure to cause the cartridge case to obdurate (to expand to seal the chamber during firing) in that instance the powder gases will leak rearward and can get into the bolt. Powder fouling, and the rust it will in turn promote if left untreated could very well cause the firing pin to stick forward, creating a situation that could be dangerous if the cartridge primer is fired before the breech bolt has fully locked.

Smokeless powder clean up

Everything we said above about cleaning your black powder gun with solvent-based methods applies to clean up with smokeless powders, except the idea of staring off with the water rinse. Omit that step entirely since water won't do a thing for you. Your solvent should be a cleaning solvent meant for cleaning up nitro-powder instead of the black powder solvent, but the methods you use and tools that aid you are identical. Of course, the amount of fouling and residue with smokeless powder ammo will be miniscule compared to what you would have with black powder or Pyrodex. But, is it anywhere near as cool? Sir, I think not!

Incidentally, I tried that moly-treatment on an S&W .38 that has a slightly rough bore, this gun used to give me leading problems but since cleaning the lead out and treating it with Brownells Moly Bore Treatment Paste, the leading has all but stopped.

Clean guns shoot straight

If you notice that a weapon's accuracy has begun to deteriorate during a shoot, stop, take a time out and give that barrel a good cleaning. If it's a revolver you are shooting, clean the cylinder chambers and base pin area too. After you are finished cleaning, if you are going to shoot the gun soon, dry the bore and the chambers thoroughly with clean, dry patches before you load up again. Sometimes with a freshly dried and clean bore that first shot will be a flyer, think about firing one prep-shot before you do any for-the-record target shooting. This is sometimes known as a dressing shot. It will absolutely dry and slightly foul the bore, it will also give it a coat of bullet lubricant so that any successive shots have what they call a normalized bore to slide through.

Endnotes

[1] Gunsmithing Guns of the Old West by David R. Chicoine, Krause, 2004

[2] The Chemistry of Powder & Explosives by Tenney L. Davis, Angriff Press, 1943

Chapter 9

Cowboy firearms manufacturers and importers

Here is a list of some of the popular firearms makers, sellers and importers who do business today selling the Guns of the New West along with a just a few originals. (indicates firearms featured within this book)*

American Arms Inc.,
715 Armour Rd., N. Kansas City, MO 64116

American Derringer Corp.,
127 N. Lacy Dr., Waco, TX 76705

Ballard Rifle and Cartridge, LLC,
113 W. Yellowstone Ave., Cody, WY 82414

Browning Arms Co., One Browning Pl.,
Morgan, UT 84050 (801) 876-3331

* Cimarron Firearms Co., P.O. Box 906,
105 Winding Oak Road, Fredericksburg, TX 78624
(830) 997-9090 or 877-SIXGUN1
Internet: http://www.cimarron-firearms.com

* Colt's Manufacturing Co., P.O. Box 1868,
Hartford CT 78624 (860) 236-6311 www.colt.com

CVA, 5988 Peachtree Corners East, Norcross, GA
30071 Phone: (770) 449-4687

* Dixie Gun Works, Inc., P.O. Box 130,
Gunpowder lane, Union City, TN 38281
(800) 238-6785 http://www.dixiegun.com

* EMF Co., 1900 E. Warner Ave., Suite 1-D,
Santa Ana, CA 92705 USA (949) 261-6611
http://www.emf-company.com

Euroarms of America, Inc., 208 Piccadilly
Street, Winchester, VA 22601 (540) 662-1863

Freedom Arms,
P.O. Box 150, Freedom, WY 83120

H&R 1871 Inc,
60 Industrial Row, Gardner, MA 01440

* Marlin Firearms Co., 100 Kenna Dr.,
North Haven, CT 06473 (203) 239-5621
www.marlinfirearms.com

Navy Arms Corp.,
815- 22nd St., Union City, NJ 07087 (201) 945-2500.
http://www.navyarms.com

Old Town Station Ltd.,
P.O. Box 15351, Lenexa, KS 66285 (913) 492-3000
www.armchairgunshow.com

Remington Arms Co., Inc., 870 Remington Dr.,
Madison, NC 27025 (800) 243-9700
www.remington.com

C. Sharps Arms and Montana Armory, Inc.,
P.O. Box 885 Big Timber, MT 59011 (406) 932-4353
http://www.csharpsarms.com/

* Stoeger Industries (Uberti),
17603 Indian Head Highway, Accokeek, MD 20607,
(301) 283-6300, www.uberti.com

* Sturm, Ruger & Company Inc.,
200 Ruger Rd, Prescott, AZ 86301 (520) 541-8820
http://www.ruger.com

Thompson/Center Arms Co., Inc.,
P.O. Box 5002, Rochester, NH 03866. (603) 332-2333
http://www.tcarms.com.

Traditions Performance Muzzleloading,
1375 Boston Post Rd, P.O. Box 776,
Old Saybrook, CT 06475 (860) 388-4656,
info@traditionsfirearms.com or http://www.
traditionsfirearms.com/

* Uberti: *see Stoeger Industries above*

* U. S. Fire Arms Mfg. Co., P.O. Box 1901,
Hartford, CT 06144 (877) 227-6901 e-mail:
usfa@usfirearms.com, http://www.usfirearms.com

U.S. Repeating Arms Co., *(Winchester firearms)*
275 Winchester Ave., Morgan, UT 84050
(801) 876-3737

Sources for parts, repair and restoration services for replica and/or antique firearms

Barrel lining and rifling

Randy Redman, **Redman's Rifling and Relining,** 189 Nichols, Omak, WA 98841 (509) 826-5512

Color Case Hardening

Bill Adair, 2886 Westridge, Carrollton, TX 75006 (972) 418-0950 BILL.ADAIR2@verizon.net

Color Case Company, Box 27, 14435 Unity Rd., New Springfield, OH 44443 (330) 542-2062

Doug Turnbull, P.O. Box 471, Bloomfield, NY 14469 (585) 657-6338 www.turnbullrestoration.com

Grips and Checkering

Checkering: Bill Hoffman, 246 Hatchway Rd., Fort Mill, SC 29715 (803) 802-3943 (checkers ivory grips)

Grip maker: Jerry Meacham, 8433 Cavett Ct., Charlotte, NC 28269 (704) 875-2224 (Custom Colt pattern one-piece ivory grips, pre-war Colt ivory carving.)

Plating and/or stripping

C&R Hard Chrome and Electroless

Nickel Service, Inc., 940 Hanover St., Gastonia, NC 28054 (704) 861-8831 fax (704) 865-3018 Bill Cottingham

Re-Marking and lettering

Bill Adair, 2886 Westridge, Carrollton, TX 75006 (972) 418-0950 BILL.ADAIR2@verizon.net

Ken Howell, R&D Gun Shop, 5728 E. County Rd. X, Beloit WI 53511

Colt specialists:

Repair (originals), restoration, appraisal: **David R. Chicoine** (704) 853-0265 bnpress@quik.com

Parts; Colt, Ed Cox, PO Box, 21417, Keizer, OR 97307 (503) 390-1698 www.coltparts.com

Parts; SAA repair, restoration, custom work: Peacemaker Specialists, Ed Janis, P.O. Box 157, Whitmore, CA 96096 (916) 472-3438. www.peacemakerspecialists.com

Parts; SAA, Art Pirkle, 1344 W. 17th Place, Yuma, AZ 85364 (520) 783-9108 no catalog.

Parts and repair; SAA,: Smith Enterprise, 1701 West 10th St., Ste.14, Tempe, AZ 85281 (480) 964-1818. www.smithenterprise.com

Smith & Wesson specialists:

Repair (originals), restoration, authentication and some parts: David R. Chicoine (704) 853-0265 bnpress@quik.com Internet; www.oldwestgunsmith.com

Parts; Smith & Wesson obsolete models: Jim Horvath, 117 So. Alexandria, New Orleans, LA 70119 e-mail Driftdive56@aol.com

Winchester specialists:

Parts; Buckingham's Winchester Parts, 501 Eaton Brazil Rd.,Trenton, TN 38382-9663.

Repair, restoration, appraisal: David R. Chicoine (704) 853-0265 bnpress@quik.com

Parts; Columbia Precision Parts, P.O. Box 301, Timnath, CO 80547 (303) 686-2865

Parts; Fred Goodwin, Sherman Mills, Maine 04776 (207) 365-4451 (Winchester lever gun parts)

Parts; Art Pirkle, 1344 W. 17th Place, Yuma, AZ 85364 (520) 783-9108

Parts; Western Rifled Arms, P.O. Box 236, Rochester, WA 98579 (360) 273-7716

Parts for various older guns:

Parts; Ballard, Remington, Stevens, Winchester Screws: Cedar Creek Screw and Machine, P.O. Box, 1531, Woodland, WA 98674.

Parts, Colt, Remington, many other obsolete and replica firearms: Dixie Gunworks, P.O. Box 130, Union City, TN 38161 (901) 885-0700

Parts and wood; Marlin, Remington, Stevens, Winchester: Precision Gun Works, 110 Sierra Rd., Kerrville, TX 78028 (210) 367-4587.

Parts, Colt and Ruger SA: Belt Mountain Enterprises., P.O. Box 3202, Bozeman, MT 59772 FAX (406) 388-1396

New (n) and/or obsolete (o) gun parts, all makes:

n/o: Bob's Gun Shop, P.O. Box 200, Royal, AR 71968 (501) 767-1970 www.gun-parts.com

n/o: Brownells Inc., 200 S. Front St., Montezuma, IA 50171 (641) 623-4000 www.brownells.com

n/o: Jack First Inc., 1201 Turbine Dr., Rapid City, SD 57701 (605) 343-9544 www.1stingunparts.com

New (n) and/or obsolete (o) gun parts, all makes: *continued*

n/o: Numrich Gun Parts Corp, West Hurley, NY 12491 (914) 679-2417 www.e-gunparts.com

n/o: SARCO, 323 Union St., Stirling, NJ 07980 (908) 647-3800

n/o, imported replica firearms: VTI Gunparts, P.O. Box 509, Lakeville, CT 06039 (860) 435-8068 http://www.vtigunparts.com

Restoration services

Restoration services: Bill Adair, 2886 Westridge, Carrollton, TX 75006 (972) 418-0950

Repair, restoration: Colt, S&W, Marlin, M-H, Remington, Sharps, Winchester, etc.: David R. Chicoine (704) 853-0265 bnpress@quik.com or www.clt.quik.com/bnpress/gunsmith.htm

Repair, restoration: Colt SAA. Peacemaker Specialists, Ed Janis, P.O. Box 157, Whitmore, CA 96096 (916) 472-3438. www.peacemakerspecialists.com

Restoration services: Doug Turnbull, 6680 Rt. 5 &20, P.O. Box 471, Bloomfield, NY 14469 (585) 657-6338 www.turnbullrestoration.com

Tools

Brownells Inc., 200 S. Front St., Montezuma, IA 50717 (800) 741-0015 www.brownells.com

Other:

Real, old-time collodian photography.

Will Dunniway, P.O. Box 77384, Corona, CA 92877-0112 (909) 264-9839 Cell, email ~ dunniway@collodion-artist.com. Web sites ~ www.dunniway.com or www.collodion-artist.com

Some sources for gunleather and clothing:

Leather:

*****James Allen,** 75 Jones Rd., Heflin, AL 36264 (256) 463-5320

Bianchi International, 100 Calle Cortez, Temeculah, CA 92590

John Bianchi's Frontier Gunleather, P.O. Box 2038, Rancho Mirage, CA 92270

Ted Blocker, 14787 SE 82nd Dr., Clackamas, OR 97015

*****El Paso Saddlery,** P.O. Box 27194, El Paso, TX 79926

GALCO International, 2019 W. Quail Ave., Phoenix, AZ 85027

Idaho Leather, 18 S. Orchard, Boise, ID 83705

*****Kirkpatrick Leather Co.,** P.O. Box 677, Laredo, TX 78042

Lefty's Leather, P.O. Box 1654, Upland, CA 91785 (909) 981-8087

Bob Mernickel, 12-9053 Shook Rd., Mission, BC Canada V2V 5M2

Old West Reproductions, 446 Florence Loop South, Florence, MT 59833

Red River Outfitters, P.O. Box 241, Tujunga, CA 91042

Roy Rugers, 502 E. Garrison Blvd., Gastonia, NC 28054 (704) 867-3529

Milt Sparks, 605 E. 44th St., Boise, ID 83714

*****Texas Jack,** P.O. Box 906, Fredericksburg, TX 78624

Tombstone Outfitters, 3430 Old Due West Rd., Marietta, GA 30064

Trailhands & Gunslingers, P.O. Box 2270, Walnut, CA 91788

Wild Bill's Originals, P.O. Box 13037, Burton, WA 98013

Wrangler Leather, P.O. Box 1209, Afton, WY 83110

*****Wes Terner's Outfitter** 1426 Fairmont Loop, Coeur d'Alene, ID 83814

Yoder Custom Leather, 525 William St., Hamburg, PA 19526

Products featured within this book.

Clothing:

C&C Sutlery, 3953 Fuller Rd., Emmett, ID 83617

Cowboy Corral, 219 N. Hwy. 89a, Sedona, AZ 86336

Red River Outfitters, P.O. Box 241, Tujunga, CA 91042

Texas Jack, P.O. Box 906, Fredericksburg, TX 78624

Tombstone Outfitters, 3430 Old Due West Rd., Marietta, GA 30064

Bibliography

Action Shooting Cowboy Style
by John Taffin, Krause, 1999.

A History of the Colt Revolver
by Haven and Belden, Bonanza, 1950.

A Study of Colt Conversions
by R. Bruce McDowell, Krause, 1997.

A Study of the Colt Single Action Army Revolver
by Graham, Kopec & Moore, 1976.

Big Bore Handguns by John Taffin, Krause, 2002

Big Bore Sixguns by John Taffin, Krause, 1997.

Cartridges of the World, 9th ed.
By Frank C. Barnes, Krause, 2000.

Civil War Breech Loading Rifles
by John D. McAulay, Andrew Mowbray Inc., 1987.

Civil War Guns
by William B. Edwards, Thomas Publications, 1997.

Civil War Pistols of the Union
by John D. McAulay, Andrew Mowbray Inc., 1992.

Colt Firearms from 1836
by James E. Serven, Stackpole 1979.

Colt's Pocket 49'
Robert M. Jordan & Darrow M. Watt, self pub. 2000

Colt's Single Action Army Revolver
by Robert H. "Doc" O'Meara, Krause, 1999.

Cowboy Action Shooting by Charly Gullett, Wolfe.

Cowboys and the Trappings of the Old West
Manns & Flood, Zon Intl. Pub, 1997

Evolution of the Winchester
by R. Bruce McDowell, Armory, 1985.

Flayderman's Guide to Antique American Firearms, 8th ed. by Norm Flayderman, Krause.

Guns by Dudley Pope, Spring Books, 1965

Gunsmithing Guns of the Old West
by David R. Chicoine, Krause, 2004

History of Smith & Wesson
by Roy G. Jinks, Beinfeld, 1977.

Loading the Peacemaker
by Dave Scovill, Wolfe, 1996.

Marlin Firearms
by Lt. Col. William S. Brophy, Stackpole, 1989.

Metallic Cartridge Conversions
by Dennis Adler, Krause 2002

Packing Iron
by Richard C. Rattenbury, Zon International, 1993

Pollard's History of Firearms,
Claud Blair, Ed., Macmillan, 1983.

Remington; America's Oldest Gunmaker
by Roy Marcot, Primedia, 1998.

Remington Firearms: The Golden Age of Collecting
by Robert W. Ball, Krause, 1995.

Sam Fadala's Muzzleloading Notebook
by Sam Fadala, Winchester Press, 1985.

Sharps Firearms by Frank Sellers, Sellers, 1982.

Shooting Colt Single Actions
by Mike Venturino, MLV Enterprises, 1995.

Shooting Lever Guns of the Old West
by Mike Venturino, MLV Enterprises, 1999.

Shooting Sixguns of the Old West
by Mike Venturino, MLV Enterprises, 1997.

Shotguns by Keith by Elmer Keith, Bonanza, 1957.

Single Shot Rifles
by James J. Grant, Gun Room Press, 1947.

Sixguns by Keith by Elmer Keith, Stackpole 1955.

Smith & Wesson 1857-1945
by Neal & Jinks, A.S. Barnes and Co., 1975.

Smith & Wesson Sixguns of the Old West
by David R. Chicoine, Mowbray, 2004

Standard Catalog of Firearms 2003
by Ned Schwing, Krause, 2003.

Standard Catalog of Smith & Wesson, 2nd edition
by Supica & Nahas, Krause, 2001.

Standard Catalog of Winchester
edited by David D. Kowalski, Krause, 2000.

The Colt Single Action Revolvers, a shop manual, Vols I & II by Jerry Kuhnhausen, 2001.

The Complete Blackpowder Handbook
by Sam Fadala, Krause, 1996.

The Handgun by Geoffrey Boothroyd, Bonanza, 1970.

The History of Winchester Firearms 1866-1980
by Duncan Barnes, Winchester Press, 1980.

The NRA Book of Small Arms, Vol.1
W.H.B. Smith, NRA, 1953

The Peacemaker and its Rivals
by John E. Parsons, Morrow, 1950

The Pitman Notes (Vols 1-5)
by Major John Pitman, Thomas Publications, 1992.

The Story of Colts Revolver
by William B. Edwards, Stackpole, 1953.

The Story of Allen & Wheelock Firearms
by H.H. Thomas, Krehbiel, 1965.

The Top Shooters Guide to Cowboy Action Shooting
by Hunter Scott Anderson, Krause, 2000.

The Whitney Firearms
by Claud E. Fuller, Standard, 1946.

The Winchester Book
by George Madis, Art & Reference House, 1971.

The Winchester Handbook
by George Madis, Madis, 1981.

U.S. Cartridges and their Handguns
by Charles R. Suydam, Beinfeld, 1977.

Winchester Lever Action Repeating Firearms
by Art Pirkle, North Cape, 1994.

Winchester Repeating Arms Company
by Herbert G. Houze, Krause, 1994.